# OUT IN THE
# MIDDAY SUN

# OUT IN THE MIDDAY SUN

The British in Malaya
1880–1960

## MARGARET SHENNAN

JOHN MURRAY
*Albemarle Street, London*

First published in 2000
by John Murray (Publishers) Ltd,
50 Albemarle Street, London W1X 4BD

A catalogue record for this book is available from the British Library

ISBN 0-7195-5716 X

Typeset in Adobe Garamond by Servis Filmsetting Ltd
Printed and bound in Great Britain by The University Press, Cambridge

*To the memory of my father,*
*who first went out to the Straits Settlements in 1926 and retired in 1953,*
*and to his generation of British expatriates*
*who loved Malaya, but endured outrageous fortune*

# Contents

## Contents

# Illustrations

## Illustrations

The author and publisher would like to thank the following for permission to reproduce illustrations: Plate 1, John Murray; 2, National Portrait Gallery, London; 3, 4 and 5, *Twentieth Century Impressions of British Malaya*, 1908, pp. 582, 585, 671, by permission of the Syndics of Cambridge University Library; 6 (Y30311B/1), 7 (Y30311B/6), and 8 (Y30311B/12), Lillian Newton Collection, RCS, by permision of Cambridge University Library; 9 (Q22743), 10 (Q82506), 41 (FLM 908) and 42 (HU 2781), Imperial War Museum, London; 11 (BAM 1/63), RCS, by permission of the Syndics of Cambridge University Library; 12, 15, 16, 18, 21, 27, 32 and 39, Gordon Snell; 13, 14, 25, 26, 30, 31, 34, 37, 38 and 50, J. A. S. Edington; 17, Christopher Cannell; 19, 20 and 53, Norman Price; 24, 36, and 45, Ms Ray Forsyth; 29, E. R. Read; 35, Brian and Colin Kitching; 40, Dr Erina Batt; 43, Derick Cullen; 44, D. J. Anderson; 46, Bodleian Library, Oxford; 47, 48, 52 and 55, H. P. Bryson Collection, Mrs Catherine Small; 49, Miles Templer; 51 and 57, Mrs Fenella Davis; 56 and 59, Brian Stewart CMG; 58, Edward Morris. Plates 22, 23, 28, 33 and 54 are taken from the author's collection.

# *Acknowledgements*

In writing this book I have relied on the generous advice, information and goodwill of many people whose help I wish to acknowledge. In the first instance, my warmest thanks go to Ms Terry Barringer, librarian of the Royal Commonwealth Society Collection at Cambridge University, who gave me invaluable guidance and assistance, particularly on my numerous working visits to the library. I also thank Mr Lewis Hill, Director of the Centre for South-East Asian Studies at the University of Hull, Mr Michael Hughes at Rhodes House Library, Oxford, and the staff of the Imperial War Museum Archives, London, including Mr Peter Kent at the Photograph Archive. I am grateful to the staff and the Trustees of the Liddell Hart Centre for Military Archives at King's College, London, for permission to quote from the Vlieland papers; to Dr Gareth Griffiths for advice and for permission to quote from the resources of the Oral History Archive of the British Empire and Commonwealth Museum, Bristol, archivist Mary Ingoldby. In addition, I thank the Syndics of Cambridge University Library for their permission to publish material from the Royal Commonwealth Society's collections; and the staff at Lancaster City Library and Lancashire County Services, Lancaster University Library and the Sydney Jones Library, University of Liverpool, for their assistance.

A number of people offered me private family papers, manuscripts and letters, and I am most grateful to them for providing hitherto unpublished material. In particular, my heartfelt thanks go to Ray Forsyth and John Soper for allowing me to make significant use of the unpublished works of their father, Mr J. R. P. Soper. I am similarly indebted to M. J. Gent, OBE, for offering me the unqualified use of

# Acknowledgements

Marian Gent's manuscript; to Derick Cullen for use of his family collection of letters and other papers; to Jack Warin of Adelaide for use of his father's 'Changi Diary'; also to Susan Tanner for lending me the copy of Captain Henry Malet's 'War Diary' and a rare commemorative booklet on the Convent School, Cameron Highlands; to Norman Price for allowing me to use his mother's 'Malayan Memories' and other family papers; and to both Colin and Brian Kitching for permission to quote from their father's work in the Royal Commonwealth Society Collection, and for kindly presenting me with a copy of the diary of Tom Kitching, *Life and Death in Changi*, published by Brian Kitching, while letting me quote freely from the text. I am grateful also to Geoffrey Barnes for permitting me to quote from his autobiography, *Mostly Memories;* similarly to Jonathan Sim with regard to Katharine Sim's book, *Malayan Landscape*, and to Pelanduk Publications regarding Dato Mubin Sheppard's biography of Tunku Abdul Rahman. I thank Suzanne, Duchess of St Albans, for clarifying some personal details and also for permission to quote from her autobiography, *The Mimosa and the Mango* (now part of a condensed version of her three-volume memoirs, *Mangoes and Mimosa*, published by Virago). Mary Elder was kind enough to lend me a copy of *God's Little Acre* with its invaluable insight into the Emergency, and I thank John Edington for providing me with numerous personal items and for his constant advice and willingness to answer a stream of questions.

Many former residents of Malaysia offered photographs from their personal collections, with permission to publish them as illustrations, together with other memorabilia from the colonial period, and I thank them sincerely and regret that only a proportion could be incorporated in the book. I should like to record my thanks to Derek J. Anderson for permission to reproduce a drawing of Changi Gaol, formerly in the possession of his grandfather, Alexander Godfrey Donn, a prisoner-of-war in Singapore; Douglas Benton for a rare photograph of Guy Hutchinson; and Gordon Snell for full use of his family albums. Others to whom I owe thanks are listed in the acknowledgements to the illustrations.

Several people gave me valuable advice in the early stages of the project, in particular, A. J. S. Anderson of the Scottish Malaysian Association, Kenneth Barnes, Peggie Robertson, John Gullick, Kay Larsson and Professor Mary Turnbull. I am grateful to John Loch for putting me in touch with John Davis of Force 136. I also received valuable information in telephone and face-to-face conversations with ex-Malayans, and in letters and newspaper cuttings. In conclusion, I record my thanks to the Revd Derek Allton, John Anderson, Ron Armstrong, Ken Barnes, the late Colonel Christopher Barrett, Jette Barrett, Roger Barrett, Dermot Barton, OBE, Margaret Barton, Dr Erina Batt, Gordon D. Brown, Christina Browne, Christopher Cannell, Dr D. R. Clementi, Derick Cullen, John Davis, CBE, DSO, Anne Douglas, Robert W. Duffton, Deirdre Edington, John A. S. Edington, Mary L. Elder, Ray Forsyth, Sir Leslie Froggatt, James Gilbert, D. M. Gold, Dulcie Gray, CBE, Ian Harness, Maureen Heath, Michael J. Henebrey, Valerie Henebrey, Brian Hunt, Tom Kerr, Donald Macpherson, Margot Massie, John Menneer, G. T. M. de M. Morgan, MC, OBE, Edward Morris, Peter Morris, Harold Naysmith, Mrs Jane O'Donovan, Dr Michael Pallister, J. R. Pippet, Norman Price, Anthony Pybus, Sheila Rawcliffe, Edward R. Read, Alastair Reid, James Robertson, MBE, Professor Peter Rowe, Elizabeth Scott, Catherine Small, Gordon Snell, Brian Stewart, CMG, Susan Tanner, Miles Templer, William W. Vowler, Christopher Watkins, E. James Winchester, Simon Wright and Alexander Wylde. If there are any inadvertent omissions, I offer my sincere apologies.

Margaret Shennan

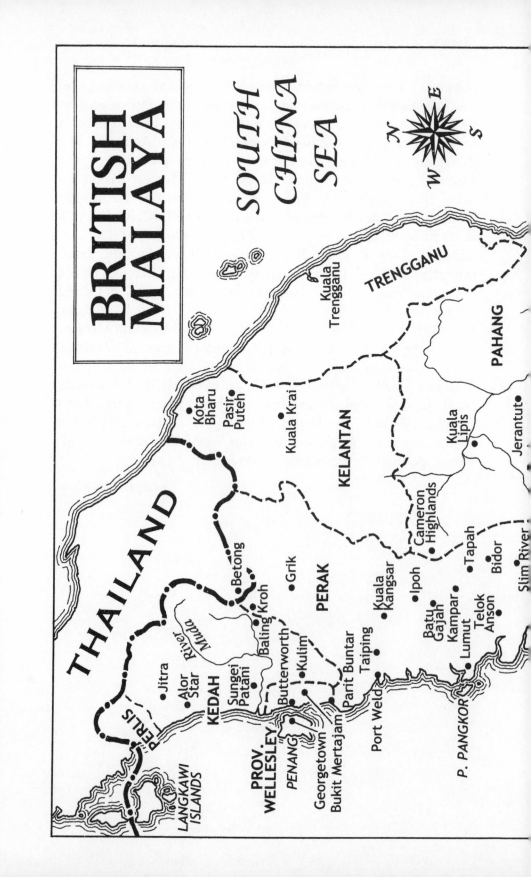

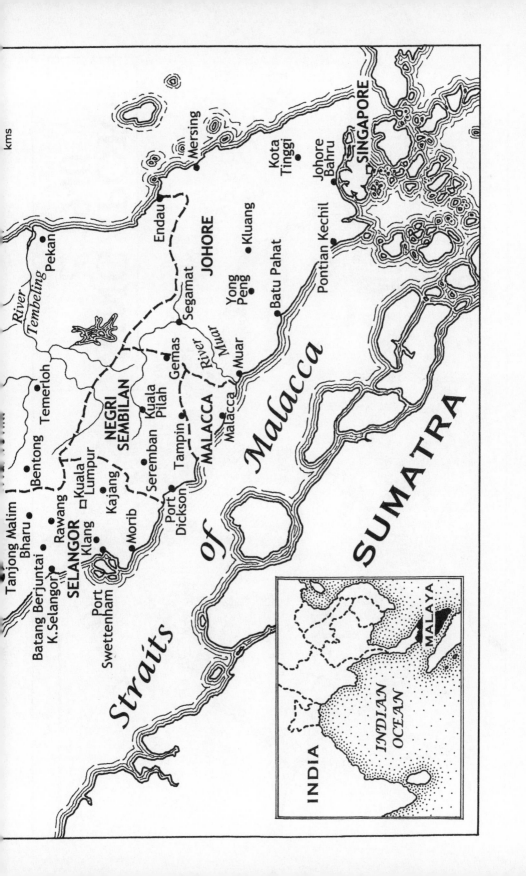

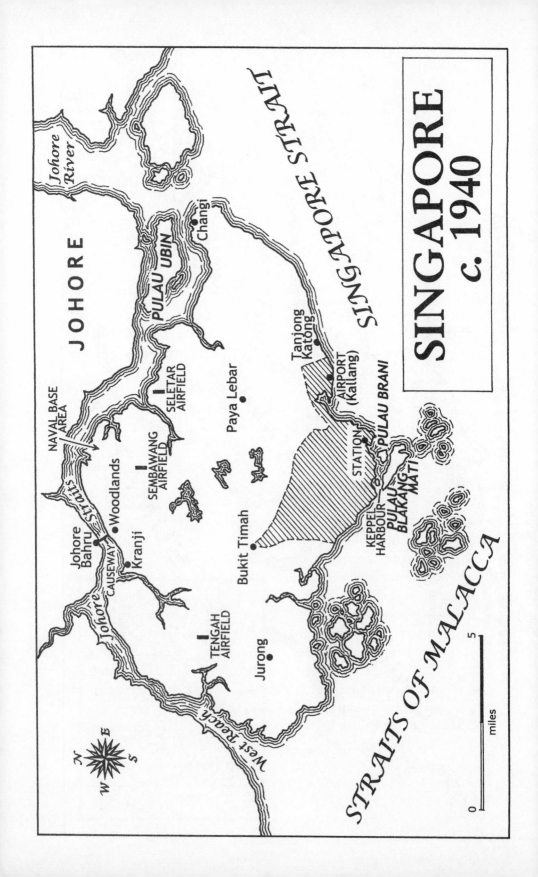

# Introduction

In the past century the British appear to have been driven by a compulsion to put into words their experiences and perceptions of life in the East. Malaya, in particular, has stimulated a mass of literature, both fiction and non-fiction. Many British expatriates wrote letters home or kept a diary to be turned later into a period memoir, with descriptions of events, people, the beauty of the tropical scenery, the trials and surprises of the climate. Travellers kept accounts of their journeys; journalists and writers found inspiration in Malaya's exotic setting, its humdrum and quixotic characters, or the tragedies of a benign but flawed colonial regime. If the Raj boasts Rudyard Kipling, E. M. Forster and Paul Scott, Malaya has, among others, Joseph Conrad and Henry Fauconnier, Somerset Maugham, Anthony Burgess, Paul Theroux, J. G. Farrell, Neville Shute, Alan Sillitoe and Leslie Thomas. Alongside these are some less well-known raconteurs and observers: Isabella Bird and Emily Innes – both underestimated, despite the sharp eye for detail of the one and the laconic humour of the other; governors Frank Swettenham and Hugh Clifford, and the official J. T. Thomson, who like Swettenham was a gifted artist and whose paintings of Malayan scenes have a directness akin to Lowry's pictures of industrial England. And more recently, in the twentieth century, civil servants such as Richard Winstedt, R. J. Wilkinson, Victor Purcell and J. M. Gullick have demonstrated their expert knowledge in contributions to academic scholarship.

Malaya, as the British knew it, embraced the Malay peninsula, the south-easterly appendage of Burma and Thailand, and its adjacent islands, including Penang and Singapore. Three-quarters or more of this equatorial country was covered by tropical rainforest, thanks to temperatures in the range of 70 to 90°F, high humidity and an average annual rainfall of 100 inches. The landscape is dominated by a core of parallel jungle-covered mountain ranges, peaking at over 7,000 feet, which serve as the watershed of a valuable river system. In the centre and north, hilly outcrops of limestone support stunted vegetation, scrub and secondary forest clothe the lower slopes, and swamps line the western coast.

In the century and a half of British involvement, the country was made up of a dozen political units and was peopled not only by Malays but by large immigrant communities from China, India and Indonesia. In the post-colonial period, since 1957, social, economic and political development has been rapid, and with the exception of Singapore – now an independent state – what was once Malaya is the western part of a larger Federation of Malaysia. There is a historical logic to this union, for in cultural terms the Malay peninsula has long been a part of the Malaysian archipelago, which lay between the two historic spheres of influence in the East: the Indian subcontinent and the Buddhist lands bordering the South China Sea. Mass immigration from these two regions into Malaya during the British period of influence was to build a new, multiracial, multicultural country with a complex administrative system, consisting of a Crown Colony and two protectorates. This system ended with the collapse of British power in 1941–2 and the Japanese occupation from 1942 to 1945. After the return of the British in 1945 a temporary military administration was instituted. On the restoration of civil government in 1946, the colony of Singapore became politically separate from the rest of Malaya, under both the ill-starred Malayan Union (1946–8) and the Federation of Malaya. The island was then briefly (1963–5) merged in the Malaysian Federation which continues to this day.

The Malay people had migrated southward into the peninsula from the interior of Asia in around 2000 BC. Earlier, in prehistoric times, an ethnically distinct people had followed the same route. Some of these aboriginal tribes moved on to the Indonesian islands and as far as Australasia, but those who settled in the mountainous rainforests of the Malay peninsula would be known by the Malays as *orang asli* – 'the original people'. The Malays themselves spread across the whole Malaysian archipelago to establish, after several centuries, a unifying *Melayu* civilization based on Sumatra. They were followed from the third to the fourteenth centuries by successive waves of migrants: Greeks, Arabs, Persians, possibly Egyptians and Phoenicians, and more significantly Indians, who brought a thousand years of Hindu culture to the peninsula and to the island of Tumasik (known later as Singapore). All these voyagers reached Malaya by sailing with the prevailing monsoon winds – north-easterlies sweeping westward from China or south-westerlies bringing traders from India. Over the centuries the balance of power in South-East Asia fluctuated , but the several small states of the Malay peninsula were generally reduced to vassal status by large and dominant empires based in Siam (present-day Thailand), Sumatra or Java. After Tumasik had been sacked by Siamese imperial forces at the end of the fourteenth century, its ruler, Paramesvara, escaped to a fishing village on the west coast of the peninsula, creating a new Malay state of Malacca.

In the fifteenth century Malacca's position at the crossroads of the Asian trade routes made it a prominent trading power, an entrepôt for the spices of the Moluccas and Banda islands, fine Indian textiles and Chinese silks and porcelain. In addition, this city-state forged a distinct Malay tradition, based on the Islamic faith, a literary cultural identity and a hierarchical political system with officers of state presided over by the Sultan, a structure adopted later by emergent states elsewhere in the peninsula. In 1500, on the eve of European intrusion into the Far East, Malacca led the Malay world, its control extending to the states of Pahang, Trengganu, Kedah and Johore.

In the past the European historical tradition tended to underplay the achievements of Asian states and cultures like Malacca. Interest focused on the wealth of the East, the precious metals and stones, silks, 'spices' (aromatic condiments, medicines, dyes, perfumes and cosmetics) and the exotic products of tropical seas and forests, such as coral, pearls and sandalwood. This accounts for the lure of mysterious countries such as Cathay (China), Cipangu ( Japan) and the region east of India dubbed the Golden Chersonese, identified with the Malay peninsula. Also, by emphasizing European technological superiority – the seizure of Malacca by the Portuguese in 1511 and by the Dutch in 1641 – other aspects of the evolving Malay world were overlooked. The modern sultanate of Johore, for instance, was formed by members of the Malacca royal house, escaping from the Portuguese to the southern end of the peninsula. Later their seat of power was moved to the Riau–Linggi archipelago, to the south of Singapore Island, leaving Johore in the hands of the Sultan's minister or temenggong.

By the middle of the seventeenth century, Malacca had lost its earlier economic vitality. The Dutch, whose power base was further south in the Malaysian archipelago, found it difficult to enforce their monopoly over the export of tin from Malay states such as Perak. In the developing power vacuum, the Bugis people of Celebes – a race of skilled sailors, warriors and traders – began to settle along the coast of the Malacca Straits, into Johore's territories in the Riau islands and the region between Perak and Malacca, which in 1745 became the separate state of Selangor under a Bugis sultan.

Economic opportunity also attracted other waves of immigrants to Malayan shores at this time: Arabs and Indians to Kedah; Chinese to the centres of mining and agriculture in the eastern states of Trengganu and Kelantan, Perak in the north and Riau; and the Minangkabau people of Sumatra to a cluster of small states lying between Malacca and Selangor, of which Sungei Ujong was the most prominent (and from which Negri Sembilan later emerged). Both Dutch and Bugis influence diminished in the eighteenth century, amid protracted civil war, political fragmentation and piracy on the high seas. Siam re-exerted its overlordship of the northern Malay states. British traders such as Francis Light, based in India, saw new opportunities for developing trade with China by utilizing the tin and spices of the Malay peninsula.

British trading power was established in India by the mid-eighteenth century, but the East India Company had no base in the Far East. Light, who was on amicable terms with the Malay Sultan of Kedah, coveted the small island of Penang, which guarded the northern entrance to the Malacca Straits. In 1786 he acquired it from the Sultan for an annual payment of $6,000 Spanish dollars and took possession on behalf of the Company. This takeover marked the beginning of British power in the Malay archipelago. The extension of British control was a gradual process, and continued to 1914. In 1795 the British captured Malacca from the Dutch (though it was temporarily returned in 1818). Then, in 1800, the East India Company secured from the Sultan of Kedah territory on the Malay mainland facing Penang. It was named Province Wellesley, after the Governor-General of India.

The next important milestone was the acquisition in 1819 of Singapore, when Stamford Raffles negotiated the right from the temenggong to establish on the island a second fortified trading post of the East India Company. Initially this provoked opposition, particularly from the Dutch, though they and the British settled their differences by the Treaty of London in 1824. The Dutch recognized the Malay peninsula and adjacent islands as a British sphere of influence, and in 1825 the East India Company was confirmed in possession of Malacca and Singapore. Shortly after, the Company's four Malay settlements were unified into a single territory known as the Straits Settlements, with the status of a presidency, and placed under the administration of the Governor of Penang (1826–30). In that time another political issue was settled. The Anglo-Siamese boundaries of influence were agreed by the Treaty of Bangkok in 1826. The small northern Malay states – Kedah, Perlis, Kelantan and Trengganu – were recognized as coming effectively under Siamese control, while the remaining states, including the larger states of Perak and Pahang, were acknowledged as within Britain's sphere of influence.

In the next four decades the government of the Straits Settlements underwent further change. For financial reasons, they were brought directly under the East India Company's administration in Bengal from 1830 to 1832. However, the Company's star was in decline, and, having lost its monopoly of the China trade in 1833, it was reduced in 1834 to a managing agency for the British government in India. From 1832 the routine administration of the Malay territories was conducted in Singapore, the new capital of the Straits Settlements.

The island of Singapore, some twenty-six miles wide by fourteen miles deep, is larger than Penang (and larger than the Isle of Wight, which it curiously resembles in shape). Stamford Raffles had foreseen that, with its natural deep-water harbour and strategic position, it would flourish as a free port and eventually overtake Dutch centres of influence in the East. Yet the Bengal government increasingly resented the burden of responsibility for the Straits Settlements and saw no advantage in involvement with the Malay States. Malaya was dismissively referred to as 'Farther India', to emphasize its distance and obscurity. After the Indian Mutiny of 1857, when the Company was deprived of its governing role, the Straits Settlements were brought under the Indian Office in London. Finally, in 1867 they were designated a Crown Colony, to be administered directly by the Colonial Office. This was a turning point in the evolution of British Malaya.

With the impetus of steam navigation and the opening of the Suez Canal in 1869 the economic prospects for the Straits Settlements were good. But two major problems could no longer be ignored by the administration. Merchants in the Settlements were increasingly worried by the social anarchy in the Malay peninsula, especially the factional fighting in the rich tin-mining areas of Perak and Salengor, and by the threat to shipping from sea pirates in the Malacca Straits. Also, the British government was concerned about the looming colonial aspirations of Britain's European rivals, France and Germany, in the Far East. In 1873 Sir Andrew Clarke was sent out to Malaya to investigate the internal situation and propose solutions. Clarke went further. A mechanism was needed to sanction British intervention without offending individual sultans. After meeting a group of Perak chiefs and local Chinese leaders off Pangkor Island, a settlement was reached regarding the Sultanate of Perak. The formula was embodied in the Pangkor Engagement of 1874 – another landmark in the establishment of British power in the peninsula. While retaining his rights on matters of Malay religion and custom, the Sultan of Perak agreed to accept the 'advice' on all other questions and the 'protection' of a British Resident. At first there was some hostility to this foreign interference, and the over-zealous first Resident of Perak, J. W. W. Birch, was murdered by a group of resentful chieftains in November 1875. Meanwhile, however, the rulers of Selangor and Sungei Ujong were also persuaded to accept the principle of British protection – a tactful euphemism for governing authority – and the same principle was applied to all Negri Sembilan and Pahang in the 1880s. Thus, while the Straits Settlements continued to be ruled directly as a Crown Colony, as the result of the Pangkor agreement a system of *indirect* rule was initiated in some of the Malay States, which became British protectorates. Subsequently, between 1874 and 1914, as we shall see, this status would be extended further, with structural variations, to all the Malay States. To say more at this stage would be to pre-empt the following chapters.

It would have been possible to choose the Pangkor Engagement of 1874 as my starting point for this book, but that might imply a concern with constitutional or political structures rather than with people. However, by 1880, the starting date I have chosen, the principle of British involvement in the Malay sultanates embodied in Pangkor was established, and the arrival of Sir Frederick Weld brought a strong

Governor (1880–7) under whom British influence was firmly exercised. Nevertheless, 1880 is a date of convenience, and I have not hesitated to dip into preceding years – for Isabella Bird's account of her travels in 1879, for example, or Emily Innes's experiences which spanned 1876 to 1882 – when I believe earlier material sheds light on the state of the country in 1880. Similarly, 1960 has been chosen as the cut-off point because it marked the end of the twelve-year Emergency which began in 1948 and was the main preoccupation of the British for its duration, although strictly speaking Britain's political role ended in 1957.

A few further points of explanation should perhaps be made. To avoid confusion I have used throughout the spellings of names and places in the source material which relate to the British period. The 'Malays' were of the Malay race and (with the *orang asli*) were the indigenous inhabitants. 'Malayans' were people who lived in Malaya, and might be of Asian or European origin. 'European' was a term much used by the British to describe themselves, and I have used it in that sense to give some variety to the text. However, it obviously also applies to other European nationals living in Malaya, such as the resident communities of French, Danes, Dutch, Germans and Portuguese, particularly in the years before 1914 or 1942. In some situations, the designation 'European' was also used as a shorthand substitute for 'white people' to include people from the Dominions, Commonwealth countries and the United States. The word 'Asiatic' is used only in verbatim quotations; elsewhere I use 'Asian'.

This is not an official history based on a study of government records; nor is it an in-depth social analysis. It is an unofficial account, a collage of the British in Malaya, their lives, thoughts and reactions to events happening around them. In choosing this approach I was influenced by the words of J. S. Potter, an executive of the Guthrie's agency who worked in Malaya for twenty-three years: 'I have long felt that some eye witness accounts should be recorded for posterity and in justice to the large numbers of fellow Malayans who can no longer speak for themselves.'[1] Reflecting on conversations, listening to taped interviews, and trawling through letters and memoirs, the force of his remark came home to me: so many British expatriates have wanted to put their side of the story, express their opinions, reveal their experiences and, in many cases, correct misunderstanding and disparagement.

In 'England Expects', the American humorist Ogden Nash wrote:

Englishmen are distinguished by their traditions and ceremonials,
And also by their affection for their colonies and their contempt for their
colonials.[2]

One is reminded of the aphorism attributed to Noël Coward, that
Malaya is 'a first-rate country for second-rate people'. Somerset
Maugham visited the country in the 1920s, then woundingly disparaged
its easygoing, hospitable society. The British who had been his hosts
were furious, and a retired expatriate remembers to this day his parents'
anger at this public betrayal of private generosity. It is a curious tradition that the most hostile jibes about colonial society should come not
from Asian nationalists, but from writers, journalists, academics and
public figures of the English-speaking world. Why, I wonder, over the
years did the British in Malaya face an indifferent public at home and
an unsympathetic British press? Why should a nation that has always
mistrusted intellectuals and set higher store by doers than thinkers
brand Malayans as philistines? How did a community of activists,
engineers, miners, surveyors, planters and businessmen, who prided
themselves as golfers, cricketers, tennis and rugby players or big-game
hunters, so offend the scribes? Perhaps the explanation lies partly in
envy – envy of those who escaped from insular Britain to achieve social
status and material gain. Perhaps, too, British Malayans connived in the
criticism because of the peculiarly British liking for self-deprecation.
There was a tendency to talk down anything but sporting talent, while
bemoaning the lack of mental and cultural stimulus in the tropics. (In
casual conversation in 1930s Perak, Katharine Sim, a customs officer's
wife, concluded, 'It is doubtful if even Shakespeare's genius could have
blossomed in the perpetual dank heat of the palm house at Kew.')[3]
This attitude contrasted noticeably with that of the French, in whose
colonies literature was honoured; ironically, a French planter, Henri
Fauconnier, won the Prix Goncourt in 1930 with his novel, *Malaisie*
(translated as *The Soul of Malaya*).

The enormous gulf between the political and cultural norms of imperial Britain and those of the twenty-first century makes it difficult to
view the record of colonial society objectively. Not surprisingly, 'protection' has become 'occupation'; 'responsibility' is dismissed as 'hypocrisy',
'employment' as 'exploitation'. In response to anti-imperialist rhetoric,
former members of the Malayan Civil Service have defended the young
idealists who enthusiastically came out to Malaya to promote the welfare

of the people, but, fifty years on, the post-colonial climate cannot empathize with colonial elites, and the new norms of political correctness reinforce differences of perspective. So the orthodox perception of British Malaya remains: of a smug, superficial, patronizing community, which deserved no better than it received. On the other hand, survivors from the colonial era remain convinced that it was a good and well-ordered world, served by a code of liberal Western values, many of which are universally tenable today. Perhaps the 'voices' of British Malayans, which speak out of these pages, allow us to understand their world a little. After all, for much of the twentieth century Great Britain itself has been a flawed democracy, a society of haves and have-nots, and in the last analysis the British in Malaya were arguably no more philistine, class-ridden, pleasure-seeking, exploitative or condescending than their families, friends and peers back home.

PART I

# The Building of British Malaya
## 1880–1920

# I

# *The Meeting of Two Worlds*

In 1879 a mature, middle-class Scotswoman, Isabella Bird, descended upon the Malay archipelago on her way back to England from a lengthy visit to Japan. An indefatigable traveller, she toured the parts of the Malay world which were then within the British sphere of influence. It was an interesting time. The inhabitants of the Malay States were just emerging from several decades of anarchy. Piracy and civil mayhem – the result of succession disputes among the rajas and internecine quarrels over the profits of tin mining – had impoverished village communities, until the British intervened to restore the peace.

Isabella's first ports of call were the areas which had been least affected, the Straits Settlements. As she tasted the bustle and congenial lifestyle of Singapore and Penang, she admired the abounding hospitality of the capital and the overpowering greenery, with its kaleidoscopic arrangement of colours. As for Penang, like many before and since she was awed by the island's beauty: 'This is truly a brilliant place under a brilliant sky.' Meanwhile, the little Chinese steamer *Rainbow*, over fifty years old but still ploughing the Straits of Malacca, took her to the old town which bore their name. She stayed at the historic Stadthaus, the former residence of the Dutch Governor but reduced under the British to a condition of faded stateliness. Once Malacca had been the greatest Malay city-port of South-East Asia. Now it was 'very still, hot, tropical . . . a town "out of the running", utterly antiquated, mainly un-English, a veritable Sleepy Hollow'. It had slipped into a time warp. Trade was invisible; no British or French mail boats called; 'there is neither newspaper, banker, hotel, nor resident English merchant'.[1]

Moving on, Isabella explored the interior of the west coast, the so-called 'Native States' of Sungei Ujong, Selangor and Perak, with their new protected status. (The east-coast state of Pahang, the fourth state to come eventually under British protection, was beyond her reach.) She made her way by boat and by horse-drawn gharry, on foot and somewhat insecurely on an elephant's back, along muddy rivers and jungle tracks. During the itinerary she met most of the new British administrators and made a quick stop at the Dindings, a strip of coastal Perak and a group of small islands ceded to England by the Pangkor Engagement, 'a dream of tropic beauty', where she watched 'scarlet fish playing in the coral forests, and the exquisite beauty of the main island with its dense foliage in dark relief against the cool lemon sky'. And towards the end of her tour she squeezed in a brief excursion to what was once a part of mainland Kedah, but since 1800 had been the British territory of Province Wellesley: 'only thirty-five miles long by about ten broad, but it is highly cultivated, fertile, rich, prosperous and populous . . . miles of coco-nut plantations belonging to Chinamen all along the coast', with 'sugar-cane and padi, and then palm plantations again'.[2]

Curious and quick to observe everything around her, whether it was of a personal, social or political nature, she was also aware of the danger of forming hasty and inaccurate judgements. Her sharp gaze alighted on contrasts in prosperity between the Straits Settlements, a British Crown Colony since 1867, and the Malay States, which were still undeveloped under their own native rulers. And she noted, too, the stereotyped attitudes, the 'great mist of passion and prejudice', inherent in Britain's policy towards the Malay chiefs and their people.[3] It was a situation compounded, in her view, by British ignorance; and in this she anticipated the opinion of Sir Frank Swettenham, later Governor of the Straits Settlements: 'In the first years of the colony's history, from 1867 to 1874, it is almost inconceivable how little was actually known of the independent Malay States in the Malay Peninsula . . .' he wrote; 'there was probably not a European . . . who could have given correctly the names of all the States in the Peninsula.'[4]

Malaya has never gripped the imagination of the British nation as vividly as the splendours of the Raj or the arcane riches of China. To the English middle class, a post in the Malayan administration lacked the cachet of the Indian Civil Service or the attractions of Ceylon (as Sri Lanka was then known); and the Church of England found Muslim Malaya an unpromising mission, less rewarding than India or China with their hungry hordes.[5] As the Empire grew, the Victorians had many distractions, and the Malay States were undoubtedly a low priority. In fact, five of the traditional states – Johore, Kedah, Perlis, Kelantan and Trengganu – remained outside British influence until after 1909. The cavalier attitude of politicians and the press was mirrored by the lack of awareness on the part of ordinary British citizens about what was going on before and after British intervention. Even Isabella Bird admitted, 'I felt humiliated by my ignorance of Province Wellesley, of which in truth I had never heard until I reached Malacca!' Nor was the name Sungei Ujong familiar until she arrived there. And, writing from Selangor's capital, she warned her sister, 'You will not know where Klang is, and I think you won't find it in any atlas or encyclopaedia.' Nonetheless, she deplored British indifference:

> Public opinion never reaches these equatorial jungles; we are grossly ignorant of their inhabitants and their rights, of the manner in which our interference originated, and how it has been exercised; and unless some fresh disturbance and another 'little war' should concentrate our attention for a moment on these distant States, we are likely to remain so, to their great detriment, and not a little . . . to our own.[6]

In the Victorian age, the task of managing the inhabitants and the environment was left to a small number of British officers, and a few developed a serious interest in Malayan anthropology and culture. Frank Swettenham was one of them. A giant among builders of British Malaya, it was his years as Resident of Selangor in the 1880s and of Perak in the 1890s that taught him about Malay life, which he sketched prolifically in words and drawings.[7] He argued that 'To begin to understand the Malay, you must live in his country, speak his language, respect his faith, be interested in his interests, humour his prejudices, sympathise with and help him in trouble, and share his pleasures and possibly his risks. Only thus can you win his confidence.'[8] But Hugh Clifford, who arrived in the Malay States as a mere seventeen-year-old in 1883 and ultimately rose like Swettenham to be Governor of the Straits Settlements, felt this was a pious hope: that regrettably 'It is possible for a European to spend years on the West coast of the Peninsula without acquiring any very profound knowledge of the natives of the country or of the language.'[9]

Traditional Malay society was composed of two classes: a governing elite of rajas and other titled chiefs, presided over by the ruling Sultan, and the ordinary Malays – the *rayats* – peasants and fishermen living in coastal or riverside villages under their headman or *penghulu*. A kind of feudal relationship prevailed between ruler and ruled. This gave immense prestige and authority to the ruler, reinforced when subjects fell into slavery and debt-bondage. There was a wide gap in social status between the *rayats* and their chiefs, but the Malay community was small enough for all to feel bound together by age-old custom and heritage. The Sultan and his chiefs lived close to their people, enjoying customary prerogatives and revenues. At Pekan, in Pahang, for instance,

> At the royal palace there was a large bronze gong. Whenever His Highness desired his followers to be assembled for any service such as to accompany him on a hunting expedition, they beat this big gong repeatedly, and soon a crowd of followers would assemble at the royal palace ready to carry out any royal command. This gong when beaten made a loud and deep booming sound . . . It could be heard for miles around.[10]

The township housing the ruler's home was primitive by the standards of European princes: not until the approach of the twentieth century did Sultans hanker for grand palaces. In the 1870s, Abdul Samat, Sultan of Selangor, lived surrounded by pariah dogs in a modest cluster of riverside buildings at Langat, a town disparaged by a colonial official as 'nothing but a mud-swamp, with one mud-path . . . between two padi-fields'; while Isabella Bird's initial and lasting impression of Klang, the first town of the state, was of 'a most misthriven, decayed, dejected, miserable looking place'.[11] Though Selangor was rich in tin ore and gutta-percha, the mechanisms did not exist for the Sultan to exploit his state's potential. For Malays, status depended on other considerations. Abdul Samat was the owner of three houses 'in the purest style of Malay architecture . . . The wood of which they are built is a rich brown red. The roofs are very high and steep, but somewhat curved. The architecture is simple, appropriate and beautiful.' Luxury was a relative quality in the tropics. Half-shaded windows allowing a constant, gentle breeze and relief from the glare of day were perceived as luxurious refinements. But the richness and harmony of the Dato Bandar's home in Sungei Ujong were also evident in the ebony chairs, silk drapes and Oudh rugs subtly woven in mixtures of rich but toned-down colours. The beautiful house of the exiled Mentri (ruler) of Larut was 'built of wood painted green and white, with bold floral designs . . . shady inner rooms with their carved doorways and *portières* of red silk, the pillows and cushions of gold embroidery laid over the exquisitely fine matting on the floors'. Wealth was measured, in addition, by the precious gems and jewelled artefacts worn about the person. Abdul Samat's status was secured by 'a "godown" [warehouse] containing great treasures . . . hoards of diamonds and rubies, and priceless damascened *krises* [daggers], with scabbards of pure gold wrought into marvellous devices and incrusted with precious stones'.[12]

Malay notions of power and justice differed fundamentally from European concepts. 'In the eyes of Malay Justice – which is a very weird thing indeed,' wrote Hugh Clifford – 'if you cannot punish the right man, it is better to come down heavily on the wrong one, than to allow everybody to get off scot free.'[13] To the Englishman in government service, the universal practice of offering bribes smacked of the deliberate perversion of justice, and he also found it difficult to accept the oppressive system of debt-slavery. When British administration was established, slavery was abolished, but not before the barbaric treatment meted out to recaptured slaves had impressed on Europeans that 'the Malay nature is "treacherous, blood-thirsty and cruel"'. On the other hand, the British use of hanging to dispose of convicted pirates was deplored by the Malays. 'They say "it is the death of a dog", and that Allah disapproves of human beings being killed in that manner".'[14] The Sultan's power, too, was a matter of cultural patriarchy rather than *force majeure*. Abdul Samat was respected as the father of his people and a potentate of ancient lineage; but, as a former pirate leader who had turned to the British for help in an inter-tribal war, his power to control was effectively limited after 1874 by dependency on the British Resident's advice on all political and financial matters.

After James Innes was appointed in 1876 to be collector and magistrate at Abdul Samat's seat of Langat, Emily Innes could not help observing her husband's relationship with the Sultan and commenting with laconic humour on the conflicting values of their two societies. 'It was Mr. Innes's duty to see that this old man did not get into mischief, and to warn him that Queen Victoria did not approve of piracy, slavery, pawnbroking, and other little failings to which he was addicted.' But age had made the Sultan forgetful: he 'sometimes got into trouble through his benevolent wish of pleasing everybody. He gave grants and monopolies of all sorts of things to all sorts of people, and then forgot that he had done so, and gave them over again to others.' In the confined surroundings of Langat, where the Inneses lived for several years,

> Now and then we came on the old Sultan, seated astride on a carpenter's bench, or else squatting on the ground, amid a crowd of dirty followers, watching a cock-fight . . . He was usually dressed in nothing but a very scanty little cotton kilt, or a pair of still scantier bathing-drawers, and was at first sight hardly distinguishable from an old Malay peasant; but on seeing us he would skip nimbly off the carpenter's bench . . . and come to meet us. He would then make a few condescending remarks, and finally wave us off with his hand in a most dignified manner . . . Although his appearance was by no means majestic and . . . he might seem to be a little wanting in oriental calm and dignity . . . I was present once on the homage-day, when all his subjects, rajas included, came crawling to kiss his hand. None of them dared approach him without grovelling on the ground . . . and anyone having to cross the room in his presence, crawled sideways on all-fours like a crab . . . As time went on we grew to have not only a feeling of warm friendship, but even of respect for him. He was invariably kind to us, and I believe to everybody.[15]

However, the subordinate class was subject to feudal services and the discretion of the local headman, and faced 'injustices and unfairness due to discriminations against which the unfortunate peasants seldom could get redress'.[16] Despite this, a young education officer, a newcomer in 1887, found the ordinary Malay to be dignified, honest and good-humoured, and he strongly resisted simplistic European judgements:

> The story-books of my childhood always described the Malay as *treacherous*. This, as I understand the word, I believe he never was. That he would strike at any enemy with the greatest possible secrecy I can well believe; but that it was a characteristic of him to pretend friendship while nursing enmity was not at all in keeping with my experience. Modern critics often describe him as lazy; but this word, too, is ill-chosen. As I knew him the Malay would work well enough in independence about his own affairs . . . but was, however, almost untouched by greed for gold. His motto appeared to be 'Enough is as good as a feast' and he was averse to selling his independence for a wage.[17]

Frank Swettenham (who belonged to an age which had no problem with ethnic stereotypes) drew a pen portrait of the typical male *rayat*:

18

short, thick-set, well-built man, with straight black hair, a dark brown complexion, thick nose and lips, and bright intelligent eyes. His disposition is generally kindly, his manners are polite and easy. Never cringing, he is reserved with strangers . . . He is courageous and trustworthy in the discharge of an undertaking . . . He is a good talker, speaks in parables, quotes proverbs and wise saws, has a strong sense of humour, and is very fond of a good joke . . . He is a Muhammadan and a fatalist, but he is also very suspicious. He never drinks intoxicants . . . is by nature a sportsman . . . is a skilful fisherman, and thoroughly at home in a boat. Above all things he is conservative to a degree, is proud and fond of his country and his people, venerates his ancient customs and traditions, fears his Rajas, and has a proper respect for constituted authority.[18]

Custom – *adat* – was 'the fetish of the Malay, hence their proverb, "Let our children die rather than our customs."'[19] *Adat* governed succession and inheritance, ancient traditions and modes of behaviour; it was bound up inevitably with the Islamic religion. Custom was also the main barrier to the Europeanization of the Malay people, which to Hugh Clifford's regret was beginning by the 1880s to change the amiable and gentle-mannered Malay, 'with his love of the *dolce far niente*', into a 'sadly dull, limp, and civilised' being.[20] 'Malays are never vulgar,' Emily Innes observed. 'Vulgarity and snobbishness seem to be growths peculiar to civilization.' She saw how civilization had introduced Tunku Paglima Raja to the stimulating effect of Bass's pale ale; and it was teaching the Viceroy of Selangor 'to forsake the ways of his ancestors, to drink "berendi" [brandy] and to wear a mouthful of white teeth "like a dog", instead of filing and blackening them according to the good old Malay custom'.[21]

In her outstation, Emily was constantly brought face to face with divergent Malay and European conventions. 'The manners of the English seem abrupt, unpolished, and disagreeably frank to a Malay, who is always slow and dignified', she acknowledged, 'and in whose code of politeness it is a first law that people should rather tell each other pleasant falsehoods than unpleasant truths.' On the other hand, like many Europeans, she was baffled by aspects of Malay culture: by the oriental habit of laughing when conveying bad news; by 'the Malays' incorrigible unpunctuality'; by the inertia of he who 'would like to lie under a banana tree all his life and let the fruit drop into his mouth'; by the fact that 'It is thought good manners in Malay circles to tell people that they are rich and fat, and to depreciate oneself by alleging that one is poor and thin'; by it being 'no rudeness if a Malay raja calls on a lady with bare legs, feet, arms and shoulders; but . . . it is an insult to her if a Malay takes off his cap in her presence'. Hygiene was another unpredictable subject. In a conversation with Tunku Paglima Raja over the respective merits of eating with fingers or forks, Emily confessed, 'he had rather the best of the argument': *his* fingers had never been in anyone's else's mouth and could never be mislaid or stolen!' But, when a certain raja visited her for tea and 'proceeded to cut his bread-and-butter and his toe-nails alternately with his knife', she ended 'by reflecting philosophically that the Malay code of manners is different from ours'.[22]

On her various visits in 1879, Isabella Bird was impressed by the kind hospitality of the kampong dwellers. She noted they were passionately fond of pets and of taming birds and animals. She was interested, too, in their mimetic skills and in their linguistic sophistication, their recourse to proverbs and their love of puns. She was aware that 'In these *kampongs* the people have music, singing, story-telling, games and religious ceremonies, perhaps the most important of all . . .' Even in the outback – the *ulu* – she caught a glimpse of vigorous customs at work. 'Buffaloes are sacrificed on religious occasions, and at the births, circumcisions, marriages, and shaving of the heads of the children of the wealthy people.' Such practices indicated that 'They have an elaborate civilisation, etiquette, and laws of their own.'[23] Here was evidence of

> a rich and varied culture. The peasant or labourer, even though he lives in relative poverty and may have little education, is and feels himself to be a *cultured* man in the literal sense. He knows the oral traditions and perhaps the written literature of his own community. Its family and religious ceremonies, its festivals, traditional theatre and music enrich the content of his life. The distinctiveness of each community's culture is . . . a link with the past and a present possession to be treasured and enjoyed.[24]

All the same, it was easy to idealize the lifestyle of the Malay people. In a semi-subsistence economy of agriculture, fishing and animal husbandry, some areas were more advanced than others. In the tamed landscape of Malacca or Selangor, the well-spaced kampong houses were raised above the ground on stilts for protection from wild animals and flooding. Isabella Bird noted that

Each dwelling is of planed wood or plaited palm-leaves, the roof is high and steep, the eaves are deep, and the whole rests on a gridiron platform supported on posts, from five to ten feet high, and approached by a ladder in the poorer houses and a flight of steps in the richer. In the ordinary houses mats are laid here and there over the gridiron, besides the sleeping-mats; and this plan of an open floor . . . has various advantages. As, for instance, it ensures ventilation, and all the debris can be thrown through it, to be consumed by the fire which is lighted every evening beneath the house to smoke away the mosquitos . . . Scarcely any kampong is so small as not to have a mosque.[25]

It was customary practice for the Malays to feed themselves by growing rice about their homes. Houses were grouped 'under the shade of coco-palms, *jak*, durian, breadfruit, mango, nutmeg and other fruit trees. Plantations of bananas are never far off . . . food is above them and around them.'[26] As fishermen, the Malays generally sited the kampongs near rivers, to benefit from the natural life of what Hugh Clifford called 'the most lavish water-system in the world'.[27] In addition, Malaya's coastal waters brimmed with shark, swordfish, tenggini, red fish, smelt and shellfish. It was perhaps this natural bounty which gave foreigners the impression that the Malay was easygoing to the point of laziness. But this is a partial picture. The truth in some regions was darker. In East Pahang and the Kemaman district of Trengganu, well into the twentieth century, the fishing people were crammed together in shacks – in contrast to the wide spacing of houses on the west coast – and were bitterly poor. There was a serious lack of self-sufficiency. In Trengganu few of the coastal and river fishermen grew any crops; instead they obtained rice and provisions from Chinese dealers in dried and salted fish. In East Pahang the people relied on rice imported from Kelantan and Patani. Perak drew on additional supplies from Burma.

As the nineteenth century progressed, the natural predominance of the Malays was counterbalanced by ever increasing numbers of economic immigrants from China.[28] Chinese fishermen already had a footing on the coast, but newcomers were attracted by prospects of tin mining in the foothills of the interior. By 1876 the state of Selangor was home to 15,000 Chinese but only 2,000–3,000 Malays; the small state of Sungei Ujong housed 10,000 Chinese to 2,000 Malays. In Perak lawlessness was endemic. During civil strife in 1871–4 some 3,000 men on both sides were massacred in one day's fighting in Larut in 1872; the main street of attap buildings was destroyed, to be rebuilt in 1874. The Chinese brought their own cultural baggage with them, which differed radically from the Malays'. 'Lean, smooth-shaven, keen, industrious, self-reliant, sober, mercenary, reliable, mysterious, opium-smoking, gambling, hugging clan ties', Chinese workers voluntarily endured a harsh camp life, living in communal 'kongsi' houses around the mines, where they toiled, quarrelled and conspired together in a struggle for the survival of the fittest.[29] The downside to this industrious, thrifty people was their involvement in secret societies and their addiction to gambling, and to the opium-smoking which wasted many to comatose skeletons. The task of calming the warring groups of Malays and Chinese called for tact, patience and restraint on all sides. It was achieved by the use of judicious force by the British authorities and by the introduction in 1877 of a special government agency, the Chinese Protectorate, to deal with problems in co-operation with the headmen in the Chinese communities, who held the title of Kapitan China.

The impact of the Chinese upon Malaya was decisive. It was through them that urban life developed in much of the peninsula. Alongside their mining villages they set up shops and workshops, and from these beginnings grew the main towns of the 'protected' states. By 1880, Taiping, formerly the Malay village of Larut, had become 'a thriving, increasing place, of over six thousand inhabitants, solely Chinese, with the exception of a small Kling population [from southern India]' and 'scarcely any Malays'. It had at that time

> a street about a mile long, with large bazaars and shops making a fine appearance, being much decorated in the Chinese style; halls of meeting for the different tribes, gambling houses, workshops, the Treasury, a substantial dark wood building, large detached barracks for the Sikh police, a powder magazine, a parade ground, a Government storehouse, a large, new jail, neat bungalows for the minor English officials, and on the top of a steep, isolated terraced hill, the British Residency.[30]

But the chaos almost overwhelmed Isabella Bird: 'trains of carts with cinnamon-coloured, humped bullocks . . . gharries with fiery Sumatra ponies dashing about, crowds of Chinese coolies, busy and half-naked . . . and all the epitomised stir of a world which toils, and strives, and thirsts for gain'.[31] To Emily Innes, on the other hand, a two-day break there made a welcome change and she 'looked back upon it as one of the few bright gleams in my dreary jungle life . . . We had some delightful walks and drives in the neighbourhood.'[32] However, Taiping was soon to be overtaken by the rising town of Ipoh. Once a Chinese village, lying in a vast semicircle of limestone cliffs, Ipoh was the natural focus of the rich tin deposits of the Kinta valley and during the 1890s became the leading colonial town of Perak. Meanwhile, Kuala Lumpur, which overtook Klang as the capital of Selangor in 1880, was another town created by the enterprise of the Chinese. Beginning as a crude mining village at the muddy confluence of the Klang and Gombak rivers, its development from 1869 was in the hands of Ah Loi, the most prominent man in Selangor and a reformed character since the days when he allegedly purchased the heads of his enemies in the market place.

> He has made long roads for the purpose of connecting the most impor-
> tant of the mines with the town . . . he has so successfully secured peace
> and order in his town and district . . . He employs on his estate –
> in mines, brick-fields and plantations – over four thousand men. He
> has the largest tapioca estate in the country and the best machinery.
> He has introduced the manufacture of bricks, has provided the sick with
> an asylum, has been loyal to British interests . . . and has dispensed
> justice to the complete satisfaction of his countrymen.[33]

In 1873 Kuala Lumpur was still a Chinese town with two streets and numerous thatched houses, but in 1883 a visitor observed that a colonial town was emerging: 'The main road has been improved; neat, inexpensive police stations and good bridges have replaced decayed old ones, whilst several new buildings are in progress.'[34]

These public works were evidence of the improved administration of the British, although how the system functioned effectively with such a small establishment is surprising. It appears that in 1879 there were only three European residents of Sungei Ujong, and only two – James and Emily Innes – lived in the Langat district of Selangor. At the evening service held in Klang, the European population who formed the congregation totalled seven men and two women. In Perak Europeans *and* Eurasians together numbered eighty-two, and the 1881 census showed only thirty-two Europeans in all Malacca. It was a measure of Perak's advance towards civilization, in Emily's eyes, that by 1880, in addition to the arrival of 'that delightful sign' of progress, the telegraph, there were several new European residents. She remembered the barrage of curiosity at her own arrival at Klang in 1876 – 'Chinese, Indians and Malays – running together to look at me, as if I were a wild animal' – while the Malay policeman explained 'that I was the first English 'mem' [lady] ever seen in the country'.[35] A bridge of mutual acceptance and trust had to be built; meanwhile, the possibility of a 'native outbreak' was ever present, haunting the dreams of isolated Europeans.

Outside the Straits Settlements, the pioneer immigrant of the Victorian age had to make do with primitive transport. Much use was made of river craft; the roads were simple tracks with wooden bridges. It was one of Emily Innes's complaints that there was no regular communication at all between Langat and the outside world, and in the event of an emergency there was no European within a day's journey.[36] Up-country, change was slow to come and transport remained primitive even in the First World War; there were only one-horse carts or bicycles available to the District Officer of Jelebu in 1913–14.[37] The river estuaries of the Straits' seaboard were difficult to navigate, as countless steamer captains were to testify over the years.

The eastern shoreline of the peninsula was a very beautiful coast, where, according to Hugh Clifford, 'The waves dance and glimmer, and shine in the sunlight, the long stretch of sand is yellow as a buttercup.'[38] In contrast, large reaches of the west coast from Johore to Kedah were lined with mangrove swamp or *mangi-mangi*, 'a belt miles in breadth, dense, impenetrable'. At low water the mango trees, 'from forty to fifty feet high . . . of dark, dull green . . . are seen standing close packed along the shallow and muddy shores on cradles . . . of their own roots five or six feet high . . . [They form] huge breeding grounds for alligators and mosquitoes, and usually for malarial fevers.'[39] Selangor typified the West Malayan pattern: a belt of low-lying swamp and dense jungle behind, with high jungle-covered hills in the far distance, a vast area of unexplored, beast-haunted country. Living in this *ulu*, Emily Innes learned that 'The diseases most common to Englishmen in the tropics are [malarial] fever, cholera, and sunstroke, any one of which may carry off a strong man in a few hours.' The last was alleged to have killed the Resident in Sungei Ujong, Captain Murray, and the first two were a particular scourge on rubber estates, where workers lived in close proximity.[40] Public health was an unknown concept in these early days. Isabella Bird was horrified by the sight of Selangor village, for instance:

'a most wretched place'. 'Slime was everywhere, oozing, bubbling, smelling, putrid in the sun, all glimmering, shining and iridescent, breeding fever and horrible life.'[41] In fact, for middle-class Europeans life here was as risky as it was for the poor in early Victorian England. But at least the British government allowed the Inneses a water-boat 'to fetch us our drinking water, so that we never drank the water of the swamp . . . the primary cause of a terrible epidemic of cholera'.[42]

Those living up-country faced daily hazards which can only be hinted at here: venomous mosquitoes that 'rose up at sunset in their thousands from the swamp . . . thirsting for our blood', bites from fiendish ants, scorpions, all manner of snakes, spiders, centipedes and lizards. 'Carpenter beetles buzzed into our soup, locusts whirred into our tumblers, hornets entangled themselves in our hair.' The river banks were home to loathsome reptile life, the jungles to man-eating tigers who 'came moaning around the house [at Langat] about once a week generally, but sometimes for several nights together . . . Other growls and roars we heard sometimes, probably those of black panthers and leopards.'[43] Tinned food usually formed the staple diet, but there was also the monotony of 'turtle soup, stewed turtle, curried turtle, and turtle cutlets *ad nauseam*'.[44] Otherwise fresh food was limited to local river fish, skinny fowl, the occasional piece of fresh pork butchered for a Chinese holiday, and whatever fruit was grown locally. Bananas, limes, pomegranates, custard apples and mangosteens were sometimes available, with a few vegetables, such as sweet potatoes, caladium, tapioca, a kind of spinach, Indian corn, and brinjal or aubergine. It was particularly galling for those up-country to be held to ransom by Singapore food suppliers. 'Redress – from a jungle – is unattainable,' Emily bitingly observed as she sent home to a co-operative store in England for 'groceries, tinned meats, drinkables etc.'.[45] British import agencies could be remarkably efficient. On a visit to a tin mine near Larut, Isabella Bird was surprised to be presented by her Chinese host with Huntley & Palmer's coconut biscuits. In view of their official duty to provide hospitality, senior government servants had access to special supplies. At the Residency at Kuala Kangsar, Hugh Low offered his guests 'fresh beef, fresh game, mutton and venison, preserved *pâtés de foies gras* and other luxuries from Crosse and Blackwell's', not to mention 'iced champagne [which] made it difficult to believe we were in the heart of a Malay jungle'.[46] And in 1890 the old doctor at Taiping treated Charles Bowen of the Straits' Civil Service to '15 courses and 6 different kinds of wine' at Sunday tiffin.[47]

However, no matter how underdeveloped they might be, there were times when the Malay States engulfed Europeans with their magic. Isabella Bird penned eulogies about the beauties of the Malayan dawn and the 'sumptuously-coloured sunsets'. She waxed eloquent over Perak's lotus lakes and the glory of the Pass of Bukit Berapit as 'the apes were hooting their morning hymns, and the forests rang with the joyous trills and songs of birds. "All Thy works praise Thee, Oh Lord!"' Even the densest jungle had an awesome attraction:

> The loveliness was intoxicating. The trees were lofty and magnificent . . . the glorious tropical sunshine streamed in on gaudy blossoms . . . and on pure white orchids, and canary-coloured clusters borne by lianas; on sunbirds, iridescent and gorgeous in the sunlight; and on butterflies, some all golden, others amber and black, and amber and blue, some with velvety bands of violet and green . . .[48]

Her words of wonder were echoed thirty-five years later by a new recruit to the Kelantan service. Touched by the magnificence of the scenery, Alan Morkill sensed the presence of his Creator in the primordial grandeur of the rainforests.[49] But young officers tracking down pirates along the west coast were faced with an implacable terrain which turned their task into a nightmare; and on survey work in untamed Perak the young Frank Swettenham and his four companions resorted to elephant transport to negotiate land which European pioneers would never cross again in his time in Malaya:

> It had been raining at intervals all day, and the track . . . was a succession of holes . . . full of water . . . After an hour's progress it became darker than I have ever known it before, and darkness in dense jungle feels at least doubly dark . . . we were sitting back to back, on some wet grass, in an open pannier, with no covering of any kind, and to make us thoroughly miserable, it began to pour with rain – buckets of tropical rain – and never ceased till late the next morning . . . Floundering through mud and water, tumbling over fallen trees, and tearing through briars and thorns, all in pitch darkness . . . in constant fear of being carried off by tigers . . . We crossed three considerable rivers in flood. We saw nothing, but we . . . heard him [the elephant] ploughing through the water, and held on for our lives as he crawled up the opposite bank . . . I feel it is impossible and absurd to attempt to describe . . . the misery we endured.[50]

As for Emily Innes, the prospect of a second posting to Langat in 1881 filled her with dismay: 'So now we were once more back in our butcherless, bakerless, tailorless, cobblerless, doctorless, bookless, milkless, postless, and altogether comfortless jungle.'[51]

Compared with those who struggled with conditions in the Malayan interior, life was easy for the Europeans in the Straits Settlements. By 1880 Singapore, the most cosmopolitan of Eastern cities, was home to fifty-four language groups and dialects. 'How I wish I could convey an idea, however faint, of this huge, mingled, coloured, busy, Oriental population,' Isabella Bird wrote to her sister. 'The native streets monopolise the picturesqueness of Singapore with their bizarre crowds.' She was to enthuse similarly about Penang. 'The sight of the Asiatics who have crowded into Georgetown [the capital] is a wonderful one, Chinese, Burmese, Javanese, Arabs, Malays, Sikhs, Madrassees, Klings, Chuliahs, and still they come in junks and steamers and strange Arabian craft.' Isabella had listed the Chinese ahead of the other races because by 1879 they were 'commercially the most important of the immigrant races as they have long been numerically and industrially': there were nearly 20,000 Chinese in Malacca, 45,000 in Penang and 86,000 in Singapore – 'enough to give Singapore the air of a Chinese town with a foreign settlement!'[52] Far from being a homogeneous community, the Chinese belonged to different groups reflecting their origins and occupations. Domestics and unskilled labourers were invariably Hailams or Hainanese. The Hokkiens were masterly traders, especially in rice and 'Straits produce' – tin ore, aromatic woods, wax, shell and nipa palm products – through which they also developed a hold on shipping. The Teochews specialized in cash crops, such as gambier and pepper. The Cantonese were both labourers and artisans – tailors, launderers, engineers, goldsmiths. And last but not least there were the Babas or Straits Chinese, descendants of earlier waves of migrants from China who had settled in Malacca, Riau or Penang before in many cases choosing to move to Singapore once the British had taken over in 1819. They were well integrated in the Malay world, having learned to speak the language and intermarried with the locals; often better educated than other Chinese groups, many Babas could also speak some English and were familiar with European culture.

While the majority arriving from China were poor coolies or hawkers, a few triumphed over poverty and adversity to become extremely rich. The most famous local *towkay* or capitalist of the Victorian age was a Canton migrant who settled in Singapore in 1830 and diversified from shops and businesses into speculative ventures. Hoo Ah Kay was better known as 'Mr Whampoa, C.M.G., a China-man of great wealth and enlightened public spirit who is one of the foremost men in the colony'.[53] He rose to higher political office than any other Chinese resident of Singapore, and, imitating the most successful Europeans, built himself a magnificent mansion and gardens in Serangoon Road. Long before his death in 1880 he was regarded 'almost as much an Englishman as he is a Chinaman'.[54] Some of the minorities also did well. In Penang one of the oldest communities were the Indians, mostly Tamils and Chettiahs, the latter being moneylenders whose activities expanded into banking. There were some 15,000 Indians living on the island in 1879, though they were reinforced in the next twenty years by the arrival of Jaffna Tamils from Ceylon. An Arab merchant and banker, Noureddin, was 'the millionaire of Pinang and is said to own landed property here to the extent of £400,000', Isabella Bird reported.[55] The Armenians were another small but significant commercial group, headed by the Sarkie brothers, who owned the Crag Hotel on Penang Hill and built the Eastern and Oriental Hotel in Penang's Georgetown and the Raffles Hotel in Singapore in the 1880s.

The division of economic functions between the various racial groups is said to explain the comparative peace and harmony that prevailed in the Straits Settlements. But, however numerous and visible the Asian peoples, it was the English who held the reins of power. Even a junior officer in the Straits' Civil Service quickly became aware of the authority he exercised:

> It seems a little new to me that whenever one goes in or out, up the streets or anywhere, the sentries or police always present arms, besides the enormous power one has of ordering police or Government servants to do anything one wants and, as long as on duty, travelling on Government steamers or Government horses.[56]

How much greater, therefore, was the deference enjoyed by the Governor. He was the fount of colonial power, ruling in the Straits Settlements with the help of an Executive and a Legislative Council. In the 'Native States', the Residents personified British authority with the Governor's approval. The function of the Resident, according to the terms of the Pangkor Engagement which Governor Andrew Clarke had presided over in 1874, was to offer British protection and to advise the Malay rulers on political matters, justice and finance – indeed, on everything except the sensitive issues of religion and custom. The system, which had first been introduced in Perak, Selangor and Sungei Ujong, was extended to include the other small states lying between Johore and Selangor, which joined together in stages to become the Negri Sembilan (the 'Nine States') in 1895. Meanwhile, through the good offices of Hugh Clifford, Pahang, the largest but poorest of the Malay States, came under the British sphere of influence in 1888. Although the 'taming of Pahang' was interrupted by local resistance – referred to as the Pahang War – by 1895 British administration was successfully established on the east coast of the peninsula.

The details of this political process do not concern us here; but the outcome in 1896 marked the penultimate stage of the unification of 'British Malaya', when the four 'Protected' states of Perak, Selangor, Negri Sembilan and Pahang were joined together as the Federated Malay States (FMS). While each state retained its own Sultan as constitutional head, and had its own Resident and Advisor, the new federation was effectively centralized under a Resident-General in Kuala Lumpur and the overall authority of the Governor of the Straits Settlements, wearing a second hat as the High Commissioner of the FMS. 'In many respects, the Straits Settlements and the federated states were a unified British colony, although the sovereignty of the states remained a legal fact.'[57] To oil the wheels of the new structure and reconcile the Malay chiefs to their loss of real power and dignity, they were paid monthly political allowances by the colonial government. The establishment of State Councils also guaranteed a system of consultation between the chiefs and British officials. In the longer term, education was targeted to ensure the future participation of the Malay aristocracy in the administrative branch of the Civil Service.

The joint celebration of symbolic events also played a part in the coming together of the two worlds, East and West. In response to the new constitutional arrangements a lavish official conference or Durbar of the Malay rulers was convened in 1897 at Kuala Kangsar, capital of Perak. This gathering of Malaya's grandees came just a month after Queen Victoria's Diamond Jubilee, which 'has been a tremendous affair all through the Straits Settlements; the Chinese especially have shown their loyalty', gloated a colonial civil servant, 'in spending heaps of money on processions, arches, fireworks etc.'.[58] As a Singapore resident pointed out, 'One had got so used to the fact that Queen Victoria ruled. No one out here could remember any other ruler . . .' This explains the experience of a bemused Emily Innes. 'Malay men sometimes called on me. Their first question usually was, "How is Queen Victoria? Are you any relation of hers? and have you heard from her lately?"'[59] Emily was reporting this in the aftermath of the Queen's elevation as Empress of India, which raised her status in many peoples' eyes to a position 'fixed and unalterable, a necessity without which the Empire could not live'.[60] In 1887 her Golden Jubilee had been celebrated by the people of the Protected States and the Straits Settlements in what was considered an appropriate way:

> On Monday the festivities began and did begin with a vengeance; the first day they consumed nearly drs. 300 worth of champagne alone not to mention whiskies and sodas and 2,000 or 3,000 pounds weight of ice. The sports were very good . . .
>
> On the second day we had a grand breakfast at which old D[enison, the District Officer] made the finest and most loyal speech I have ever heard in my life, in the afternoon we had aquatic sports and a dinner in the evening. And the next two days were spent in finishing up the sports.[61]

Now, however, with the convergence of two major royal events in 1897, the celebration of the Queen's sixty years as sovereign and the first Durbar following the inauguration of the Federated Malay States alongside the Crown Colony of the Straits Settlements, the achievements of the Victorian age seemed to have reached a unifying climax.[62]

While the hybrid colony developed in the long years of the Pax Britannica, the British grew in confidence, feeling secure in their position in the Far East, despite the colonial aspirations of France and Germany. The political classes were satisfied that British intervention in Malaya was necessary and constructive, though a few administrators had the foresight and empathy to envisage a degree of partnership. It was said of Hugh Low, Resident in Perak, that 'He obviously attempts to train and educate these men [the rajas] in the principles and practice of good government, so that they shall be able to rule firmly and justly.'[63] He was acting in the spirit of Queen Victoria's portentous instruction to Disraeli in 1875 to bring on the people of these states to the stage where they could govern themselves. But the popular view was voiced by Sir Frederick Weld (Governor in 1880–7) when he famously declared, 'I doubt if Asiatics will ever learn to govern themselves; it is contrary to the genius of their race, of their history, of their religious system, that they should. Their desire is a mild, just and firm despotism: *that* we can give them.'[64] Indeed, the British believed that 'The Malays highly appreciate the manner in which law is administered, under English rule, and the security they enjoy in their persons and property . . . It is possible that they prefer being equitably taxed by us . . . to being plundered by native princes.'[65] Or, as another administrator put it, in terms that reflected the spirit of that age, 'It is just the Irish tenantry all over again but the difference is that they would sooner come to us with their grievances than their own Rajas . . . One generally finds about twenty Malays waiting round the house in the morning who have all different yarns.'[66]

Seeking confirmation that the British were indispensable, Isabella Bird asked her Kling boatman what brought so many migrants voluntarily to Malaya 'from the Red to the Yellow Sea'. He answered without hesitation. '"Empress good – coolie get money; keep it." This being interpreted is, that all these people enjoy absolute security of life and property under our flag.' On the other hand, she had the acumen to realize that 'This is by no means to write that the Malays love us, for I doubt whether the *entente cordiale* between any of the dark-skinned Oriental races and ourselves is more than skin deep.'[67] Emily Innes agreed. 'Malays – the patriotic ones – do not love us; why should they?' Why, indeed. A deep chasm lay between the civilizations of Europe and Asia, with all the possibility of racial intolerance. Tunku Chi of Selangor 'hated the English . . . with all her heart' for having 'civilised' her husband, the Viceroy.[68]

The 'inscrutable Chinee' was not just a popular theatrical stereotype: to many British colonials he was a genuine enigma. After a river excursion into Perak's tin-mining country, where he observed the Chinese at work, a young government officer wrote home, 'They are a most extraordinary people. I cannot understand them at all yet and they always smile with a smile that is childlike and bland and with few exceptions one can never believe one word they say.'[69] Isabella Bird discovered part of the explanation. In a frank exchange with a Chinese acquaintance whom she considered both able and highly educated, she was told that the Chinese (with the possible exception of the Babas) regarded the British as 'the incarnation of brute force allied to brute vices!' As for the Malay people, she wrote, 'we do not understand them, or they us, and where they happen to be Mohammedans, there is a gulf of contempt and dislike on their part which is rarely bridged by amenities on ours'.[70] Only the Tamil Indians and Ceylonese showed blind admiration for Europeans.

The responsibility for racial harmony lay unquestionably with the British administration, although, as products of the age of nationalism, officers clearly thought in terms of racial stereotypes, as one of them revealed:

> the Malays are far more reasonable [than the Irish] but just as cunning and tell more lies. I am beginning to like the Chinese in a sort of way they are as obstinate as pigs and are always in court with paltry cases; as to paltry cases the Klings are the worst and they are all regular lawyers and never speak the truth by accident.[71]

However, 'If I may venture an opinion,' stated Isabella Bird firmly:

> all Colonial authorities in their dealings with native races, all Residents and their subordinates, and all transactions between ourselves and the weak peoples of the Far East, would be better for having 'the fierce light which beats upon a throne' turned upon them. The good have nothing to fear, the bad would be revealed in their badness, and hasty counsels and ambitious designs would be held in check.[72]

Whatever the prejudices and shortcomings of the British, a visit to Saigon in 1861 convinced Franklin Kendall, a shipping assistant with P. & O., that as colonial administrators they were far superior to the French:

> 'The French . . . do not understand what they are doing at all . . . They seem to delight in harassing and annoying the natives as much as they can. They knock down their houses, burn their rice, make them work like so many convicts . . . and stop all their trade. Their only idea is 'La Gloire' . . . Then again, they don't look after their own men at all; they make them work in the sun without awnings, lie down on the damp ground without tents, pay them very badly and feed them worse . . . The way too in which business is mismanaged and the public money squandered is so patent to any sound-thinking man . . . I do not mean to say that we English are by any means immaculate, but we have a semblance

at any rate of management and order in the way we do things, which Johnny Crapaud has not.[73]

Two decades later Isabella Bird heard that Saigon 'has the wild ambition to propose to itself to be a second Singapore!' – a preposterous idea, since on the Mekong dockside 'nothing looked very busy' and 'the cafés were full of Frenchmen, Spaniards, and Germans, smoking and dozing with their feet upon tables'. During her walkabout there, Isabella came across a young French artillery officer who was 'eloquent upon the miseries of Saigon'. Swiftly she decided, 'I do not envy the French their colony.'[74] The English, however, were admired by their European rivals. In a conversation with the French Ambassador, the German Chancellor Karl von Bülow is said to have remarked, 'My dear Ambassador . . . You know very well that if we both were condemned to spend the rest of our lives in a colony, you wouldn't live in a German one and I certainly shouldn't live in a French one. We'd both choose an English one.'[75] Faced with different Asian cultures and with an existing system of native rulers in the Malay States, the British responded to the challenge of colonial government by introducing into Malaya their own notions of justice, policing and ways of life, and the whole mental paraphenalia of a 'self-confident culture, convinced of its superiority and its "civilised" status'.[76]

But the last word, like the first, should perhaps belong to that astute eyewitness Isabella Bird. In her judgement, the other powers were 'almost nowhere in this strange Far East'. She had no doubt about Britain's place in the world at the height of the Victorian era. With apologies for sounding 'hifalutin', she wrote with conspicuous pride and all the moral certainty of a nineteenth-century Imperialist:

Russia, France, Germany and America, the whole lot of the 'Great Powers' are represented chiefly by a few second-rate warships, or shabby consulates in back streets, while England is 'a name to be conjured with', and is represented by prosperous colonies, powerful protective forces, law, liberty, and security. These ideas are forced on me as I travel westward.[76]

# 2

# *Pioneers and Progress*

From the 1880s Malaya was gripped by an enterprise fever that affected many parts of the globe in the late nineteenth century. A free immigration policy drew in Asian immigrants to fill the labour void. Tin was still the magnet of opportunity for thousands of Chinese, and the race to develop the Perak tinfields of the Kinta valley foreshadowed the Klondike gold rush. Shiploads of Tamils from southern India and hundreds of Javanese came as indented estate labourers. In other fields, too, opportunities expanded. Jaffna Tamils from Ceylon filled clerical posts or laboured on the railways; Sikhs, Punjabis, Bengalis and Pathans found positions as watchmen and police, or in transport and business. Europeans learned of new openings in established agencies or fledgling companies which seemed to offer attractive prospects for engineers, managers, administrators, salesmen, shippers and professional experts. They were still a small fraction of the population, a modest 6,500 in 1901, of whom three-quarters were residents of Singapore and Penang. Who were these pioneers from Europe, what brought them across the globe in search of work, and what did they achieve?

The Malays did not distinguish between Europeans, regarding them all as simply '*orang puteh*' – 'white men'. In fact the majority – about 85 per cent – came from the British Isles. They were predominantly young, unmarried men, sons of the middle classes: officers and officials, soldiers and sailors, professional or skilled men, men with no formal qualifications, men with university degrees, public-school men, set to become so-called boxwallahs, officewallahs, junglewallahs and competition-wallahs.[1] Of the others, a small number came from continental Europe, from farming, mining or seagoing backgrounds. A few were Americans of European ancestry. Some were of settler stock from the Dominions – Australians and New Zealanders. A proportion came from other parts of the Empire. A stream of Ceylon planters, for instance, arrived at the beginning of the century. To take an example, Bill Fairlie was a Scotsman who began as a coffee planter in East Africa. He moved to Ceylon, where he planted tea for twelve years, and finally came to Malaya, ending by managing a tea estate in the Cameron Highlands.[2]

This diverse body of expatriates disembarked at Penang or Singapore to join a European merchant class in the Straits Settlements that was considered a well-integrated, gregarious, international community, with 'none of that abominable clique system of Bombay or Calcutta' which a young shipping assistant, Franklin Kendall, had encountered before transferring to Singapore.[3] Young men experienced the camaraderie of living in communal lodgings or messes. Non-British Europeans turned for company to their consulates.[4] At the same time the British, having imported the old Regency tradition of social and sports clubs, relaxed and mingled in a range of institutions, such as the Singapore Club or the Tanglin Club, founded in the 1860s, or the newer golf and swimming clubs established in the 1890s.

Some social changes appeared after the Straits Settlements became a Crown Colony, in 1867. Official circles grew in size and self-importance; governors were conscious of their position as representatives of the Queen. By 1880 colonial officialdom was somewhat stuffy, according to Isabella Bird – imbued with a 'high sense of honour' and a 'righteous *esprit de corps* which characterises our civil servants in the Far East', though, travelling in a semi-official capacity, she appreciated the advantages to be gained from this enhanced status.[5] In particular, she was struck by the conviviality she encountered everywhere among the Malays: 'Their hospitality was very graceful. Many of the wealthier Mohammedans, though they don't drink wine, keep it for their Christian guests, and they offered us champagne', while her Chinese host in Larut 'in anticipation of our visit . . . had conveyed champagne, sherry, and bitter beer!' Government officers received a social allowance, so they were obliged to entertain fellow Europeans even in jungle outstations; but it was a duty that was taken seriously. One of the few compliments Emily Innes ever paid the Resident of Selangor was that he was hospitable; and Isabella Bird was also grateful to his gracious wife, who, despite a lack of facilities, managed to produce an excellent English afternoon tea: 'Before we left [Klang] Mrs Douglas gave me tea, scones, and fresh butter, the first fresh butter that I have tasted for ten months.'[6] Friendly behaviour became a tradition in Malaya. As a resident of Penang, Gerald Mugliston, recalled 'the good fellow- and sportsmanship and the hospitality among the European community, and the wish, from highest to the most lowly, to try to do everything possible to help a youngster on his way'.[7] Sometimes cultural differences between Europeans were the subject of gossip or jest among them, but they rarely caused friction before the First World War. Rivalry and sectarian differences mattered little. So when the tiny Christian congregation in Klang gathered for Sunday service one evening in 1879, the hymn, '"I heard the voice of Jesus say", was sung with equal enjoyment by Catholics and Protestants in the wilds of the Golden Chersonese'.[8]

Forty years earlier scarcely a European had been seen in Province Wellesley, and even in the 1850s 'there was only one white man to be found in the interior between Singapore and Bangkok'.[9] The fact that the first European pioneer in the region was a Frenchman made no difference to the British. Leopold Chasseriau enjoyed a unique reputation for boldness and initiative. Born in Bordeaux in 1825, he began as a sugar planter in Mauritius before moving to pastures new in Malaya around 1848. First he opened up a plantation in Province Wellesley, the Jawee Estate, but over a drink with an Englishman he then bought several thousand acres of jungle around Ayer Rendang in northern Malaya. A descendant tells his story:

> Having picked up a partner on the way, Great-Grandfather set off at once with a gang of men and elephants to clear his newly-acquired property . . . Pirates, alerted by the bush telegraph, were awaiting them by a bend in the [Batu Kawan] river, and the poor partner, taken by surprise, was struck through the heart with a kriss, and that was the end of his adventures. But Great-Grandfather was ready with his pistol, and within a few minutes the corpses of the pirates were drifting down the river, escorted by a fleet of hungry crocodiles. Undeterred, he carried on with his pioneering alone, and from then on, continually called upon by Rajahs of the surrounding states to restore order, he became, willy nilly, the policeman of Northern Malaya, marching his battalion of armed men and elephants wherever a new war broke out.[10]

After several years, Leopold Chasseriau returned to France to find a wife and brought back his imperturbable seventeen-year-old bride, fresh from her convent, to his estate, renamed Malakoff after the key fortress captured by the French in the Crimean War. There he grew sugar cane and tapioca. Although she was probably the only Western woman in the whole of Malaya's interior, Madame Chasseriau took to pioneering like a trooper. It seemed as natural to sleep at night with a pistol under her pillow as to stable war-weary elephants in the garden and to use her bungalow as an emergency hospital for locals wounded in fights. Meanwhile, the indefatigable Leopold, tall and strong as an ox, combined the role of the Malay rulers and the future British Residents in the Malay States. He 'suppressed the bandits and administered justice, and if a few corpses were hanging from the surrounding trees by the end of the morning session, there were no complaints. His methods and his justice were feudal and effective.'[11] After a further long spell in France the Chasseriaus returned again to Malaya in the 1870s, sold Malakoff, and settled down instead on a thousand acres of newly cleared jungle on the island of Singapore. Then, like a true entrepreneur, Leopold struck a bargain with the Governor, Sir Andrew Clarke. In return for a concession of another 2,000 acres he offered to clear the town streets of its human refuse. Every day at dawn a train of forty bullock carts and 500 men left the Chasseriau estate on Bukit Timah Road to bring back the 'odiferous but invaluable fertilizer'. His crops of coconuts, sugar cane, tapioca and coffee flourished, and to play safe he 'kept tigers on the estate to gobble up the jungle pigs who root up the tapioca tubers'.[12]

In the frenetic climate of pioneering, fortunes were quickly made and lost. Until mining techniques changed dramatically in the twentieth century, the Chinese used cheap, labour-intensive methods to dominate tin production. Attempts in the 1880s by European prospectors and companies to break into mining in Perak and Selangor fell down on cost-effectiveness, and by 1892 their efforts had all but failed. The sole exception was the Society of Kinta Tin Mines, which was the first to operate in Kinta and also built the first hydroelectric power-station in Perak around the turn of the century. Meanwhile, other industries were developing. A formidable Dutchman, Theodore Cornelis Bogaardt, who joined the British agents Mansfield & Co. in 1872, was succeeding in his shipping ventures with the Straits Steamship Company and the

Blue Funnel Line. Danish sea captains made a niche for themselves in coastal steamer traffic. A German, Herman Muhlinghaus, was co-founder with a Scotsman, James Sword, of the powerful Straits Trading Company, which owned smelting works in Province Wellesley and on the island of Pulau Brani in Singapore harbour.

The German pioneers were unquestionably a thrusting group. The German house Behn Meyer, founded in 1840, became one of the most famous in the East. With offices in Singapore and Penang, from the 1880s it held the agency for the prominent German shipping line Norddeutscher Lloyd. The high profile of the Germans impressed the Mancunian Edwin Brown, who travelled out in 1901 on Norddeutscher's SS *Hamburg* to join Brinkmann & Co., and became one of only two Englishmen in the Singapore branch. In no time he became acquainted with members of the other leading companies: Huttenbach Bros, Kumpers & Co., Puttfarcken & Co., Schiffmann Heer, Rautenberg, Schmidt & Co. and of course, Behn Meyer. Germany's commercial presence had been steadily growing over half a century (especially in the years since Isabella Bird had made her disparaging remarks about other European powers), but the portents were already there in 1860 when the shipper Franklin Kendall began to feel outnumbered. 'Talk about Australia being full of Scotchmen, what would anybody say of Singapore? Jellicoe [his colleague in the P. & O. office] and I are almost the only two Englishmen in the place, the rest being with very few exceptions about 75% Scotch and 25% Germans.'[13]

His tongue-in-cheek remark said a lot about the composition of Singapore's commercial sector, which had a marked and enduring Scottish presence. The Scots' invasion of the East had begun in the 1720s and was confirmed later in the century when Henry Dundas, 1st Viscount Melville, recruited large numbers of his fellow countrymen to the East India Company. The Scots in the East were proud of their nationhood. Penang had been 'quite appropriated by the Scotch', a visitor observed.[14] But Scottish celebrations were held throughout the Straits Settlements. In Singapore, 'New Year's Eve was always a very hilarious and noisy evening. There were so many Scots . . . that Hogmanay and First Footing was carried on with all the Scottish traditions and drink', while Burns Night and St Andrew's Day were occasions for 'highly exaggerated exhibitions of Scottishness peculiar to the Scot in exile . . . They are the necessities of life to the exile, these festivities, with their fantastic meals of haggis, Athol brose, salt herring, all of them manufactured apparently for export to places such as Penang.'[15]

To keep their end up, Penang's English community celebrated St George's Day with equal enthusiasm, inviting all their Scottish friends to a grand ball at the Town Hall. For all their clannishness, the Scots were much admired. The Jaffna Tamils, an 'industrious, thrifty, conservative, intelligent, morally earnest' people, actually cherished being called the 'Scotsmen of the East';[16] and an Englishman, looking back over his Malayan career, marvelled at the providential impact of the Scots. 'I'm astonished and struck by the fact of the large number of Scotsmen with whom I've been great friends,' he added.[17]

A scan of the leading companies in the Straits Settlements makes clear Scotland's contribution to Malaya. The best known, Guthrie's – founded in 1821 by Alexander Guthrie – was managed for the duration of the century by a trio of dynamic Scotsmen: James Guthrie, Thomas Scott and John Anderson. It was the longest surviving company in Malaya, but there were plenty of other influential firms with Scottish associations – A. L. Johnston & Co., managed by the Scots-born William Henry Read (in partnership with Robert Bain and James Cunison Drysdale), Syme & Co., Fraser & Co., McAlister & Co. and Paterson, Simons & Co., to name a few. Typically, the Scots provided the first two governing Residents of Singapore: Colonel William Farquhar of the Madras Engineers and Dr John Crawfurd, once of the East India Company medical service. Malaya's best-known hill stations, Fraser's Hill and Cameron Highlands, bear Scottish names. In a nautical context, Captain John Blair of Alloa – 'as honest good a Scotsman as ever left the land of cakes' – became Manager of Singapore's Tanjong Pagar docks in 1866, while in 1880 rare visitors to Selangor included Scottish engineers of small coasting steamers.[18]

With the opening up of the Malay States to commercial exploitation, a steady flow of Scots planters, young 'creepers', surveyors and engineers came to build roads or plant rubber.[19] None took to pioneering better than Jimmy Irvine, who was greatly admired in his adopted home town of Penang. He sailed from Clydeside in 1873, and within a short time was

> the friend of Malay sultans, owner of an engineering business, maker
> of bridges, roads in the jungle, planter of padi fields, builder of wharves
> on the rivers. He had fought in the Perak Wars, started a steamship

service, founded a ship chandlers' and contractors' business, and yet had time to become a great authority on the natural history of the peninsula.[20]

Irvine represented the post-Pangkor generation of pioneers, as did Grant Mackie, a Scot 'of great character in whom the spirit of adventure was strong'. Born in 1852, he was a son of the manse who began his Malayan career as a road constructor but after many years in the country struck tin and became extremely rich. Grant was a contemporary of James McClymont, a Girvan lad who began as a clerk on the Port Dickson–Seremban railway and rose to be General Manager of the Sungei Ujong Railway, meanwhile acquiring a large fortune from investments in rubber and other ventures.[21]

In the 1890s coffee planting became the fashion, but after 1900 a new wave of pioneers came to develop rubber. Possibly as many as one-third of these planters were Scottish, though whether, as Somerset Maugham implied, they spoke in a broad, unintelligible accent is a moot point. Scottish directors sometimes selected educated lads from modest but respectable backgrounds – though many had been to English or Scottish public schools: Bruce Lockhart, for instance, went to Fettes, his best friend, Freddie Cunningham, to Glenalmond before coming out East in 1907.[22] There were a number like James McClymont, who spoke with a broad Girvan tongue, or the manager of a Kedah estate who had a chip on his shoulder about arrogant English public-school 'creepers'; although those same English subordinates admired their boss as an 'utterly fearless Scottish highlander . . . the soul of honesty and conscientiousness' and a dab hand with a 22-bore rifle to boot.[23] Estates such as Lauderdale in Perak, Caledonia in Province Wellesley, Highlands and Lowlands and Lothian in Selangor advertised their Scottish ownership; names like Watson, Duncan, Findlay and Macfadyen recall the many early Scottish proprietors. In the more obscure role of estates' doctor, Dr Malcolm Watson made his name as a noted malariologist while carrying out valuable research on the habits of mosquitoes on the rubber plantations around Klang, Selangor. In the opinion of an English planter, 'without Watson's brilliant discoveries and leadership the plantation industry in Malaya would never have survived'.[24] Scotsmen could be found in the remotest places. In 1913 the minuscule community of Kuala Klawang in Jelebu ('an enchanting little mountain nest') included two mine owners called Macgregor and Hamilton (the latter Bruce Lockhart's cousin) and two mine managers, Laidlaw of the Titi tin mine and Ross of the Kenaboi gold and silver mine.[25] And the list of notable Scots Malayans could run on and on. It was a time when dozens braved 8,000 miles at sea – an 'awesomely hazardous' voyage – knowing little of what to expect at journey's end, for 'A man might never return from tropical exile.'[26]

James H. Drysdale was another of these determined pioneers. Despite a family connection with Malaya, he succeeded through his own initiative.

> I arrived in Singapore in March 1872 as fourth engineer of the S.S. *Tanah Merah* after rather a long voyage, having sailed from the Tail of the Bank [Clyde] on New Year's morning at 3 o'clock, and run into a gale in the Irish Channel, which compelled us to run back to Belfast for repairs. As three engineers were the full complement for a steamer of her size running on the coast, I was dumped on Tanjong Pagar wharf with all my belongings, namely an old-fashioned carpet bag of clothes and ten bright guineas in my pocket, to make a career for myself in the East. Fortunately I was gifted with a nature which made me tackle any work that was given me with right good will.[27]

Variations on his unceremonious landing and uncertain future were enacted time and time again. A missionary teacher never forgot the empty feeling of being 'a lonely stranger at Tanjong Pagar' after disembarking from a P. & O. liner.[28] It was the sight of the coaling station which overwhelmed Maurice Hillier when he reached Singapore on Christmas morning, 1887:

> Torrential rain was falling from a leaden sky as we entered the harbour . . . I looked from my porthole on to a dirty, shabby wharf, covered with sodden stacks of coal, backed by a row of dingy sheds. There was not a soul to meet me, and the outlook was miserable in the extreme. I waited awhile, but as no one turned up, eventually managed to secure for myself a ramshackle gharry, and behind a wretched little pony with an air of dejection altogether in keeping with my own spirits, made my way along the Tanjong Pagar Road to the town. Any Old Timer in Singapore will know that I got no glimpse of the promised paradise along that dreary stretch, and my heart was in my boots.

Fortunately, once inside his hotel Hillier met a holiday atmosphere which dispelled his depression, and later he discovered a certain beauty in his surroundings. 'The green sward of the esplanade with the trees and the cathedral spire in the background made an unforgettable picture.'[29]

Those who had company on the outward voyage were less aware of loneliness. Travelling out with Christopher Harrison on board P. & O.'s SS *Syria* to Penang in 1907 were four other young Englishmen: one a lawyer who built up a practice in Ipoh, and three would-be planters like himself. Harrison was all too conscious of his immaturity: 'I was only 18 and very pink and white!'[30] At much the same time another eighteen-year-old creeper went out on the SS *India* to Penang. Leopold Ainsworth was another public-school boy, but he arrived alone, knowing no one and with 'nothing to help me on my way except for ten pounds in my pocket, and a five years' contract for service on a rubber and coconut plantation in the native Malay state of Kedah'.[31] Within a space of hours, Ainsworth experienced grandeur and bathos in quick succession. The beauty of Penang touched him deeply, but he was soon brought down to earth when he ate his first meal at the estate manager's home. The first course consisted of tinned soup with a crust of dead ants. This was followed by tinned soft roes on toast, tasteless but badly fried in coconut oil. Next came a kind of tinned beef, 'exquisitely tough and stringy and flavoured with a sharp metallic tang'. In place of bread he was given 'large dry biscuits of the dog variety, very hard and tasting of cardboard and straw'. The smell and taste of the semi-molten tinned butter was indescribable. The final course, banana fritters, looked better but was ruined by the flavour of coconut oil, and the whole meal ended with coffee, 'its horrible flavour due to the cook's invariable habit of using one of the manager's socks as a strainer'.[32]

After this inauspicious beginning, while he worked for £15 per month, Ainsworth, like Drysdale, began to find Malaya a congenial place. He branched out on his own, starting as a planter with thirty acres of his own land under rubber, then becoming successively an independent factory owner, rubber trader and surveyor, before returning latterly to rubber planting as the Manager of a 5,000-acre estate in Kedah owned by a large American firm.[33] Drysdale, meanwhile, had married the daughter of an English doctor, a humanitarian pioneer in Borneo. In time they had four children, and, apart from home leave, they put their roots down in Singapore. He forged a career in a newly established firm of engineers, founders, and bridge- and shipbuilders.

Messrs Riley & Hargreaves expanded and diversified until it had five branches in the Far East and employed up to 1,000 men. James Drysdale became the Manager of the company's central store in Singapore.[34]

Similarities may be drawn, but there was no single profile of the pioneer. Ainsworth and Harrison, public-schoolboy planters, were no more typical than Drysdale, the Scots engineer, or Franklin Kendall, the P. & O. assistant from an ancient Cornish naval family. According to hearsay,

> In the early days . . . when Malaya was being opened up, the men who went out from Britain to work there were all kinds, rich, poor, honest, dishonest. These early pioneers either passed quickly from sight or they eventually retired home with, very often, a considerable Fortune – acquired by 'Fair means or Foul'. Having got home they then became 'big noises' in the City.[35]

A sizeable number came because they had family contacts or school friends in service in India or Ceylon, if not in Malaya itself. Colonial life and service ran through generations. In addition to the well-known names – Maxwell, Birch, Clementi, Braddell – there were many other examples of Malayan dynasties.

The Blundell-Newton connection began with the Hon. Edmund Blundell, Governor of the Straits Settlements from 1855 to 1859, who had started his career in 1821 with the East India Company in Penang. His daughter married Kenneth Bruce Stuart Robertson, Singapore's Deputy Commissioner of Police, and their daughter married a direct descendant of Isaac Newton, the legendary scientist and mathematician. Howard Newton (whose name was given to Newton Crescent and Circus, and a station on the Singapore–Kranji railway line in 1903) served in Singapore's Municipal Engineers Department for almost twenty years, until 1895.[36] In turn, two of Howard Newton's daughters married into prominent Singapore families, the Maysons and the Griffith-Joneses.

John Theophilus, who worked in Malaya for forty years, recalled his and his first wife's Malayan antecedents:

> Around the 1860s Colonel Talbot was in charge of the garrison in Singapore, and he had to my knowledge, three sons and a daughter; and a young cadet called Frank Swettenham came – who eventually of course

was Sir Frank . . . Well, old Colonel Talbot and his wife were very good to Swettenham, and he helped these three Talbot chaps when they grew up. All of them came out here. It was the end of the eighties, I suppose. One of them was head Policeman and President of the Lake Club in Kuala Lumpur – you will see on the board here, from 1903 to 1908, I think; that's the eldest one, Henry Talbot. Jack Talbot was an accountant; and he ended up as Accountant-General; and the third one . . . was a District Officer. Now, my first wife's parents got married in Taiping. Her mother was a Miss Scott, who came out with her cousin, Miss Talbot, both unmarried ladies; and this Captain Edye of the Malay States Guides, he heard that Miss Scott had money and he said, 'I'm going to marry her!', and he jolly well did! Miss Talbot then met a fellow called Evan Cameron who was running the Straits Trading Company in Seremban, and Evan married Miss Talbot . . . There was a certain Edward Merriweather [*sic*]. He came out in the early nineties or late eighties, but he ended up in 1915 as Chief Secretary, Singapore, and he was knighted then: Sir Edward Merriweather. He was a distant cousin of my family – my mother's side of the family . . . His wife was a Miss Braddell – you may have heard the name. The Braddells were a Singapore family, generations of them.[37]

Another distinguished figure was E. W. F. Gilman, who retired in 1931 as Resident Councillor of Penang after thirty-two years' service. He had connections on both sides of the family with early pioneers. His great-grandfather, John Gilman, had been an East India merchant. His grandfather, Dr Oxley, whose name is commemorated in Oxley Road and Oxley Rise, rose to be Senior Surgeon and Sheriff of the Settlements. Another notable pioneer family were the Russells. In the 1880s seven of them disembarked at the port on the Klang river and made their way by gharry to Kuala Lumpur. 'My grandfather came out as a Government printer, and he was for a number of years editor of the *Selangor Journal*,' recalled a third-generation Russell, who came to Malaya in 1953.

And then he was the first editor of the *Malay Mail*; and he had five sons . . . and these boys were apparently the first English family to be brought up in Kuala Lumpur . . . The sons were brought up rather in the Chinese fashion, being educated in different things. The eldest boy, George, was an engineer; Phil was an architect, Don was a mining engineer, and my father [Archie] . . . made finance his particular field. They started a partnership and they constructed roads from one place to another, and they built the railway station in Kuala Lumpur; and Phil, the architect, certainly designed some of the buildings here, too, like the old Hong Kong Bank building, which was where J. A. Russell and Company had their first office.[38]

The Crawford family played the part in the tin and rubber industries that the Russells were to play in tea. 'They were all true pioneers, and became experts in their particular fields by the gradual accumulation of hard-earned knowledge.'[39] When James Richard Crawford, an engineer, arrived in Perak in 1885 Sir Hugh Low was Resident. The family connection with Perak was to last ninety years. After a spell in construction work he made Ipoh his base, invested in a plot of jungle off the Gopeng Road, and built a family house in 1905. 'He could have owned half of Ipoh!' exclaimed his son.[40] By 1910 he had his own foundry business. Malaya was on the brink of an economic boom. He sold his business and went into rubber instead, but also bought the Ulu Piah tin mine in partnership with his brother Robert and two Frenchmen. The venture paid off handsomely and paid for his children's education.

Undoubtedly many Europeans were attracted by the hope of quick profits, others by the lure of space and of the unknown. And the prospect of an outdoor life drew some from industrialized England. Robert Munro, 'a cheerful, sporting soul', threw up a career as an insurance broker in the City to take up the quiet life of a planter at Jugra in Selangor.[41] Freddie Cunningham was encouraged to leave Scotland because he was 'the so-called brainless son of the family'.[42] A few, like the Polish-born mariner Joseph Conrad, arrived by chance – in Conrad's case, after the barque on which he was sailing caught fire in the Indian Ocean. Oliver Marks, a Ceylon tea planter, happened to visit Malaya in 1890 with his cricket team. He gave such a brilliant performance on the sports field that he was offered a job in the Civil Service, decided to accept, and rose in twenty years to be Resident in Selangor. Misfits from English society often found their niche in Malaya. 'A good many of the men here are regular rolling stones who have at last landed in well-paid billets here.'[43] And, in a cruel jibe, a senior manager told his junior, 'Some people come out to Malaya as planters because they would be unemployable elsewhere.'[44] Former naval and army officers were taken into government service. Curiously, the old landed Catholic families of England, whom history had consigned to the role of social and political outcasts since the Reformation, also found a new *raison d'être* as colonial servants. From their ranks came several respected administrators, including a Governor of the colony, Sir Frederick Weld, and two of his relatives, F. J. Weld and Sir Hugh Clifford. Indeed at one time so prominent was the Catholic caucus that there were mutterings of anti-Protestant discrimination in Singapore![45]

There are two common perceptions of the pioneers. One is that they were just ordinary men and women caught up in an extraordinary world; the other is that they needed to be rugged individualists to survive. Exceptional lives are more likely to be documented. Madame Chasseriau was perhaps unusually resilient and brave; but Louisa Isemonger, wife of the Police Magistrate in Province Wellesley in the 1870s, was a 'gentle, thoughtful, well-informed and studious' woman who 'interested herself in the Malays and has not only acquired an excellent knowledge of Malayan, but is translating a Malayan book'.[46] Two with saintly courage were the dignified, long-suffering Mrs Douglas of Klang, who, in addition to her wifely duties in that difficult outpost, tended to her handicapped daughter 'with a loving, vigilant, and ceaseless devotion of a most pathetic kind'; and Sophia Cooke, the dedicated missionary who became a household name in Christian circles. For over forty years until her death in 1895 she ministered to such unlikely opposites as poor, homeless and unwanted Chinese and members of the armed forces and the European police force in Singapore.[47] Alan Morkill, who became District Officer in Negri Sembilan, recalled that 'Splendid work was done by the Lady Dispenser, Miss Kibble. Malays would not allow their women to be attended by male doctors and the Government brought out a few of these devoted women to serve their needs.' Miss Kibble doubled as a midwife, and 'no hired car driver would take a fare from "Missy Kibble" in Kuala Pilah'.[48]

Fame of a different kind came to two explorers. William Cameron was a government surveyor who crossed mountainous primeval jungle with his elephants and in 1885 mapped the Perak–Pahang border around what became known as the Cameron Highlands. Louis James Fraser, commemorated by Fraser's Hill, was a partner in the Singapore firm of Maclaine & Fraser before he went up-country, trying his hand as a speculator, ore trader and mule-train operator in the mountains between Selangor and Pahang. Tough men of all sorts figured among the rolling stones: mercenaries like a certain Captain Tristram Speedy, who stood six feet five, sported Abyssinian garb, played the bagpipes, and brought his own sepoys from India to quell the riotous miners of Larut. Captain William Brown talked of a 'hard-core generation of adventurer captains' and of 'the circle of "Muck-a-mucks" and the Sahibs' whom he encountered in the 1890s in Penang. The Europeans there

> were a confident, hard-working pioneer bunch mostly, free of the tight grip of respectability and correctness that held down so many other white men in the East. Engineers unashamed to wear dungarees were running the island's ship repair business. Planters had the look of men whose agricultural knowledge came from fields. And ships' officers whose home port this was, were the hard-bitten, salt-water men whose navigation had more relation to the sea than to trigonometry.[49]

Not all who came out East, however, were resilient and successful. For every affluent entrepreneur like Jimmy Irvine, others were defeated by the challenge. While in Perak, Isabella Bird came across two disconsolate-looking Ceylon planters, prospecting for coffee, but was unmoved: 'An enterprising son of an Edinburgh "Bailie" has been trying coffee-planting beyond the Perak [river], but he has got into difficulties with his labourers, and is "getting out of it".' (A Malay or Chinese labour force could not be galvanized into working on remote estates; not until the introduction of Tamil coolies in large numbers was the problem resolved.) It was obvious to Isabella that only practical men with 'Good sense, perseverance, steadiness, and a degree of knowledge of planting' were likely to succeed. 'The two "prospectors" look as if they had heard *couleur de rose* reports, and had not "struck ile". Possibly they expected to find hotels and macadamised roads . . .' she concluded dismissively.[50] Bruce Lockhart knew several men who did not make it. Harry Cumming, the brother of a rubber magnate, had been a failure. (He was later blown to bits at Gallipoli.) There was also Robert Engler, 'a mystery German of good family, who had been an officer in a crack cavalry regiment and had become a remittance man . . . He never did a stroke of work, but drank beer by the gallon.' And there was the sad case of 'Monkey' Holland, who was too easy-going, kind, generous and hospitable to make a fortune from rubber planting.[51] Good connections were no guarantee of success, for 'Monkey' was the brother-in-law of Lord Forteviot.

In the jungle, muscle was more important than brains. Yet muscle allied to an upper-middle-class background was considered the best combination. Those sharp distinctions of speech which were a feature of the English class system were brought into focus by the intimate life-style of the European community, but less so among the Scots, where difference in speech went unnoticed and everyone was acceptable. In English circles, however, accents and speech mannerisms were a subject of uninhibited comment and even affected job opportunities. As one public-school planter observed, 'the unfortunate lad who drops an "h" can't get on, no matter how good he is'.[52] The police force was one of the few government departments where 'the class standard was lower'.[53] Back in 1880, Emily Innes remarked how tough Cockneys found employment in untamed Selangor as 'English policemen of the rough-and-ready order, whose 'arts were in the right place, according to their own account, but whose *h*'s were decidedly in the wrong'. She was mildly amused that 'One of these who constantly acted as interpreter for the Resident, infected all the Malay rajas in the country, so that they began to talk and write Tuan *H*innes and the *H*office.'[54] Maurice Hillier, on the other hand, found it sad that stories should circulate about a Harbour Master of Malacca who had 'difficulty with his aspirates'. A 'sturdy pompous individual' and 'very much an old sea dog' in his manner, he became a little garrulous at a Residency dinner attended by the Governor. Commenting on present and former residents, he observed, 'It's a curious thing but when I came to Malacca there wasn't a haitch in the place; there was h'Irving and h'Isemonger and h'O'Brien and h'Elcum and h'Everingham: and now they're all haitches 'ere; there's 'Arvey and 'Odge and 'Ogg and 'Ellier and 'Owell and 'Armer and a lot more: It's very strange!'[55]

In the days before a modern civil service, the administrators were a mixed bunch. Most were military or naval officers; few understood Malay or the people of Malaya. Colonel Butterworth, for instance, an early Governor of the Straits Settlements, was a pompous eccentric, nicknamed 'Butter-pot the Great'.[56] Among the early Residents there were men whose bluff, insensitive manner offended the Malay code of politeness. Captain Bloomfield Douglas of Selangor was 'tall, vigorous . . . with white hair and a florid complexion' which belied his pusillanimity; he had an unfortunate habit of bawling at subordinates 'in tones that would have done admirably well for giving orders during a storm at sea'.[57] Like Captain Speedy, he was eased out of the service. Another officious type was 'Mr. X.', Acting Postmaster-General in Singapore.

He was of portly figure, had a shining red face adorned with white whiskers and moustache and somewhat resembled the 'Indian Nabob' of the early Victorian era. He was a good whip and made an impressive figure when he drove his pair of horses in a high mail phaeton round the esplanade of an afternoon, wearing a white top hat and having on the back seat two Indian syces clothed in gorgeous livery . . . One day a business man strolled into his office without having the politeness to take off his hat. 'Can I speak to the postmaster?' said he. 'If you take off your hat,' said X., glaring at him, 'you can speak to the Postmaster-General. I am that person.'[58]

Yet there were also selfless and dedicated officers, such as Police Superintendent Haywood of Malacca, who was 'very brave and used to danger', and Mr Syers, who was later promoted to head the police force in the Federated Malay States, a fluent Malay speaker and Superintendent of Military Police in Selangor, a thoroughly efficient man, sensible and conscientious, with a concern to understand the people, the flora, fauna and geology of the Malay States.[59]

Of the early Residents, Hugh Low of Perak proved a model colonial servant, and the success of the Residential system was attributed to him. In thirty years' experience in the East, Low brought

not only a thoroughly idiomatic knowledge of the Malay language, but a sympathetic insight into the Malay character to his present post. He understands the Malays and likes them . . . His manner is quiet and unpretending as can possibly be, and he speaks to Malays as respectfully as to Europeans, neither lowering thereby his dignity nor theirs . . . He is altogether devoted to the interests of Perak.[60]

Equally admirable was the first Resident of Negri Sembilan.

I do not think Martin Lister had an enemy in the world . . . He was a good man and did his duty in this world and was loved by every Malay in the State. When I told the Malay Sergeant-Major of Police yesterday [of his death] he burst out crying in the office and the Malays are slow to show feelings . . . the Malay Chiefs . . . all loved him. And so thought the Chinese of Kuala Pilah who erected an arch in his memory and carefully tended the little garden in which it stood.[61]

These early Residents were 'jacks of all trades', with onerous responsibilities but considerable autonomy. Captain Murray, resident of Sungei Ujong, regarded the state as his little kingdom over which he presided as 'judge, "sitting in Equity", Superintendent of Police, Chancellor of the Exchequer, and Surveyor of Taxes, besides being Board of Trade, Board of Works, and I know not what besides. In fact *he is the Government.*' In addition, he was also thoroughly honourable, and was both beloved and trusted.[62] The District Officer also had a duty to know his patch. Denison at Telok Anson was a typically conscientious officer of the 1880s, described by his subordinate as 'the most hard working man I have ever met'.[63] He liked working in remote outposts, and enjoyed the compensatory perks. It was said of him, 'Old D— of Telok Anson drinks nothing but champagne now, his allowance of whisky used to be at least a bottle and a half a day. He is about as hearty an old man as I ever met.' And 'I don't think he ever sleeps; he is always out first thing after daylight with a little short stick under his arm poking into every nook and corner all over the town'. His position gave a District Officer both authority and independence. As one of them confessed, 'the people are all more like my children than anything else, and when one is the father of some thousands of children it is hard to have to move'.[64] It was the autonomy and self-reliance of these pioneers which probably explains the number of 'characters' littering Malaya's colonial past, for often there was a fine line between individualism and eccentricity, conscientiousness and obsession.

C. C. Brown, the British Adviser in Trengganu, was a case in point. An intense, scholarly Malayophile, he always insisted on conducting meetings in Malay, even when no Malays were present! One of the most colourful characters was a mine-owner and planter called Athelstane Braddon, known to everyone in Negri Sembilan as 'the Abang' (Elder Brother) as he had a younger brother, 'Adek', in Seremban, said to be the most brilliant doctor in Malaya and a pioneering researcher into beri-beri. Between them they lived in Malaya for close on a century. The Abang had been in Jelebu for as long as anyone could remember. He had a shrewd business head, sported a powerful Hupmobile (the only car in Kuala Klawang in 1913), built himself a five-hole golf course, and converted a rice-godown he owned into the local club. After fitting it with all amenities, he charged the members $5 a month. But such was the force of his personality that any peccadilloes met with amusement rather than disapproval.[65] Braddon was a true *Tuan Besar*, as was Theodore Hubback, a handsome, rugged individual, son of a Lord Mayor of Liverpool, who began in the Public Works Department in 1895. Later he made his name as an expert on large fauna and protector of wild life. As honorary Game Warden of Pahang from 1920 and pioneer of conservation, he was involved in the politics of big-game hunting in conjunction with the Malay princes, agriculturalists and hunting enthusiasts.

Among the pioneering District Officers, Hubert Berkeley was considered unorthodox, even in the tolerant society of British Malaya. A grandson of the Earl of Kenmare and descendant of an ancient Catholic line, he ruled his fiefdom of upper Perak like a feudal prince. Berkeley was suspicious of any European posted to his district, but treated the young Financial Assistant J. W. S. Reid well once he knew he was not a Secretariat spy. 'H. B.' was, in Reid's opinion, 'a very great English gentleman', albeit an eccentric figure in his sarong and *baju* of highly variegated tartan and his straw boater crowned with a ribbon inscribed 'H.M.S. Malaya'.[66] When Alan Morkill succeeded him as District Officer, Berkeley had been in Grik for twenty-one years. 'He had woven a legend about himself and I had the impression that he saw himself as an old time Malay chief . . . Many were the colourful stories about him.' One that was often repeated concerned Berkeley's outside latrine, a two-holer, where he invited guests to sit alongside him while he belaboured them with earthy anecdotes and jokes. 'I took over from him three riding horses and six elephants,' observed Morkill; 'there was also a barouche and pair in which he drove daily to a hot spring with his sais [*syce* – coachman] dressed in his family's heraldic colours. When showing me round he pointed to the Courthouse and said, "Here we administer justice, not law."'[67]

Berkeley worked tirelessly to promote local agriculture. In his long career he was unfailingly judge, counsellor and father-confessor to his people. Few Britons handled the Malays so well or were loved so much by them. He hated all reminders of urban civilization – modern communications, industry and machines – and identified totally with the time-tested Malay way of life. Cars were his bête noire: 'Nasty, smelly things, not to be compared with a good horse.'[68] His hostility to change was total, but he fought a losing battle, and when he finally left upper Perak the district 'began to feel the hot breath of modernization . . . He was one of the last of a dying breed.'[69] C. D. Bowen, who served in the Civil Service from 1886 to 1919, saw the dangers facing the pioneer who could not keep up with the times, admitting 'I used to be a Raja in Selama, till the carriage road was finished and with that came civilisation.'[70] Bowen identified two signs of economic progress: agricultural self-sufficiency and improved communications. From the 1890s he brought padi planters into Perak, and later as District Officer he supported agricultural improvements in the Port Dickson area of Negri Sembilan.

The credit for transforming Selangor and Perak, however, went to the Resident, Frank Swettenham, with the backing of British and American capital. The creation of a road and rail network to support tin production and a new rubber industry was the key to development, as Bowen observed:

> Now Swettenham's policy is to open this country as fast as ever he can with roads, railways etc., he has made Selangor as prosperous as Perak and it is a country that has not half the resources of the latter. Government in a country like this must help capitalists or they will not enter it; now the way to help them is to open up the country with roads and railways thereby providing transport.[71]

The construction of new port facilities on the Malacca Straits was the final strategy for modernization. Port Weld was the first of the new railway ports, built to receive the Larut tin for transshipment to Penang. James Richard Crawford, a locomotive engineer who helped to construct the eight-mile rail link with Taiping, drove the first train when it was opened in the presence of the Governor, Sir Frederick Weld, amid official fanfares. For the next decade Port Weld was Malaya's leading west-coast port. With the opening up of the Kinta valley came another port development in the 1880s. Telok Anson was 'a well laid out town of brick and plank houses of about 6,000 people with public buildings . . . [and] with daily steamer service to Penang and the coast ports south-wards ending with Singapore'.[72] By 1892 a start had been made on Swettenham's plan to link this port forty miles from the mouth of the Perak river with the tin towns of the interior. C. D. Bowen noted that

> The railway from Telok Anson to Batang Padang and to Kinta is progressing rapidly and as it progresses the whole face of the country is

changing. One can drive now where only three years ago one had to ride an elephant through jungle paths; there are now quite 200 miles of mac-adamized roads in Perak irrespective of bridle paths. The Europeans are increasing. When I first came [in 1886] there were about eighty or 90 Europeans in the State, now there are nearer 500. Very soon there will be a large planting population in this part of the country and Perak bids fair to be a second Ceylon.[73]

To complete the port structure of the Protected States two more outlets were developed. Port Dickson served the trade of Negri Sembilan, and by the early 1900s Port Swettenham replaced Klang as the port of Kuala Lumpur and Selangor after the rail link was built in 1889. The growth of inter-state communications accelerated after 1896. By that time it was clear that Kuala Lumpur would become the princi-pal town, railway centre and capital of the Federated States. By 1900 good progress had been made thanks to an ambitious programme, started in 1888, which would embellish the town centre, surrounding the parade ground with palatial buildings. But rubber and railways guaranteed its prosperity, with central workshops, yards, offices and a spectacular railway station – a spatial 'cross between an extravagant Oriental palace and a mosque'.[74]

The rail system was one of Britain's major pioneering legacies to Malaya. By the early twentieth century there were a hundred stations in the peninsula. Some were more patently functional than Kuala Lumpur's: Tank Road station, the original teminus in Singapore, for instance, 'had a tower which made it an aid to ships navigating the harbour', and the terminus at Prai in Butterworth was a 'clock-towered station in white stone'.[75] By 1906 some 350 miles of track curved its way from Gemas on the Negri Sembilan–Johore border to Prai, a projected new port opposite to Penang. Singapore had had its own system since 1903, and when the Johore line was finished in 1909 Malaya's railway system was completed. Only the causeway link with the rest of Malaya and the extension to Siam had to wait until the inter-war years.

The economic prosperity of the Federated Malay States after 1896 convinced Sir Frank Swettenham that Britain should extend her polit-ical influence to the rest of the peninsula. Promoted to Governor of the Straits Settlements and High Commissioner for the Malay States in 1901, he urged the need to rescind the 1826 Anglo-Siamese treaty which had guaranteed Siamese suzerainty over Kedah, Perlis, Kelantan and

Trengganu – something that earlier governors like Clementi Smith had also wanted to end. His able successor, Sir John Anderson, was sympathetic to business interests which he felt would be advantaged by greater union between the Malay States and the Straits Settlements.

The northern states had long been within Britain's sphere of trading influence, Kedah in particular. But the propensity of the rulers of Kelantan and Trengganu to grant dubious concessions opening north Malaya to French or German interference was unacceptable to British interests. The rajas, however, were jealous of their Islamic-Malayan culture and resisted being drawn into the Federated Malay States. Anderson introduced changes in the government structure of the Federated States, but his significant achievement was an agreement with Siam in 1909 that the northern Malay states should be transferred to the British sphere of influence. When the terms were revealed, the Malay rulers felt they had been betrayed. In Sultan Abdul Hamid's vivid language, Kedah had been 'bought and sold like a buffalo'.[76] But the Sultans were powerless to affect events. Britain withdrew her extraterritorial rights in Siam and provided a generous loan for railway building in return for Siam's concession. Kelantan, Trengganu, Kedah and Perlis entered a new relationship with Britain as the Unfederated Malay States. The Sultans retained their independence, but agreed to the presence of a British Adviser as a guarantee of British 'protection'. This left Johore standing alone, but in the end the economic arguments for co-operation in the peninsula under a system of British advice and protection were persuasive. In 1914 the independent-minded Sultan Ibrahim agreed to join the Unfederated States and to accept a British 'General Adviser'. Forty years of intervention had come to fruition. Despite its curious tripartite constitutional structure, all Malaya was, to varying degrees, under British authority.

Meanwhile, by 1914 modernization had made life more pleasant and comfortable for the well-to-do. While the small townships and the east-coast states had an unchanging air, public works – hospitals, schools, roads, bridges, law courts, hotels and all other indicators of modern civilization – changed the appearance of the major towns in the Edwardian era. By 1905 the luxury of fresh meat, fruit and dairy produce had arrived in Singapore – courtesy of the Cold Storage Company – and by 1914 the same service had reached Penang, Kuala Lumpur, Ipoh, Taiping, Telok Anson and Klang. Large new stores increased the choice of high-class goods for European customers. Whiteaway Laidlaw & Co., drapers, had a showpiece store in Singapore from 1900, selling household goods, shoes and crockery. Branches were opened in Penang and Kuala Lumpur soon after. Pritchard's of Penang, starting as tailors and outfitters, diversified into other lines and became rivals of Robinson's and John Little's of Singapore and Kuala Lumpur. With twelve large bottles of Heidsieck champagne at $54, ¼ lb of pâté de foie gras at $2.25, cashmere socks at $7.50, a dozen, and gentlemen's dress shoes at $5.00 a pair, the cost of living may have seemed high, but the expanding retail trade was a sign that planters, middlemen, business people, anyone outside the official sector, now had money to spare.[77]

Captain Brown of the Pilot Service admitted that his profit-related salary rose dramatically during Penang's boom years, from $600 a month in 1906 to $2,500 a month by 1912. Boxwallahs had learned from the Chinese how to negotiate perks and bonuses for services rendered. 'Everybody was everybody else's confederate in the great business of handing out discounts and tips' as the investment of capital was caught up in 'the long traditional kumshaw [kick back] usage of the Orient'.[78] Profits soared when the demand for Malayan tin and rubber rocketed after 1908. When rubber boomed at the equivalent of 62p a pound in April 1910, shares bought originally for £25,000 reached the unheard of sum of £500,000. One man retired as the head of his firm at the age of thirty-nine with personal shares worth £90,000. Like many of the pioneers, 'till he came to Singapore he had never earned more than twenty-five shillings a week'.[79]

'Trade boom came on trade boom, ports grew overnight, plantations pushed the jungle back and flourished like the jungle. It was almost an impossibility not to make money.'[80]. The last generation of eager young pioneers to come with £10 in their pockets were heirs to a decade of rampant change, and for the vast majority change was equated with material progress. By general consent the years between 1900 and 1914 were the great high noon of the Europeans in the East.

# 3

# Private Lives, Public Values

On 21 January 1901 a Malay *ayah* escorted her young charge on their customary walk to the grounds of St Andrew's Cathedral in Singapore. Lillian Newton was six years old. 'I was aware that my dress was made of black dotted material and I had a black ribbon in my hair. "Why?" I asked. "Because Queen Victoria is dead," was the reply.'[1] For a brief while, Singapore was like a city struck by plague. Business was halted, and the crowds moved noiselessly through the streets. But in many ways Victoria lived on in British Malaya. When the Duke and Duchess of Cornwall (the future King George V and Queen Mary) visited the colony three months later to the day, everyone turned out to celebrate. Rich Chinese merchants sponsored a brilliant street procession in their honour, a swaying stream of coloured lanterns, tumblers, monster stilt-walkers and a gigantic Chinese dragon. Little changed in the Edwardian Empire. Behind the enduring public face, private individuals wrestled with the same preoccupations, the same anxieties and personal constraints, overlaid by traditional Victorian values.

Between the old Queen's Diamond Jubilee in 1897 and the outbreak of the Great War, Singapore became a cosmopolitan city of around a quarter of a million people and the seventh greatest port in the world. As *the* principal entrepôt for South-East Asia's raw materials and Europe's products, the town held out the prospect of ever rising profits to the thrusting entrepreneurs of Collyer Quay and Raffles Place, the commercial centre which, like Venice, had been built on reclaimed land. Singapore harbour sheltered every conceivable craft, from sampans, junks, schooners, launches and tramp steamers to stately warships, great cargo ships and ocean liners. It was obvious why the port was dubbed 'the Clapham Junction of the Eastern Seas'.[2] In the town itself the main streets were well maintained and lit. The people enjoyed a stable currency and improved docks, communications and municipal utilities. Three symbols of civic pride – the Anderson Bridge and the new Memorial Hall and Theatre, named after Victoria – were opened in Edward VII's reign. Only the occasional economic blip was detected on this graph of confidence, prosperity and success.

Beyond the urban crescent of old Singapore, new residential suburbs had appeared by this time, with wide, tree-lined roads and bungalows, villas and mansions hidden by leafy greenery. Behind this screen were tennis courts, croquet lawns, and fruit and flower gardens. Orange Grove, the home of the Newton family, was a typical rambling property in the fashionable district of Tanglin. In 1902 a beautiful flame-of-the-forest tree sheltered the front 'like a giant red parasol'. 'In the garden grew beds of cannas, various colours; a row of Vanda Joachim orchids . . . stephanotis, white clematis and pink honolulu grew in clusters on a sort of trellis table; yellow alamandas were creeping up a pillar of the portico. There were also pale pink lilies which bloomed . . . either side of the drive.'[3] From Singapore town a network of roads radiated outwards. There were hints of rural England and Scotland in their names: Orchard Road, Scotts Road, Balmoral Road, Grange Road, Tanglin Road. Havelock Road, Neil Road and Outram Road were named after heroes of the Indian Mutiny. Stamford Road, a stately thoroughfare beginning at the Esplanade, turned at its other end into a country way. River Valley Road recalled 'the quiet beauty of a Devonshire lane', and it scarcely altered in the next three decades.[4] 'It would have been difficult to find a better place wherein to spend one's youth,' remarked Marjorie Binnie long afterwards, recalling the Edwardian years when she lived there with a widowed aunt.

It was an adventure to cross the Island on Sunday, picnicking at Woodlands or crossing over to Johore Bahru. Expeditions to one of the seaside Government bungalows were very popular. Changi, the loveliest, with its garden to the sea, the traveller palms and great shady trees, was often filled to overflowing and lucky the tenant staying there for a fortnight or longer, for it seemed the most perfect journey's end in those days. To escape from the turmoil . . . to this shady verandah, these lofty cool rooms, looking over calm waters to green islands, was indeed – journey's end.[5]

All around the Singapore coastline Europeans found sandy playgrounds where the government rest houses were located – Seletar, Ponggol ('which was almost tumbling down but provided shelter enough for happiness – and honeymoons'), Tanah Merah ('a few brown wooden bungalows standing on a sort of cliff') and Pasir Ris, facing the island of Pulau Ubin, where there were crocodile shooting, wild-pig hunts, fishing, bathing in the *pagar*, and dancing on the pier in the moonlight.[6] In her formative years Lillian Newton went on holiday with the Drysdale family to the island's most accessible resort, Tanjong Katong or Turtle Point, where she learned the delights of underwater swimming, diving and *agar-agar*, an edible seaweed jelly. Later, as a young woman, she sometimes visited friends, the Youngs, on Pulau Bukum. Despite the oil storage tanks for which the island was known, there were still unspoilt niches, including a coral reef with first-class bathing.

In the years before the First World War, pleasure was unpretentious. Singapore's Europeans enjoyed a variety of sports – even shooting parties to eliminate flying foxes and the occasional prowling tiger – and there was a good deal of home entertaining (in which the hard work was done by servants), besides intermittent special events to liven the social calendar. Lillian Newton recalled her mother's At Home days, when the tennis and croquet courts were thrown open. 'They were always jolly and friendly affairs. Tea was served outside in the garden and at six o'clock at sunset, when the light suddenly faded, cold drinks were served – stengahs (whisky and soda), lime squash, ginger beer and ginger ale.'[7] From their long family association with Singapore, the Newtons had many friends in club and cathedral circles.

> Mother was a member of the Ladies' Lawn Tennis Club, situated in Dhoby Ghaut, opposite the Scots Kirk in Stamford Road . . . After tennis the members would play bridge in the pavilion – it was very popular at that time, having superseded the more dull whist . . . Mother loved playing cards, she was a bit of a gambler, a very good loser and popular with all the players . . . We went to the club quite often.'[8]

Elizabeth Newton and her older daughters, Maud and Edie, used to attend the monthly dance at Tanglin Club in Stevens Road. They danced the waltz, lancers and gallop, and young Lillian loved seeing them dress up for these occasions. All the ladies 'looked very pretty in their evening dresses in bright colours in muslin, voile, chiffon, silk or satin; full, frilly and very décolleté. Their hair in knots on the top of the head and a curled fringe in front over the forehead.' After 1911 it would be her turn, too, to put her hair up and go to club dances. The introduction at Tanglin Club of 'a wonderful new dance, the foxtrot' was something she would not forget, and there were other highlights, such as dancing the reels at the St Andrew's Society Caledonian Ball on 30 November, and trying out the tango, which the Governor's aide-de-camp had taught her.[9]

But 'At Home' days in Malaya were not all tea and stengahs. Perak Ladies' Rifle Association, for instance, organized periodic 'At Homes' where pair-shooting, surprise-target and vanishing-target competitions were held. Up-country in the tin-mining and planting areas, where the close proximity of wild life in the jungle created a social culture accepting of danger and the need to hunt and kill, some women were evidently as enthusiastic as European men about handling guns. The Malay States Guides allowed the Perak Ladies to practise on their rifle range, and, of the twenty or so who did, some became experts with a .303 service rifle at a distance of 150 to 200 yards and held their own in competition with the men's teams.

Sport and pleasure were important for morale, but life in a tropical colony had its drawbacks and discomforts too. A comfortable lifestyle depended on seniority, a sufficient income or inherited resources, and even in the European community there were clear variations of wealth. Salaried officials with dependants could find themselves worse off than those in business. As Assistant Municipal Engineer of Singapore municipality (rather than of the colonial government), Howard Newton did not have a large salary, but he was scrupulous in resisting the bribes that greased the palms of a number of commercial men. To pay for his family's passages on their last home leave he had been forced to sell the house near Government House which he had built for his bride, and they travelled second class on a P. & O. ship. It was not uncommon for married men with large families to feel the pinch: the Newtons' friends the Lloyds (Mr Lloyd was a well-known auctioneer) had eleven children and could never afford to go home on leave or send the children to English schools. Despite her respectability and colonial connections, widowhood forced Elizabeth Newton to swallow her pride and make economies. As the proud owner of a Wilcox & Gibbs sewing machine, she made clothes for her daughters, including 'twelve of everything, petticoats, nightdresses, drawers, camisoles, all white calico trimmed with lace, tucks and frills' for Maud's trousseau in 1906.[10] Even her widowed mother, old Mrs Robertson, born a Governor's daughter yet a practical person and a fine needlewoman, took knitting orders for pregnant mothers in Singapore society to make extra pocket money. Elizabeth Newton also made a tough but necessary decision. To supplement her income, she decided to take boarders in her home in Tank Road from among the numerous unmarried male assistants in mercantile firms looking for accommodation. It was the first of a series of boarding houses she ran.

Among the social constraints were conventions of dress which took little account of a tropical climate. Ladies wore white gloves for their afternoon drive and other functions; both men and women wore gloves for dancing. On Sundays, at her mother's insistence, Lillian wore black cotton stockings and high boots, and at Raffles Girls' School she had to endure starched Eton collars and cotton bow ties. It was still an age of chemises, tight stays, camisoles, voluminous drawers trimmed with lace or Swiss embroidery, and full petticoats tied round the waist with tapes and trimmed with frills, lace-edged and tucked; and over all a white drill skirt and blouse with starched or boned collar. Lillian's contemporary Marjorie Binnie was living with her aunt, Mrs Howell, a long-standing resident of Singapore and an expert horsewoman, when she received a sharp lesson in matters of dress and decorum. Marjorie recalled a Saturday afternoon when she visited Abrams' riding stables alone and the trainer

hailed me with an offer to go with him on his extraordinary chariot which he used when breaking in horses to carriage use. It was the queerest looking affair, and we sat perched on high on a very tiny seat, side by side, behind four galloping steeds that tore down Orchard Road. Anyway, I thoroughly enjoyed our wild gallop round the Padang, back up Orchard Road, everything hastily getting out of our way . . . I clinging half to him and half to my very small seat (I was a buxom wench in those days). My hair was flying over my head, hairpins having long since been lost in the wind . . . and my hat had been blown off into the sea. We slowed down to turn into the stable yard and thanking the old chap very heartily I walked home to give my Aunt a tremendously vivid account of my adventure. I do not want to remember her icy reception

. . . Suffice it to say that I was in future extremely careful about 'behaving in such an extraordinary manner, so unfitting to a decently brought up girl' . . .

Oh dear! But we must remember that in those days a young girl was very much in the public eye, and the unwritten law was that she must NEVER let herself be talked about. *That* was sheer lunacy, and death to the hopes of ever making a good marriage.[11]

Any suggestion, however, that the small British Malayan community was preoccupied with form over substance gives an inaccurate picture. The charge of philistinism levelled against those who went out to the colonies grew from the brief impressions of outsiders, visitors passing through, rather than from those with knowledge of Malayan life. A glimpse inside the Residency at Sungei Ujong in 1879, for instance, revealed that 'The drawing room has a good piano, and many tasteful ornaments, books and china'; the dining room had 'exquisite crystal, menu cards with holders of Dresden china [and] four classical statuettes in Parian', all belonging to Captain Murray, the Resident.[12] Moreover, there was apparently quite a market for pianos with brass fittings made expressly for a tropical climate. The planter Robert Munro (referred to in his family as 'Coconut Munro' for co-writing a definitive *Guide to Coconut Planting*) was a talented musician whose 'singing of a comic song to his own accompaniment was almost professional. He had, in fact, intended to be a professional pianist, and would have been but for a shooting accident to his finger.'[13] The civil servant Andrew Caldecott was 'a good Malay scholar with literary tastes . . . had a piano and played it well. More wonderful still, his bungalow was decorated with attractive water-colours of his own painting.'[14]

In particular, Singapore was alive with musical talent and interests in the years 1880 to 1914. A dominant influence was Edward Salzmann, once of the Royal Italian Opera Company in London, who held the position of organist at St Andrew's Cathedral from 1874 to 1917. As choirmaster, C. B. Buckley was his right-hand man until Edwin Brown took over the post. 'C. B.' was a natural impresario and the originator of the brilliant Christmas musical and theatrical 'treats' laid on for thousands of Singapore's children. These men gathered round themselves a cluster of fine amateur musicians, singers and instrumentalists, led by A. P. Ager of the *Straits Times*, a gifted violinist, the lawyer Ambrose Cross, who acted and wrote plays as well as being a proficient accompanist, Mr

Whitefield, manager of the Robinson Piano Company, an accomplished pianist, Howard Newton, Lillian's father, a fine tenor and an experienced performer, and Mrs Salzmann, a distinguished contralto. In March 1891 the Singapore Philharmonic Society was founded on the initiative of Major St Clair (who later produced a popular series of children's concerts), and from that time its soloists doubled for performances of serious works such as Rossini's *Stabat Mater* and productions of Gilbert and Sullivan, then newly in vogue. Both Penang and Singapore boasted flourishing amateur dramatic societies, but professionals of the musical and theatrical world also came to perform. Matheson Lang and his company played Shakespearian plays.

> Marie Tempest played to crowded houses; Maud Allen danced her Salome dance! Musicians like Marie Hall visited Singapore . . . The Bandmann Company played all the musical comedies of the day, *Belle of New York, Our Miss Gibbs, Dollar Princess, Pink Lady, Chocolate Soldier, Arcadians, Quaker Girl.* We had all the musical scores and would sing the various favourite numbers round the piano when we had the singsongs of those happy days.[15]

The Newtons were very much involved in the amateur musical and theatrical activities. All three daughters had inherited artistic talent, and Maud and Edie attended the Guildhall School of Music in London. Lillian's interest grew during her years at Raffles School. On Saturday mornings Maud ran a dancing class, for which her mother played the piano. She was tall and graceful and was called 'The Gibson Girl' because of her likeness to Camille Clifford, the original Gibson girl on the London stage. 'We all learnt among other items the skirt dance as danced by Lois Fuller and Isadora Duncan,' Lillian wrote. Gilbert and Sullivan became a family passion too. Both Maud and Edie, who had made their stage debuts in 1903 and 1906 respectively, took part in the production of *The Pirates of Penzance* at the opening of the new Victoria Theatre in 1909.[16]

Governing this lively and talented community were long-standing Victorian standards and attitudes. Majorie Binnie had learned how greatly appearances mattered. In Malaya, European women were treated with respect by men of all races. But the concomitant was that traditional values such as propriety, modesty, purity, obedience and godliness had to be upheld in everyday behaviour. These values were put under extreme stress when a major murder case rocked the people of the Malay States and the Straits Settlements in 1911: the trial of Mrs Ethel Proudlock.[17]

Certain facts seem indisputable. Mrs Proudlock was the wife of the Acting Headmaster of the Victoria Institution in Kuala Lumpur. She fitted naturally into the town's European society, a pleasant, unassuming middle-class mother in her early twenties who sang in the choir of St Mary's Church. Her husband, William, who had taught in Kuala Lumpur since 1902, was President of the Selangor State Band and a member of a local football team. The pair were apparently happily married, and had a three-year-old daughter. Ethel's father, Mr Charter, was a Public Works Department official in the town. On Sunday 23 April 1911, after attending evensong, Ethel Proudlock went back home to their bungalow near the school. Her husband was dining out. She changed into a cool pastel gown to write some letters, before being interrupted by the arrival of one William Steward, a thirty-four-year-old bachelor and mining engineer with whom the Proudlocks were acquainted through their mutual membership of the Selangor Club. A short while later Ethel Proudlock killed Steward with repeated shots of a revolver. When her husband arrived home soon after with a colleague, Ethel Proudlock was dishevelled and hysterical and, though barely coherent, admitted to having shot a man. Taken into custody in Pudu Gaol, after a magistrate's hearing in May she was in due course committed for trial on the charge of murder. 'In the history of the Federated Malay States the case is without parallel,' wrote the editor of the *Malay Mail*, which reported the whole episode.[18]

The British were stupefied. There were fewer than 1,500 European residents of the state of Selangor in 1911 and the spotlight was now turned upon them as a group as much as on the central figures. Proudlock was a government official, Steward, formerly a Manager of South Salak tin mine, a mining consultant. Kuala Lumpur was a conventional colonial community. Even in the 1920s it was a place synonymous with collars and ties, stiff suits, regular office hours, and the Selangor Club – known familiarly as 'the Spotted Dog' – which enforced traditional standards of good behaviour. In the aftermath of the case, some residents feared the consequences for their reputation and relations with the Asian races, and there was apprehension as to how the British public would react in view of the disdain in which Malaya was held at home.

The Proudlock trial opened on 8 June at the Supreme Court. Trial by jury having been abolished in the Federated Malay States in 1899, the case was heard by Mr Justice Sercombe Smith, assisted by two planters serving as assessors. Ethel Proudlock pleaded 'Not Guilty' to the murder charge, claiming that she had acted in self-defence when Steward tried to rape her. When struggling to escape his molestations, her hand came into contact with the gun; she picked it up and shot him twice. Steward apparently made to leave the bungalow. After a brief interval there were further shots before he collapsed beyond the bungalow steps. The rickshaw man who had brought him to the house heard the noise and saw Ethel Proudlock standing over the body, gun in hand. She, on the other hand, remembered nothing at all after the initial shots. Her defence asserted that she was incapable of cold-blooded murder, that she had acted under great provocation, and that her terror and stress were exacerbated by embarrassing gynaecological problems. But the prosecution questioned the truthfulness of the defendant's testimony, imputing that she had invited Steward to the bungalow that Sunday evening while her husband was dining elsewhere, that the two were involved in an affair, and that Mrs Proudlock was, in effect, that unmentionable Edwardian sinner, an adulteress. However, no proof of the allegation was established by the prosecutor. Conversely, it emerged that Steward had a Chinese woman living with him at his remote South Salak home. The defence, on the other hand, could not establish from the medical examinations of both parties that there was evidence of rape. On 16 June the verdict was announced. Mrs Proudlock was found guilty of murder and sentenced to death by hanging. As her distraught husband tried in vain to console her in the court, she sobbed uncontrollably until led away for transfer to the death cell, unaware that a recommendation for mercy was to be made.

The European community was outraged by the verdict. Some had been appalled that Mrs Proudlock had been denied trial by jury, others at the imputations against European womanhood. Testimonies to her virtue were publicized; other theories about Steward's killing circulated. In view of the imminent coronation of George V in London, appeals and petitions of Europeans, Indians and Chinese were prepared for submission to the new King and Queen. Then amid the heated public furore the case took a new twist. The London *Times* reported on 29 June that the prisoner 'has written a letter in which she reiterates her innocence and states that she is unable either to bear the horror and suspense of her present position or to face another trial. She therefore withdraws the appeal against her sentence, of which she had given notice, and asks the Sultan of Selangor to have pity on her sufferings and to pardon her.'[19] The reasons for this unexpected change of strategy on Mrs Proudlock's part raised many questions, but the fact that a European woman's fate now depended on a Malay potentate fuelled further disapproval in Britain. Rumour and innuendo began to circulate, focusing on Ethel Proudlock's character and her putative relationship with William Steward, including the possible motive for the crime. However, the pressure for clemency was strong. The Sultan and the State Council met to consider her case on 8 July and decided to grant Mrs Proudlock a free pardon. She was immediately released from gaol and prepared to leave the country. At Penang, she and her daughter boarded the first ship home, reaching England at the end of August. Her loyal husband had to remain temporarily in Kuala Lumpur. He faced a libel case arising from police treatment of his wife, in the course of which it was revealed that he had lived with a Chinese woman before his marriage to Ethel Charter. After losing both the lawsuit and his job, he followed Ethel back to Britain in November 1911.

The Proudlock case led to a very public scrutiny of colonial mores. Much was revealed during the trial. William Proudlock learned that there was a question mark over Ethel's parentage. Mrs Charter was not Ethel's mother; by implication, Mr Charter had had another liaison. Was Ethel Proudlock the innocent young English woman she appeared? Did she kill William Steward in revenge for rejecting her for a Chinese woman? Was she herself Eurasian, as has recently been suggested? As for Steward, was he, in the journalist Horace Bleackley's words, 'one of the innumerable satyrs with which those Colonies where the male population is largely in excess of the female population are infested'?[20] And did the Colonial Office deliberately destroy official correspondence from the High Commissioner because of the risk to racial harmony and British prestige? The bitter taste left by the case was seized on by Somerset Maugham when he visited Malaya in 1921. He was told the story by none other than Mrs Proudlock's lawyer before using it as the basis for a famous short story, 'The Letter'.[21]

As the Proudlock case confirmed, throughout the Straits Settlements and the Malay States in the pioneer years the European residents were primarily youngish, able, active single British men: it was undoubtedly a male-dominated society. Those who lived in the towns – Kuala Lumpur, Ipoh, Singapore, Penang – could enjoy the collegiality of their clubs. But for those up-country the options for leisure were very few. The civil servant Richard Winstedt, who became a distinguished expert on Malay culture, recalled a young man's problem: 'No home life, no women friends, no libraries, no theatres or cinemas, not always big enough community for bridge or tennis, no motor-cars, no long walks on account of that labyrinth of trackless jungle'.[22] The pioneer Hugh Clifford, too, understood the trauma of isolation as a result of years administering Pahang, from 1887 to 1899. 'Educated white men have inherited an infinite capacity for feeling bored,' he wrote feelingly; 'and a hot climate grills boredom into irritability . . . It is said that "a white man, who has lived twelve consecutive months in complete isolation among the folk of an alien Asiatic race, is never the same again".'[23] Monotony and loneliness turned some men into eccentrics, others into alcoholic depressives. 'The wear and tear of that old jungle work together with whisky in excess killed many a man in this country,' admitted another officer who knew.[24] The image of the heavy-drinking planter, conjured up with devastating effect by the pen of Somerset Maugham and others, could be applied to this isolated, disorientated minority during these years before the First World War. Despite a duty of $1.50 per gallon on spirits in the Malay States, Walker's whisky and Bols gin were still affordable to salaried Europeans. Nothing relieved 'the steel cap clamped round one's temples during the day' better than a few evening stengahs, the official Victor Purcell testified, although that did not imply he became a 'soaker'.[25]

Drink could be a short step to unsocial behaviour, which was noticeable in a mixed-sex community. Lillian Newton remembered some unpleasant situations at her mother's boarding houses. On one occasion, at their first house on Tank Road, 'I was very frightened of [the young male assistants]; they used to come back in the evenings from the clubs very drunk and one night . . . the sober men had to guard our bedroom door from one young man, very drunk and rampaging around the house.' This was not an isolated instance. At their house in Cairnhill Road,

> One evening, one of the men found it necessary to get dead drunk and there were terrible scenes in the dining room. Edie and I sat holding hands in the bedroom while all this was going on. We were very fright-

ened. On these occasions Mother just expelled the young man the next day, and of course it was a financial loss to her. There were many of these episodes over the years, all very horrid and distasteful. Some of them kept up a vendetta.[26]

The boarders at Cairnhill Road were not the only problem. Sometimes returning from school by rickshaw Lillian encountered a man exposing himself, which terrified her so much that she could not bring herself to report it. Another day 'we met a very drunken soldier, quite alone and on foot brandishing his bayonet'. When their neighbours left in 1912 – they were a noisy couple with a penchant for parties – 'a mess of Dutch batchelors took over the house. They entertained prostitutes from time to time. Again no sleep, the noise was fearful and they were one of the reasons for our leaving.'[27]

This incident raises the question of sexuality and the male lifestyle. Alcohol, sex and race were three issues constituting aspects of the downside of successful colonial expansion, and, as Clifford implied, it was difficult to reconcile public standards of morality based on Victorian values with human instincts and emotions. On remote estates away from the proximity of neighbours, different opportunities for solace presented themselves. Despite the deep stigma attached to homosexuality by European society, there was evidence of white *tuans* exploiting their coolies by imposing homosexual practices upon them, to the concern of the government agencies charged with protecting the welfare of Asian communities.[28] However, the strength of public homophobia has obscured the extent of homosexuality, particularly in the early twentieth century. Drawing from life in his prize-winning novel *The Soul of Malaya*, Henry Fauconnier only hinted at a homosexual relationship between Rolain, a European planter, and his Malay servant. Yet he was less coy about depicting heterosexual affairs, when the wife of Rolain's Tamil gardener, Palaniai (a 'sweetmeat of India', a chocolate 'wrapped in variegated paper and filled with a sugary liqueur'), became his hero's lover.[29]

The pioneer generation admitted a range of sexual relationships. In view of the length of overseas contracts, a contemporary asked, 'was it any wonder that the white exile took to himself one of the complaisant, amusing, good-tempered and good-mannered daughters of the East?'[30] Although there were *public* scruples about sexual relations with non-whites, single European men habitually took Asian concubines. The system was known colloquially as 'Keeps'. Up to 1914 it was common practice for civil servants to keep Malayan mistresses – until the Secretary of State for the Colonies forbade it, forcing several officers to marry their Malay paramours, including Charlton Maxwell, brother of the Chief Secretary of the Federated Malay States. Up to this point a very high proportion of planters also had native mistresses. From his work among the planting community in Selangor, Dr Malcolm Watson put the figure as high as 90 per cent at the beginning of the twentieth century.[31] It would seem that, with the exception of the Malays, Asians were for the most part tolerant of the European's *droit de seigneur*, and, while individual women may have suffered, the benefit, according to the old school, was that 'the European of those times gained a more intimate and sympathetic knowledge of those he ruled'.[32]

The incidence of British men with Asian mistresses or wives emerges in anecdote. Robert Munro of Permatang Estate, Selangor, for instance, had a Tamil mistress who bore him two daughters, Maria and Eve, whom he adopted, and a posthumous son, James. Munro married his mistress shortly before he died mysteriously in 1919. In the 1920s a Johore planter, Joe Allgrove, came across another planter called Nicoll and an Australian miner called Skine who had Tamil wives of long-standing, the latter with three Eurasian daughters. At the same time the civil servant Hugh Bryson met an elderly Irish planter in the Kota Tinggi district who had married an Indian woman, and a character called Jack Le Doux was known to have a 'Javanese-born wife, who was a bit of a tartar'.[33] The tea planter Bill Fairlie heard of a man named Baker with a Tamil wife, but labelled him an oddball for riding buffalo-back, growing his hair exceptionally long, and calling his 'three most glamorous daughters, [all] coffee-coloured . . . Hovis, Bermaline and Turog!'[34] Bruce Lockhart, however, committed a social solecism in Negri Sembilan when in 1907 he took the beautiful Amai as his mistress, for Malay culture was disapproving; he was forced to leave Malaya in some haste. A change in attitude was in train even before the 1920s, when company managers forbade assistants to keep a woman, especially when she was on the company labour force. The view began to prevail that 'the type of planter or tin miner who "kept" a girl' was 'generally of a slightly lower mental poise and strength than the rest', as one planter put it.[35]

In Singapore and Kuala Lumpur before 1914, European men had

greater freedom and choice: for instance, in Singapore there were some 236 Chinese, 48 Japanese, and 10 European brothels. European men seemingly preferred their own kind, and the brothels of Malay Street and Malabar Street housed Hungarians, Poles and Russian Jewesses, a retinue recruited by professional pimps from among the poorest people of Central and Eastern Europe, who drifted East by way of Bucharest, Athens and Cairo: 'white wrecks of European womanhood', one man described them, 'silent, immobile, passionless [who] trade their bodies for the silver dollars of Malaya'.[36] In the absence of East European women, a young planter was told, 'the answer was Japanese': before 1914 'it was the custom for the lonely European to get in touch with the Japanese Consul in Singapore and a strict financial arrangement was made. A Japanese girl came out, lived as the man's wife and was suitably pensioned off at the arranged time. These "pensioners" [were] the Japanese "Marys" who ran the Jap Hotels in K.L. and elsewhere . . .'[37] But before that, in their role of surrogate wives, Japanese women had a reputation for 'absolute fidelity and perfect housekeeping'.[38]

These liaisons were not only an indicator of British ambivalence towards the subject of sex but also illustrated the double standards operating in Malaya in the matter of race, which extended for the most part to Eurasians as well as Asians. In the Dutch East Indies, Eurasians were treated as Europeans. In Malaya there was a meaningful distinction (except in early census returns). The British in the early twentieth century tended to be dismissive of Eurasians (which was why Ethel Proudlock's nationality was a sensitive matter). The barrier was a subtle mix of historical, social and economic factors. Eurasian descendants of past settlers were regarded as pseudo-Europeans, clinging to their European surnames and speaking English with an undesirable sing-song inflection described as 'chi-chi': hence the importance attached by the British to being 'pukka'.[39] In some quarters there was strong disapproval of Eurasians trying to pass as pure whites. H. N. Ridley, the pioneering scientist, depicted them as 'weak in body, short-lived, deficient in energy and feeble in morals'.[40] Malacca, in particular, symbolized to the British the heritage of two failed colonial societies. 'Portuguese and Dutch rule have passed away, leaving as their chief monuments . . . a race of half-breeds' and a population who were indolent and poor and, to Isabella Bird, seemed to 'take an endless siesta behind their closely-covered windows'.[41] Finally such thinking was translated into a colour-bar policy by rulings of 1904 and 1910 debarring non-Europeans and Eurasians from administrative posts in the Civil Service, and holding them largely to inferior grades as mechanics, clerks and typists (or, in the case of a group of Scottish-Eurasians, to serving as train drivers). Efficiency was the excuse for a policy designed to protect the prestige of white men in a complex, multicultural Malaya.

The double standards in race relations were a matter of concern to Europeans who genuinely believed in racial equality. Despite a Bishop of Singapore's optimistic recollection 'of the friendliness which existed among Europeans, Eurasians, Chinese and Indians', Lillian Newton remembered differently a growing social and racial divide condoned by adult society around her.[42] Having been brought up in a staunchly Anglican family to be tolerant and charitable, she made no distinction between creeds and races in her friendships. Among her best friends were the Lloyds, a Catholic family, and the Cornish Methodist family of Polglase, who were teetotallers and opposed to dancing and theatre-going. Later she made several Chinese friends as a result of working at the Methodist Mission in Chinatown. She was also proud of the fact that, unlike other European families, the Newtons respected the holidays of their servants, Chinese New Year or Hari Raya. Her education at Raffles Girls' School from 1903 to 1909 was a genuinely multi-ethnic experience. 'I noticed that some of the children were Eurasian, Chinese or Jewish but that did not worry me. They were nice and kind, very quick and smart and I got on well with them and with the other European children.' But she was perceptive enough to detect a gulf between her own attitudes and those of her mother's circle. 'These were two worlds and it was very puzzling to me . . . The people I met at home were all white people and those at school were all different colours . . . I wondered why I did not meet them at the houses we visited.' Her bemusement was highlighted by the Sunday services at St Andrew's Cathedral. To ventilate the interior, 'the punkahs [fans] were pulled by Indian coolies who sat outside on the ground. It always worried me that *we* went into the church to pray to God but the Indian coolies, the rikisha men and our *syces* all stayed outside. Two worlds again, very puzzling to a little girl.'[43] While Europeans mingled in public places with Asians and Eurasians, genuine socialization was eschewed.

When Lillian reached her teens, the golden angsena trees on the main

Esplanade of Singapore became diseased, and were felled and replaced by flame of the forest. It was a symbolic change in a scene that for decades had seemed immutable. For the Chinese community there was one hugely significant break with the past, as the Newtons became aware in 1911 when their Chinese houseboys gave up wearing their hair in pigtails, as the Manchu dynasty had previously decreed all its subjects should: 'there was a fearful noise in the servants' quarters and suddenly one after another appeared with short hair. A barber was busy in their quarters. They told us this was to show that they had thrown off the oppression of the Manchu dynasty for ever.'[44]

Change had both benefits and drawbacks. The Tanglin Club altered its rules so that ladies could become members. Electricity did away with oil lamps and hand-pulled punkahs; motor cars drove horses and traps from the streets, but created a new hazard – the red dust rising from newly built laterite roads, which could ruin clothes within five minutes. 'The roads were pleasanter without their ungainly hulks and smelly exhausts,' Marjorie Binnie insisted.[45] The expansion of the tin and rubber industries and the commercial agencies brought a steady influx of male Europeans.

In small, disjointed ways, too, Lillian noticed that things were evolving and a degree of social alienation had set in. 'In the early days I realized the [Ladies' Lawn Tennis] club was a very friendly place, where everyone knew everyone else, but during those two decades times changed . . . New people were arriving from Europe every week . . . To the newcomers we were just a widow keeping a boarding house and her daughters.' She now observed examples of a distasteful chauvinism in the attitudes of their young British paying guests to their non-British boarders. One of their Chinese boarders, Dr Chadwick Kew, had a dental practice in Singapore, and the Kew brothers had practices in Hong Kong and Shanghai besides. He was a very good dentist, Lillian maintained – and a good family friend – but he was effectively ostracized by the British boarders. When Hans Valois, 'a most charming Belgian, a wonderful cello player, came to board' at Orange Grove, 'immediately five of the Englishmen gave notice to leave . . . I relate this as an example of the snobbery and prejudice of those days.' There were other disturbing instances of the emerging white, male, British macho culture in Edwardian Singapore. Mrs Newton used to take Lillian to the home of the Young Women's Christian Association, where there was a choir of Chinese girls. She was struck by their evangelical fervour and was fascinated

> by the lusty way the girls sang [the Sankey and Moody] hymns, with their gay choruses, so unlike the hymns at the services at the Cathedral. Once again my two worlds appeared. I was puzzled and shocked when the [British boarding] men at Orange Grove made fun of our 'banana' meetings and the hymn, which I think was their own invention, '*Oh, for a man . . . a mansion in the sky!*'[46]

In the Christian European community there were people who deplored the boorishness and intolerance of the young male xenophobes of the British Empire. But insensitivity towards other races was not unique to the colonial mentality: it was ingrained in European civilization. On New Year's Day 1914 Lillian Newton excitedly proclaimed she was going home to England for the first time in her adult life. It was an adventure for a twenty-year-old woman, so she travelled with friends of her mother who would be unofficial chaperones. In March she sailed on the P. & O. SS *Nore* with high expectations. She could not know that European xenophobia was about to burst forth in an appalling orgy of self-destruction and that, before the summer was out, England would be plunged into the First World War.

# 4

# Pyrotechnics in Penang

In the middle of June 1914 the men of the German cruiser *Emden* entertained the crew of HMS *Minotaur*, flagship of Britain's China Command, at the port of Tsingtao, Germany's new showpiece city of the East. The two sides played a friendly football match, and it was a 2:2 draw until the British sailors sneaked three more goals in extra time. Happily, the Germans won the gymnastics contest, and the whole occasion was judged a success. Two weeks later, tensions in the Austro-Hungarian Empire erupted when on 28 June the imperial heir, Archduke Franz Ferdinand, and his wife were assassinated in Sarajevo by a Bosnian Serb.

At first it was hoped that the fallout would be localized in the Balkans, for, despite the sometimes strident rivalries between the nation states and the scramble for colonies in the 1880s and 1890s, Europe had enjoyed a century free from general conflict. To the people in Malaya this incident seemed a distant, unimportant event, until the dismal repercussions began to unfold. Exactly a month later Austria-Hungary declared war on Serbia, and German troops invaded Luxembourg and Belgium. Within a month Europe had divided into two armed camps: France, Britain and Russia, joined by Japan, facing the German and Austro-Hungarian Empires. An unfortunate minor incident had unleashed an international conflict, the first 'world war' in history.

To protect the interests of the Empire, Britain had already signed a treaty with Japan in 1902, and, confident of her ally, British battleships had been virtually withdrawn from Far Eastern seas after 1905. 'Nowadays', it was observed in 1908, 'it is only occasionally that Singapore is visited by a warship of the squadron.' On the other hand, 'The approaches to the harbour are laid with mines and are

73

commanded by heavily-armed forts on the outlying islands of Blakang Mati and Pulo Brani.'[1] This was as well, because, with the British Grand Fleet based in European waters, Britain had to rely in South-East Asia on the assistance of Japanese, French and Russian ships and the new navies of Australia and New Zealand. Vice-Admiral Jerram, in charge of China Command, had one old battleship, four cruisers and eight destroyers to cover the coasts of Asia from Weihaiwei on the Yellow Sea to Socotra and the Gulf of Aden. However, unlike Penang, which was defended only by Volunteers, Singapore was a garrison town with regular infantry troops and units of artillery and engineers as well as a Volunteer corps. In the Federated States some initiatives had been taken in 1902 to form the Malay States Volunteer Rifles (MSVR), in view of the growth of the country and the inadequate protection in the event of an emergency.

But no emergency was seriously expected in the Far East. With hindsight, however, a Singapore resident recalled a strange incident at the German community's Teutonia Club in Scotts Road:

> Shortly before the War crashed upon us some of the Members gave a fancy dress dance at which a guest appeared as the Tricolour, draped in the flag that usually waved from the Messageries Maritimes. 'So soon we shall trample upon that,' said Hans [Becker?], but even with the clouds all about us we only laughed and swore that War could never be.[2]

A Civil Service administrator, T. P. Coe, a member of the Malay States Volunteer Rifles, remembered the atmosphere in Kuala Lumpur at the outbreak of war:

> August Bank holiday, 1914, found us winding up a week-end rifle meeting on the range. The atmosphere was less electric there than in the town (the clubs were terrible) but single galley-proof sheets found their way out from time to time from the Malay Mail Office with the latest news, which became more and more disquieting. The principal local fear was that with business at a standstill and the market for tin and rubber closed there would be riots among the entire cooly [*sic*] population . . . the fear was a very real one. We were semi-mobilized of course from the outset – with some wonderful orders. I received a postcard from my sergeant ordering me to be prepared to parade at any time at very short notice, 'with haversack packed with spare boots, puttees, shirts, socks, breeches, shaving material etc.'! Not much room for iron rations after that! We did some semi-intensive training, with route

marches . . . and one or two demonstration marches through the town.
Contingents were also taken to Singapore for special training.[3]

The Volunteers were willing amateurs. While, in Coe's words, 'there
was interest in rifle-shooting' and some civilians became quite competent marksmen, the 'general standard of drill, discipline and turn-out
. . . was modest in the extreme'. 'D' Company, to which he belonged,
'was a mixed crowd – Government Officers of all Departments, ages
and grades; planters, miners and merchants of equal diversity; and a fair
sprinkling of the type of "tough" that was numerous in Malaya when it
was a get-rich-quick country'.[4] A rubber planter from another company
admitted frankly, 'On parade we were a queer bunch. The soaks had to
be held up in line by their neighbours; the rest might be described as
"the halt, the lame and the blind".'[5]

The Malay States Volunteer Rifles had had their first taste of military
police-keeping at Chinese New Year 1912, quelling striking rioters in
Kuala Lumpur. Coe felt the experience was beneficial in preparing the
British for trouble. 'The riots did us a lot of good and gave a fillip to
recruiting. Young men of military age who had rather sneered at volun-
teering joined up on tasting for the first time the experience of not
having been "in" a local show.'[6] Now, as the news of German successes
on the Western Front percolated to the Far East, patriotic pride was
aroused and keen colonials felt a moral pressure to return home to
enlist. In the first six months of 'the Kaiser's War', as it was then called,
1,000 Britons left Malaya to fight – gratifying proof of national soli-
darity. Among the first contingent of forty Volunteers who left in
November 1914 was William Price, an assistant at the Kuala Lumpur
branch of Whiteaway Laidlaw. In 1917 a further 338 men returned home
to join up, and in 1918 yet another 143. But, as it became more difficult
to get passages home to Europe, men were encouraged to join the
Indian Army Reserve of Officers. Once home, experienced Volunteers
with the appropriate middle-class background could expect a commission in Kitchener's Army. Coe himself left Malaya in 1915 and won the
Military Cross as a serving officer. So too did Captain William Price,
for leading a reconnaissance party to destroy a couple of German
machine-gun posts in northern France. The commandant of the
MSVR, Lieutenant-Colonel Hubback – the Government Architect in
Selangor in more peaceful days – rose to command a brigade in France.

As Malaya waved goodbye to its virile youth, and married men took their wives and children back to England, the local economy began to suffer. The 'rush to the Colours by nearly all young and healthy men, many of whom were never to return, became so serious that [rubber] estates were denuded of staff,' one planter recalled.[7] The Civil Service too lost forty-five of its younger officers – some 20 per cent of its strength – and eleven of these were to be killed in action. Over 700 Britons from a variety of occupations – a third of the FMS European male workforce – left the Federated States to serve in the armed forces, and of these over 200 were to lose their lives in the war. Some of the older and married men who remained in Malaya felt frustrated by being away from the field of action. Most did their bit by working longer hours to make up the deficiencies in manpower, and by joining the Volunteer defence forces, never expecting to see active service. However, when Singapore was thrown into crisis in 1915 the Volunteers were called on to help restore order. For Walter Lowther Kemp, who fell in with the Singapore Volunteer Rifles, any opportunity to be a soldier came as a tonic. The newly formed company had had very little training – 'I had to teach half of them how to put on their bandoliers and load their rifles,' he declared, but 'one . . . feels that we have had at least a little bit of a show ourselves instead of being entirely out of everything'.[8]

In a country as racially diverse as Malaya, reactions to the war were bound to vary. It was difficult to gauge the attitude of the silent Asian majority – urban workers, domestic servants, coolies in plantations or mines – but a distant war was unlikely to impinge upon them. The business and professional communities, however, were keen to demonstrate their loyalty to the British Crown. The booming revenues of the Federated Malay States had already funded the battleship HMS *Malaya* for the Royal Navy, and collectively and individually wealthy Chinese residents contributed generously to the war effort.[9] The Straits Chinese British Association pledged 'to render whatever services they were capable of to King and Country "in the hour of sore trial"', and published a handbook on citizenship, *Duty to the British Empire*, which was distributed free to workers and to its educated members. At the outbreak of war, Chinese and Malay companies of Volunteers were mobilized and provided guards at key points on Singapore Island; in 1916 additional Chinese companies were raised in Malacca, Penang and

Perak. The small Ceylonese community made their own enthusiastic contribution through the all-Ceylon Tamil Fund. In total, fifty-three planes were presented to Britain by Malayan subscribers of all races.[10] The Sultan of Johore showed his support for the British cause by presenting a squadron and by investing £1 million in government bonds. The fact that the Malay States repeatedly expressed their loyalty towards the Empire was significant, since as Sunni Muslims under the caliphate of Turkey they might have been tempted into a jihad or holy war out of sympathy for the Turks, Germany's allies. The same was true of the Indian Muslims. In fact, in March 1915 the Muslim community of Singapore – Arabs, Indians, Javanese and Malays – sent a special message of loyal assurance to King George V.

As the Allied campaigns took shape, the Straits Settlements experienced a friendly invasion which greatly swelled the European population. It was witnessed by Arthur Thompson, a Major in the Royal Engineers:

> One of the most interesting events in the early War Days was the arrival in Singapore of 4000 Russian Troops. 'The Czar's Own', specially recruited, every man was exactly 5′ 10″ and not less than 38″ Round the Chest. Dressed in White Smocks and Baggy Black Pants and Knee high Soft Boots, they made an impressive sight as they went on a Route March. They had no Band, but the Leading Platoon of each Battalion (or the equivalent) seemed to be a selected Alto Choir; they sang a Line, then the whole of the men thundered a heavy chorus. It sounded simply wonderful. They were en route to France. I met them on the Wharf and took General Lokvitzsky, their G.O.C. up to Head-quarters. With other British Officers I was invited to Lunch. The Russian Officers had been picked from the whole Russian Army and all claimed to be Princes. Lokvitzsky warned me they would try to make me drunk, and advised me to take a sip of Champagne after every sip of Vodka . . . Thanks to L., I was more than able to hold my own.[11]

However, in addition to friendly Allies in transit, Singapore's European community included some nationals who were distinctly *personae non gratae*. In particular the well-established German colony was now treated as the enemy. Some Britons found this difficult: they had come to admire the German residents for their contribution to the city's cultural life. Marjorie Binnie remembered an emotional evening not long before the war, 'one night of singing – a German party whose voices thrilled us into silence, as they sang hour after hour, folks songs, patriotic songs, love songs, unaccompanied by any music as we rested in a fleet of Malay sampans on a phosphorescent sea'.[12] On the other hand, it was noticed in commercial circles that Germany's suave merchants of earlier days had been superseded by a new generation of brash, hard-nosed businessmen, not endearing to their British rivals. On a trip to Borneo in 1904, a Scotswoman witnessed the spread of German influence: 'all the shipping in the Straits and British Borneo is getting into the hands of the Germans. Formerly at Bangkok it was practically British, now 95% is German and 5% British.'[13]

Edwin Brown's arrival in Singapore three years earlier coincided with a public spat. From the harbour 'I . . . remember seeing the German flag flying proudly from the top of one of the houses . . . The residence in question was one occupied by a German "mess" . . . the Free Press waxed wroth in a leader upon the fact that the visitor to Singapore saw the German flag first, and the mess were prevented from flying it any longer.'[14] Another resident was struck by how much the Germans made themselves at home in pre-war Singapore:

> There was a large colony of Germans in Singapore at that time. They had their club, the Teutonia Club in Scotts Road, and they always had a Gala night on New Year's Eve and well into New Year's Day. On one occasion some bachelors from a mess decided to visit us. They brought with them a small barrel and the gong from the furnished house they rented. They piled in, eight of them, into a gharry to drive to our house to first-foot us. Just as they reached the German Club it struck twelve. All piled out and with the Indian driver made a ring round the gharry and pony in the middle of the road and sang Auld Lang Syne.[15]

After the outbreak of war, however, it was discovered that this jovial community in Singapore provided a smokescreen for espionage activities. Britain's natural allies, the Australian and New Zealand forces, acted promptly in occupying the scattered German Pacific colonies in Samoa, New Guinea and the Bismarck archipelago, and Germany's base at Tsingtao was quickly besieged by the Japanese with British support. But the captured German wireless station of Herbertshohe on Neu Pommern Island (renamed New Britain) provided evidence of how far Germany had anticipated hostilities before the declaration of war.[16] A series of wireless stations was already in place; auxiliary ships such as the *Comet* were equipped with radio installations, as was discovered when she was intercepted off New Guinea. Special land-based offices had been set up in major ports – Tokyo, Tsingtao, Shanghai, Manila, Batavia ( Jakarta) and Singapore – under the command of naval officers, in order to gather intelligence, maintain communications and facilitate essential supplies such as coal for steam-powered vessels.

Suspicion built up that the Dutch, who were technically neutral, were abetting the German naval effort by providing German agents with a safe haven for anti-British activities and by turning a blind eye to their transmission of ship movements. On 1 August, three days before war was declared, Captain Minkwitz of the German freighter *Choising* quickly left Singapore for the Dutch East Indies, carrying confidential mail from German agents in Singapore which he delivered in Batavia on the 5th. He was allowed to stay in the roads for a month.

Lillian Newton, who knew many of Singapore's German-speaking community through her musical connections, had her eyes opened by one curious experience.

A strange concert we went to at the German Club was one given by the band of a German battleship, when one of the soloists, a sailor, played a xylophone. There was a lady solo pianist, very brilliant, the wife of an employee in a German mercantile firm. When the 1914 war broke out this couple made a quick departure from Singapore. I saw the man in Batavia when I was visiting my Robertson cousins during the war. He was sitting at a table near ours at the Club in Batavia and we were all listening to the band. It was then known that he was a spy, the German mercantile firm was his disguise. He stayed in the Dutch East Indies for the duration of the war. Mother and I often talked about the concert, the wife of the spy, the sailor who played the xylophone, and wondered what had happened to them.[17]

So, rightly or wrongly the Dutch appeared to defer to Germany, and the Allies' suspicion of Mata Hari, the female spy executed by the French for espionage in 1917, was not lessened by the fact that as the wife of a Dutch colonial officer she had lived in the Dutch East Indies from 1897 to 1902. Yet the British authorities, inexperienced in handling a war emergency, were lackadaisical in dealing with enemy residents. Singapore's German civilians were installed complete with their servants in the Teutonia Club, and the head of Behn Meyer, Herr Diehn, was allowed into town to take care of the company's affairs. In time the authorities woke up to the error of their ways. These civilians were transferred to Tanglin Barracks as internees, although as middle-class Europeans they were still well treated. In the Federated Malay States measures were equally slack; no attempt was made to confine German civilians until events forced a change of policy. Initially, however, sixty-five German men, women and children were allowed to go about on parole. Later, in 1915, they were brought by ship to Singapore for intern-ment. 'We treated them with every consideration,' the officer in charge of the operation confirmed, 'although of course we had sentries at different places to keep them in one part of the ship and the daily routine was prescribed for them.'[18]

However, another section of the alien population – Singapore's European prostitutes – fared less well than middle-class Germans. As a safety precaution, the authorities halted official recognition of the brothels and closed them down. Roland Bradell accepted the logic. 'Our European *maisons tolérées*, which used to play a very essential part behind the scenes of the white settlements in the Orient, were all closed during the Great War, principally owing to the fact that their inhabi-tants were almost all of enemy nationality.' So prostitution was driven underground; and the result, according to Braddell, was widespread venereal disease, broken health and ruined careers, even though the image of Singapore and Kuala Lumpur was improved.[19]

As it happened, prostitution came briefly under the glare of publicity during the first confrontation of the war in Malayan waters. Shortly after war was declared, the German light cruiser *Emden* (of football fame), under the command of Captain Karl von Muller, was diverted from the main German East Asiatic squadron in the Pacific, to serve in the Indian Ocean. Like the French corsairs of earlier times, the *Emden*'s captain had orders to carry out the maximum damage to British mer-chant shipping. He also hoped to track imperial troop carriers crossing Indian waters, and believed that the presence of a German cruiser off their shores would demoralize the Indian people. In three weeks during September 1914 Muller carried out a series of outrageously successful attacks in the Bay of Bengal. The *Emden* captured, commandeered or sank eighteen British merchantmen, causing havoc in the sea lanes between Calcutta, Burma and Singapore, and Muller even dared to shell the vital Burmah oil installations in the port of Madras. *The Times*, reporting 'More Successes for the Emden', published a full list of ships that had fallen victim to the raider. Small wonder that Britain's naval Commander-in-Chief, China, Vice-Admiral Jerram, was greatly exercised by the need for a blackout on information as vital contingents of Indian, Australian and New Zealand troops were being shipped over to the European zone.[20]

While Winston Churchill at the Admiralty fumed at the failure of China Command to anticipate the *Emden's* movements, Muller planned his next manoeuvre: a hit-and-run attack on the shipping in Penang harbour, using a camouflage device. It was no secret in Malaya that

a number of war-ships, whose mission it was to assist in the hunting down of the Emden and bringing her to book, had their base in the harbour of Penang. These ships were the English cruiser Yarmouth, the Russian cruiser Zemtchug [*sic*], a small French gun-boat . . . and two or three French torpedo boats. The captain of the Yarmouth apparently took precedence over the Commanders of the other vessels . . . and when the Yarmouth was in harbour there was strict discipline aboard her, and vigilance was shown not only on her, but on the vessels of the Allied Powers. The Yarmouth, however, often went on extended cruises in the Indian Ocean in search for the Emden, and in her absence matters became very slack indeed amongst the ships left behind. Evidently the captain of the Emden learnt of this state of things from Dutch sympathisers and determined to take advantage of it. This he did in a very sporting way.[21]

The German commander planned to pass the observation post overlooking Georgetown in the murky light before dawn and anchor in the man-of-war anchorage. By erecting a fourth funnel of canvas and wood, he hoped that land-based observers would be deceived into thinking the *Emden* was HMS *Yarmouth*. Although the Empire was at war, the lights of Penang were still burning, which increased visibility. It was just after 5 a.m. when the cruiser was clearly revealed, flying the Royal Navy's white ensign. A few minutes later, just before opening fire, the flag was exchanged for German colours (in accordance with the rules of war). A British eyewitness, R. K. Walker, takes up the story:

I was manager of a Rubber Estate in Klang and had been given a week's leave in late October. My wife and I decided to go to Penang Hill. We left Port Swettenham on Sunday and arrived on Monday morning by sea in one of the Straits Steam Ships at Penang, and after lunch at the Hotel, we were taken up the hill by coolies and were given a Bungalow named the 'Dove-cot'. We spent a quiet and peaceful time until the last day, I think it was Saturday the 28th Oct., when we were woken by heavy Gun Fire from the harbour area. I at once slipped on a coat and made for the veranda overlooking the harbour, quickly followed by my Wife. There was a little mist in the harbour, but we were able to see what was happening.[22]

At the same time three men sharing the Medical Officer's house in Butterworth, across the straits from Penang, were also wakened by the din. Maurice Hillier recalled the scene:

The first salvo brought us quickly out of our beds, and into the veran-dah of the house with our field glasses. We had, so far as the dim light permitted, an excellent view of the Harbour . . . It was obvious that the Zemtchug was being heavily shelled, and we soon came to the conclu-sion that the other ship was not the Yarmouth but the Emden. During the engagement two shells came over our heads, one pitching on the golf-course directly behind our house ploughing a furrow in the turf there and then ricochetting away into the rice-fields: the other falling directly in the rice-fields . . . it was generally thought that the two shots . . . were aimed at the Butterworth Oil Tanks. Personally, I believe that they came from the Russian. They were fired during the fight, and I think the unfortunate crew of the Russian vessel panicked, and fired every available gun they had regardless of the direction of their shots.[23]

The Russians were not the only ones to be thrown into confusion when gunfire shattered their sleep. Some of the locals wrongly believed the intended target was the Butterworth tin-smelting works owned by the Straits Trading Company, which was well within gun range. Watchers on Butterworth beach panicked when a shell burst behind them, getting inside the smelter, and some residents of Georgetown were also bemused by the noise. An elderly British woman – 'a lady of near eighty, of the old pioneer stock, very much a grande dame with her straight figure and shining mass of white hair' – rushed out of her house in a state of complete confusion and 'yelled alternately, "I'm shot!" "No, I'm not!"' On reaching the waterfront she was humiliated to find that she was completely bald and 'in plain view of all Penang'! The glorious silver wig which had fooled people for years had been left behind in the rush.[24]

This personal disaster, however, was nothing compared with that of the *Zhemshug*. Walker saw

the Cruiser 'Emden' with a 'Rigged-up' . . . Funnel slowly coming from the right firing salvo after salvo with her 4″ guns at point blank range at the Russian cruiser 'Zemshug', anchored some hundred yards from the harbour, in front of the E. & O. [Eastern & Oriental] Hotel . . . The noise was terrific.

The *Zhemshug* received two devastating torpedoes ten minutes apart, as well as a bombardment of shells which turned her hull into a sieve: 'the Russian Cruiser . . . suddenly blew up in dense flame and smoke. She quickly sank, leaving only her masts showing above the water. The loss of life must have been terrible. the "Emden" quickly increased speed and made for the open sea.'[25]

The *Zhemshug* had gone down within fifteen minutes of the first missile striking, with casualties reported to be 89 dead and 123 wounded, of whom many were critically injured.

Major Arthur Thompson of the Royal Engineers added detail to Walker's account:

The 'Emden' did not disclose her identity until she opened Fire upon the unfortunate vessel, most of whose officers were on shore. The Captain saw his Ship sink from the E & O Hotel Verandah. The Crew were having a great time. The Bodies of a Dozen or more Japanese Girls were amongst those washed on Shore. The 'Zemchug' did not have an earthly chance and did not get off a single shot until she sank. The 'Emden' steamed round her using both Broadsides until she went down. What the 'Emden' did not know or discover, they were so intent on the 'Zemchug', was two French Torpedo Boats were tied up at the Wharf within 200 or 300 yards of her when she came round. Unfortunately neither vessel had their Compressed Air up and were unable to fire a Torpedo. A third T-boat, 'Le Mousquet', returning from the Watch they were keeping on the German vessels who had taken refuge in the Sabang Bay of Pulo Weh, was met by the 'Emden' going out and simply blown out of the Water without leaving a trace.[26]

The only survivor, according to Maurice Hillier, was 'an Annamese sailor, who, clinging to a hen-coop, was washed ashore on the Province Wellesley coast'.[27]

Meanwhile, Hillier later reported, one of the Butterworth observers

– a Mr Ballantyne, Secretary of the Penang Harbour Board and a member of the Penang Volunteers – knew that 'it was his duty to report himself immediately at the Volunteer Headquarters in Penang. He had struggled into his uniform as quickly as possible, and started for the pier at Butterworth, hoping to find some means of crossing, when to his surprise the Ferry Boat arrived.' The indifference of some of the Asians to the sight of European naval guns blazing across the harbour caught the British by surprise:

> the Ferry boat which, morning after morning, left Penang to cross to Butterworth at twenty minutes to five, crossed at the usual time although this naval fight was proceeding in the harbour only a few cables' length away . . . he [Ballantyne] went on board and commandeered her to go to the assistance of the drowning men. To this both the Malay 'Nakhoda' (skipper) and the Chinese supercargo strenuously objected, but by threatening them with his bayonet he made them obey him, and he picked up and took to Penang twenty-two of the Russian crew. Many others were rescued by launches and boats from the Penang side and all were taken to the Hospital.
>
> Many Penang ladies immediately gave their services in assistance to the Hospital staff in this emergency, and pyjamas and other clothing were requisitioned by telephone from numerous male residents.[28]

Another who had gone to the help of the sailors was the senior harbour pilot at Penang. As soon as the *Emden* disengaged, Captain William Brown moved in:

> I took a launch over the spot where the Russian had sunk, nosing it into a clear patch among the floating living and the dead. Boats had rushed from the shore and the shipping. I picked up twenty men, one of them in five piece, hanging together by threads of muscle, yet still alive. The Emden stood off and watched while the rescued men were landed and the dead placed in rows on the quay.[29]

As a member of the Volunteer Coastal Defence Service, Brown was ashamed that 'The town and harbour were at Muller's mercy.' But there was no time to brood. He had to locate and warn the Penang patrol launch, *Sea Gull*:

> Not a very comfortable job . . . but as it happened, just as my launch left the quay, the *Emden* unexpectedly got under way, and moved ahead of me to the north. I steamed in her wake. Muller, it seemed, was not

disposed to waste a shell on the pilot launch, and ignored me . . . his cruiser put on speed as she neared the open water. Her guns roared again, and we ducked.[30]

The victim proved to be the little *Sea Gull*, but, although she was damaged, she managed to make the shelter of the Penang shore. On her way out, the *Emden* had also fired across the bows of a Glen Line steamer entering port, but then allowed it to carry on unharmed. It was quickly obvious to the Butterworth observers and the pilot, continuing his pursuit, that the cruiser had the French torpedo boat in its sights. They saw the *Emden* catch her main target just after 7 a.m. Unable to match the *Emden*'s guns, the unfortunate *Le Mousquet* was 'battered into shapelessness' and went down, as Major Thompson confirmed. As was his custom, Muller ordered his boats to pick up any survivors.[31]

The Walkers, meanwhile, ended their holiday and came down from Penang Hill to stay overnight at the E. & O. Hotel. Their curiosity was aroused when they saw the other guests:

During meals we noticed the Russian Captain and his Wife of the ill-fated Cruiser, were staying at the same Hotel, both seemed much distressed. Later on in the day we left Penang by one of the S.S. Co's Ships for Port Swettenham and found the Russian Captain and his wife aboard proceeding to Singapore. What happened to them we never heard.[32]

Major Thompson knew rather more of the sequel. 'Baron Clodt, a Russian naval aide-de-camp to the Czar, came out to conduct an Enquiry. He cut a dazzling figure, White Uniform, Gold Epaulettes, Aigulettes [*sic*], Sword, Belt and Decorations.'[33] The Baron presumably had no difficulty in establishing the facts, for it was observed by a number of prominent people in Penang that the Captain of the *Zhemshug*, Baron Cherkassov, ran a slovenly ship. By absenting himself from the vessel, he condoned inefficiency and dereliction of duty in his officers, while the corpses of the Japanese prostitutes were evidence of poor discipline board. At any rate, a Vladivostock naval court in 1915 found Cherkassov guilty of gross negligence and he received a sentence of 3½ years in a house of correction, losing his decorations, his rank of Admiral and his status as a member of the Russian nobility.

The episode showed that, far from being on a war footing, Penang's defences were totally inadequate to withstand the kind of attack that had damaged Madras. On the other hand, a single ship – even one with an exceptional commander – could not keep up the initiative indefinitely. Even before Muller's raid on Penang the British had scored a heartening success against him. On 12 October, HMS *Yarmouth* had caught his two coal supply-ships, the *Markomannia* and the Greek-owned *Pontoporus*, off the Dutch-Sumatran island of Simaloer. The *Markommania* was sunk and sixty Germans were taken prisoner, including fourteen of the *Emden's* men who were aboard the *Pontoporus* at the time. The *Yarmouth* transported the captured crew back to Penang, and later they were taken on to Singapore. A second piece of luck came two months later, on 11 December, when the armed merchant cruiser *Empress of Japan* sighted the British collier *Exford*, known to have been captured earlier by Muller's ship. This time seventeen former *Emden* crewmen were seized. They included Lieutenant Julius Lauterbach, a burly one-time master of a Hamburg–America liner, who knew the China Sea and Singapore like the back of his hand. The *Empress* took the *Exford* back to Singapore, and on 15 December the German prisoners were marched off to join the German civilian internees in Tanglin Barracks.

A month before the recovery of the *Exford*, the *Emden* saga had been finally concluded. Mr Walker of Klang succinctly recalled:

> The 'Emden' left Penang and sailed down the Straits of Malacca and then on to the Cocos [or Keeling] Islands in order to destroy the Wireless Station. Before she did so a message was sent to the Australian Navy. At once the Cruiser 'Sydney' was ordered to proceed to the Cocos Islands at full speed. (This was on the 9th of November). After a short battle the 'Emden' was destroyed, and the Captain and the Crew surrendered.
> So ended the escapade of the German cruiser.[34]

Still imbued with the traditions of nineteenth-century chivalry, the British Admiralty directed that the *Emden's* survivors should be accorded the honours of war and her officers should retain their swords. In the meantime, the story of the *Emden* and the Battle of the Cocos Islands was reported in the British press in a way that betrayed a certain admiration for the enemy captain. Like the German air ace Baron von Richthofen, Muller belonged to an age of gallantry in tune with British sentiments of 'playing the game'. In this he differed from his subordinate, Julius Lauterbach. As a captured officer, Lauterbach was treated leniently by the British authorities in Singapore, but when offered parole he declined to accept, since to do so would have denied him the right to escape. Later, the authorities in Malaya judged to have under-estimated the danger behind the coldly dispassionate mentality of Lauterbach and others, just as they were slow to appreciate the implications of modern warfare. But, as the Great War dragged on in Europe, gentlemanly values were submerged in the impersonality of massive artillery bombardments and the obscenity of trench and gas warfare.

# 5

# *Mutiny!*

With the removal of Muller from the scene there was a sense of relief in Penang and Singapore: more so when news came through that almost the whole German fleet under Admiral Graf Spee had been defeated in the Battle of the Falkland Islands on 9 December. Christmas 1914 passed, the New Year came, and ostensibly all was well.

Since the withdrawal in 1914 of the 1st Battalion of the King's Own Yorkshire Light Infantry for service in France, Singapore had relied for protection on a battalion of the Indian 5th Light Infantry, a mixture of Pathans and Rajputs, who were due to transfer to Hong Kong on the troopship *Nore*. This would leave much of the responsibility for defence in the hands of the Volunteers. Meanwhile, the job of guarding the German prisoners of war and internees at Tanglin Barracks fell to soldiers of the 5th, based at Alexandra Barracks, about seven miles from the town. It was easy to be wise after the event but the Bishop of Singapore was dismissive of the Rajputs, 'descendants of Hindus who had been forcibly converted to Islam . . . These people, as I knew them in India, were always a discontented lot.'[1]

A young British resident later remembered how there was an unpleasant mood abroad early in 1915:

> my Aunt, Mrs E. F. Howell, who had lived for many years in Singapore and who knew a fair section of its races, had been told by one or two of the officers in the Regiment, friends of hers, that trouble was brewing . . . My Aunt did not take their warning very seriously beyond advising me, her niece, not to wander too much alone, whether riding horse or bicycle. I was eighteen at the time, and certainly did not pay great attention to my Aunt's friends and their warnings, although I did

once or twice remark to my Aunt that some of the Indian soldiers guarding part of the road to Tanjong Katong, down which we often rode on
our way for a bathe, looked extremely unpleasant.[2]

As it happened, Mrs Howell was well informed. 'Every Officer in the
Command knew there was something wrong in the Regiment,' Major
Thompson wrote later:

> The Regiment was very short of British Officers, and it was unfortunate
> that there was a certain amount of discord between the most responsible.
> The trouble . . . was a legacy from the former C.O. and was in the nature
> of a feud between the two most forceful men amongst the Pathan
> Officers . . . This had become very acute, and had spread down until
> even the Sepoys had become partisans.[3]

There was also uncertainty about the Regiment's transfer, as rumours
circulated that their destination was to be France or Mesopotamia, not
Hong Kong.

Just as serious a problem for the military authorities was morale and
discipline in the Sikh battalion of the Malay States Guides, who, with
the Mountain Battery of Indian mountain tribesmen, were also part
of Singapore's defence command. Two of the Malay Guides were
befriended by an Arab-Indian merchant of Singapore, Kassim Ismail
Mansoor, who fed them anti-British propaganda encouraging them to
abscond. The Sikh Guides were also turned against the war by an agi-
tator, a Singapore Sikh named Jagat Singh. Thompson recalled that,
although they were

> officered from the Cream of the British Indian Army . . . they [the Malay
> States Guides] never moved from Taiping [in Perak], except for the
> Annual Manoeuvres. When War came (1914) they came to Singapore
> but they did not want to go to War. They owned all the Coffee Shops in
> Taiping, 90% of the Bullock Carts in Perak. Many were Money
> Lenders . . .
> The Sikhs refused to volunteer for Active Service [in December 1914]
> and we were all relieved to see them returned to Taiping.[4]

In all, given the rumbling discontent, there was a disaster waiting to
happen – or, as Major Thompson said, 'the only thing that would have
been "inexplicable" would have been if something had not happened'.[5]

For all that, when the trouble came to a head at Chinese New Year,
Monday 15 February 1915, it seemed to catch the British community

entirely by surprise. Despite her friends' warning, Mrs Howell and her niece found that 'suddenly it happened'.

> We had been riding one late afternoon in Tanglin, and on our way home . . . in Orchard Road were passed by dozens of cars filled by men in khaki, some with rifles, more without. 'Probably some manoeuvres by the Volunteers,' my Aunt remarked, wondering why some of the men gestured violently to us to hurry and others called to us that there was trouble and we should hurry home. It still did not occur to us that any-thing serious was happening.[6]

Victoria Allen remembered there was 'a curiously tense atmosphere' that afternoon, 'like that preceding a violent thunder storm, only more so, and very disturbing'. It was a fact noted by several other people. Yet when her brother-in-law returned from a walk he mused, 'Can't think what's happening.'[7] One woman 'had heard shooting all afternoon, but thought it only the Chinese New Year crackers firing'.[8] Several loud reports like rifle shots were heard by people in the Tanglin area, and some wondered if there had been a break-out by the German POWs. Since it was a public holiday, the Lowther Kemps were due to play tennis with friends that afternoon and were dressed in their whites; 'when we got there we heard that there had been some trouble with the 5th Light Infantry'.[9] The news caught up with Major Thompson at Singapore Cricket Club. He 'had been tempted to linger at a Cricket Match being played on the Padang. About 3 p.m. I noticed Mr Richard Page [an official] stop his car outside the Municipal Offices and cross over to the pitch. Stumps were immediately drawn and the players returned to the Pavilion.'[10] That something serious had occurred was now obvious, but some people found it hard to assimilate.

Lieutenant M. B. Shelley was then part of a contingent of the Malay States Volunteer Rifles undergoing a month's training at Normanton Barracks. (He rose later from District Officer to the heights of Chief Secretary of the Federated Malay States.) There had been a strenuous morning's musketry practice – followed by tiffin – which had sent the men off to sleep.

> I was, perhaps, the only one in that camp who heard a few shots fired about 3.15 p.m. I was seated on my bed writing a letter and I remember wondering what the shots meant, but I gave no further thought to them. About a quarter of an hour later two officers of the 5th desperately out of

breath, rushed up to the guard tent of the M.S.V.R. and called to turn out the men. One of the guard came running up to my tent and repeated the message. I went at once to Captain Smith's tent, and found him asleep.[11]

Shelley wakened his CO, who assumed it was 'a false alarm, just to give the M.S.V.R. men a little more practice in turning out quickly'. Captain Smith replied, '"Tell them to go to hell", and he turned over and went to sleep again.'[12] Mrs Howell and her niece, Majorie Binnie, were equally sceptical, despite the fact that on returning to their flat 'we were met by our Chinese boy, who urged us vehemently not to stop but to go into the town as the "sepoys" were killing all the "orang puteh" (Europeans)'. Marjorie admired her aunt's sang-froid:

> a typical Victorian, not to be hurried or flurried unduly, [she] ordered our baths and dinner to be served immediately afterwards. I remember feeling very excited and somewhat alarmed at the idea of mutinies and massacres, but as my Aunt did not seem unduly perturbed I bathed and changed . . . Then the 'Cookie' appeared . . . and urged us not to wait – not even to finish our dinner. My Aunt took no notice except that she ordered the boy to put the heavy iron bar . . . across the front door, and see that it was securely in its sockets . . . Just as we finished our dinner, heavy footsteps came clattering up the stairs. Frankly, I was terrified.[13]

So, too, was a Tanglin resident who miraculously avoided a fusillade as she and her husband drove at breakneck speed into town. 'I never felt more frightened in my life . . . The Indian Mutiny flashed into my mind,' she confessed; 'also the fact that we had no white troops . . . they did not hesitate to kill women in the Indian Mutiny.'[14]

The Allens had 'decided on an early dinner, determined to be ready for any emergency'. Mr Allen, a Singapore Volunteer, rang the Drill Hall and was told to report there immediately.[15] An English woman and her husband [S——], a senior officer at the gaol, were told 'two soldiers from the Indian Regiment were "running amok" and shooting all Europeans . . . the doctor at the hospital (the very nice man who operated on S—— and was so kind) shot dead in his car just below our house'.[16] Two more women fled from Tanglin when 'a volunteer wounded in the throat rushed down from the barracks and said . . . "For God's sake get the women and children away, the Fifth have mutinied and are shooting down the guard."'[17] Major Thompson, meanwhile, had learned that a full-blown mutiny had broken out:

there was serious trouble with the Native Troops and [an official] had been requested to instruct all volunteers to report immediately to the Drill Hall. Leaving the . . . Cricket Club for Headquarters I met the G.O.C. [Brigadier-General Ridout], who told me 'the lid was off' at Alexandra [Barracks] – MacLean commanding the Mountain Battery, Malay States Guides; Elliott and Boyce of the 5th having been shot down, the other British Officers barely escaping with their lives. It was reported that the Guard over the German Prisoners of War at Tanglin Barracks had been attacked and several killed, also a number of Civilians had been murdered around Pasir Panjang . . . Unfortunately Major Galway and Captain Izard of the R[oyal] A[rtillery] had been murdered at Sepoy Lines whilst on their way to Jardine Steps from the Garrison Golf Club.[18]

Various versions of the Mutiny began to spread. One person after another came into the Europe Hotel with tales of horror going on outside. Mrs Howell heard one account from a breathless cleric on the staff of St Andrew's Cathedral – his were the heavy footsteps up her stairs – when he urged the two women to leave.

'Don't wait another moment – go down to Johnson's Pier and you will be put on a launch going out to the P. & O. *Nile* or other ship. The 5th Light Infantry mutinied about 3 o'clock and have been shooting up people – don't know how many – the place is full of wild rumours but I can't wait – I'm rounding up all women and children round here – most of the Tanglin people are already down at the Pier or at the Singapore Club. Don't stop to pack, and cut through the Cathedral grounds, it's shorter that way . . .'[19]

They quickly snatched up a few odds and ends and hurried off, but decided to avoid the Cathedral grounds and keep to the seafront, 'as if by chance we did meet the mutineers, we could at least jump into the sea and swim for it, said my undaunted Aunt'. Later they heard 'that the ringleaders did not intend to mutiny until nightfall and then to split into parties, and take the various residential districts by surprise and assault until the whole island had fallen into their hands'. Yet they remained confident that help would arrive to quell the rising.[20] However, those who had a fuller picture knew the situation was more complicated.

Major Thompson, appointed Provost Marshal at the height of the Mutiny, found that a plot had been hatched by some of the *Emden*

POWs, led by Lauterbach, who were set on escape. By an unfortunate accident – or was it incompetence or crass stupidity? – the Indian soldiers chosen to guard the prisoners from the *Markomannia* and the *Emden* were unreliable, and a number of the Germans, who spoke Hindustani, played on their susceptibilities. 'There was no check on this Guard, except a perfunctory daily visit by the Commandant of the Prisoner of War Camp [Major Cotton or Captain Gerrard, second-in-command] . . . and apparently the Guard and the Prisoners mixed freely. The Corporal of the Guard used to salute a picture of the Kaiser which had a place of honour in this Barrack Room.' It was the section of the Pathans led by this Corporal of the Guard, 'a man of strong personality . . . the man who turned the rankling dissatisfaction into open mutiny', who led the assault on Tanglin Barracks. Thompson was later shown a tunnel which had been almost completed, the burrowed soil from it having recently been removed to make a flower bed by unsuspecting coolies. The tunnel was never used, but sixteen POWs escaped in the chaos when the Tanglin sentries were attacked. Six were recaptured, but ten, including Lauterbach, successfully escaped by boat from the Jurong river across the Straits of Malacca to the Dutch East Indies. Thompson concluded that a handful of Germans had bamboozled the Pathans, who were already excited by anti-British propaganda coming from India. 'The Mutiny, in my opinion, was the work of a few desperate men who were fooled by certain Germans into believing the "Emden" would come to their assistance if they would aid them to capture the town, and that they could then reach safety in the independent Mohammedan State of Johore.'[21]

Be that as it may, in the first twelve hours there was a fair degree of confusion on all sides. A town guard of older civilians of all races was hastily formed, yet no one thought to alert the Inspector-General of Police about the Mutiny until late on the Monday afternoon. Despite the introduction of martial law, in the coming hours more British soldiers and harmless civilians were shot, making a total of forty-four European victims. One of the first to die was a young man in the MSVR, Private Leigh, who had gone into town on his motorcycle to fetch the mail and was fired at as he passed the quarter-guard of Alexandra Barracks. Another fatal casualty was Private Drysdale, son of the pioneer James Drysdale and a childhood friend of Lillian Newton. Three young newcomers to the agency house of Guthrie's –

MacGilvray, Dunn and Butterworth – were shot dead while lounging in the garden of their bungalow at Pasir Panjang, and a planter, harmlessly reading the paper, received a bullet through the forehead. His whisky tumbler was found intact beside him. However, what most shocked the European community was the murder of a pair of newlyweds, particularly the shooting of 'such a sweet, pretty bride'. 'Mrs Woolcombe had thrown herself across her husband when their car had been stopped by mutineers who had fired at Mr Woolcombe and a second shot killed his wife,' Marjorie Binnie remembered, deploring what had happened.[22] In a separate incident, a woman caught up in the Mutiny related, 'Another car was attacked and in it one woman and three men. Her husband stood up to protect her, but was shot, and the other men too. Three dead men were on top of the poor soul, but she got out and . . . took shelter in an empty police station, from where she was rescued.'[23] At a different section of the town, one of the Volunteers, who walked in his sleep, was challenged by a sentry. On failing to receive an answer, the sentry shot and killed the unfortunate man. Yet a Mr Gibson, who was 'accustomed to taking long walks, often talking aloud on his way . . . in the fierce heat', was spared by the mutineers as a lunatic: a case of mad dogs and Englishmen![24]

Women and children evacuated by launch from Johnson's Pier to ships in the roads were bemused, unprepared, many fearful of the worst. Victoria Allen and her small son, who had boarded the Straits Steamship coaster *Ipoh*, found the conditions tough: 'twenty women and children were using the captain's own cabin as a dressing room, and mattresses were placed on the deck for those who hoped to sleep'.[25] For three days on the *Nile*'s open deck, 'We slept where we sat; the ship was packed to overflowing,' Majorie Binnie reported.[26] Others were more outspoken and petulant about their experience: '. . . we numbered 2,400 people on that boat [the *Nile*], mostly black people. What we suffered is beyond description. The blacks [including Eurasians] simply took everything, food, berths, cabins, lavatories, and as we white women would not and could not fight them, we fared badly.' Yet, to ease their misery, 'Our quartette played bridge in the smoking room. I wish you could have seen one of our number storm the bar for a bottle of whisky and carry it down the deck.'[27] However, even this aggrieved woman was more fortunate than some public-service families. A woman with two babies told of her alarming, not to say bizarre, experiences:

Night was coming on and it would have been madness to stop in our isolated house, with the jungle so close round, so we went down to the gaol to see where the whole family could go for the night, and this room amongst the punishment cells seemed to be the safest place, except the old prison, which was already crowded with all the warders' families and wives and children of men at the docks. We took the babies and the amahs [nursemaids] and all the absolutely necessary impedimenta wanted, down the hill in the pitch darkness, with a guard of three warders armed with loaded rifles, and felt and looked just like the cinema pictures of Belgian refugees.

In the morning . . . the firing suddenly began again just outside the gaol, and the order was given for all women and children to go to the old prison. I was making the babies' food at the moment and dashed across with the boiling milk and any other indispensable article of infants' food and clothing I could carry . . . Such an awful scene of horrible dirt and squalor we found there; the building is old and not in use generally except for executions – the floor thick with dust and the ceilings with cobwebs. Every room had families of poor, tired women and filthy, tired, howling, hungry children – one ghastly child of three, half-witted and having screaming fits and convulsions all the time, added to the general air of misery . . . the mutineers were firing from the hill opposite and we had to keep away from the window.[28]

In the confusion, the police and military responded slowly. On the first night the Central Police Station was manned against an expected attack by a small number of Volunteers 'armed with old sniders, 1869 pattern, with long bayonets'.[29] When the Mutiny began, Colonel Martin, the 5th Infantry's CO, found himself cut off from his troops, marooned in the officer's quarters (as was Mrs Cotton, wife of his second-in-command). He managed to escape across the rifle range to his residence, to meet up with a force of the MSVR sent to assist him. There they were all bottled up for a nerve-racking night. The Mutiny failed to escalate thanks to the presence of mind of two men: the Rajput bugler of the guard, who blew the alarm and ensured that the Germans were denied the sepoys' rifles, and a naval intelligence clerk, who responded coolly to a warning message. In the GOC's name he contacted Captain Marryat of HMS *Cadmus* moored in Keppel Harbour and ordered him to send every available man, including a machine-gun party from the sloop. A detachment of sixty men was landed at the P. & O. wharf, and it was their firepower which on 15 February stopped an advance on the city that had started in the area of Pasir Panjang and Alexandra Roads. In addition, the next day they helped a party of Singapore Volunteer Rifles to flush out the mutineers and send them scooting from their barracks like hunted hares, to melt into the jungle behind Alexandra Barracks. These same British naval gunners were, however, an unpredictable bunch. As dawn broke over the CO's residence, where the Colonel and the Volunteers were besieged, 'the rattle of machine gun bullets on the roof of the house warned us that the over-keen Cadmus men had mistaken us for the enemy'. Reports also spread that the same gunners 'went on their way shooting all kinds of dark-skinned but quite innocent people – milk and food vendors plying their trade in the streets', for 'every Tamil coolie and Bengali bullock-cart driver was a potential enemy'.[30]

With a loose cordon placed around Singapore town and Alexandra Barracks back in control by the second day, the main objectives were to restore order at Tanglin Barracks and then to round up the renegades. The first task was easily accomplished. It was fortunate that, in Major Thompson's words,

> The behaviour of the former Singapore German Residents in the P.O.W. Camp was excellent. One or two members of the Guard, who were in the Camp when the attack took place were hidden away; Captain Pahnke, Marine Superintendent of the North German Lloyd took command, confined the Seamen element to their Barracks and placed armed sentries over them. On my arrival, I was greeted with many sincere expressions of regret and horror at what had taken place.[31]

What finally saved the day for the British was their opponents' failure to carry out their original strategy. When the Germans failed to co-operate, the rising disintegrated. On the second day, the 16th, one of the ringleaders, the Indian corporal, was wounded and captured by a gunner from the *Cadmus* and incarcerated in the gaol with ninety-eight other mutineers. (The English refugees in the gaol heard him reciting the Koran and saw 'his picturesque white draperies and turban . . . soaked in blood'.)[32] On the same day the mutineers who had attacked the guard put up a white flag. Major Thompson was instructed

> to get them into a position where they could be surrounded, and demand their unconditional surrender. On my arrival I was surprised to find myself in the midst of a detachment (60–70) of the 36th Sikhs.

They were greatly excited, and as nervous as cats. However, by making them fall in and do a little squad drill, I got them in hand, and then got their story from the Halvildar-in-charge.

Thompson explained in their defence that 'The attack on the Guard was over before they realized what was going on.'[33]

Meanwhile Lieutenant Shelley of the MSVR came face to face with some forty mutineers near the Keppel Harbour. They

> were marching down the road . . . the leader was carrying a white flag . . . there was only one thing to be done, and that was go to out and call upon them to surrender. So I hastened up the road to meet them . . . The funk which I felt . . . was pardonable when it is remembered that the last thing known about this regiment was that they were wandering abroad shooting all Europeans at sight. When they were some 20 paces away from me I gave three commands in quick succession – 'Halt', 'Ground Arms', 'Quick March', and they carried out the orders with precision, like the well-drilled soldiers that they were.[34]

Other groups of mutineers were at a loss to know how to surrender. A party of 200 sepoys tried to persuade the Manager of a rubber estate to help them by telephoning Colonel Martin, but the telephone failed. The party hung around Seletar Police Station for some time, and then, having dejectedly broken up, made off in the direction of Johore. 'One mutineer was found outside Raffles' Hotel disguised as a Chinese coolie . . . Two others were caught near the Europe Hotel, sitting on the padang by the sea . . . Some were found disguised as Malays, but most were caught in the jungle, hungry and miserable.'[35] The Sultan of Johore had shown his loyalty at the outset, by personally accompanying a detachment of his own Johore forces by train to support the British. He also lent his Tanglin mansion, 'Tyersall', as accommodation for MSVR officers; and he willingly co-operated over the transfer to prison of a party of sixty-five captured mutineers, most of whom, the evidence showed, had been involved in the conspiracy.

The rounding up of the renegades carried on into March. All that time intermittent sniping could be heard, and there were frequent false alarms. Although Lady Evelyn Young, the Governor's wife, had left for Johore, 'Government House was very nervy and expected attack each night,' one of the officers recalled.[36] Mrs Howell had predicted that the British would rush in reinforcements, and she was right. The

Shropshire regiment arrived shortly after 'a party of 150 Frenchmen landed from one of their warships, then about 180 Japs from two of their ships and 40 Russians', all hastily organized by the Admiralty.[37] Convinced that most of the 5th Infantry were loyal, Major Thompson had some 700 of them transported to the quarantine station on St John's Island, where the task of rehabilitating the battalion began. The mutineers were housed in the overcrowded cells of the Central Police Station or on a coolie hulk in the harbour awaiting trial by court martial, a process which continued into May. Before this, however, another rising had developed in rural Kelantan. Questions were bound to be asked: 'Was the Ruling House involved? Was it engineered or encouraged by enemy agents?'[38] In fact, the unrest was apparently unconnected with the Mutiny, but it shared an undercurrent of pro-Muslim, anti-British feeling. It also left those British families who lived 'up-country' somewhat uneasy.

Kelantan could be reached from Singapore only by Danish coastal steamer, and the voyage was often a nightmare. About the size of Yorkshire, the state had a population of about half a million concentrated on the coastal plain. There were a few British rubber estates, a large coconut plantation, also British, and a British-owned trading company, along with six British officials. The rebellion of April 1915 – known as 'The Outbreak' – was led by a charismatic named To' Janggut, described by Haji Hamilton, the chief British police officer involved, as a religious fanatic with a heavy beard and of mixed Indian ancestry.

The first indication of trouble came when the British Adviser in Kota Bharu, William Langham-Carter, received a warning from the Malay District Officer at Pasir Puteh that two Malay policemen had been shot dead while serving a summons on To' Janggut for refusing to pay tax. There were rumours of a more widespread rising involving 5,000 Malays, who surrounded the residence of the District Officer, Abdul Latif. The possibility that European bungalows might be burned down and the involvement of a Kelantan chief – the ruling class of some of the *rayats* disliked the new British land reforms – forced the British Adviser into decisive action. Haji Hamilton summarized what happened:

> Langham-Carter, a delightful person but a bit weak in a crisis, wired to Singapore for help. And H.M.S. *Cadmus* rushed up and fired a few shells at random into the coconut groves along the coast, doing a little damage

to the property of inoffensive villagers, and may even have caused casu-
alities . . . Langham-Carter collected all the Europeans together in Kota
Bharu which became an armed camp. And the country police [Malays],
being out on a limb, did the sensible thing and 'went bush'. The Malay
Volunteers from Singapore were hurriedly despatched.[39]

There was some division in the administrative top brass as to how to
proceed, until Langham-Carter and others, with a body of Sikhs, went
off

in the direction of where To' Janggut was beating his war drums . . . by
sheer luck [they] came up against some of To' Janggut's men who were
in a straggling kampong on the other side of a stretch of padi-fields.
There was a little sniping to which the Police replied and then advanced.
But there was no further opposition and the Malays walked away leaving
a few dead, including To' Janggut, shot clean through the heart, which
ended the stories of his invulnerability, and the rebellion.[40]

One of those with the police party, W. E. Pepys, later wrote:

The 'Engagement' only lasted about 15 minutes and when all was quiet
again we went over to see what was behind the hedge and found about
seven bodies including that of To Janggut (who suffered from elephan-
tiasis) lying appropriately enough beside an elephant gun . . . About
seven of the leading rebels were proclaimed and given a week to surrender, after which we knocked down their houses by the simple expedient
of cutting a coconut tree to topple down on to them.[41]

One of To' Janggut's accomplices was caught and condemned to be
executed by firing squad. 'Brahim Taling was blind-folded and tied to
a stake; he faced his end with courage, protesting that he was not to
blame. No others were present, there was no demonstration, no evidence of sympathy.' Alan Morkill, watching the scene, came to regret
that his presence had somehow condoned the death penalty. Before
this, at the Sultan of Kelantan's request, To' Janggut's body was displayed, hanging by the feet from the crossbar of a goalpost, on the
padang at Kota Bharu.[42]

The Outbreak was over by the time a company of the Shropshire
Light Infantry arrived to restore order. 'A few suspects had to be found
and the country was patrolled,' Morkill observed.[43] Meanwhile, the
dénouement of the Mutiny was played out in Singapore. There was no
clemency for the thirty-seven condemned mutineers. They were shot in

batches over a period of days at Outram Road Gaol (except for Mansoor, who was hanged). The public execution of the ringleaders was meant as a warning to the Asian races. The horror of the responsibility for the execution fell to the men and officers of the Volunteers. Lieutenant Shelley of the MSVR was ordered to lead the firing squad that was to shoot two of the ringleaders. Years later he produced a stringent account of incidents which had been 'impressed upon my memory as though they had occurred but yesterday':

> That's your job,' said Captain Smith turning to me. 'But what am I do do?' I asked. 'That's for you to find out,' was the reply. Slosher, the R.S.M. – and Old Guardsman – he would know all about it: he knew all there was to know about everything. So off I went to find Slosher. Slosher *did* know *nothing* about it, but of course he wouldn't admit it. 'We must first select the party of ten men,' said the practical Slosher, 'And give them a little practice.' So the ten men were selected.[44]

Shelley's problem was the more acute since an efficient operation was essential 'to look more impressive to the natives'.[45] Finding no mention of firing parties in the little red book on musketry practice and ceremonial, he quizzed officer friends at the Europe Hotel as to procedure and learned that it would ultimately be his duty, as officer in charge, to deliver the *coup de grâce*. When the time came,

> the two mutineers were brought out from the gaol and placed in position against the stakes. They were handcuffed with their hands behind their backs, but were not blindfolded. An enormous crowd had gathered to watch the execution and the Colonel proceeded to read out in a loud voice the offence . . . The Colonel's words were then translated by Interpreters into three or four native languages. During the last three or four minutes the two mutineers and the firing party had been standing face to face. The two Indians appeared to be undergoing the Ordeal with great fortitude . . .
>
> Turning to the firing party I gave the order 'Load!' . . . one or two of the men were nervous . . . One man . . . was very shaky . . .
>
> When I saw that all the rifles were loaded and the men ready I gave the order 'Aim!' and, following quickly, the order 'Fire!' A good volley rang out and the Indian on the left dropped in a crumpled heap. But the Indian on the right – a very tall, well-built man – remained standing. The expression on his face was one of such terrible agony that it will for ever remain impressed on my memory.[46]

Shelley's unemotional extract describes the stark reality of a harrowing duty done. But as electrifying as the sight of this act of *force majeure* was the unnerving sound that rose from the gaol and filled the air: the 'weird and blood-chilling wail of the Moslem death-chant'.[47]

The official attitude towards all the convicted mutineers was expressed by a British barrister present at the trial of the merchant Mansoor, who was condemned to death for treason: 'He lived as a British subject within the benevolence of the British nation and he sought to betray that nation and bring untold sufferings to its people here.'[48] Then, with a little hindsight, alternative judgements emerged. 'The whole thing was so senseless and so wicked; these brave fellows were just cat's-paws, persuaded by lies into the doing of something that never could have affected the war in any way, and that could never have had the slightest chance of success.'[49] And Majorie Binnie was unequivocal in her condemnation of their punishment: 'Of the trial and execution of several of these [mutineers] it suffices to say that it was a chapter unworthy of British decency and fit, perhaps, to be associated with the savage punishment of Indian soldiers fifty years or more earlier when they were blown from guns after the Indian Mutiny.'[50]

Curiously, there was some sympathy for a few of the German internees. 'Poor old Saloman!' wrote Edwin Brown:

> If ever a man suffered 'the slings and arrows of outrageous fortune', it was he . . . He was suspected here, quite unfairly, of being a secret agent because he had been decorated by the Kaiser with some minor order . . . he remained [in Tanglin Barracks] on parole with his wife until the end of the war, watching his property and possessions disappear, shunned by people who had called him friend, a broken-hearted man. There must have been many Germans like him.[51]

It was clear that British colonial opinion was divided. The wife of an Englishman present at the public execution was satisfied 'that it was very well done'.[52] In an enthusiastic letter to his mother and sister, Lowther Kemp of the Singapore Volunteer Rifles wrote, 'Now that is all over I am very glad that it happened – except of course for the murders – as we had a great deal of fun out of it . . . The whole thing has been very interesting and amusing . . .'[53] Whether he reflected a widespread view is hard to establish, but in 1917 there appeared a publication called *Mutiny Musings and Volunteer Sketches*, by W. Arthur

Wilson, with an introduction by Brigadier-General Ridout. The advertisement reminded the public that 'NEARLY 3 YEARS AGO THERE WAS A MUTINY IN SINGAPORE. IT WAS A TIME OF TRAGEDY BUT THERE WAS LOTS OF HUMOUR, TOO.' Prospective readers were promised 'It gives you all the Fun of the Mutiny, and some of its Pathos, in Brilliantly Witty Sketches and Verses', at $1.00 a copy.[54] This sort of levity suggests that there was not too much soul-searching among the British community. It seems that, once the Mutiny and the Outbreak were past, they breathed a collective sigh of relief and carried on as normal, helped by the fact that most households had been untouched by the crisis. In fact the British were surprised and indeed moved by the honesty and devotion of their domestic servants. The Allens' 'splendid Madrassi' boy had visited the *Ipoh* daily with clean clothes and other supplies. Victoria Allen spoke for many when she said, 'the servants . . . Indian, Malay, Chinese, Javanese, were marvellous'. And, once their neighbourhood of Cairnhill Road was declared safe, they 'returned to find the house spotlessly clean, flowers beautifully arranged in all the vases, silver gleaming, and tea laid' – all of which, she declared, would be gratefully remembered.[55]

But the Mutiny had unforeseen repercussions. It had, for instance, shown up the deficiencies in police communications, the inadequate telephone system, and the lack of officers with understanding of the Indian people or languages. The most urgent need was the reorganization of the Singapore Police Force. In addition, through the introduction of martial law,

> We were enabled to establish a Military Censorship on mails passing through the port; take off to examine or intern suspects who otherwise could not have been touched. Details of Plots having their origin in Berlin, Chicago, Switzerland and San Francisco were obtained, funds were impounded, Garrisons strengthened at threatened points. Gun running was stopped, all as a result of discoveries made in Singapore.[56]

A spate of war legislation included a number of enactments imposing restrictions on trading with the enemy and on the import and export of goods. Not only was the flow of German trade with Malaya extinguished, but a deadly blow was struck against German commerce with Siam and the Dutch East Indies. The war marked the end of the rich German community in Singapore.[57] In Penang, too, new security measures were introduced following the *Emden* episode, with far-reaching consequences. The Japanese navy took on the role of policing the Straits and seemed to take charge of Penang. There was tension between Japanese naval officers and Penang's experienced master mariners, such as Captain MacIntyre, the Harbour Master, and Captain Brown of the pilot service, who resented what they took to be Japanese officiousness. Not for nothing were the Japanese referred to as 'The Germans of the East'![58] And, with the gloomy experience of Japanese surveillance, suspicion grew as to Japan's long-term aims. The Hon. Robert Young, a member of the Penang Legislative Council, believed even then that the Japanese were planning to take over Malaya.

Once the crisis of 1915 was over, however, the residents of Malaya saw how fortunate they were to be far removed from the theatres of conflict. They threw themselves into patriotic fund-raising. Mrs Lee, wife of the Chinese millionaire Lee Choon Guan, devoted her time to organizing fêtes in aid of the British Red Cross and raised a substantial fund from the Chinese community. Among Britons the war became a *raison d'être* for amateur-dramatic enthusiasts. The revue *My Word*, which was performed in Singapore's Victoria Theatre in December 1915 before the Governor, Sir Arthur Young, and officers of the armed forces, 'played to a packed house bubbling with enthusiasm . . . like a firework show with a fizz and a whizz, with any amount of verve and élan', and the Amateur Dramatic Committee was able to hand over £600 to the Officers' Families Fund. Following their next event, in 1916, it was the turn of the Star and Garter Homes for Disabled Soldiers and Sailors to receive a cheque. But such annual events were crowned in April 1918 by the 'Pageant of Empire'. Given in aid of the War Emergency Fund, this was an ambitious celebration of the traditional music and dance of member countries presented by the 'Children of the Empire'.[59] Those who took part in, and supported, these lavish theatricals had the satisfaction of doing their bit to keep up national morale.

The war years were a catalyst for change: new opportunities and changes in the economy, transport, the role of government, social habits, dress, and experience of women as well as men threw into relief the old regime of pre-war Malaya. Not all these developments were welcomed by people who remembered pre-war days. T. P. Coe, returning as a veteran in 1919, was shocked by the social tensions, the effects of war-weariness and inflation.

The country seemed to be in a parlous condition. Wages and prices, but not salaries, were up double. Standards were up accordingly, e.g. a respectable European could no longer ride a push-bicycle. Rice control was complicating Government finances and domestic life – even the Sunday curry had become a matter of conscience . . . Above all there was the great gulf between those who had not been to the War . . . and those who had.[60]

Many other European men felt the same. They had worked throughout the war without leave and were tired. They had seen their salaries frozen or their earnings fall, and had expected better of colonial life. Captain William Brown was typical of the old guard. He dubbed these the sad years, for they lacked the camaraderie of the past: wives were driven back to England by Penang's dullness, so there was no one to organize social evenings at home. Penang life was far different from the pleasant social activity of pre-war years.

In 1917 a new threat reached Malaya: the killer epidemic of influenza. 'I first heard of the 'flu in the papers when conditions were described in China where pneumonic plague was said to exist,' C. R. Harrison recalled. He was by now a prominent rubber planter in Selangor.

At that time Chinese labour was being recruited for work in France behind the Front. They were sent by ships which travelled all over the world to dodge the submarine menace and when the recruits became ill on board they were dropped at the nearest port of call for treatment. This in my opinion is the chief reason for the spread of the disease throughout the world. When the influenza arrived in Malaya it spread very rapidly and soon there was little or no work done on the estates.[61]

Harrison's methods for dealing with it were pretty crude, but the results were satisfactory in reducing fatalities. He isolated sick rubber workers, gave them blankets, and fed them on brandy and milk, until he himself went down with influenza, double pneumonia and malaria, which he was lucky to survive.[62] Meanwhile, 'Death stalked through the island [of Penang]. It affected all the people of Malaya equally, cut down strong and weak, old and young . . . The treatment among them for the hot fever and aching bones was bathing in cold water. It was fatal. Families were wiped out in a day.'[63] Reaching Europe in 1918, the grisly march of so-called Spanish flu decimated the ranks of exhausted veterans, who died in France while awaiting mobilization. One was

Lillian Newton's only brother, Willie. He had been in the war from the first day, and had risen to the rank of Captain. Still in uniform, he succumbed to influenza on 22 February 1919.

When at last it came, the Armistice was greeted joyously by all the races with bells and sirens and happy chanting. St Andrew's Cathedral was the setting for a moving Armistice Day service. Just as at home, Malayans commemorated the dead on war memorials. The old generation retired or, feeling themselves outsiders, kept a lower profile. Youthful newcomers introduced a mood of optimism. Peace spurred an immediate post-war boom, boosting Malaya's staple industries. In 1919 Singapore celebrated the centenary of its foundation as a British territory. The city seemed to symbolize renewal and to offer Malayans the hope of a new era of prosperity and development in the 1920s.

PART II

*Golden Years*

*1920–1940*

# 6

## *Halcyon Days*

Looking back over the 1920 and '30s, there was a special quality to the life of the European community in Malaya, and many who experienced it felt in retrospect a warm glow of remembrance and gratitude. Time and again old Malay hands, like Harold Tomlinson, spoke of the magic of the country that held them in thrall. 'Malaya casts a spell over the susceptible and may never let them go,' he wrote, recalling his life in Singapore after the Great War.[1] And that idiosyncratic personality Sjovald Cunyngham-Brown, posted in 1932 to Negri Sembilan, would never forget

> It was here [in Seremban] . . . that I first fell under the spell of Malaya that has held me ever since. My time there was short . . . but it was enough for me to fall for everything: for the mountains and plains and the streams, and the empty coasts of sand so golden in the dusk; for the charm of the inhabitants . . . the elegance of their gestures, and when young, the ineffable grace of their physique.[2]

In applying to the Civil Service after graduating from Cambridge in 1933, John Peel had no higher ambition than to follow in the footsteps of his father, Sir William. 'As I'd been born in Penang . . . I knew what a delightful country it was . . . quite frankly, it was one of the ace countries of the Empire, so I put Malaya first and was lucky enough to get it.'[3] Leslie Froggatt, an experienced marine engineer working for a subsidiary of Alfred Holt's Blue Funnel Line in the 1930s, also quickly felt at home in the land of the Malays, whom he regarded as Nature's gentlemen (an expression much loved by English colonials). He savoured the feeling that his feet were 'squarely planted on the sun-baked soil of Singapore'.[4]

Initial impressions were deeply indelible. 'One seldom forgets the first sight of Malayan shores,' wrote Mrs Gun Munro: 'low shores . . . lying on the edge of deep blue water . . . a land of perpetual summer.'[5] The approach by water lay between 'the mountains of Malaya as blue, as languorous, and as majestic as my fancy ever pictured them'; and Pulau Pinang, the off-shore sentinel of the peninsula, a long curved hump rising from the sea, as if it were the half-submerged back of a water buffalo, 'a small sleepy version of Hong Kong set in the Indian Ocean'.[6] Against the backdrop of Penang Hill and the screen of luxuriant vegetation, the bustling streets of Georgetown – the walls of Fort Cornwallis, wharves, shops and pagodas – appeared cocooned in a mass of coconut trees areca palms and sugar cane. Beyond the commercial centre lay bays and beaches, residential avenues of angsenas, 'from which tiny blossoms fell gently to the ground like golden snow', and flame of the forest curving upwards as if the talons of a dancing girl.[7] Marine Drive, in particular, lingered in the memory of one old-time planter: to him it was quite simply one of the most beautiful roads in the world. Ainsworth's sentiments were echoed in 1927 by a journalist glimpsing Penang for the first time. 'I did not think I had ever seen anything so beautiful in my life before, not even in cherry-blossom time in Japan': he was overwhelmed by the 'white sandy beaches, coconut-palm fringed, with the green-blue sea caressing them gently, rhythmically, soothingly'.[8] A few years later, in 1934, another newcomer recalled the unchanging scene: 'Bright sunshine, blue sky and white clouds above a bright green fresh foliage glistening after recent rain.'[9]

'Penang was a place that never failed to delight,' enthused Katharine Sim, one of many English women who cherished memories of happy times there.[10] Mabel Price lived in the East for thirty-three years from 1929, most of this time in Penang, where her husband, William Price, was Manager of Whiteaway Laidlaw's spacious store on Bishop Street. She recalled:

I don't know another island in this world where life went along more like a song . . . It was, and still is, I think, a beautiful island, known to many as the 'Pearl of the Orient' . . . A paradise where life for all creatures was easy, while no calamity or disaster had stalked . . . within the living memory of the oldest inhabitants. Where the poor man could live in security and happiness without fear of the unknown; where the ambitious found an easy outlet for his endeavours to the mutual advantage of himself, his family and the community of which they were happy members.[11]

To drive around the island was like doing a tour of the whole of Malaya. 'Past beaches of white sand with black-humped "elephant" rocks and bending palms, little cliffs and Chinese temples, sampans and fishing stakes and *kramat* (holy) places.'[12] And, away from the rocky coast, 'the usual Malay kampong village with fruit trees and the high-gabled attap roofed houses. Only in Penang and Malacca are they still to be seen at their best, with richly carved woodwork. Then up over a pass through a patch of jungle and through some Spice Gardens where a few nutmegs and some cocoa was still grown. Down the other side we came on paddy land, with water buffalo wandering about tended by tiny naked Malay boys.'[13]

On the northern coast nestled Tanjong Bungah, a picturesque settlement housing 'the most ideal bathing place I have ever seen', wrote an old-stager, 'even when compared with Waikiki Beach, Honolulu'.[14] The setting of Penang Swimming Club had natural beauty and character: 'the Clubhouse is the old rambling wooden house by the Pagar on the beach, but the new Pool has been formed by building a retaining wall among the rocks below the low cliff. To sit beside the pool is to be sitting among the spray . . . A lovely place.'[15] Another visitor recalled how

> Sometimes we went to swim in the salt-water pool, twenty feet or so above the sea, where from a terrace full of scarlet salvias, balsams and gay zinnias, the view across the Straits to Kedah Peak was enough to melt the stubbornest heart – to annihilate thought to a coloured ecstasy. We stayed in the warm water for hours. When the sun had set the Peak glowed gold and, as the light swiftly vanished, it melted in the brief tropic twilight to a delicate blue line, a pale mountain of the moon, like a Chinese drawing in silk.[16]

Malaya was noted for such spectacular views, and even this vision from Tanjong Bungah was surpassed by the scene from the summit of Penang Hill:

> Kedah Peak and the pale, silvery paddy lands of Province Wellesley lay across the Straits: out to sea the sun shone through the clouds on some fishing boats, and before us, vivid against the dark, misty blue of distant mountains, were the great scarlet-gold cups of a tulip tree. At dusk going down in the train, we watched the lights coming out in the town

beneath and the moon rising above the clouds. Cicadas screamed and whirred, like Chinese food clappers and electric bells, while all the tree frogs boomed. *Penang was so beautiful.*[17]

Everyone had their favourite places. 'Each town in Malay has its special setting and charms – Penang has its Crag and seafront . . . Taiping is like a lovely park with its neat drives and stately residences brooded over by the Larut Hills; Kuala Kangsar is uniquely placed on the banks of the Perak River; and Kuala Lumpur queens it with her spacious maidan, palatial government offices, and her numerous-crowned hills.'[18] One of Taiping's popular attractions was the bathing pool of cold, clear water which nestled at the foot of Maxwell's Hill. Surrounded by 'a riot of vines and flowers', with 'attap thatched houses for dressing rooms and an open bar beside the pools', it was a

> truly spectacular Swimming Club. There were a string of pools, stepped, so that the water ran through them all. They were fed from a small river which ran down beside the pools, and far upstream, in the jungle, you could see an impressive waterfall. The top pool was reserved for a shute, down which you came seated on a heavy wooden sledge-like device which could accommodate up to four adults . . . The main pool, with spring board and diving platforms, was on the bottom step.[19]

Ipoh, lying in a great semicircle of limestone cliffs, was also known for its striking setting: 'looking down . . . towards the Kinta river, one cannot fail to be impressed by the beauty of the distant mountain scenery. Chabang with its conical peak (5,600 feet) cuts the skyline on the east like a cobalt edition of Fuji-Yama without the snow-cap.' As for the town, it had solid public buildings, 'comfortable shady bungalows . . . a select Malay suburb' and a 'Chinatown, a fascinating place with its . . . kaleidoscopic colour and movement, spicy odours, and exotic street stalls'.[20]

However, for capital-dwellers like Leslie Froggatt there was nothing to compare with Singapore. Its facilities overshadowed anything else in Malaya: the new 1920s buildings, public gardens, first-rate hotels, fine European shops, much-vaunted defence installations – and the equally compelling attractions of the Orient in North Bridge Road and Change Alley, where cheapjacks sold all kinds of goods for next to nothing. Singapore was in fact a Chinese city, with 400,000 Chinese inhabitants by the 1930s. But Europeans saw it differently. 'If you are English, you get an impression of a kind of tropical cross between Manchester and Liverpool', though Bruce Lockhart qualified Roland Braddell's verdict: 'an international Liverpool with a *Chinese* Manchester, and Birmingham tacked on to it'.[21] There were always temptations and choices galore: champagne and oysters, moonlight matinees or moonlight picnics, subscription concerts, and the Swimming Club – with five shining cocktail bars, terraces resplendent with sunny umbrellas, a perfect dance floor and a blue-tiled pool worthy of a film set, where the 'costumes of the women lose nothing by comparison with those of Paris Plage and Deauville and iced-beer softens the rigours of sun-bathing'.[22] No week was complete without a little outing or *makan angin*, east to the beaches beyond the Sea View Hotel or westward to the Singapore Gap to take in the panorama across the harbour. Here was escape from the stew of Oriental smells once emanating from the river and the shanties of Old Singapore, though much had changed for the better by the 1930s, and it had become 'a gloriously clean city'.[23] 'Singapore is one of the sweetest smelling spots I've known,' claimed Leslie Froggatt:

> There is nothing evil in the smell of the East . . . At first it loses heavily in comparison with the wild and garden flowers that go to make the scent of England, but gradually it seeps in, at once fascinating and repellent . . . It is a mixture of garlic and temple flowers, durian and incense, teak wood swelling in the river and Yardley's talcum powder so popular with the Indians.[24]

Katharine Sim, young and recently married, spoke with equal enthusiasm of the little coastal backwater in Perak where her husband was a customs officer, as she revelled in the sunlight and peace of Malaya and her artist's eye imbibed the natural colour around. 'Those Lumut sunsets were never to be forgotten and they flame now in my memory, framed as they were in the "golden gates" of the two western headlands . . . the colours rioted madly, changing every second in breath-taking glory, from rose to blood, to gold and bronze and copper-green . . . We could not speak, it was far too beautiful.'[25] Even a down-to-earth expatriate like Guy Hutchinson, who had every right to be waspish about the rotten time he and other Selangor planters had had during the Great Slump of 1930–2, could not wait to get back in 1934: 'I, for one, gave thanks', he wrote, 'for the pleasant times and places that my lot was cast in.'[26] And in 1931, from the ranks of that cynical breed, the visiting British politician, came paeons of lavish praise for Malaya's undying charms, the very 'apple of the eye' to 'an efficient and far-sighted administration'.[27] To conclude, here was 'as happy a land as one could ever hope to find – a Tory Eden in which each man is contented with his station, and does not wish for a change'.[28]

Visiting the Far East in 1922, Charlotte Cameron put her finger on the reason for this contentment. 'The Europeans', she observed, 'have a very good time.'[29] In a society where a white man was treated as a minor god, few questioned the rights and wrongs of their assumed superiority. On the other hand, British Malayans did accept the need to 'do their social bit' in return for a standard of living that was more lavish than they could normally expect in Britain. 'Malaya is rich, and can afford to pay her sons well for their work. So they live well,' the visitor from the Houses of Parliament remarked.[30] He seemed unaware of the slumps of 1922 and 1930–2 that had hit the salaries and prospects of white planters – and of the fact that the Chinese community included entrepreneurs who were far wealthier than Europeans. (There was no European equivalent to the Chinese Millionaires' Club in Kuala Lumpur.) But the fact remains that the standard of living of most Westerners rose in the inter-war period, and the Far East continued to lure British men and women with its profitable, vibrant, titillating image. To paraphrase an American observer, what was noticeable by the late 1930s was not how few Europeans lived luxuriously but how few did not.[31]

Luxury was gauged in several ways. Privately owned cars were certainly one indicator, and from the middle of the 1920s men on renewed contracts, whose salaries warranted the expense, proudly sported their Rover, Buick, Hillman, Ford, Vauxhall or Morris, or occasionally a showy Chevrolet. The automobile, even second-hand, was 'in my time a sort of status symbol', wrote Hugh Bryson of the Malayan Civil Service, who worked in rural Trengganu in the late 1920s. 'Even though there were so few miles of road almost all the "top" people had motor cars.' As an official – he was then Settlement Collector in the state – Bryson felt entitled to have his own vehicle, but as well as status it brought a practical benefit: it was 'a godsend in the monsoon weather because there was no other means of covered transport from house to office'.[32] It also enabled men and women in rural districts to take part in club life and other entertainments in the main towns. In addition to a car, a retinue of domestic servants sustained the kind of privileged life-style which had disappeared from middle-class Britain. The married European generally had a cook, a 'boy' or two to clean and run the household, a *syce* or chauffeur to drive and look after the car, an *amah* or *ayah* as nursemaid for the children, and, lower in the pecking order, a gardener or *kebun*, a *dhobi* or laundryman and a *tukan ayer* to take care of water and sanitary needs – all for a salary bill in 1930 of no more than $150 to $180 a month, less than an average monthly budget for food and drink.[33]

Except in the most remote estates and mining areas, the choice and quality of food improved in the 1930s with the growth of refrigerated transport. 'Today', gloated Bruce Lockhart in 1935, 'Singapore gets fresh meat from Australia, fresh butter from New Zealand, swede turnips from Sumatra, potatoes from Palestine, tomatoes from Java, rhubarb from New South Wales, oranges from China', and a dozen other items from elsewhere, such as Edam cheese and Droste chocolates from Holland.[34] Although the ubiquitous pale-blue tins of Crosse & Blackwell were still in demand (with surprising contents such as Oxford sausages, kippers and cheese), gone were the days when stuffed eggs, mulligatawny soup, scraggy chicken and *ikan merah* (red mullet) formed the staple menu of every gala dinner. Instead, by the 1930s inter-national cuisine was standard fare in the main establishments. At Singapore's Sea View Hotel, a visitor could dine off 'an excellent *petite marmite, homard à l'américaine*, and roast pheasant', complemented with bread sauce and *pommes pailles* – a feast that left little room for *pêche Melba* and angels on horseback. 'Here was a revolution', the same visitor concluded: cold storage, electricity, the automobile, and air con-ditioning for Singapore's plutocracy – all inventions that removed life's main discomforts in the tropics.[35]

In general, people accepted unavoidable irritations with a shrug – the mould-inducing, enervating humidity, mosquitoes and prickly heat. They acknowledged Malaya's deficiencies: for instance, in many areas the absence of antidotes and blood transfusions in the event of acci-dents, and the dearth of picture galleries and serious theatre – though it was untrue, as one ex-Malayan wrote, that 'music, drama and the arts [were] *entirely* missing'.[36] When these were weighed against the benefits, Leslie Froggatt felt there was much to be thankful for:

There's no denying it, it was an easy life, and a pleasant one. Food was varied, plentiful and cheap. Liquor and cigarettes came in practically duty free, so that we drank whisky and smoked and thought nothing of it. If you had money to spend, you had the finest selection of English, American and oriental merchandise imaginable, embroidered silks and tapestries, carved teak furniture, and leering black wood buddahs, fine egg-shell china handpainted in the most extravagant designs, long ivory back-scratchers and masses of ornaments and curios in ebony, jade and moonstone, pewter mugs, bright hand carved silver from Siam, and skin bags of every kind. We had everything we could want from East and West.[37]

Singapore in the 1920s was as gay and bohemian as any Western capital. In modern terms it was a swinging city, where the nouveaux riches and spoilt darlings of the world of Scott Fitzgerald, Cole Porter or Noël Coward blotted out memories of the Great War by 'having fun'. These years marked the start of America's cultural influence over British Malaya. Up to this time, before westernization of the East removed a lot of the local colour, it was the Orient which symbolized mystery and glamour. Europeans were intrigued by traditional Asian arts: by the Chinese lion and dragon dance and the Malay *wayang kulit*, the shadow play of moving puppets, often depicting heroic tales from the ancient Indian epic of the *Ramayana*. On special occasions a *ronggeng* would be performed with great suppleness, a communal friendly dance and 'the soul of democracy'. 'The Girls . . . dance around by themselves and the Males come up, at intervals, and dance in front of them. There is a sort of "game" in that the Girl must not let herself be touched by the Man' on account of the Muslim ban on physical contact.[38] And, despite the glamour of America, Europe still determined much of colonial taste in the 1930s. In Singapore the dance bands were composed mainly of Austrian and Russian players. Gramophones churned out Richard Tauber, John McCormack and the lilting cadences of Heykens's *Serenade*. Brass bands delivered medleys of Delibes, Hahn, Auber, Edward German, 'and the most tum-pety-tum medleys from Gilbert and Sullivan'.[39] Expatriates dreamed of home and flaunted their national pride with their extravaganzas on St Andrew's, St George's and St Patrick's Nights.

America, however, projected unselfconscious wealth and novelty. (Among the memories of two young English boys living in Malacca in the 1930s was a neighbour named Rita Williams, 'a rather glamorous American who used to wear sun glasses and tied silk scarves around her head. She owned a large Alsatian . . . We used to pretend it was a tiger.')[40] The USA was also Malaya's biggest customer, buying over half the country's rubber and tin by the mid-1930s, by which time Americans exceeded the French, Danish and Dutch as the largest non-British white group in the Federated Malay States. The impact of American dynamism was felt in the fields of popular culture – jazz, musical shows and Hollywood films – sustained by the transatlantic craze for commercial advertising. After talking pictures superseded silent films in the 1930s, the cinema claimed its weekly or bi-weekly attendance, as even Malaya's small townships acquired a fleapit or 'tin tabernacle'.[41] The small town Segamat in north Johore, for example, boasted 'a very good little cinema, with the back half-dozen rows, the $1.50s, with rattan arm chairs.. These were quite comfortable provided you did not go in shorts: if you did you got badly bitten by "rattan bugs" . . . It was the great time of Jeanette MacDonald and Nelson Eddy, and the Fred Astaire–Ginger Rogers films.'[42] A few years later, a new resident wrote home enthusiastically, 'Segamat is only a small place and there are only 12 Europeans here . . . We have had several good pictures here lately, including "The Wizard of Oz", "The Lady Vanishes", "Good Girls go to Paris", and "Fast and Loose". The last was very enjoyable, with Robert Montgomery and Rosalind Russell.'[43] The large towns offered film-goers a choice. Singapore had the Capitol, Atheneum, Alhambra, Pavilion and Cathay cinemas; Kuala Lumpur the Coliseum Theatre and the Prince's Cinema, where England's outstanding film hits competed with Hollywood's MGM productions. In the streets of Singapore, billboards made a powerful impact, from alluring posters of Mae West in *I'm No Angel* to bold multicoloured street signs pushing Tiger Beer, Tiger Balm, Gold Flake, Capstan and Cold Storage freshly baked bread. The American obsession had struck eastward: 'Singapore possesses a number of first-class advertising agencies . . . Singapore is the home of hand-painted hoardings . . . both striking and pleasing to the eye.'[44]

The post-war hunger for 'making whoopee' produced a rage for dance halls. They sprang up everywhere, in poor imitation of those in the New World in Singapore and Kuala Lumpur's Bukit Bintang Amusement Park. Once through the huge, flashing neon-lit gateway of the 'world', as such entertainment parks were known, customers of all classes and all races entered a magical, vulgar campus of deafening noise and mass entertainment, theatres, opera, cinema, dance hall, sideshows, booths, refreshment stalls and a stadium. Dance-hall cabarets were much in demand among unattached European males looking for a Chinese or Eurasian partner.

In Penang, weekends were the time for stepping out, as the planters, like the cowboys of the American West, came into town from nearby Perak and Kedah. During the 1930s the Runneymede Hotel acquired a high reputation. Guests revelled in deep fresh-water baths and foyers bright with flowers: 'banks of hydrangeas and hollyhocks, and on every table, sweet-scented, old-fashioned red roses. The rooms were constantly filled with the gentle sough of the waves and the whispering of the casuarina trees which grew along the low sea wall.'[45] But a man could choose to go to the big, white Chinese dance hall, the Elysée, or the old palatial E. & O. Hotel, which in those days had professional dancers known as 'taxi-girls', some of whom doubled as illicit prostitutes after the Great War.

However, Singapore led the way in providing pleasure, as in most things. 'We danced at the Tanglin and the Coconut Grove . . .' Katharine Sim recalled. 'We danced at the Raffles . . . under the stars . . . the little tables under the dome of the night, the soft lamps, the tall palm-trees waving gently against the velvet blue sky.'[46] Whatever your taste, 'If you wanted to turn night into day, and set your candle burning at both ends, Singapore was as good a place as any,' according to Leslie Froggatt.[47] A resident recalled the high jinks of the 1920s:

Dancing, from the tango to the Black Bottom, was the order of the day. Singapore's four major hotels provided tea and dinner dances every week of the year; and the magnificent ballroom of Raffles Hotel was renowned throughout the East. There were several good dance bands in the city and others visited the Colony from time to time. The popular tune of the day was 'Bye-Bye Blackbird', and the Charleston was to be seen in full jiggle on every dance floor. An American, Dick Adamson, came with his band from San Francisco to give us a new song, 'Singin' in the Rain'. Prudery was no longer the order of the day . . .

Among the hotel orchestras of that day I recall a very good Filipino band . . . One of the more exotic musical entertainments of 1929 was provided by Madame Kaai's Hawaiians . . . like the rest of the audience,

I found myself enchanted by the atmosphere of the show and much impressed by the quality of the singing. This kind of entertainment, would, it seemed to me, have proved a great success in London and elsewhere in Europe.[48]

A different experience was provided by the travelling companies which came on tour in the inter-war years. Probably the best-known was the Manila Show, with its lively and witty impresario, Hiram Schramm, 'the first showman to bring the "Fire Dive" and "The Wall of Death" to the Far East'. Schramm was a regular visitor to Government House and was extremely popular among both Asians an Europeans alike.[49] A group that played up-country in the small townships like Segamat was Harmiston's Travelling Circus, which included excellent wire acts, some Malay clowns, and a gifted Filipino juggler. But, in preference to this rather unsophisticated form of amusement, the residents of the Straits Settlements had other treats. On Sunday evenings the resident orchestra gave popular concerts on Penang's E. & O. Hotel lawn. Meanwhile

> Singapore was regularly visited by professional theatrical companies, both English and American. Then there were the occasional visits of internationally famous artists, among them Fritz Kreisler, [the pianist] Josef Hoffman [*sic*], Anna Pavlova and Clara Butt. One of the most distinguished theatrical companies was the Charles Macdona Players which produced a whole series of Shaw plays, including *St. Joan*. The quality of the acting was as good as anything to be seen in London and several of the younger actors and actresses of this company afterwards achieved great success in London and New York.[50]

At the same time, in contrast, Malaya's flourishing amateur tradition continued in its irrepressible way. The amateur operatic societies of Penang and Singapore gave regular performances of Gilbert and Sullivan operas, supported to capacity by friends and admirers, and self-made amusement went on much as it had done in the pioneer days. An executive with Guthrie's was pleased to find that Kuala Lumpur had a music club, and his neighbour, a stockbroker, possessed an organ in his bungalow, which he played every evening. One of the leading lights of Ipoh in the inter-war years was a gifted Irish lawyer, John Woods, who had a fine singing voice and helped to organize the dramatic and musical societies, the concert parties, and the social and cultural programmes of the YMCA and YWCA. Malayans did not advertise their talents. Amateur artists such as Renée Parrish and Katharine Sim drew and painted for their own pleasure. Rupert Pease, a rubber planter from Port Dickson, was 'a water-colourist equal only to Russell Flint and might even in time have surpassed him'.[51]

The gregarious found their outlet in partying. It was easy to condemn their domestic treadmill of parties, but, when home was so far away, the ritual of celebrating birthdays, anniversaries, reunions and farewells, or indeed any kind of *Hari Besar* (Big Day), was comforting. 'On 18th December, 1926, Eleanor's birthday, we invited all to a house-warming', wrote a Pahang planter:

> Our Chinese 'cookie', Tan Po Sing, had excelled himself, and what with a brace of pheasants brought . . . from Kuala Lumpur Cold Storage, meringues which Eleanor had taught him to make, and Pêche Melba, with lashings of beer, Bristol Milk sherry, gin and whisky, we had a rousing good party. Before dinner one always serves *pahits* – gin and bitters or sherry – together with *makan ketchil* or *hors d'oeuvres* including ground-nuts fried in oil. Pahit parties are a feature of Malayan life.[52]

There were many variants of these 'jollies'. Evening parties were so frequent in Singapore that, as one visitor found, 'if you are at all agree-able and appreciative you cannot have other than an enjoyable time', being plied with gin-slings, stengahs, and million-dollar cocktails, 'frothy with white of egg and streaked with crème de cacao'.[53] At week-ends there were get-togethers for tennis, picnics, swimming, golf or Sunday curry parties. Up-country entertainment might bear no com-parison with the formal decorative balls at Raffles or the Runneymede, but could still be fun. Guy Hutchinson recalled a Christmas Eve bachelor party for Waifs and Strays without families in 1930s Johore, a roaring success thanks to a tree loaded with presents, a borrowed gramophone, a huge turkey and plum pudding, and a case each of champagne and whisky and two of beer. After the concentrated feast-ing, the organizers were happy to spend Christmas Day playing golf and making do with cold snacks. Fancy dress was all the rage. John Woods of Ipoh wrote in a letter home in April 1926:

> We had an Old English Costume dance on the Saturday night, at which a lot of the local people were got up as Inn-Keepers and bar-maids (all men) in old English costume and they did all the serving themselves,

and an old Inn was built up in one corner of the dance hall in Telok Anson Club. The Band of local talent was also old English, in uniform, white trousers, red coats and very tall hats. A most picturesque show altogether.[54]

Any event was a good excuse for a party. When the circus arrived in Segamat, Guy Hutchinson revealed, 'we got most of the European performers to come out to the club for a drink and it was a most cheerful party'. Normally people from the district gathered once a week on Club Nights for a chat, some supper and a little harmless gambling.

On Club Nights there were usually two tables of Bridge mostly supplied by the wives . . . Some folk used to go home after games on a Thursday but usually 15–20 would stay on and I would supply 'Sausage and Mash' or 'Melton Mowbray Pie' with plenty of good cheese – we had a name for giving good measure for both eats and drinks at Genuang. Russian Pool was the great game at the Bar. Tommy Despard was our leading light . . . [Robbie] Bell and Tommy used to play every Thursday and 'almost to a full house' as they were both good, amusing and heavy betters on the results, it was good to watch. After grub those who were left usually played Poker Dice for drinks and cash – it was before 'Liar Dice' came to the fore.[55]

The club was the hub of British Malayan society, John Soper recalled:

There existed a sort of club fetish: unless one was content to lead a very secluded and quiet life it was almost essential to join at least one club wherever one happened to be stationed. In outstations the local club usually catered for games and social activities, but in the large towns there might be separate clubs for golf, other sports, and swimming, all of which would offer other facilities for entertainment.

Between 1936 and 1941, while serving in northern Malaya, Soper 'joined nine [clubs] and this was by no means exceptional'; when Tom Kitching, Singapore's Chief Surveyor, took a count, he found that he had been a member of twenty clubs in the course of his career.[56]

Civil servant Victor Purcell was a member of Penang's Turf and Hunt Clubs, the latter an unlikely import in a country lacking both hounds and wide open spaces. But horse riding was a passion for some British Malayans. The cost of maintaining a horse in Malay was not heavy – around £1 a week – and Sir William Peel, for instance, rode every day of his life in the tropics. As British Adviser, Kedah, he got up at six and would go out for a pre-breakfast ride with the Regent of Kedah. Together they would settle the affairs of state on horseback. Another first-class horseman was W. S. Edington, a Scottish farmer's son who had served with the cavalry in the Great War. In 1919 he came out to Johore as a mining engineer with Lingui Tin, and, though the Tengkil mine, where he was first Assistant and then Manager until 1942, was in the heart of the Johore jungle, he always maintained at least two horses for his personal use.

Polo, flying and rallying, though minority sports, also attracted a loyal and enthusiastic following. From 1934 the government gave subsidies to establish flying clubs, where qualified instructors taught 'men and women of all races at the low cost of 28/- [£1.40] per hour'; at Kuala Lumpur, for example, Sunday lessons were given in a Gypsy Moth. The Kuala Lumpur Car Club members were mostly bachelor planters who enjoyed hill climbs and motorbike racing. Among them, Guy Hutchinson recalled, was 'an ingenious and original character called Puckridge. He had constructed from a Model-T Ford a car he called "Ustulina" (this is a root disease of the rubber tree).' 'Puck' led a more charmed life than his four-wheeled creation with its erratic steering, but together they caused much hilarity in Selangor's planting community.[57] Horse racing also had its keen European following, and was massively popular with the Chinese (though most of the horses and jockeys came from Australia). Race week drew crowds to the racecourses at Penang, Kuala Lumpur and Ipoh, but it was the magnificent new course at Bukit Timah in Singapore which attracted the largest numbers, with its modern stand and tote. Some judged it the finest in the East, race meetings being regarded as social occasions and fashion parades almost as much as sporting events.

For families, the most popular sport in the inter-war years was swimming. The boom led to a noticeable expansion of swimming clubs and a growing number of private garden pools. 'We used to go to the [Singapore] Swimming Club regularly and meet the other families there,' the author Gordon Snell recalled.[58] For young Norman Price and his brother, Penang Swimming Club was a second home, while 'There was a very nice small swimming pool at North Labis Estate, made by damming a stream that flowed in from their Jungle Reserve', which Guy Hutchinson and his planters' circle frequented.[59] Ray Soper remembered how pleased she was to be invited into her next-door neighbours' private pool, less hazardous than sea-water swimming off the Butterworth shore. The coastal pool of Tanjong Kling, near Malacca, was a simple *pagar*. The Club had a 'distinctive conical thatched roof. The pool was filled with sea water . . . Diving platforms, springboards and a wooden chute had been installed and fresh sea water was pumped in through a pipe covered with wire mesh to keep out fish, sea-snakes and flotsam and jetsam.'[60]

The sporting hallmark of the British presence, however, was the golf course. Since pioneer days, golf had become Everyman's game. Favoured by the growing class of rich Chinese and unathletic Europeans who played for social reasons, the sport still produced some fine low-handicap players. (In his long career out East, Gerald Mugliston, who won the Malayan Golf Championship in 1910, appeared to know most of them personally.) It was commonplace for European men to beat the twilight with a round after work, in addition to playing at weekends. In the 1930s Bill Price, Assistant Manager at Sungei Nyok Dockyard, played regularly on Butterworth Club's little course, since by chance the first tee abutted his back garden. All the towns had their courses; most townships and even individual plantations possessed nine holes. Here again, Singapore led the way. In 1935 Bruce Lockhart noted, 'The island has half-a-dozen golf-clubs, and in Bukit Timah a course, both in the quality of the turf and in its test of golf, which has no superior in the East.'[61] Gordon Snell writes, 'My father was a very good golfer and would play regularly at the Singapore Golf Club. When I returned to Singapore many years later and experienced the intense heat and humidity, I wondered how any golfer could survive more than a few holes!'[62] However, Leslie Froggatt, also an enthusiastic golfer, confirmed how keenly vigorous sports were pursued: 'this much-abused climate prevents no one from indulging daily in such strenuous games as rugger, hockey, tennis, badminton and squash'.[63] In addition to most of these games, 'Fred' Watkins of the Post and Telegraph service enjoyed the solo sport of clay-pigeon shooting, in preference to shooting snipe.

Younger men concentrated on team games, which brought players together. October to January were the months for hockey and rugger; soccer and cricket filled the rest of the year. 'Games in abundance provided one's spare time activities and means of making friends with members of all races. I played mainly cricket and rugby football, but at other times also association, hockey, tennis and some golf . . . The grounds provided for playing games were all universally good and I enjoyed this feature of Malayan life to the full,' wrote J. S. Potter.[64] Work never prevented men from enjoying life and playing games regularly, Hugh Bryson confirmed, and the good sportsman commanded enormous respect among all races in Malaya. Occasionally, sporting skill could still land a man a job: in 1937, for instance, Norman Bewick, a cricketing rubber planter from Muar River Estate, left planting and, 'largely thanks to his prowess at games', became Private Secretary to the Sultan of Pahang.[65]

The Malays were natural sportsmen, Alan Morkill found – highly proficient at boat racing and their own form of football and boxing – and the Indians were skilled ball players too. Geoffrey Barnes remembered as a child that 'Kebun [the family gardener] was a keen footballer. On Sunday evenings . . . he and some Tamil friends would sometimes play wild games of "kickball" with us in the garden then and I loved these games.'[66] Events such as the Malaya Cup inter-state competitions raised interest to new levels. Cricket was also taken seriously. The leading Oil Palms company in Johore, employing a large staff of assistants, worked them very hard, even at weekends; but an exception was made if there was an important cricket match. Alan Morkill, as a District Officer in Negri Sembilan in the 1920s, 'played cricket against other districts and our team included Eurasians, Indians, Ceylonese, a Sikh bowler and a Japanese wicket-keeper . . . it was best if you won the toss to bat first. After fielding for a morning in a sun temperature of 105 degrees F. the quantity of drink required for revival during the lunch interval proved a handicap.' All the same, 'These were pleasant occasions and all races took part.'[67]

Sport, it was said, was the key to Malaya's social stability. Instead of ethnic violence, there was at worst some rough tackling on the field. Bryson recalled:

Games were undoubtedly useful in helping to break down any sort of racial or social barriers that might exist. In my early days in Perak, Johore and Selangor I played both soccer and hockey with and against mixed sides . . . when a suggestion was made about 1924 that the Malaya Cup soccer sides should be confined to non-Europeans . . . this was rejected by the Asian representatives on the selection committee, who held that merit and skill should continue to be the criterion . . . When serving in

Kedah in 1936–38 I was appointed . . . one of the Vice-Presidents of the Kedah Football Association, the sole non-Malayan member . . . [Also] I played rugger and . . . visited Penang, Kuala Lumpur, Seremban, Malacca, Perak at various times . . . and as the Asians began to take an interest in this then almost entirely European pastime, I was known to them . . . I think only once in 30 odd years did anyone say to me, 'I remember you as District Officer or whatever'; it was always 'as scrum-half'.[68]

Like Bryson, Guy Hutchinson never forgot the sportsmen he encountered in Malaya: Jackie Horner, a government surveyor who had been an All Black rugger player, Parker from Malacca, formerly skipper of Glasgow University 2nd XV, 'a very good three-quarter', 'a real star at Genuang, a young New Zealander called Mabin – he played full back for the Federated Malay States . . . he was very good indeed' – and R. A. M. Stradling, an English minor-counties cricketer. Cricket, in fact, superseded rugby as Hutchinson's passion when he felt he was a bit 'long in the tooth' for rugger in the Far East. North Johore had some keen cricketers, and

> we at Genuang were the headquarters of the Cricket XI. We had a fine level grass Padang and Dunlops had provided some very good Matting Wickets like those used in Australia. Our Club House made an ideal grandstand . . . We had a really good side . . . We had regular fixtures with the Army, Singapore, Tampin and Malacca. These were our big fixtures . . . We could and did put out a side that could beat Singapore Colony and also the Army in Malaya – no mean feats – two day matches both and what fun! The Club would be packed.[69]

Club life, then, whether it was associated with sport, parties, dances or just a few stengahs and a game of billiards or mah-jong, filled a social need, and if you were a member of one club you became an honorary member of any other in Malaya and had temporary rights to sign chits for credit. There was a world of a difference, however, between the small country clubs and those in the capitals. The old Singapore Club, with its wooden verandah and comfortable tiffin rooms, had been replaced by 'a magnificent building, stately and large enough to dominate Pall Mall' in London's clubland, in Bruce Lockhart's view.[70] In addition to its golf club, Kuala Lumpur sported two famous European institutions: the sprawling Selangor Club, curiously half-timbered and even more curiously called 'the Spotted Dog' or simply 'the Dog', and the exclusive

Lake Club in the Lake Gardens. The Dog's extensive membership had a choice of tennis, football, cricket, billiards, cards and dancing, while the Lake Club catered for tennis, bridge and dancing; both had dining facilities. Penang Club, the doyen of them all, founded in 1858, had a special charm, according to its members, and beyond its airy rooms and polished floors there were sneak glimpses of the harbour. Sungei Ujong, on the other hand, had a different claim to fame: its bar was reputedly the longest in the East. During the 1930s it 'was crowded three tiers deep on Saturday nights; sports cars of the younger generation of planters, lawyers, doctors, chartered accountants and administrators jostled in the car park with the stately Daimlers of the "old and bold", and you would hear the cheerful noise of laughing conversation half-a-mile off,' Sjovald Cunyngham-Brown recalled.[71] The typical up-country club, however, resembled Genuang or Butterworth, not Sungei Ujong: 'just a large estate bungalow, built on high pillars with a good changing room underneath, and upstairs a bar and billiard room facing the road, and overlooking the Padang was a large, open-sided verandah which was the main lounge' – an unpretentious focal point for a small community.[72]

The British in Malaya had a capacity to enjoy whatever was on offer. The changing colours of the tropical landscape and the profusion of plant and animal life appealed to country-lovers, but even man-made settings were greatly admired. Penang's Botanical Gardens, 'laid out in a hollow of the hill, with winding walks and waterfalls, and every kind of tropical flower', were a natural paradise where Mabel Price remembered wild monkeys coming from the jungle to be fed by visitors.[73] Guy Hutchinson had always been keen on natural history and was

> delighted to see the very beautiful types of Moth and Butterfly that were to be found everywhere, especially along the jungle boundaries of the [Sepang] estate. I saw regularly the pug marks of Panther, Tiger, Deer, and even Tapir . . . and the estate swamps were full of wild pig. There was a breed of Black Monkeys . . . I have never seen anywhere else; and some very large, black and chestnut squirrels. I also saw Wild Dogs (the 'Red Dog' of Kipling's Jungle Books).[74]

Alan Morkill, another with a deep interest in natural history, was delighted to be posted in 1920 to the unspoilt district of Kuala Pilah in Negri Sembilan. In a garden of sweet-smelling shrubs, he and his wife kept a pet hornbill and a Sambhur hind. '*These were golden days*':

tame animals and birds . . . contributed so much to the pleasures of life.'[75]

The coastal scenery offered other fascinations. At Kuala Krau, on the Perak coast, 'We saw a large family of sea otters playing in the mangrove roots in the estuary, and elegant white egrets pecked fastidiously on the mud beaches . . . After the rain the Tiauk birds or rain-birds were calling in their strange cry, a throaty "Talk! Talk! Talk!" . . . Huge sea hawks and occasionally hornbills as big as turkeys perched on the paroquet tree.'[76] On the night drive from Taiping there were nightjars or tocs-tocs with flashing red eyes; on Penang Hill coloured moths fluttered 'like miniscule [*sic*] Pompadour's fans', and even Tanglin's suburban gardens were flight paths for golden orioles, kingfishers and Singapore robins.[77]

Pleasure, relaxation, sport, all contributed to good health and helped to counter the sapping effect of the changeless heat and humidity. Next to the cost of living, physical symptoms induced by the climate were a frequent topic of conversation. Happily there was no shortage of counsel. 'The key was plenty of exercise with natural perspiration,' an army officer advised, 'alcohol in moderation, a sensible diet and to be sensible about drink – plenty of light beverages – with some salt occasionally – keep bowels open.'[78] In their instruction on health and nutrition, the Girl Guides of Malaya were taught, 'Green salads and vegetables should take a prominent place in our daily diet.'[79] A spot of local leave with a change of climate was also advocated. A few small hill resorts, such as Penang Hill, Maxwell's Hill above Taiping, and Treacher's Hill near Kuala Kubu, already catered for government administrators, but after the Great War it was clear that these were quite inadequate to meet the growing needs of the European population. After persistent pressure, a new hill station was built in the early 1920s at Fraser's Hill, on the Selangor–Pahang border.

Bukit Fraser, 4,100 feet above sea level, was approached by hairpin bends from the Gap where the road crossed Malaya's central mountain range. With magnificent scenery rising from a sea of grey mist, Fraser's Hill also possessed the only pub in Malaya, the Maxwell Arms, which served as the clubhouse for the nine-hole golf course. Scattered bungalows, their gardens bright with flowers, perched on jungle-clad slopes around the course, and in the 1930s a school for European children opened. Golfing and walking were the chief attractions, but out on the trail everything gave way to the close unending din of the jungle:

even the monkeys high up in the trees above us went on with their squabbles as we passed. Sometimes we met an iguana in our path staring fixedly with those strange cold eyes in that great unwieldy head, and I couldn't count the lizards and little snakes that waited only half concealed as we passed. And all the time the cicadas filled the air with their never-ending song. From Pine Tree Hill, you can look down on miles and miles of thick jungle country, hills wrapped to their very peaks in cloaks of everlasting green, the home of the Saki tribes, and the big game of the forest.[80]

Travellers could take a welcome break at The Gap Rest House: here in 1929 the Hutchinson brothers sat before a huge wood fire and were served a grand high tea of fried ham. Fraser's Hill became the leading resort for government officials, and for some executives of private companies which leased land there. A generation of newly-weds chose it for their honeymoon. However, the limited scale of the development made it somewhat claustrophobic. 'Some preferred a trip to Brastagi in Sumatra where they could not only enjoy a change of climate but also escape the government atmosphere which prevailed at Fraser's Hill as it did in Kuala Lumpur, Taiping, and other towns.'[81] Brastagi was situated at 5,250 feet, close to spectacular sights such as Lake Toba and the volcano Sibajak. It was both drier and different in scale from any of Malaya's resorts, and was popular for horse riding as well as walking and climbing. Some British firms, including Alfred Holt and Harrison & Crosfield, invested in properties there where their European employees could take local leave.

By 1925 the government was persuaded of the need for a larger hill station in Malaya, and a site was selected on a high plateau ringed by peaks on the Pahang–Perak border. An access road from Tapah to the Cameron Highlands was completed by 1931. Development continued throughout the 1930s, and a prominent part was played by the Executive Engineer for Pahang, J. B. W. Fairchild. A secondary road linked the settlements of Ringlet, Tanah Rata and Brinchang, a nine-hole golf course and an official Rest House and Experimental Agricultural Station were built, and by 1935 private enterprise was responsible for three hotels, a dozen residences, two private schools, a dairy, market gardens and tea estates.[82] The long-term goal to establish the Cameron Highlands as an alternative seat of government on the lines of Simla in India was overtaken by events. However, some retired planters put down their roots there, becoming smallholders and growing vegetables and soft fruit for the Malayan market. At the same time, the entrepreneurial Russell family, having ascertained that there was a safe market for high-ground, good-quality tea, had acquired in 1927 a vast saucer of some 800 acres of land and set about developing it rapidly under an experienced Manager, Bill Fairlie. The Boh Tea Estate became a self-contained community on Cameron Highlands, with a temple, mosque, workers' housing lines and dispensary, and became a profitable concern.

By the mid-1930s the resort was proving very popular for local leave. The Green Cow Tavern at the entrance to the Tellom valley held the accolade of being the highest hotel in the peninsula. The Cameron Highlands Hotel, overlooking the recreation area in Tanah Rata, was praised for its comfortable, modern facilities, while the Eastern Hotel offered cheaper accommodation – $7 compared with $15 a day. Soon after came the Smoke House Inn, a typical 1930s mock-Tudor mansion, famous for its log fires and strawberry and cream teas. Like all the hill stations, Cameron Highlands offered the luxury of cool nights, hot-water baths, and the chance to dispense with mosquito nets and enjoy the surrounding flora. Visitors remarked on the improvement in their energy. Returning to Johore, a Yorkshire woman wrote enthusiastically home to her mother:

> I was able to do plenty of walking and climbing. The climate up there is very healthy . . . You seem to be in another world . . . much nearer to England. The houses [are] mostly like English homes, with lawns and English flowers, roses, gladioli, violets, asters, antirrhinums, carnations, and many more . . . Several times we had strawberries . . . a great treat and the cream was fresh. Rhubarb was another treat and of course salads, and these were superior to ours.[83]

Nostalgia was a powerful sentiment. The hill stations left some visitors 'feeling caught between two worlds, snatched up out of the tropics into a kind of No-Man's Land', as Katharine Sim put it.[84] For many, however, the reminders of England were good for morale, and the sight of familiar features in the Asian landscape filled emotional needs. They warmed to English gardens, pseudo-Tudor 'magpie' façades, English-looking churches. By cosily calling their houses 'The Cottage' or 'The Nest' or after a familiar place, Lomond, Dulverton or Claughton, the

British felt themselves nearer home. A few, however, rejected this sentimental attachment to their origins and took Malaya totally to their hearts, adopting a Malay name and Malay faith and culture. While not going that far, Victor Purcell certainly regarded Malaya as a happy escape from London's soot and fog and from strap-hanging in the Underground. In the case of many newcomers in the inter-war years, his attitude struck a chord. For this post-war group of British Malayans, colonial life was a novel experience – sometimes frustrating, but definitely rewarding in material and social terms. Twenty-three years in Malaya taught J. S. Potter that pre-war colonial life was unique, the best of both worlds, a symbiotic mix of British suburban life embellished by the tropics. Gordon Snell, reflecting on his family's experiences, broadly concurred. 'I suppose we were cocooned in a European style of life, the way that British colonists tended to import a lifestyle to wherever they went.'[85] 'It was a halcyon period', mused the veteran Purcell. 'All golden ages are legendary and some are entirely mythical, but all the same I feel that Malaya's "golden age" of between the wars had a firm foundation in fact.'[86]

# 7

## *Pyramids of Power*

In the inter-war years, the binding sentiments of British Malaya were loyalty to the British Crown and trust in the permanence of an omni-present Empire. Reminders of the imperial inheritance were visible in street names and public buildings: Georgetown, the urban heart of Penang Island, Victoria Dock, Victoria Theatre, King Edward Place, Empire Dock, Empire Hotel, Empress Place, and so on. 'Singapore', preened Roland Braddell in 1934, 'seems so new, so very George the Fifth.'[1] Patriotism was alive and well, a young journalist observed: 'On Armistice Day, everybody wore a poppy. Even rickshaw coolies and road sweepers insisted on contributing their mite. Here was love and respect for a nation which hundreds of thousands of Asiatics had come to accept as their own.'[2] And, after the Depression had weeded out dis-pensable individuals and sections of the manpower, 'those who were left', in the eyes of one colonial servant, 'had very much "an Empire outlook" – "working for King and Country". They never thought of themselves, certainly in the Civil Service, as doing anything but *serving*.'[3] The same could be said of men in other fields. An English officer in the Federated Malay States Police, who was posted in the 1930s to the remote rural district of Jelebu, where he was the only European, accepted the need 'to do the dangerous things' on behalf of the British Raj.[4] Guy Madoc's father had risen high in the police force in South Africa: for some the call of Empire was a family vocation. As an ex-planter put it, on hearing that his sister had taken a teaching post near Simla, 'Mother would be quite on her own with the whole of her family doing "outposts of Empire stuff", two in India, one in Ceylon and one in Malaya.' He mused after retirement, 'It is funny how this sort of thing runs in families. My father's family were the same and so were the Hendersons, as I found when I married Jessie, only with her it was both sides of the family . . . I wonder what these and families like them are doing now that the Empire has . . . dwindled.'[5]

England itself seemed so far away, until George V broke new ground by broadcasting Christmas messages to the Empire in the 1930s. Reminding his expatriate audience of the memories and traditions of the Mother Country, the King saw himself as the revered head of a great family, a role his successor George VI pledged to maintain, while fostering the 'mutual trust and affection on which the relations between the Sovereign and the Peoples of the British Empire so happily rests'.[6] Royal occasions were warmly celebrated. The Silver Jubilee in 1935 was marked by the usual balls and presentation of gifts, but also by the establishment of a National Park bearing the King's name.

The following year saw a succession of dramatic imperial events: the death of George V, the accession and abdication of Edward VIII, and finally the accession of King George VI and Queen Elizabeth. In Malaya, talk of the house of Windsor and the role of Mrs Simpson ebbed and flowed over *pahits*. Malayan-born Dulcie Gray believed firmly that 'the King should put his country first'. But her mother, Mrs Savage-Bailey, an ardent royalist, claimed not to be surprised by his behaviour: when the Prince had stayed with them in Kuala Lumpur in 1922 she had found him a difficult guest, 'out all hours with highly unsuitable girlfriends'.[7] But opinion was divided, and after the Abdication a government officer – 'a real old bachelor of about 45 years of sin! but a most likeable rogue' – amused the European community of Segamat by regularly drinking after dinner 'to the King over the Water'. No matter: royal occasions always gave the rubber planters of north Johore a good excuse for a jamboree. Guy Hutchinson recalled,

> We were a bit 'quick off the mark' when Edward VIII came to the throne, but never mind, we got in our Official Party before the Abdication . . . There must have been about 40 people present, all the local Europeans that could be got together at the one time, but unfortunately a number of married couples were away on 'local leave'. There was an Official Party for all the townsfolk going on on the Padang, which we were to join – I think we had the Police Band in attendance and I know there was a large 'Ronging [*sic*] Group' . . . We all had cock-

tails in the lounge . . . We then went outside and had a cold supper at small tables set about the lawn . . . Jean [Mrs Bird, wife of the Assistant Adviser] and I then went down to the Padang – I had never danced a Ronging – but to celebrate Edward VIII I most certainly did now. It was great fun.[8]

The coronation of King George VI and Queen Elizabeth on 12 May – Empire Day – 1937 was the most memorable royal event of the decade. The presence in London of the rulers of Johore, Pahang, Trengganu and Negri Sembilan at the Crown's invitation emphasized the importance of the Malay States to Britain, while in Malaya the British community celebrated with a full panoply of parades and parties, dancing, illuminations, fireworks, flags and flowers. Public holidays were taken seriously, with the King's Birthday heading a long list of annual events. It was an occasion for town parades, when the civil authorities joined with the armed services in tropical dress uniforms and the public watched British and Indian troops in a military display on the *padang*. Only the participants – like Victor Purcell – knew of the behind-the-scenes pantomime of struggling into 'the most absurd get-up imaginable': tight black leather boots, a large helmet, a white tunic and trousers which 'were so very, very tight that you simply could not sit down in them', flanked by a sword 'fit only for picking winkles out of their shells'.[9]

As he watched the parade in Malacca a young British resident had 'the feeling that we were all representatives of a ruling race backed by the power and prestige of the British Empire'.[10] Occasional visits by royalty, such as that of the Duke of Gloucester in April 1929, and calls by ships of the Royal Navy, reinforced colonial pride, enhancing it with a theatrical aura. From the terrace of the Singapore Club, with its superb view of the harbour, Bruce Lockhart felt a stirring of pride as 'closing in the whole scene, a line of British cruisers and destroyers, headed by H.M.S. *Kent*, stood out like black swans in the fading sunlight'.[11] On his trip to Kuala Lumpur in 1922 the Prince of Wales was given a 'Fairyland Welcome', with 'Enchanting Eastern Scenes'. In addition to a reception of former service men and women at Government House, he received 'a wonderful reception from the Chinese and Malays who thronged the streets during every hour of the day and night' in the hope of catching a glimpse of him, *The Times* reported. As he drove to the European Club, the Prince 'witnessed a Chinese torchlight procession a mile and a half long . . . Gigantic fishes, fowls, tigers, lions, ships and castles brilliantly lighted with myriads of tiny lights . . . in bewildering array.' The story was similar in Singapore and Penang. 'All the communities vied with each other in lavish decorative displays' in streets lined with thousands of children 'cheering and singing "God Bless the Prince of Wales"'.[12] An old sea dog, watching the Prince's arrival in the harbour at Penang, reflected (with some prescience in view of things to come) that 'It was far above being an empty, flag-waving holiday, a mere Royal occasion; in it lay a deeper significance of the term British Empire, than the actual centre of that Empire has ever felt.'[13]

If ceremonial was a traditional way of fostering faith in Crown and Empire, from the end of the nineteenth century education became its most potent accessory, providing a core ideology of patriotic imperialism in school textbooks, classroom aids and teachers' manuals. The daughter of a colonial officer living in Province Wellesley during the 1930s was a typical child of Empire, imbibing her heritage through geography and history lessons learned at her mother's knee.

> I would gaze at the globe – it had come in the mail to our colonial outpost on its shining metal stand – and wonder at all the blobs of pink, all originating from the tiny dot of England. That's how I began to grasp my inheritance. The globe had so much pink on it. We could leave 'home' and find similar patterns of life and values in quite contrary places. I felt paternal toward our subjects – it wasn't a feeling of superiority, it was just that we were innocently and benevolently in charge. It gave me a feeling of really belonging to the world, to the veil of pinkness spread across it. Instead of having a bus pass I had a world pass – a right of passage because I was British.[14]

These lessons in imperialism were reinforced by the initial month-long sea voyage out East. British passengers and freight were carried 8,000 miles via the historic naval bases of Gibraltar and Malta; then from Port Said through the Suez Canal – thanks to Disraeli, 44 per cent of the Canal shares had been owned by the British government since 1875 – and on through the Red and Arabian Seas to the ports of the Raj, Bombay and Colombo; and so to the Malaysian archipelago. Despite intensifying competition in the inter-war years from other national lines such as the Danish-owned East Asiatic boats, British ships still took between 85 and 95 per cent of UK trade to and from Singapore and China in 1937, and the Far Eastern routes continued to be dominated by P. & O., the Ben and Glen Lines and Alfred Holt's Blue Funnel Line, which prided themselves on their seamanship and reliability. An 'eager, enthusiastic, expectant passenger', sailing out for the first time in 1934, felt proud that 'we found the Union Jack flying at every port of call except Marseilles';[15] and a year later a mature traveller passing through Port Said was struck by 'the universal prevalence of the English language in a town which was once predominantly French'.[16] Captain Steele of the P. & O. fleet was more effusive: 'we linked up the British Empire, which it seems must grow greater . . . All was sunshine, strength and confidence . . . Only those who lived in those days can realize what the British Empire meant to us – the master race.'[17]

The outward voyage prepared the newcomer for the hierarchical nuances of colonial life. Social status dictated that senior officials of the Malayan Civil Service, senior managers and company directors travelled in the greatest comfort. So Nona Baker, sailing to join her brother, the General Manager of Sungei Lembing tin mine ('an important person in Malaya'), was 'treated royally enough, being put at the captain's table'.[18] First class signified wealth or status, and according to a maritime legend the adjective 'posh' originated from an acronym for the demands of these cosseted passengers to have cabins on the cool side of the ship: in other words, *p*ort side on the *o*utward run, *s*tarboard on the *h*omeward. Cadet administrators were treated better than planters and other assistants, but less generously than their superiors. In the words of a police officer, 'Government servants in those days [1930–1] were compelled to travel out to the East and back by P. & O. in some style, First Class. Admittedly we young men were sent out in one of the oldest, smallest and worst ships of the P. & O. fleet. And we were jammed three in a cabin designed for two, but nevertheless all very interesting, exciting and new to us.'[19] However, on his maiden trip in 1927 as a rubber assistant, Guy Hutchinson travelled down-market in the old P. & O. steamer *Malwa*, 'on which I had a 2nd class passage [but] the firm had done the dirt on my brother [also a planter's assistant] and sent him out 2nd class on a Japanese boat, just to save a few quid'.[20] With a solid reputation and a single-class fare which fell from £88 in 1929 to £74 in 1938, Blue Funnel Line offered an attractive alternative to planters' and business families aboard its new passenger steamships *Sarpedon* and *Patroclus*. But inequality sometimes rankled.

Talking of the relative treatment of European employees by government and private firms, 'I remember Mummy saying bitterly how "Colonial Service looked after *their* people,"' wrote one former Malayan – implying that commercial companies, being profit-driven, were less concerned for the welfare of their employees.[21]

Although Malaya was generally acknowledged to be a friendly country, social gaffes were still frowned on and correct behaviour was a factor in promotion. During the outward voyage Guy Hutchinson had received an interesting tip from his fellow passengers, who were mature Public Works engineers and Malayan Railway officials: 'all advised me to become a Mason. "You can't get on in the East unless you're a mason" was their dictum.'[22] Whether he took the advice is unclear, but when he moved south to Johore, on his second contract, Freemasonry was well established there. In 1940 a new hall was opened by the Masons in Segamat and 'members come for 50 to 100 miles to attend'.[23] Young police officers in the early 1930s were expected to follow certain routines:

> Whilst we were training at the Police Depot we were housed in the Police Mess and we were advised to buy motor cycles . . . but after about a year most Police graduated to extremely second hand and unreliable cars. The Head of the Mess was of course a Senior Officer and about the first thing he did was he said that you must pay official calls on the senior dignitaries of Kuala Lumpur . . . So we went round. Of course we signed the book at King's House which was where the High Commissioner lived . . . We signed the book of the Chief Secretary to the Government. As far as I remember, below those two ranks, the Chief Justice didn't have a visiting book, he just had cards. And then there were various other people, about ten altogether who called, and every time you were transferred of course you had to go round and drop your visiting cards in the little boxes of the senior people in your Station.[24]

As bachelor officers, they were expected to be gregarious and to join the Selangor Club.

> We were all required to play rugby football and indeed there was an annual match of the Federation leagues versus the Straits Settlements leagues . . . There was also on the Sunday evenings a paper chase and we had only been in Kuala Lumpur I think for three days when the Commandant of the Police Depot announced on Saturday, 'Sunday evenings you young officers will all turn out for the paper chase', and so we did, of course.[25]

As a rubber assistant, Hutchinson was also a member of 'the Spotted Dog', but did not qualify for membership of the prestigious Lake Club in Kuala Lumpur, to which his manager, 'Herbert', belonged.

> Mrs H. was a great bridge player, hadn't a great deal of time for junior assistants, and so wouldn't bother us much. They were members – as were most senior managers – of the Lake Club – the senior Government Officials' Club, and only used the 'Dog' for watching State Rugger matches, playing bridge (for Mrs. H.) and snooker for H., both in the early evenings. Our paths at the Club would seldom meet, which was a good thing.[26]

To join the *Tuan Besars* of the Lake Club required status, money and careful attention to etiquette, beginning with the customary dropping of cards into boxes. 'Woe betide any candidate . . . if he failed to "call" on the wife of any Committee member', for it was the women who vetted the candidates, according to one newcomer who mastered the system. But charm and breeding also carried weight, and 'many young men, particularly if they were good dancers, found themselves joining parties without going through the procedure, and . . . say after watching a game of tennis, you could join a table of wives and husbands on whom you had not called and be welcome'.[27] Rising stars of the Civil Service were readily admitted to the European elite.

Lifestyles and friendships were governed by occupation and a man's position in the hierarchy. Fresh from England, Nona Baker was quick to notice that 'A man's position was of immense importance in a rigidly graded society.'[28] Isabella Bird had found that the unchanging stuff of gossip in Singapore included

> speculations as to when or whether Mr —— will get promotion, when Mr —— will go home, or how much he has saved out of his salary; what influence has procured the appointment of Mr —— to Selangor or Perak, instead of Mr ——, whose qualifications are higher; whether Mr ——'s acting appointment will be confirmed; whether Mr —— will get . . . leave; whether some vacant appointment is to be filled up or abolished, and so ad infinitum.[29]

These preoccupations were intensified in the 1930s by economic ups and downs and the tendency to promote middle ranks on the basis of 'Buggins's turn'. Wherever the British gathered, conversation was punctuated by references to the company or departmental pecking order.

'My father was a Chartered Accountant and was Number Two for a group of rubber estates,' wrote a former Malayan about a small community where the General Manager, factory engineer and planters all lived near each other on Gula Kalumpong estate, fifty miles south of Penang.[30] In most European communities it was natural to discuss the authority and deficiencies of the 'Number One', the prospects of his deputy, the 'Number Two', and the assistants, who were only 'Number Three' or 'Number Four' (the latter often being the newest recruit from England). Rank brought personal prestige – all-important to a group of people who were hyperconscious of being colonial rulers.

Imperial power, in the British mind, was primarily a matter of prestige, sustained by force of arms if and when the British presence was challenged. Shared respect for the symbols of power sustained good relations between the British and the Malay princes who were bound to Britain by treaty. In 1933 the Colonial Office confirmed that Britain stood firm by the principle that 'the maintenance of the position, authority and prestige of the Malay rulers must always be a cardinal point in British policy'.[31] Although their powers were restricted – in the Federated Malay States 'the British adviser ruled and the Malay ruler advised, it was said' – the Sultans were not the helpless puppets they have sometimes been painted, particularly in the Unfederated States, which, according to Hugh Bryson, were 'less under the "fetters" of Singapore'. Kedah, for instance, 'was sometimes described as the place "where the black man ruled the white"'.[32] In the inter-war years Sultan Ibrahim of Johore was assiduous in defending his authority. He always addressed the High Commissioner as 'Governor', managing to intimate that, while accepting him as the head of a Crown Colony, the Straits Settlements, Johore's position as a sovereign state was unaffected. A British official in Johore candidly observed that the Sultan 'ruled his State with a rod of iron' and did not always listen to the suggestions of Mr Walter Pepys CMG, his General Adviser. 'A magnificent man and a magnificent monarch', in Sjovald Cunyngham-Brown's eyes, Sultan Ibrahim raised and commanded his own Johore Military Forces and 'held a court in Johore Bahru of almost medieval splendour' like a true autocrat.[33]

Malay society, then, retained a hierarchical structure as much as British colonial society. 'At the top was the Sultan, below him and usually related were the Tungkus,' wrote Alan Morkill, who, as District

Officer, came up against all levels of Malay society. 'Below them were Ungkus (also known as Rajas), Niks, Wans, and Inches (Plain Mr.).'[34] Europeans adopted Malay terms to denote status. *Tuan Besar* was reserved for top brass – the Managing Director, Senior Manager, Resident or Adviser, all of whom were treated with enormous respect, as Nona Baker realized when she reached Singapore and was accommodated in a sumptuous hotel. *Tuan* ('Sir') was the mode of address used for most Europeans, while the assistant or junior was *Tuan Kechil*. Recalling how it was in 1920s Trengganu, an official stressed that a car was the proof of authority.

> Even though there were so few miles of road, almost all the 'top' people had motor cars; it was . . . a sort of status symbol. The Sultan had a large yellow (the royal colour) American car in which he used to be driven along the road at about 15, maybe 20 miles an hour, and no one was permitted to overtake him, and we were all expected to pull into the side of the road if coming in the opposite direction, until His Highness was safely past.[35]

As might be expected, there were times when matters of protocol were publicly aired. The same official, Hugh Bryson, remembered an incident of precedence over the opening of the Johore Causeway, joining Singapore to the peninsula, in 1924:

> The High Commissioner, Sir Laurence Guillemard, was to cut the ribbon; all the Sultans were to be guests of honour. Date, time, etc., all had been fixed when the bombshell fell. His Highness the Sultan of Johore would not attend and objected to all arrangements. What had happened was that the General Manager's staff [Federated Malay States Railways Department] had sent out printed and numbered cards to the official guests; bad enough when dealing with Rulers but apparently the crowning insult was that the Johore invitation was number 65, or some such low down figure! The affair was postponed for some official reason and fresh formal invitations, written in the correct Court style in Jawi script [were sent] to each Sultan, and the Causeway was in being.[36]

Being British did not necessarily protect a man from the Sultans' wrath if he had plainly transgressed on a matter of protocol, especially if he was not a person of social standing in the European community. There was one occasion when a British official of the Posts and

Telegraphs Department was hastily removed to assuage an alleged offence against the dignity of Sultan Ishmail of Kelantan and his family. As a Johore resident, Guy Hutchinson knew 'He was a regular old Tartar was our Sultan Ibrahim.'[37] Europeans who pleased him were encouraged to remain in the state. Erina Lowson recalled how her father, a doctor in the Colonial Medical Service, was transferred in 1933 from Singapore to Johore Bahru, and 'because the Sultan liked my father, we didn't get moved again'.[38] But two cases of offending behaviour stuck in Hutchinson's memory. The first concerned a European banished from Johore for singing 'For He's a Jolly Good Fellow' during the Johore National Anthem; the sacking of a second European occurred because 'he stood the Sultan's niece a glass of sherry after she had been forbidden "alk" by the Sultan'. For his part, Hutchinson himself was careful not to transgress the Game Laws, in which the Sultan took a proprietory interest:

> It did not pay to 'buck the Sultan'. He didn't like us Europeans at that time and it was very definitely His State, and if he didn't like you then he just 'Deported you', which was alright for the 'Heaven-born' – they could be moved about from State to State in Government Service, but the poor Planter had no choice as to where his Company had their estates or vacancies on them. So we had to lie low.[39]

On the other hand, it was difficult to gauge the attitude of ordinary Malays, a naturally polite people, towards the 'occupying' British. The isolated case of a Briton being killed by a Malay running amok cannot be taken as evidence of ethnic hostility.[40] In 1928 an outburst of Islamic-inspired unrest occurred in Ulu Trengganu, reminiscent of the Outbreak in Kelantan in 1915. The situation seemed briefly threatening when 'a party of probably sixty Malays dressed for battle', some with 'old muzzle-loading guns', converged on the *penghulu's* house. Hugh Bryson, the local government officer, 'had never seen Malays in such surly, truculent mood before'.[41] But the insurrection quickly collapsed when Malay police shot a dozen of their attackers at Kuala Telemong, and the ringleader, a respected religious teacher, was banished to Mecca. On another occasion in the 1920s Alan Morkill, the District Officer, Tampin, had 'an unpleasant brush with a local tungku' over the young man's attempt to subvert the course of justice and revive 'the bad old days when the Tungku's whim was law'. The resentful Malay hit Morkill on the shoulder with a heavy stick 'for which he was carpeted and had to apologize in the presence of the British Resident'.[42] But such happenings were rare.

Soothing the sensitivities of the Malay princes was a function of senior officials. On a visit to London in 1924, the Oxbridge-educated Sultan of Perak, Alang Iskander, made waves by voicing his dissatisfaction to both George V and the Colonial Office: his particular complaint was that the State Councils in the Federated Malay States did not have the political teeth of those in the Unfederated States. In this instance he was being candid, not disloyal; indeed, his Resident described him as 'a great gentleman and a great friend'.[43] Another visitor to Buckingham Palace, the Yang di-Pertuan Besar of Negri Sembilan, impressed the King: 'that splendid sultan . . . I shall always remember him'.[44] 'Full of common sense and humour', the Yang Tuan was popular with British officialdom. He 'was a picturesque figure and looked the part of a prince', although he punctiliously consulted his major chiefs, the *Undang*, and 'exercised his almost non-existent authority by force of personality and charm'.[45] Sultan Ibrahim of Johore was regarded as the most politically astute and most Europeanized of the Malay rulers, bearing in mind his special penchant for the lights of London and Paris. He marked the Silver Jubilee of King George V with a contribution of £500,000 towards Singapore's defences, and the royal palace at Johore Bahru contained numerous life-sized portraits of Queen Victoria and members of the British royal family, besides the legendary Ellenborough gold plate.[46]

As a group, the Sultans behaved as capable, dignified, instinctively conservative Malay potentates. Though 'they vary in capacity, generally speaking, they fill the position of Ruler very well', observed one Governor, Sir Laurence Guillemard, with Anglo-Saxon condescension.[47] His Excellency the Governor-cum-High Commissioner was in the best position to judge: he exuded authority and panache. His high-plumed helmet and gold-encrusted military-style dress uniform signified on formal occasions that he was both the representative of the Crown and commander-in-chief in Malaya, the effective head of the power structure. However, there were times when the competing dignities of His Excellency and His Highness devolved into an element of farce. When stationed at Kuala Pilah in Negri Sembilan in the early 1920s, Alan Morkill witnessed one such occasion.

Early in his term of office the High Commissioner for the Malay States made a tour of the country. I was instructed to warn H[is] H[ighness] . . . of the impending visitation. A vote was included in the State estimates to meet the cost of the ceremony, by tradition a banquet . . .

Protocol required that he be received with a salute of 21 guns and a brass muzzle-loading cannon had been set up on the hill behind the Palace and firing over its roof. After the first few rounds a shower of rain damped the powder and there was an interval. Meantime the High Commissioner was greeted by H.H. and the banquet, consisting of curried goat and rice washed down with warm crème de menthe – a concession to the alcoholic habits of the Europeans . . . – reached the point at which H.E. rose to speak. By this time the powder was dry and the bombardment was continued. 'Your Highness, Ladies and Gentlemen, this is the first occasion on which I . . .' Bang! and down came a shower of dust and assorted coleoptera from the roof with a lizard or two for good measure on to the table below.

Age long tradition demanded that H.E. must continue as if nothing unusual had occurred; British aplomb must be shown. 'And I hope that it will not be my . . .' Bang! The timbers of the roof trembled and down came a second instalment. Responding to an agonized look from the A.D.C. I left to stop the bombardment and when I returned the fare-wells were being said. All was quiet and smiles.[48]

Whatever their private thoughts about the British, in these inter-war years the Sultans played the game courteously with the authorities, both literally and metaphorically. They entered into European social life and shared the British passion for sport. Hugh Bryson recalled from his east-coast service in the 1920s that, in addition to the European golf course in Kuala Trengganu, the Sultan had a golf course of his own adjacent to his summer residence, and it was during games of golf that the good relations were cemented between Sultan Sulaiman and his British Advisers. Sultan Ibrahim of Johore had an unrivalled reputation as a sportsman: athlete, cricketer, tennis player, horseman and renowned big-game hunter. Others were keen but had more modest skills. The Yang di-Pertuan Besar of Negri Sembilan occasionally visited the club at Kuala Pilah, where he 'enjoyed a game of Snooker which he described as *bola sa-ribu* (a thousand balls)'.[49] The new Sultan of Perak in the late 1930s was a tennis enthusiast, and the Sultan of Pahang was a popular visitor to the European club at Sungei Lembing. 'He . . . sported a con-

1. Mrs Isabella Bishop: as Miss Isabella Bird, this observant and well-travelled Scotswoman wrote one of the first accounts of life in the western Malay States, shortly after they were brought under British protection

2. Sir Frank Swettenham: the architect of the Federated Malay States, Swettenham's administrative career of thirty-three years was crowned by his appointment as High Commissioner of the Federation and Governor of the Straits Settlements. He retired in 1904, the year in which John Singer Sargent painted this portrait

3. The pavilion of the Singapore Cricket Club: its commanding position on the Padang reflected the significance of the club to European colonial society. Founded in 1861, it had a membership of 666 by 1907, and its imposing new pavilion provided a theatrical setting for members and their ladies

4. Ladies' Day at the Penang Swimming Club: the outstanding natural beauty of its location at Tanjong Bungah made the club one of the island's major attractions. The original clubhouse was an 'old rambling wooden house by the Pagar on the beach'

5. Guthrie & Co., Singapore: after eighty years of successful commercial trading in the East, the Scottish firm was housed in new head offices and acquired new godowns on Havelock Road by the Singapore river. As a result of expanding business in the rubber boom of 1906-12, Guthrie's also opened an office in Kuala Lumpur in 1910

6. *Above* A view of Singapore Harbour: in the first of a series of panoramic photographs of Singapore, F. Hill-Cottingham encapsulates 'the Clapham Junction of the Eastern Seas'. Prominent on the left is Cavenagh Bridge, built in 1869 across the Singapore river

7. *Below* Singapore street in the midday sun: a typical street in the Chinese commercial quarter is the setting for this atmospheric study. Few pedestrians brave the noonday heat, conveyed in the contrast of bright light and deep shadow

8. View of a rubber estate: a manager and his assistants on their rounds on a Singapore estate in the early 1920s

9. The wreck of the *Emden,* 1914: after a successful raid on Penang Harbour, the Emden sailed towards the Cocos or Keeling Islands to destroy the wireless station there. However, the German ship was outgunned by the Australian cruiser Sydney in a short battle on 9 November 1914 and her superstructure and funnels were destroyed. The captain and crew surrendered, and the holed wreck was beached off North Keeling Island

10. The end of the Singapore Mutiny, 1915: on 15 February a mutiny of men from the Indian 5th Light Infantry in Singapore shocked the British community. The mutineers were soon rounded up and later thirty-seven Indians were executed. This shows the scene outside the walls of Outram Road Gaol, immediately after the last group was shot by a firing squad of the Singapore Volunteers

11. A tour of Empire: the Prince of Wales's visit to Malaya, 1922. Following protocol, the newly arrived Prince (later Edward VIII), standing with his entourage under the shade of a ceremonial canopy, greets the line of colonial officials and dignitaries

12. The King's Birthday Parade, 1931: another royal occasion, the King's Birthday, was one of the numerous public holidays in the annual calendar. In Singapore the march-past was held on the Padang, against the backcloth of St Andrew's Cathedral (*right*) and the City Hall (*left*)

13. Tin mine manager's bungalow, Johore: up-country life in the inter-war years could not provide the luxuries of Singapore, but this roomy wooden bungalow, built in traditional Malay style, with a large garden, was an imposing family home for the Manager of the Lingui tin mine in South Johore

14. An industrial site: an open-cast tin mine in the 1920s. This view shows the layout of the Lingui tin mine, Johore. The pontoon, a large shed housing the steam engine, can be seen on the right. From the sluice boxes (*top centre*), the tin dust, separated from the waste, is channelled down the chute into pans and then bagged to be transported for smelting

15. Life in Singapore in the 1930s: a view of the ground-floor interior of the Snell family's new residence in Adam Park, Singapore

16. A colonial residence, Singapore: the home of Mr and Mrs Snell in Adam Park, Singapore, described by Gordon Snell as 'a large house with ample grounds . . . light and airy with french windows opening on to the verandah'

17. The visit of the Duke of Gloucester, 20 April 1929: a limousine carrying the Duke is watched by curious bystanders of all races as it sweeps towards Orchard Road during his official visit to Singapore

18. A reception at Government House, Singapore, 1933: an invitation to an official garden party was highly prized. Here Mr and Mrs Snell are introduced to the Governor, Sir Cecil Clementi, and Lady Clementi

19. Swettenham Wharf, Penang: a regular port of call for passenger liners and freight steamers on the long haul between Europe, the Far East and Australasia. Swettenham Pier was opened in 1905 and named after the recently retired Governor, Sir Frank Swettenham. The original wharf was 600 feet long and had godowns for cargo

20. King Edward Place, Georgetown, Penang: the heart of colonial Georgetown nestles around the north-eastern projectory of the island. Between Swettenham Pier and Fort Cornwallis stands King Edward Place, flanked by buff-coloured government buildings, adjacent to the Victoria Memorial Clock Tower, built to commemorate the Queen's Diamond Jubilee in 1897

21. Singapore Swimming Club, Tanjong Rhu: a view of the children's pool. In the background is the large blue-tiled adult pool, 'worthy of a film set', with diving-boards and surrounding tables shaded by umbrellas, which made it one of the most popular venues in Singapore

22. The Mems taking afternoon tea: a gathering of friends and neighbours at the home of Mrs Kathleen Price (*centre*) in Butterworth. The children, meanwhile, were having tea a short distance away in the garden with their *amahs, c.* 1937

23. A children's party: the customary group photograph taken at a Butterworth party, showing young children accompanied by their *amahs* (with two mothers also present), *c.* 1934

24. A fancy dress party: in the inter-war years fancy dress balls and parties were all the rage. John Soper, dressed as Robin Hood, and his wife Marjorie, as Maid Marian, enjoy an evening's fun at the Butterworth Club with their neighbours, the Fergusons

25. Stengahs at sundown: before the darkness of the surrounding jungle closes in on their bungalow, two women in a remote part of Johore enjoy a drink on the verandah at sunset

26. Tennis at Tengkil: in the 1920s and 1930s estates and tin mines sometimes had private swimming-pools or tennis courts. Here a group at the Tengkil tin mine in South Johore arrange a foursome for a late afternoon game of tennis

27. A wedding reception in Singapore: in June 1931 a large group of European guests attend the open-air reception for Alex and Dorothy Cullen, following their wedding at the Presbyterian Church, Orchard Road, where the bride's father, Revd Stephen Band, was minister. The bridal party is at the centre front table

28. A Coronation Party, May 1937: flags and bunting flew at the special party organized for the children at the Butterworth Club to celebrate the coronation of King George VI and Queen Elizabeth on Empire Day, 1937

29. Malacca: the colonial centre close by the riverside is noted for its rose-coloured buildings, a combination of pink brick brought from Zeeland and local red laterite. By the town square stands a Stadhuys or town hall (*right*), built by the Dutch in 1641-60. In the centre is the old clock tower and (*left*) Christ Church, built by the Dutch in 1753 but converted to Anglican use by the British

30. Kota Tinggi in flood, 1930s: the worst natural disaster of the inter-war years was the Great Pahang Flood of 1926–7, but the threat of monsoon flooding was ever-present in low-lying areas. The streets of Kota Tinggi were especially vulnerable to intermittent flooding from the town's proximity to the Johore river

siderable stomach, which did not, however, prevent him from donning a pair of white shorts and playing a strenuous game of tennis on our private courts,' was Nona Baker's recollection.[50]

While sport brought about a certain bonding between the class of high-born Malays and British officials, it also helped to foster good relations generally. A young agency official found cricket and rugby a means of making friends with members of all races, whereas 'Off the playing field one's activities tended to be restricted to the European circle, which could be somewhat narrow.'[51] Within the Civil Service, inter-district cricket matches were played, and Morkill's experience of a multiracial cricket team has been noted. John Woods of the Ipoh legal firm of Cowdy & Jones, was known as 'The Father of Malayan Badminton' for organizing the sport on a multiracial basis, and his success earned him the admiration of the Asian communities.

Changes in government policy to involve non-Europeans in government also helped to make Malaya a stable country in these years. British administrators solved their consciences by admitting a small number of educated Malays into the Malayan Civil Service – men such as Dato Mahmud of Pahang, Raja Uda and Dato Hamzah bin Abdullah, 'honest, reliable, hard-working [men] who believed that their duty lay in serving the people', as Hugh Bryson judged them.[52] Yet this was a far cry from the introduction of equal opportunities, and in a frank assessment Marian Gent observed that senior British officials 'could not believe that a Malay was as competent as his British counterpart, and firmly, if politely, prevented ambitious Malays from reaching their goals'. For instance, 'Dr. Mohamed Said fought all his life for the recognition he deserved, and his resilience in the face of consistently unsympathetic treatment was remarkable – so also was the true affection that, in spite of everything, he and many Malays like him had for the British.' As a medical student he was so brilliant that he became 'something of an embarrassment to the British who rarely came across such a gifted Malay'; accordingly he was relegated for the best part of thirteen years to Pekan, a remote district of Pahang, on half the salary his European equivalent received, and it was not until the 1950s that his career took off – in politics rather than medicine. Dr Said was not alone in being confined to a subordinate position in the medical service.[53]

Outside the sphere of government, however, some non-Europeans were able to progress in their careers. Two Malayan-born journalists,

Lim Keng Hor and Leslie Hoffman, became respectively News Editor and Night Editor in the *Tribune* group of papers; and on the retirement of the European manager of Sungei Nyok Dockyard in Butterworth in 1919, Mr H. E. Ward, a Eurasian, was appointed 'Number One'. Ward, his later Assistant Manager wrote, was a man 'completely dedicated to his job, his employers and the British Crown. Nothing else mattered, and personal gain never entered his head.'[54] This Assistant Manager, appointed in 1926, was an Englishman – an unthinkable relationship a generation earlier, but in fact the two men worked in constructive partnership for fifteen years.

Niceties of power and ethnicity were illustrated in a vignette of rural Perak. Stuart Sim was a Customs and Excise officer at the little port of Lumut, where the District Officer was a genial Malay, a distant relative of the Sultan of Perak. In addition, Katharine Sim wrote, 'the Forest Officer who lived by the estuary was an Eurasian; the Police Officer and the Engineer were Europeans; both were unmarried . . . The Government Doctor was a quiet, charming Indian . . . whom we grew to like very much . . . His hospital [was] on a hill to the west of the town, high up above the estuary.' In fact, the houses of all the government personnel (except the forestry official) were built on hills behind the village, with a fine view of the estuary.

> On one was the District Officer's house . . . Between the District Officer's house and the Customs Officer's house was a valley with a wild little golf course . . . The second hill was 'ours'. The Customs Officer's house was the top one, with the Policeman's just below and beyond his, the Engineer's. Our hill was two feet higher than the District Officer's hill, therefore Oriental ideas of 'departmental dignity' required our house to be built just below the crest. It was a pity: our view would have been even more superb a few feet higher.[55]

The Sims accepted their aesthetic loss: after all, the District Officer was Number One.

In this arcane area of race relations there was no absolute consistency. S. N. Veerasamy, the first Indian on the Malay Federal Council, asserted that Malaya's glory 'was that men of diverse races and creeds live in peace, in unison and in harmony'.[56] In this respect the country was far ahead of other parts of the Empire. Returning home on leave in 1939, J. S. Potter noted 'The segregation of the races which we found in Cape

Town was a shock to my fellow passengers and myself after our experiences in the East, where no such segregation existed.'[57] The way Malaya's population mixed freely in public places was significant. Even a child aboard the Butterworth ferry noticed the absence of barriers.

> Together everyone would hurry down the pier: local Malays, bearded Sikhs, Tamils and a few Gujeratis, Siamese, Sumatrans, Eurasians, pale-faced Europeans like ourselves, Straits-born Chinese . . . There were saris and sarongs, tutups and bajus, sun-dresses and cheongsams, pyjamas, trousers, shorts, singlets and loincloths . . . All kinds of people . . . the dirty, the scruffy and the stained . . . scrubbed, shining, starched, oiled, perfumed, elegant . . . the laden and the light-handed, the bowed and the carefree . . . an amazing human pot-pourri.[58]

In the Unfederated States of Kedah and Johore, where British power coexisted with a staunchly Malay sultanate and culture, social contacts between Europeans and non-Europeans were a regular occurrence. According to Roger Barrett, who grew up near Sungei Patani, 'normally pre- and post-war Kedah society, as I remember it, was more integrated racially than other states. As children we had friends of all races and a Malay doctor and his family were my parents' closest friends until they died.'[59] Agnes Davison had the same experience in Alor Star. 'We got to know the Kedah Malays very well. Kedah Club was the centre of the social life. All the Tunkus and Malay Heads of Departments were members and joined in all Club activities. The most popular occasion was the Gymkhana.' There were numerous formal occasions when the British and the Malays mingled, but Mrs Davison felt, more significantly, 'many of them enjoyed coming to our homes and entertained us in theirs'. The younger Malays, in particular, 'were full of fun and had a great sense of humour, and were very keen to learn some of our customs and to show us theirs'.[60] In Segamat, Johore, Nancy Wynne also socialized with her Asian neighbours: 'Yesterday', she wrote home in 1940, 'I went out to tiffin with two Chinese ladies, Mrs Eng and Mrs Lim, at a Malay lady's house. She served a delicious Nasi goreng . . . Malay was the lingua franca.'[61] In Port Swettenham, in Selangor, the Rawcliffes also counted Chinese and Indians in their circle of friends.

However, as the European population increased and concentrated in the main towns, there was a certain tendency to seek the company of fellow nationals, and European clubs were regarded as places to relax among peers and forget the conventional pressures of a ruling class. In Singapore, it was said, the 'only social meeting places of Asians and Europeans were the three slightly disreputable entertainment parks, or "worlds"'; and George Peet, editor of the *Straits Times*, representing the new type of British expatriate, much regretted the increasing social polarization in the early 1930s. 'Today in the towns of Malaya there is neither time nor inclination for the study of races and languages, and the commercial or professional European living in Kuala Lumpur knows little more about the Asiatic races round him . . . than he did before he left his own country.'[62] Undoubtedly people's experiences in the 1930s differed. Hugh Bryson was adamant that 'The so-called Europeans Clubs admitted without distinction the senior Malay officers who were in the Civil Service or Police; the Selangor Club had several Chinese and Eurasian members; so had the Selangor Golf Club, the Singapore Cricket Club and the Singapore Golf Club.' Furthermore, 'once a man of different race had been accepted as a member, there was quite distinctly no sign of any discrimination'.[63] In Perak the Sims generally played tennis at Lumut Club, which had both Asian and European members, but sometimes they went to the Asian club at Sitiawan, where they played with Chinese friends. Yet the evidence remains ambiguous. In many clubs 'the majority of members were European and in much the same way the Chinese, Malay, Indian and Eurasian clubs kept their membership to their own people,' Bryson also reported.[64]

In the higher echelons of society, race was no bar to friendship. The Federal Councillor Choo Kia Peng, for instance, counted himself a personal friend of Sir George Maxwell, Chief Secretary of the Malay States, and, with a small cadre of prominent Selangor Asians, Choo helped to form the Kuala Lumpur Rotary Club, the first of many in which Europeans and non-Europeans co-operated. A British official recalled that 'At official dinners or parties given by Chief Secretaries, Residents and such high-ranking officers the guest list covered all races without any sign of discrimination.' In addition, 'It was by no means uncommon to have dinner parties with non-European guests and their wives in my earlier days (viz. 1920s).' Later some difficulties occurred because neither the European newcomers nor the Malay women could speak the other's language. There were also fewer Chinese guests at European houses, due perhaps to 'some feeling of social difference – the Malays were the owners of the country, the Chinese were immigrants who had made money; they were upstarts and therefore socially not quite accept-able'.[65] The Eurasian community, on the other hand, particularly in Singapore, was 'strong, self-respecting and very prosperous' by the 1930s, and as the English-educated Asian middle class increased in the inter-war years there was regular socializing with Europeans.[66] The Davisons regularly attended functions in the grounds of the Istana given by His Highness the Regent of Kedah. In 1939 Stuart Sim and his wife received invitations from the new Sultan of Perak to his installa-tion ball at the strawberry-coloured palace in Kuala Kangsar, and shortly after, in May, to an official luncheon marking the opening of Lumut's new mosque, where the late Sultan's son, Raja Kechil Tengah, talked to Katharine Sim 'of England and Bourne End and London's policemen'.[67] Sometimes the Sultan of Pahang stayed with the Bakers at Sungei Lembing, appearing before the locals 'a vast figure swathed in gorgeous silks'.[68]

Weddings in particular were occasions for social mixing, though guest lists, like club membership lists, reflected the social hierarchy. Guy Hutchinson, being a mere Senior Assistant, found himself socially excluded, despite having been educated at a well-known British public school.

> there were two functions that . . . I would have liked to have 'got in on', but as they were for Managers Only there was no hope. The first was a local 'do'; the big Chinese Towkay who owned the Segamat Cold Storage married his daughter off to the bigger Towkay who ran the Aerated Water Works at Seremban. All the local Managers and Government Officials were asked and most went. We, the smaller fry, saw the elab-orate lighting going up, in and around the Towkay's house outside Segamat; he put up a couple of big Marquees and a stage and imported, not only a good Malay Ronging (Dancing) group, but a modern orches-tra and a lot of the Dance-Hostesses from the 'Worlds' (Dancehalls) of K.L., Malacca and Seremban. It was quite a 'do' . . . The other 'do' was much more Regal, in fact it was at the Istana (Palace) at Johore Bahru and was to celebrate the . . . 40th anniversary of the Sultan's reign . . . a sort of answer to George V's Jubilee. The leading Planter from each dis-trict was asked and H.B. represented our, Segamat, area. It was a most palatial affair.[69]

For all his exclusion from these events, Hutchinson belonged to the small privileged class, in contrast to the layers of humanity making up the rest of the social pyramid. Among the excluded was a fringe of poor whites – unemployed, bankrupts, men whose occupations carried no prestige, such as prison warders and railway workers, and those who, voluntarily or otherwise, eschewed a European standard of living. The latter seemed somehow shocking. Encountering an elderly, barefooted Englishman in Malay dress, Katharine Sim felt 'There was something at once pitiable and repulsive about him', but he was 'the only case of "going Native" that I saw'.[70]

Even among the Asian workforce, hierarchical attitudes prevailed. The Malay *syce* with his starched uniform was socially superior to the Chinese rickshaw coolie, and it would have been thought beneath their dignity for the cook or (house) boy to do the king of sanitary chores performed by the *tukan ayer*. Similarly, although 'the majority of Malays [were] still men of the soil . . . the younger generation has come under a further influence, that of vernacular education' between the ages of seven and twelve, 'and so the semi-educated youth . . . thinks himself a better man than his father', with expectations of a 'collar and tie' job 'in keeping with his learning'.[71] In the opinion of a British officer, the political implications of this policy – in particular the creation of a Malay intelligentsia from the ranks of a peasant people – were not fully appreciated by colonial administrators, 'who hurriedly stepped in to remedy illiteracy without considering what would be the result'.[72]

During the 1930s, numbers of Malays – padi growers and fishermen by tradition – became clerks, policemen, chauffeurs and domestic servants, although they were overtaken numerically by the Chinese, who continued to dominate the commercial, industrial and clerical sectors of the labour market. The immigration of Tamils from southern India peaked in the second half of the 1920s, and they then exceeded the Chinese as industrial labourers on the railways and on rubber estates, though Indian labour tended to be more transient. While there were also small minorities of middle-income and wealthy Chinese, Sikhs and Chettiars, who could more than match the starting annual salary of £450 paid to a young British administrator, the broad base of Malayan society was paid a pittance compared with their European employers.[73]

The Asians living in rural kampongs, kongsi houses, estate lines or congested urban shophouses had no prestige. Nor, for the most part, had they political ambitions. The only political opposition which the

British community took seriously was the Malayan Communist Party, which the authorities dealt with in 1931–2 by imprisonment and extradition. The potential dangers from Malay and Indian nationalism remained outside the perceptions of the average European. There was an unthinking smugness in some British officers, who were certain that they had the affection and goodwill of the Asian races because the British had a sense of justice and took a kindly interest in society's underdogs. The certainty ran deep. Even the Chief Security Officer, when assessing the political situation in Malaya from 1939 to 1941, disclaimed any organized anti-British movement and argued that 'Malaya's population as a whole presented . . . a sufficiently peaceful and loyal front, all parties working generally for the common weal and their own great economic benefit.'[74]

# 8

# *Officials and Unofficials*

Recalling his impressions of twenty-three years as a rubber executive, J. S. Potter noted that 'In Malaya we were either Officials or Unofficials, regardless of race, colour or religion: at least, that was my experience.'[1] He was, of course, alluding to a generally held distinction between, on the one hand, the administration – civil servants, officers, police and military, and specialists in the technical and municipal services – and, on the other, those in the private sector like himself – planters, mining experts, civil and marine engineers, lawyers, journalists, and men in freight and shipping, commercial companies and agency houses. The terms 'Official' and 'Unofficial' were part of Crown Colony vocabulary. To modern ears the word '*Un*official' has a slightly pejorative ring, a hint of unauthorization compared with the 'Official'. It was linked with the notion of the superiority of the government servant and the inferiority of commerce implied in the Establishment custom of referring dismissively to the man in trade as a 'boxwallah'. These terms reflect a colonial outlook which made one despairing Malayan officer describe the whole system as 'worthy more of a Gilbert and Sullivan opera than a modern community'.[2]

Strictly speaking, the two labels, 'official' and 'unofficial', were used to distinguish members of the country's governing councils. Throughout the colonial history of Penang and Singapore, there had always been tension between the administration and the commercial fraternity. However, as the commercial sector far outnumbered the administrators, leading Europeans, followed by a few prominent Asians, were invited to take a public part in government as unofficial members of the State, Federal, Legislative and Executive Councils.

Potter, for instance, served as an *unofficial* member of the Negri Sembilan State Executive Council (the last European unofficial to do so, as it happens.) Vincent Baker, the General Manager of the Pahang Consolidated Company tin mine at Sungei Lembing, was one of the two European unofficial members of the Pahang State Council in the 1930s.

The system was far from democratic. The senior officials sat ex-officio on the councils, while at all levels the unofficial members were nominated, not elected. After reforms were made in the inter-war years, Hugh Bryson, then secretary to the Resident in Negri Sembilan, believed that the unofficials were satisfied with their power 'to have some say in running local affairs'. They could 'use their position in Council to voice criticism of Federal interference', and serve, as 'the mouthpiece of an organization – the European put forward the views of the Planters' Association, the Chinese of the business men, and so on'.[3] In the Straits Settlements, the Legislative Council was enlarged to give equal numbers to the officials and unofficials, but a proposal to extend this principle to the Executive Council was vilified in the Establishment press. It was made clear that all Legislative Councillors were 'there to co-operate with the Government – to advise; to criticize; if necessary to oppose – but they in no sense constitute a regular opposition as in our Parliament at home',[4] while the retention of the Governor's casting vote ensured that the Legislative Council remained 'more an organ of government than a guardian of public interest'.[5]

All Councillors of the Straits Settlements and the Federated States were styled 'The Honorable', which sometimes raised a wry comment – not least from Singapore's best known satirist:

> The position was usually held by a merchant, but when there are not enough merchants of distinction falls automatically to a lawyer . . . The 'F's' [Federal Councillors] have a supreme disdain for the 'L's' [Legislative Councillors] and *vice versa*. Sometimes the twain meet, on a nice expensive yacht with sumptuous tiffins and a rare array of decanters . . . official business is the only fly in the ointment that soothes the life of an Honourable. The title itself almost makes up for that: then there is the satisfaction of always being noted as one of 'those present'. Also, there are sundry dinners . . . providing fodder for innumerable letters and conversations with the introduction, 'As His Excellency said to me', or 'As I said to His Excellency' . . .[6]

Cheng Lock Tan of the Straits British Association sat on the Legislative Council in 1924–34 alongside Mohammad Euros bin Abdullah, the father of Malay journalism and President of the Singapore Malay Union. Among the unofficials on the Federal Council in the 1920s were Choo Kia Peng, the Selangor tin magnate, S. N. Veerasamy and Raja Chulan, son of the former Sultan of Perak, who served from 1924 to his death in 1933, having retired from the Malayan Civil Service. Dr Noel Clarke was a widely respected Eurasian member of the Legislative Council in Singapore. The non-Asian unofficials were also men of substance. The British community was represented on the colony's Legislative and Executive Councils by its most successful business moguls: Sir John Bagnall, Joint Managing Director of the Straits Trading Company from 1923, who fought for the interests of Malayan tin, Charles Wurtzburg, Chairman of Mansfield & Co. in 1933, 'a wise man, with many interests, a public servant all his life . . . almost revered by those who worked for or under him',[7] 'Jiddy' Dawson, a shrewd and industrious Scot from Aberdeen, General Manager of Guthrie & Co., and F. D. Bisseker, General Manager of the Eastern Smelting Company in Penang and a critic of government defence policy in the 1930s. Members of the Federal Council between the wars included a leading Selangor rubber planter, E. N. T. Cumming (a man with Establishment connections – his brother was a major-general at Camberley Staff College), the journalist J. H. M. Robson, founder and Managing Director of the *Malay Mail*, Egmont Hake, a prominent spokesman of the agency houses, and Arnold Savage-Bailey, a well-known lawyer and judge (who had been at St Paul's with Governor Clementi).[8] Behind these individuals were pressure groups and ethnic associations, as Bryson had observed, but government in the 1930s was effectively in the hands of administrative experts, and officials went along with a situation in which 'Malaya was unpestered by politics'.[9]

Outside the government arena, the terms 'official' and 'unofficial' were used loosely to distinguish between civil servants and people in the private sector – a division which has been played down in recent years. Between the wars the social composition, attitudes and behaviour of the European community changed. Malaya still attracted young public-school men – Guy Hutchinson, the rubber planter, had been to Wellington, Vincent Baker, the mining engineer, was from Haileybury, John Woods, the barrister, from Shrewbury – but many of the new expatriates had lower-middle-class or skilled-working-class origins. They came out East to work in planting, commodities, mining, engineering and shipping, swelling the 'unofficial' majority in the European community but mixing on a par with local officials in the technical and municipal services, so that the distinction became blurred. The Rawcliffes of Port Swettenham had a typically mixed circle of friends from the Selangor Pilot Association, planting, commerce, customs, Public Works and the police. Sometimes clashes of interest occurred among unofficials: between planters and executives of the agency houses, for instance – those who worked 'hands on' and the pen-pushers. Not everyone approved of the 'business man's East' and the new office class who dominated in places like Penang. In Kuala Lumpur, the Hutchinson brothers avoided white suits at Saturday tea dances at the Spotted Dog because 'these were worn by the "Office wallahs"'.[10] But distinctions were not just a matter of dress. Like many of the subtle nuances of colonial society, the difference between officials and unofficials was unconsciously observed in everyday speech. One young Malayan was intrigued: 'I knew that my Daddy was "in shipping" . . . Then such-and-such was "in rubber" and so-and-so worked "in tin" . . . Some people we knew were "in Mansfield's" . . . Another person was "in Holt's", someone else had been "in Jardine's" and a third "in Boustead's".' On the other hand, 'Some people simply *were* things . . . I could tell . . . that being "in Straits"' or "in Holt's" was different from being straightforward "Colonial Service" or "P.W.D." or "Army people" or "Harbour Board".'[11] The most patent divide was between senior members of the Malayan Civil Service and the mass of unofficials. As Hutchinson remarked with some feeling, '*the "Heaven Born" . . . lived – or thought they lived – in a world apart*'.[12]

Since rubber planters formed the largest single group of unofficials in Malaya, they must deserve separate treatment (see Chapter 9). However, by 1912 half the world's tin was also produced in Malaya, and by 1937 what had been a predominantly Chinese industry had been taken largely into European ownership and management. Mining and mine engineering were the preserve of a small number of hardy individuals, generally Australians or emigrants from Britain's Celtic fringe – Scots, Welsh and Cornishmen. Their activities were vetted by state Wardens and Inspectors of Mines responsible for protecting the public interest. Most of Malaya's tin was alluvial, and there were numerous methods of extraction, of which dredging and hydrauling had been developed by British operators, although the technicalities do not concern us here. However, the impact on the landscape could be dramatic. In 1928 at Kuala Lumpur, Guy Hutchinson 'saw for the first time the Chinese open cast tin mine with its characteristic high pier like structure'; the residue of 'the "tailings", fine white sand . . . led off to form banks of waste land that took years to cover with vegetation'.[13] Dredging was no kinder to the land: the vast machine, 'anchored in its man-made lake of milk-white water, drags up the innocent mud', and dredges, 'like corrugated monsters from Mars, lumber over the northern plains of Malaya: sinister, rattling contraptions eating the heart out of the land'.[14]

The largest operation in the country and the only underground-lode mine (except for the Australian Raub gold mine) was at Sungei Lembing, a remote site in eastern Pahang. By 1930, Pahang Consolidated Company had some 8,000 workers there, of whom only twenty-nine men (eight married) were Europeans. The General Manager, Vincent Baker, a clergyman's son, was an enlightened benefactor, 'a king and father' to his people. His ambition was to create a lasting community in the tradition of the Welsh valleys he had known. He ensured there was an eighty-bed hospital and good housing for the workers, with decent schools for their children and good amenities for the European staff. When, following the worldwide economic collapse, tin output was restricted by international agreement in 1931, he diverted men to road building to avoid making redundancies.[15] Life in this secluded, paternalistic and enclosed community 'can be paralleled nowhere else in the Malay peninsula', G. L. Peet reported in the *Straits Times*:

> The European staff live in comfortable bungalows, supplied with water and electricity and set amidst pleasant gardens. The 'mems' do their shopping at a sort of department store run by the Company . . . a remarkable place with shelves loaded with goods of every kind . . . For recreation there is a European club, with sports ground and tennis courts, and in the native town there are a cinema and a theatre. A wireless station receives the day's news from Rugby, in far-away England, and keeps the town in touch with Kuala Lumpur.[16]

In addition to the mine complex, which included a modern mill, power plant and engineering shops, there were a post office and a police station, and twice a day steamers sailed upstream from Kuantan to a riverside terminus where a light railway made the fifteen-mile run to Sungei Lembing – all provided by the Company. Concern was taken for the engineering staff and miners, who went 'many hundreds of feet underground, alternately streaming with sweat and exposed to chilly draughts' on work which was 'highly skilled, costly in machinery and labour, and occasionally dangerous'. In economic terms it was Malaya's most efficient mine, giving an output of over 27,000 tons of tin to the value of £3,755,000 for the Pahang Consolidated Company in 1929–41.[17]

A smaller-scale operation, yet one that was typical of the tin-mining industry, was Lingui Tin Ltd of Johore, owned in the inter-war years by Sime Darby (who remained as agents after Lingui Tin was bought by the Anglo-Oriental Co., based in Perak). The complex consisted of two main mines, Lingui and Tengkil, about three miles apart, with a number of minor outcrops. Steam-operated engines drove water at high pressure to sluice the tin-bearing soil, separating the tin dust from the waste. The tin was then dried and bagged for shipment. Hainanese coolies supplied the labour, and only the Chinese clerk, William Ong, spoke English.

When W. S. Edington took over the management in the early 1930s (having been Assistant Manager since 1919), he and his family were the only British residents in a remote jungle area, thirty miles upriver from Kota Tinggi, the nearest town. 'There were really no neighbours. Even Kota Tinggi . . . was a pretty wild place in those days. The only person I can remember', said his son John Edington (who left at the age of six in 1932), 'was an elderly Dutch trader, called "Uncle Peter", whose bungalow was located near the landing stage' from which both people and the bags of tin dust were transported by river to Kota Tinggi.[18] There the Lingui tin, like the ore from Sungei Lembing, was taken by boat to be smelted on the island of Pulau Brani, adjacent to Singapore's Keppel Harbour. It was here, and at the Company's other smelter at Bagan Luar, Butterworth, that the Straits Trading Company produced its world-famous 'Straits Tin', its only rival being the Eastern Smelting Company based in Penang. But the world restriction on tin output hit the Straits Trading Company as much as the mining companies, and in 1932 the Butterworth smelter was closed down, forcing a reduction of the European staff from sixty-one to thirty-five in 1935. To counter recession, Sir John Bagnall began a bold diversification policy in 1938.

A group of subsidiary companies was formed in Malaya, Siam and Britain to launch separate smelting, mining, tin-production and rubber-planing enterprises. By 1940 the Straits Trading Company was buoyant again, and in 1941 the Butterworth works reopened.[19]

The Straits Trading Company had also become part of a large interlocking commercial–shipping empire based on Singapore, whose employees formed a sizeable body of unofficials. From 1924 Straits Trading was based in Ocean Building, Singapore, the prestigious water-front offices of the shipping agency Mansfield & Co., which managed the Straits Steamship Company, a subsidiary of the Blue Funnel Line. Carrying tin ore became bread-and-butter business for the Straits Steamship Company, a household name in Malaya, for it had operated coastal services out of Singapore since 1890. After the Great War, in the hands of its dynamic Managing Director and Chairman H. E. Somerville, Straits Steamship underwent a period of expansion. Within the period 1922–32 it took over a number of ailing shipping concerns, thus extending its operations from the South China ports to Rangoon, East and South Sumatra, the Riau archipelago and Borneo. Its prime takeover was the Penang-based fleet of the Chinese Eastern Shipping Company, together with its Butterworth dockyard at the confluence of the Sungei Prai (River Prai) and Sungei Nyok (Coconut river) facing Penang harbour.

When the Legislative Council permitted vessels of under 75 tons to be manned entirely by native crews in 1922, the Straits Steamship Company seized the initiative, modernizing Sungei Nyok Dockyard to build 75-tonners, beginning with the *Rengam* in 1924, thereby greatly extending its coastal trade. Despite the impact of the Depression on company profits, the Dockyard Manager, H. E. Ward, and his Assistant and naval architect Bill Price, with a willing labour force of some 200 Asian workers, completed another dozen ships by 1941.[20] With black, blue and white funnels and white hulls and superstructures, the Straits Steamship Company's White Fleet was known throughout the East. Its regular services conveyed a diverse array of passengers and Eastern produce, from tin ore to pineapples, palm oil to coffee, machinery and car tyres to beer and cigarettes, fish to racehorses. Many of the little ships, like the *Kuala* and the *Kedah*, would play a proud role in the war with Japan in 1941–2.

However brief this glimpse of British commercial enterprise, it underlines Malaya's important contribution to the imperial economy and Britain's maritime dominance in the Far Eastern trade routes. It also reminds us that a relatively small number of European managers, technical and support staff – unofficials – helped to generate that wealth. On the other hand, the officials of the Malayan Civil Service, who ran the country, were also few in number. Malaya was a convivial posting. Following a major (and overdue) review of its pay structure, the Civil Service was mollified by a generous rise in salaries and allowances in 1920, which gave it a new *esprit de corps*. From that time its members were personally insulated against economic recession and constituted a secure, well-paid elite under the Governor. For Councillors and unofficials, 'Naturally, an invitation to Government House is the highest social honour attainable.'[21] Otherwise, the Governor's main duty was 'to keep the colony in peace, prosperity and security'.[22]

Sir Laurence Guillemard was fortunate that the international situation enabled him to keep faith with this last pronouncement for his seven-year term from 1919 to 1927. He was lucky, too, as a former Treasury high-flier, that, although 'there was lots of work to be done', there was also 'plenty of money to do it with'; and with that typically English faith in pragmatism he saw it as a special advantage that he knew 'little or nothing about the colony to which I was going or the particular problems and difficulties to be faced'.[23] He soon discovered that the country's political organization was shot through with complexities. He set his sights on tackling the centralizing trend which had reduced the power and purpose of the state governments in the Federated Malay States and had confirmed the resistance of the rulers of the Unfederated States to joining the federation. But in taking modest steps towards decentralization, giving the Malay aristocracy a role as unofficial members of the Federal Council and proposing the abolition of the position of Chief Secretary of the Federated States, the Governor became locked into a fierce personality clash with the holder of the post, George Maxwell, and met the stern disapproval of European and Chinese business members of the Federal Council. Hugh Bryson, an Assistant Secretary in Kuala Lumpur at the time, watched the unedifying spectacle as

This disagreement over constitutional matters before very long became public knowledge and the European community . . . divided into the pro-Maxwell and the pro-Guillemard factions . . . The pro-Maxwellites, like my humble self, were inclined to see the move not as de- but as re-centralization with power shifting to Singapore where we feared the big commercial interests with their London control would exercise too much control over the Malay States.[24]

When Guillemard's stormy period of office ended, the Colonial Office appointed as successor the Governor of Ceylon, a man whose familiarity with Malaya was calculated to reassure everyone. Sir Hugh Clifford was a respected but slightly eccentric patrician with a towering physique and a larger-than-life personality. As a young cadet in the 1880s he was a man of action who had stormed successive jungle stockades in the Pahang rebellion. Now, he had the aura of an enlightened autocrat, but his triumphal tour of Pahang in 1928 was thought by some to be more appropriate to the age of imperial adventure of his youth than to an era of rising interest groups. Many stories circulated about Clifford – a number of them involving his addiction to fast cars, physical danger and attractive women. After less than two years his mental health gave way and he retired. A distinguished figure, he spoke sincerely and in the grand tradition of Britain's role and responsibility for progress, but he represented the political past rather than the future.

Clifford's successor, Sir Cecil Clementi, was another charming patrician and another colonial Governor – of Hong Kong – when he was appointed to Malaya in 1929. But he was a man of a very different mettle – an 'awesome figure with a doom-laden reputation for thinking the unthinkable about imperial disengagement', as one historian has put it.[25] With more determination than Guillemard, he took on 'the buffalo of integration' to bring all the Malay States into a federation, decentralized and supported by a customs union. Clementi's time coincided with the world economic depression – a difficult backcloth against which to implement controversial changes such as a protective tariff and controls against the Chinese Communists and Nationalists, or to introduce more Malays and other Asians into the administration. While he succeeded in pushing through some measures of decentralization to devolve powers to the Federated State governments, his notion of an enlarged federation of all the states was unfulfilled (although it was to be revived thirty years later).

Clementi's pro-Malay stance won him support in the Malayan Civil Service, but others found his mode of championing Malay rights too patronizing. In the end, blasts of protest from the business community, echoed by retired Malaya hands like George Maxwell, confirmed the mistrust of the Colonial Office, who effectively sacked Clementi in 1934. The Malayan press was also critical: Maurice Glover of the *Tribune* considered him to have been 'dogmatic and immovable'.[26] However, press barons tend to see their role in provocative terms, and Glover rated Clementi's successor no better. Sir Shenton Thomas, Governor of the Gold Coast, 'was too old and out-of-date'; he was 'a one-man system' who 'made mistake after mistake'. His unwillingness to unbend served only to antagonize opinion against British rule and a system that was too bureaucratic.[27] On the other hand, Thomas prided himself on his man-management, and he succeeded in winning over many in the business community by his genial manner and down-to-earth approach. According to the Superintendent Engineer Leslie Froggatt, a shrewd, apolitical observer, 'Our Governor . . . was a very mild sort of person, could make witty speeches, and we had a certain affection for him.'[28] To the insiders in the Colonial Service he was judged to have governed well. He continued Clementi's decentralizing plans and presided over the smooth running of the administrative machine. But, as Glover indicated, not everyone was taken in by his affability, and many outside the Civil Service thought he lost touch – and respect – when he and his wife went on a long home leave in 1940.

Governors, of course, came and went. Under their command was the Malayan Civil Service, the permanent administrative machine of some 200 British officials, drawn from the public-service class of Britain – sons of clergymen, army officers, doctors, bankers, members of overseas civil services, schoolmasters and lawyers – and an additional group of around forty high-born Malays. This core body of public-school men and Oxbridge graduates was assisted and advised by another 1,500 Europeans and other races in the technical services – dealing with health, medicine, education, mines, fisheries, agriculture, customs, police and public works – and by a subordinate Malay Administrative Service giving mainly clerical support. In other words, throughout the inter-war years the whole country was effectively governed by fewer than 2,000 officers.

Subtle changes were taking place in the 1930s. The Residents had lost their political independence and were now overseers of a bureaucratic apparatus rather than movers and shakers as their predecessors had been, and the chief of staff, the Secretary to the Resident, had an important co-ordinating role. But the District Officer was still the all-rounder in the field. 'As D.O. I was a veritable Pooh-Bah,' wrote Victor Purcell, listing an incongruous portfolios of duties.[29] Sjovald Cunyngham-Brown, too, felt quiet satisfaction as he surveyed his 'kingdom' of Jasin in South Malacca, 'a hundred thousand people, nine mukim (parishes), twenty-miles-by-twenty of hill-and-dale'.[30] In fact the reputation of the service rested on the District Officer's performance.

> In his office the D.O. was . . . assisted by a clerical staff that was quite sizeable in the bigger places. These included Malay assistant collectors in land offices, chief clerks who were often Chinese, and hosts of subordinates drawn from all three of the main racial groups . . . Nothing was more essential to sound administration than constant touring throughout one's district, acquiring intimate and comprehensive knowledge of the people and their lives and devoting thought and time to their welfare.[31]

European officials were also expected to play a social role. 'The presence of the D.O. added a social cachet to weddings, to spinning contests, ronggengs etc. and few days passed without a sireh tray being dumped on the office table by way of invitation,' recalled A. B. Cobden-Ramsay, who served in Alor Gajah, Malacca.[32] When Mervyn (later Mubin) Sheppard arrived there in the mid-1930s to be District Officer, he was treated as a kind of universal aunt: 'the people expected him to do everything, quite simply because the D.O. always had done, as far back as anyone could remember'.[33] One responsibility was to ensure that cadet officers were integrated into the system. Some District Officers had a reputation for being indifferent towards beginners. In 1928 Sheppard's superior at Temerloh, deep in Pahang's interior, was a dour Aberdonian who could not even raise a smile of welcome. 'This first formal interview was totally devoid of human kindness,' Sheppard recalled.[34] On the other hand, from the moment Hugh Bryson disembarked at Penang he met with kindness and hospitality. His posting was selected for him by chance – 'Batu Gajah [in Perak] wanted a cricketer, preferably a bowler. The other man didn't play; I did, but certainly wasn't a bowler. I went to B.G.' He soon realized how lucky he was. Junior administrators did not always receive training on the ground but learned from observation and experience. Bryson found

The Batu Gajah Land office, under the direction of [T. S. Adams] the
Chief Assistant District Officer . . . was probably one of the best places
in the country for a young Cadet to learn his job. In the office I was often
given bundles of files and told to make précis of the matters there discussed, and to sort out the important facts concerning the application
for a new mining lease or rubber lands. This entailed references to other
files very frequently, to maps and plans . . . Some of this work may have
been what might be called original research, but much of it was T.S.A.'s
method of training his young recruits.[35]

The Land Officer's work included keeping records, supervising and
registering land changes, collecting rents, hearing devolution suits, and
carrying out fieldwork. Bryson found that the purely office side of his
job had its own attractions, but going off into kampongs with the
Malay Settlement Officers was a particular pleasure, for he met the
smallholders and learned, as he put it, 'about the happy ways of Malay
peasantry and Chinese shopkeepers'. Bryson also recalled another side
of their work: that 'We all had to study the law books, the statute laws
of the Federated Malay States, and to pass examinations in them before
being gazetted as Magistrates of the First Class . . . later . . . I realised
more fully the vital importance to the peace and well-being of a district
if it was to have justice quickly and impartially administered.'[36]

Since all-round competence was looked for in young officers, they
could expect to be moved around to test their potential. Bryson held
seven different jobs in his first tour of duty from 1921 to 1925:

Cadet attached to the Land Office, Batu Gajah . . . until about May 1922.
Then a year or less as Financial Secretary to the Senior Medical Officer
in Taiping. A couple of months as Assistant in the Land Office, Taiping.
Three months as Assistant Secretary to [the] Resident, Negri Sembilan,
during which time I was posted to deputise as District Officer, Port
Dickson, while the incumbent went into hospital with malaria.
Three months as Assistant Supervisor of Customs, on preventive work
connected with rubber smuggling, at Kota Tinggi, Johore. Then the
remainder of the tour in the Federal Secretariat in Kuala Lumpur, in
charge of the confidential records. I found interest in all these jobs.[37]

Similar expectations were made of cadet officers in the Chinese
Protectorate and the Labour Department. The former was a crucial
department, as the government's main window on Chinese activities.
Victor Purcell found that as Assistant Protector and later Protector of

Chinese in Penang, he had to carry out a multitude of jobs, as magistrate, prison visitor, controller of labour and secret societies, arbitrator of disputes, protector of women and girls, supervisor of Chinese education, city councillor, company registrar and liquidator, and, finally, Deputy Registrar of the Supreme Court. Proficiency was required in the language of the Asian community for whom officers were responsible, although some were inherently better linguists than others. However, the ethos of the Service was staunchly pro-Malay, and Malay was the principal language spoken by officials. When Walter Stark, who was trained in Tamil for Labour Office work, was moved to Jelebu as Acting District Officer, he knew his Malay was barely adequate; he was mildly amused when the local headman afterwards praised his successor, H. T. Martin, for his fluency: '*pandai chakap Melayu*'.[38] In addition to knowing Tamil and Telegu, Sjovald Cunyngham-Brown was directed to learn Malay by his superior in Penang. He spent two years with the Emigration Commission before being moved around as Deputy Controller of Rubber in Kuala Lumpur, a Magistrate in Singapore and later Seremban, District Officer in Malacca, and Controller of Labour in Johore.

In the course of their career, all administrative officers had some contrasting experience of working in rural outstations – the essence of the 'real Malaya' – and of undertaking general responsibilities and political paperwork in Kuala Lumpur, Penang or Singapore. However, promotion came more readily to the Malay-speakers, and instinctively the high-fliers progressed along this royal road to the Secretariat. To become addicted to the *ulu* like Hubert Berkeley was frowned upon, while to opt for specialization in the Labour Department or the Chinese Protectorate was considered perverse, as Purcell, a scholarly ex-serviceman, discovered. He was attracted by the idea of mastering Chinese and studying one of the great civilizations of the world, but was quickly disabused by his superior, who warned him he would never become a Governor or even a Resident. Instead, he would 'merely be a *specialist*!' Brilliance and expertise were not highly prized in a system requiring, as Purcell put it, 'the industry of the Benedictine, the orthodoxy of the Dominican, the diplomacy of the Jesuit, and the silence of the Trappist on all controversial issues'.[39] Purcell quickly worked out that the Eastern cadets fell into two categories, the ambitious and the nondescripts, and despite being clever (as well as ambitious) he achieved success. But Sjovald Cunyngham-Brown, contemplating his own career, concluded he would have done better 'bowing at the doors of the mighty, marrying a nice girl, seeking a post in the central Secretariat and becoming a freemason' – a neat dig at the ambitious Residents and fast-track-men in Singapore who leapfrogged over their peers in pursuit of well-defined goals, honours, high office in London or the Empire, plus a knighthood.[40]

The Head Office men had a reputation for being, in the words of a former Governor, 'pedantic and narrow-minded bureaucrats who spent their days penning tiresome and unnecessary minutes' as increasingly they took the limelight away from the District Officer.[41] Charlotte Cameron, touring the East in 1922–3, observed them at play in Singapore, at their yacht races and their dinner parties, where white was always the predominant fashion colour. On the other hand, the men of the technical and specialist branches of the Colonial Service – doctors, agriculturalists and so on – integrated in the community. According to one of their number, they were

> university graduates, selected by interview; they were generally sent on postgraduate courses at government expense before taking up their posts. The Police and Customs cadets, however, began younger and were selected soon after leaving their public schools. In the police there were two ranks: the superintendent and higher corresponded to officers and wore military 'pips' . . . the inspectors were of the warrant officer type and were separately recruited.[42]

While there was certainly criticism of the Service from within, the record of some of the specialist sections was good, according to one officer, John Soper. In the late 1930s his department, Agriculture, was 'justifying its existence and was well on the way to doing better'; Drainage and Irrigation 'deserved praise' for doing 'a tremendous amount of work, much of it extremely valuable'; the Fisheries department 'was beginning to produce good results'; and Forestry was 'run by capable men on up-to-date lines'. But, if any deserved high praise, it was the Medical and Health branch of the Service:

> The work of this department . . . probably ranks highest amongst the achievements of the administration in this country. Malaria was almost completely under control in the large towns and was being well suppressed in nearly every small township. Cholera was practically excluded

by an efficient quarantine organisation and outbreaks of small pox were extremely rare. The large hospitals were well-equipped and well patronised. Vernacular schools were subject to medical and dental inspection. Maternity and infant welfare clinics were springing up and were doing good service. Midwives were all trained and registered . . .

As to the Public Works Department . . . which was responsible for the construction and maintenance of all government buildings, roads, bridges, waterworks etc. [it] came in for more kicks than ha'pence. True some of their senior members were not ideal organisers and administrators, true all their work was not perfect . . . but taken as a whole they did a good steady job under a continual fire of nagging.[43]

Officers quibbled with government accountancy methods which required that 'Even the fitting of a water tap in a sub-overseer's quarters had to be charged separately to the correct sub-head of expenditure', but there was an official consensus that 'The system went easily and well in its time-worn grooves – familiar, tried, efficient, and therefore complaisant [*sic*], as such systems are bound to be.'[44] 'Most of us in the M.C.S., I feel, accepted the framework in which we had to operate as preordained,' an ex-member admitted.[45]

The system included what a satirist referred to as 'an ingenious cumshaw called allowances', and mention of cumshaws (or backhanders) raises the uncomfortable subject of corruption.[46] According to the official line, venality did not exist in the Malayan Civil Service, nor in the technical services. Belief in the incorruptibility of officials was touching: 'there was one thing that was common to all these men [Europeans] – They were EXPECTED TO BE HONEST. That is why they were sent out to Asia – to be honest,' argued Guy Hutchinson.[47] However, Hugh Bryson conceded that 'There was considerable corruption among the Malay officials [in the 1920s] or at least nepotism in excelsis.'[48] And, if some blatant practices, such as 'government servants getting their "rake-off" from land concessions', had been stopped, the system of payment to contractors for road building and the scandalous suppression during the 1930s of the Prai port and rail terminus by vested interests in Penang were deplored by John Soper.[49] Guy Madoc admitted there had been ten vacancies in the police service in 1930.[50]

The police were one of the specialist services to come under criticism. According to John Soper:

the lower ranks of the Police force were thoroughly rotten: the places at which inspectors of police were usually stationed were tabulated according to their bribe value, and some ran to over $300 per month, made up of small sums from a large number of concerns which did not wish their activities to be watched too closely. There was also a very doubtful racket over Chinese immigration which was never investigated, but the fact that immigration was rigidly confined to certain shipping lines and that a passage to Malaya from China cost more than ten times a similar passage in the opposite direction is very significant. The men who could allow such a state of things to continue were either utter fools unworthy of the position they held or were receiving a nice little share of the profits from the companies concerned.

And

Mines: Without a doubt was the rottenest department in the country. For many years it was well known that almost all the officials took bribes, in fact not to do so was to deny oneself promotion. Nevertheless it was not until 1940 that the pressure of public opinion became so strong that the higher authorities could abstain no longer from taking proceedings. Several prominent members and ex-members received terms of imprisonment, others were fined . . . it is difficult to decide who were the worst offenders, the officials who took the bribes as a matter of course or the higher administrative authorities who allowed the scandal to continue unchecked: it may be that some of the latter had guilty consciences and feared a 'tu quoque'.[51]

There were some who blamed unofficials in private enterprise for corrupting officials. The official 'has picked up from the merchant the knack of passing on the blame for things', a satirist suggested.[52] Others deplored the influence of the Singapore–London commercial axis upon government, and the fact that, in the words of one insider, 'The trend of general policy was heavily biassed by the opinions of leading business men, and was governed more by temporary economic and financial considerations than by any higher ideals or world concepts.'[53] Civil servants were advised to avoid lateral thinking:

Taken as a whole there was a strong inclination towards the status quo, an unwillingness to act for fear of making mistakes with the result that action was only taken when circumstances became overpowering, so that instead of sins of commission those of omission were numerous but overlooked. This outlook on life meant that only short term problems were tackled, and those with only a very limited outlook. Initiative and ideas in a junior . . . were usually frowned upon.[54]

So, too, were political views – especially radical opinions that 'our job was to teach the Malays and prepare them to take over from the European administrators'. A few natural democrats like Gerald Hawkins might talk of self-government among friends, but, as Hugh Bryson saw it, 'this move towards independence was not a policy that was given any official public support; in fact I think it would probably have got a Civil Servant into trouble if it had been charged against him that he was inciting the local people to assert their desire for freedom from British guidance'.[55] Instead, in self-defence, civil servants kept their heads down and worked longer hours, aware that they were increasingly under scrutiny. George Orwell, himself a colonial official for a time, wrote that:

By 1920 nearly every inch of the colonial empire was in the grip of Whitehall. Well-meaning, over-civilized men, in dark suits and black felt hats, with neatly rolled umbrellas crooked over the left forearm, were imposing their constipated view of life on Malaya and Nigeria, Mombasa and Mandalay. The one-time empire builders were reduced to the status of clerks, buried deeper and deeper under mounds of paper and red tape.[56]

The complaint that 'the D.O. was smothered in paper, seldom left his office, and . . . was rarely seen outside his head-quarters town' was made repeatedly.[57] Returning to Klang as District Officer in 1927, Walter Stark, for instance, found little satisfaction in the office routine of responding to letters, chairing meetings and checking Treasury books amid frequent interruptions and telephone calls. The trouble was, according to John Soper, that

The conduct of all government business was governed by a mystic volume entitled 'General Orders'; in this could be found the answer to any question, always provided that one had patience and a good clerk. Unlike the law of the Medes and Persians, these regulations were always changing: an amendment slip would arrive on average once a week, and the volume was very rarely revised and brought up to date. In an efficient office therefore most of the original pages were pasted over or interleaved with countless slips, many of which merely cancelled one another, and it was often difficult to arrive at the correct answer: in an inefficient office the slips were merely lost, and one was always behind the times. It should have been possible to devise a more permanent code.[58]

Despite the razzamatazz surrounding his office, there were times when even the Governor was just 'a human post-box for receiving the instructions of the Home Government'.[59] On the other hand, there was always someone who gladly suffered the tedium of bureaucratic minutiae in order to get on. It was said that as Colonial Treasurer and later Acting Chief Secretary M. B. Shelley 'reveled in the pomp of office . . . He loved his uniform and sword, his intimacy with the governor, the deference and the prefix "Honourable" he received as a member of the federal council, and his close association with merchant princes.'[60] So the wheel comes full circle. Though they defended their special 'interests', officials and unofficials on the governing councils – all 'Honourable' men – were kindred spirits from the same social elite.

That elite also included a group so far overlooked, namely the officers of the Singapore garrison. After the Great War, although there was only a small garrison, it played its part in the island's European community, particularly in the social scene. The GOC Troops Singapore was a member of the Executive Council of the Crown Colony. This point is made for a good reason. The argot spoken by the Europeans in Malaya was heavily influenced by the official-speak of Singapore's company of military officers and civil servants, and the practice of using initials as shorthand was universal by the 1920s. So Kuala Lumpur was referred to as 'K.L.', Kuala Kangsar as 'K.K.', Telok Anson as 'T.A.', Johore Bahru as 'J.B.', and so on, while the ubiquitous terms 'F.M.S.' and 'U.M.S.' meant of course Federated Malay States and Unfederated Malay States. In time it came naturally for every European to say 'H.E.' for His Excellency the Governor, 'C.O.' for the Colonial Office, 'M.C.S.' for the Malayan Civil Service, 'P.W.D.' for the Public Works Department, and 'D.A.I.D.' for the Drainage and Irrigation Department. Civilian expatriates soon learned that the M.E.O. was the Malayan Establishment Office, H. & S. the Hongkong and Shanghai Bank, A.P.C. the Asiatic Petroleum Company, R.G.A. the Rubber Growers' Association, and P.A.M. the Planters' Association of Malaya. One did not have to be in the Civil Service to know that R.C. was Resident Councillor, S.R. Secretary to Resident, B.A. British Adviser and D.O. District Officer, with a number of subordinate ranks being prefixed with 'A.', meaning Assistant, such as the A.D.O. or the A.A. (Assistant Adviser). On a personal level, in the 1920s Theodore Adams (later Sir Theodore) was called by those around him T.S.A. (his initials) or C.A.D.O. (Chief Assistant District Officer).

Old hands failed to appreciate how baffling such a barrage of acronyms sounded to new civilian arrivals.[61] What novice could know, for instance, that O.D.O.s were Out Door Officers of the Customs Service? In entering the curious world of British Malaya, where men were divided into officials and unofficials, the expatriate had to adjust to many unfamiliar conventions. However, in the opinion of Katharine Sim, wife of a Perak customs officer, if there was one extraordinary example of official-speak it was O.C.P.D. – 'invariably spoken as if all one word'. The O.C.P.D. was the Officer in Charge of the Police Department, which, as a piece of coded language, arguably 'beat all the other initials in this country of initials'.[62]

# 9

# *The Rubber Men*

'There is romance and comedy and tragedy in the story of rubber,' wrote a seasoned adventurer.[1] That story began in 1876 in the rain-forests of the Amazon basin, when the Victorian explorer Henry Wickham smuggled out 70,000 seeds of *Hevea brasiliensis* and brought them to Kew Gardens. In due course a batch of twenty-two saplings of Para rubber was shipped out to the botanical gardens of Ceylon and Singapore for experimental research, and a few were passed on to the Federated Malay States, where Sir Hugh Low, an amateur botanist, carefully tended them in his Residency garden at Kuala Kangsar.

Rubber took hold in Malaya thanks to three crucial events. First, the arrival of H. N. Ridley as the new Director of Singapore Botanical Gardens in 1888 brought a keen publicist on the scene. Then, following the devastation of Malaya's coffee plantations by the bee-hawk moth, perceptive European and Chinese proprietors decided to experiment with rubber. And lastly the invention of the pneumatic tyre for the automobile industry sent the demand for rubber soaring. By 1896 the first estates were planted in the Federated States of Perak, Selangor and Negri Sembilan. Malacca followed suit, and later Johore too. Cash crops were interplanted with rubber; coffee was forgotten. Rubber was king. Its production surged ahead in the boom years of 1906 to 1912. Hopes for the future ran high.

> By 1920 every rubber tree in the Far East was a descendant of [Wickham's] seeds. The trouble with the rubber tree was that it was 'too hardy': it flourished in Malaya ... An acre of rubber from a well tended European Estate would yield, year after year, about 500 lbs of dry rubber a year ... It was all too easy.[2]

The pioneering plantation owners were men of means. Even their assistants – the 'creepers' – had to be 'the sons of gentlemen', as one of their number put it, and 'must, of course, find their own passage as well as the premium . . . good birth and education sine qua non . . . Public school education preferred and good sportsmen.'[3] This socially discriminating practice died hard, but, as the costs of large-scale production increased during the Edwardian boom, many proprietors were forced to float their estates as companies. This gave the old-established merchant houses of Singapore, like Guthrie's and Harrison & Crosfield's, a golden opportunity to enter the rubber business as company agents. Taking on the tasks of raising capital in the London market and recruiting suitable Managers and Assistants from home on behalf of the company directors, they did 'all the buying and selling of everything from a bag of nails to the cases of rubber produced'.[4]

Initially rubber was not an exclusively European business.[5] British planters returning home to fight for their country in the Great War left behind a number of successful Chinese planters with commercial estates of over 1,000 acres and many smallholders – Malay and Chinese – who grew rubber in addition to their subsistence crops. This situation began to change after 1919. Peace brought a fresh influx of Europeans into rubber planting in expectation of high post-war demands. Malaya experienced a mini-boom, and by 1920 the country was producing some 196,000 tons of rubber – over half the world's supply.

The new arrivals included former British soldiers, for any European who had fought in the Great War was given a grant of 100 acres. 'The usual practice for the Ex-Service men had been to go into "kongsi" partnership with each other – four or more together – with their plots adjoining,' a planter recalled. 'It was from this type of grant that Corsican, Prang Besar (Great War), Lima Tuan etc. Estates grew up.'[6] However, the majority of new recruits were handpicked young employees, potentially good 'company men' aged from nineteen to twenty-four – like Joe Allgrove, who went out to Johore in 1920, or Guy Hutchinson, who arrived in Selangor in 1928. They were selected in London as Assistants to the Managers employed to run large company estates. Unlike the Edwardian generation, fewer had a private income or family money to cushion their lifestyle. (There were, nonetheless, some independent planters – such as the Vowlers, whose property straddled the boundaries of Malacca and Negri Sembilan.) The main credentials for young planters were a respectable background, physical prowess and personal skills – although personal introductions could be decisive, J. S. Potter found:

> When I first expressed a desire to go East at the age of seventeen, my father sent me to the only relation we had who was connected with the East . . . a director at Harrison & Crosfield in London and their Chief Accountant. [He] sent me back to school for a year; but a year later introduced me to Guthrie & Co. . . . in response to my father's stipulation of an old established Scottish firm with a young Managing Director . . . Prior to sailing for Malaya in April 1934, I had served a four and a half years' apprenticeship in Guthrie's London Office . . .[7]

Guy Hutchinson confirmed that

> It was usually through a friend of a friend of a Director that one heard of a job, and the selection was pretty severe, as there were, then, more applicants than jobs . . . If [the Directors] were Scots then they plumped for an educated lad, of poor but honest parents (the gamekeeper's sons, the village shopkeeper's son, occasionally a son of the Manse) . . . If the Directors were predominantly English they went for what is now called 'the old school tie type', the Public School or Senior Grammar School boy.[8]

Hutchinson was in a sense a hybrid of the two types. The son of a former army officer, he went to New Beacon and Wellington and thence to Glasgow, where he studied engineering. His first job in the early 1920s was in the mining industry at Bo'ness, Lothian, where James Watt had developed his steam engine in 1765. Like many of his generation, he faced economic insecurity ('coal mining had no financial future in it for me'), but he also had a vital Malayan connection. His younger brother, Mike, had been working as an Assistant at the Batu Caves Estate near Kuala Lumpur since 1925. In 1927 Guy was offered a five-year contract with the same firm, which he took without hesitation. 'First and foremost it was "an open-air job" – in a short time you became, as near as possible, "your own boss". There were no exams to pass . . . You got paid from "the word go", and on paper the pay looked good.' Besides, he reflected later, 'I think I would have done anything rather than become what is now called a "Commuter", going up and down to an office in London – What a terrible thought!'[9]

'If one kept free from malaria, life seemed full of interest,' Joe Allgrove discovered. 'For relaxation there was sometimes a gramophone . . . books, for a good many, booze, and on a number of estates, a tennis court.' This was probably all one could expect up-country in the 1920s, but 'I suppose what one has not had is not missed.'[10] Guy and Mike Hutchinson were keen sportsmen, sharing their passion for biking with others in the area:

> there was a planter, Duggie Ainger, mad keen on motor bicycles . . . and his assistant, Rex Duncan, had ridden in the amateur T.T. . . . Their estate was hilly, and Ainger had a 'Scramble' course round it. He also had a swimming pool, and on Sundays held 'open house' for kindred spirits. There used to be about a dozen of us, talking motorbikes, then having a swim, then a Curry Tiffin. A great godsend to the young was D. Ainger.[11]

The Hutchinson brothers made the most of their leisure. Finishing work at noon on a Saturday, they were off on motorbikes to 'the Dog' in Kuala Lumpur. If a rugger match was in progress on the *padang*, they usually watched before browsing through the magazines and papers, waiting for the tea dance to begin. Since there was scarcely an unat-tached woman and 'not being of the "shark" type, we did not do any dancing but hung around "Cads Corner", making comments on the dancers' on the floor. Around 9 p.m. it was off to the Coliseum Hotel, where 'you could get a very good steak or fried fish eats for a reasonable price', or to 'one of the Japanese hotels in High Street or Petaling Street that specialised in Fried Prawns, omelettes etc.' But Kuala Lumpur also had other attractions for virile young men:

> Down the Batu Road was 'the Malay kip-shop' – here you could get cold beer or a Malay girl if you wanted one. Nearby was the 'Siamese house' . . . where they had a gramophone and you could dance with the Siamese girls . . . by far the most beautiful of all the Eastern races . . . further out near the Princes Cinema were the more superior Japanese Hotels, where you could get Beer and almost any race of girl.[12]

The lack of single European women was an unspoken problem. British attitudes had changed since the pioneer years, and companies imposed constraints on Assistants which ruled out marriage before their second or third contract. 'The outcome was that to have anything to do with a woman, the bachelor had to either seduce his neighbour's wife or resort to prostitutes and so V.D. was very rife.' Guy Hutchinson was quite frank about his first foray into sex.

> I was a 'virgin' when I came out. After some months and a lot of drink I had a most unsatisfactory initiation with a Chinese pro. I was still very

worried about learning Tamil, and against all advice I decided to try and get a 'sleeping dictionary'. So I asked a 'mary' and a young Tamil girl was produced, and a trial weekend was arranged. I felt a bit of a cad, as at sixteen Rasamah looked very young. Young or not, a weekend was enough for her to give me a 'packet' and that ended 'romance', 'sex' and 'sleeping dictionaries' for me for many years. The 'packet' was 'cleared up' at 'the Sultan Street Club' in a few months, and I returned to Stengahs and Motor Bikes, as being cheaper and healthier.[13]

Meanwhile Hutchinson had discovered other disadvantages of being a young, single rubber planter. His hard-earned savings – 'my all', roughly $150' – were spent in his first three days while sightseeing on Penang with his penniless brother. (Mike had run up debts of $450 and was constantly in need of salary advances.)[14] Joe Allgrove similarly found that the cost of enforced stops at Rangoon and Penang on the outward voyage meant 'a young man arrived at Singapore 6½ weeks "out" with empty pockets'.[15] Hutchinson had to admit that his assumptions about both money and exams had been quite wrong. A European planter needed communication skills such as basic Tamil, and 'when you got out there you found that the wise took the Incorporated Society of Planters' exams – the language exams were compulsory with many Estate Managers'. At first he despaired of ever succeeding, but thanks to *Well's Coolie Tamil*, the Assistant's bible, he knew enough to do his work after three months. In addition,

> Pay . . . wasn't nearly as good as it looked. In fact it was hard for a First Agreement Assistant to keep out of debt and have a bit saved up for his leave. One found that food and servants took $150 a month. It cost not less than $20 for a Saturday night, drinks, dinner and cinema. Then there was running a motor bike – hardly one in a hundred had a car . . . And last but not least there are clothes. Shirts, shorts, vest and pants and shoes for estate work were cheap – the Chinese tailor ran up what you wanted in 24 hours . . . But a Palm beach suit, European type shirts, shoes etc. were very expensive. And then you had to have everything for your house – kitchen utensils, cutlery, china, bed linen etc. And unless you came out with about £300 earmarked for this and your first 'outfit' of estate clothes, you ran into debt – so easy to do – from the very start.[16]

Hutchinson's starting salary in 1928 was the average rate of $250 a month, rising to $350 – an improvement on the junior's salary of $225 which had been the norm when Joe Allgrove started in 1920. At that time 'there was no holiday pay, no provident funds, in fact no extras of any sort'.[17] Allgrove's generation was particularly unfortunate because by 1922 the mini-boom had given way to a slump, as the world economy failed to pull out of the economic dislocation of the Great War. The numbers of estate staff had to be suddenly reduced, or juniors found their salaries cut to $175. By the mid-1930s, when J. S. Potter was posted to Guthrie's Kuala Lumpur office and joined a mess with other bachelors, rates had returned to 1920 levels. 'My starting salary was $250 per month with no allowances. Not much! But it is amazing to look back and see how far it went. Mess Bill (all in living expenses) $130 per month. Club bills $40, transport expenses $30, left one with $50 a month for clothes and savings etc. We were well fed and lived very comfortably sharing three Chinese servants.'[18]

Although the standard of living for Europeans improved in the interwar period, life on an outstation was far less comfortable than in the towns. The jungle was never far away – 'a world of unending colonnades of gigantic trees', one planter recalled – while the rubber imposed its own kind of tyranny.[19] 'There is nothing beautiful about a rubber estate – only a monotony of regularity which corrodes one's outlook on life,' observed Bruce Lockhart.[20] 'The rubber groves are melancholy. As far as you can see are the black arches of the rubber, and the white day beyond is blinding in contrast. There are thousands of acres of rubber trees . . . and each grove is as black as the last. There is a depressing tidiness about them.'[21] Joe Allgrove recalled that in the pre-car era of the early 1920s country roads and tracks were interminably winding, there was no telephone, and malaria was still a hazard.

> Twice weekly everyone had a dose of liquid quinine. It was nothing to have 50–60 genuine fever cases at the sick muster . . . Few active planters of today have ever tasted liquid quinine. It is horrible and the horror lasts some time. Many labourers would try to miss their dose by hiding in the rubber . . . Many, having had their dose, would squat in the roadside drain and retch violently! 'Master' often took a dose pour encourager les autres![22]

Hutchinson developed malaria in the mid-1930s. After a long course of quinine, he too decided that 'the cure was worse than the disease and made you deaf and bad-tempered'.[23]

Living conditions on most estates were primitive. 'To talk of living in an attap-roofed shack, eight feet off the ground with the bathhouse below, no running water, no electric light, no fans, no sanitation and little or no "Cold Storage" or refrigerators, is almost beyond credence.'[24] And if there was no attap available, shacks were roofed in tin, which could be very hot and very noisy in rain. The Manager's bungalow was generally more spacious and comfortable. 'I remember well . . . a large, typical colonial house and garden,' wrote Susan Malet, and the Barretts' home in Sungei Patani was 'airy with wide verandahs'.[25] But in many houses bedroom walls were unplastered: there was 'only the [external] weather boarding, which overlaps and allows curious creatures to wander in from the jungle'.[26] 'Assam Java', the family bungalow of an independent planter in Selangor, tended to shake and rattle in the wind. The palm thatch housed a multitude of snakes and insects; 'rats and squirrels peered down at us . . . Miniature owls raised several families on top of the wardrobe of the nursery.'[27] Wooden structures had to be steeped in creosote: the same family had cousins in Kedah whose home collapsed after being attacked by termites. If the bungalow floor was not sufficiently raised, 'all you got were fleas' from 'the scrawny chickens that everyone's cook kept under[neath] . . . in the heat of the day'.[28]

Most planters' houses were built on similar lines. The living quarters, which included some sort of mosquito-proofed area, would be separated from the kitchen and the servants' quarters at the rear by a covered walkway. Water supplies were a matter of chance. 'Our drinking water is sent down to us once a week by launch. It is kept in a large tub,' wrote one housewife, 'and when it is wanted it is put through a drip stone filter, then boiled, and filtered again.' At 'Assam Java' there was a 'stinking, muddy pond in the garden, full of rotting rubber leaves, the only source of water apart from the monsoon rain'.[29] The result was thick tea-coloured baths and drinking water sterilized and tinctured with permanganate of potash. Laundering was primeval: clothes were whacked on a wet stone. It was much the same for company planters:

There was no 'Mod. San.' . . . Running water was not common but each bungalow had a well. Each bathroom had a 'shanghai jar', a large earthenware tub, . . . and a tin bath, the ordinary galvanized tin wash tub of pre-war days . . . There was also the 'jam-pan' or 'night commode' and a jerry. These latter were usually emptied but once a day – it all depended how near one lived to the coolie lines . . . We also kept our 'beer and soda' in a bucket down the well, where it kept fairly cool.

All kinds of expedient were necessary:

> We put the legs of tables, beds etc. in the china cups used to collect the rubber latex from the trees, and these were filled with water topped by kerosene. This kept the ants at bay . . . Now the furniture . . . by and large it was a disgrace. We had two old iron single beds, with sagging springs . . . The mattresses were 'aged', pillows ditto. Mosquito nets, a new one every three years if lucky. Each bedroom had one or more Almirahs [wardrobe/cupboard] and a strange assortment of dressing tables . . . The dining room furniture was almost always the same . . . black P.W.D. teak of early vintage . . . Then the sitting room – almost universally these had 'rattan' or cane type armchairs [and] settees . . . In 5 years I only had one new set of cheap rattan chairs. What was the reason for this? It was simply that not much cash was allowed by the directors for furniture – the ex-crofter type of director seemed to rule this department.[30]

The only compensation was the sense of space that went with a large garden; and, though the grass was often poor, the soil of Malaya somehow sustained a profusion of flowers. 'Assam Java' had trellis on three sides and a bounty of moonflowers, orchids and firecracker vines, marred only by a hidden subculture of insects. But, whatever the conditions, there were always planters who managed to make their homes cosy and contrived to be happy, even house proud, against the odds.

Rubber planting was a physically demanding pursuit, the daily routine much longer and more exhausting than any office job in the East. A French planter's daughter remembered how 'Papa walked every-where . . . On and on he trudged with only a stick to ward off cobras.' He would be away seven or eight hours, checking, examining, inspect-ing.[31] According to Guy Hutchinson, 'Managers differed greatly. Some worked day and night; others did not appear to do very much outside their office and factory', content to leave the rest to their Assistants. Hutchinson was fortunate in his superiors. 'Plum' Warner, a dynamic little man, was 'a very good planter' who made sure Hutchinson had a 'very thorough training'. Herbert, Manager of Batu Caves Estate, was 'a decent . . . inoffensive-looking type' who gave a young man his head, and Hedley Bragg, the Manager of Tenang Estate in Johore, like 'Plum', became a close friend. 'H.B. was the type who would discuss everything with you, walk everywhere with you and then leave you to get on with it: just the sort of Manager that I could work well with.'[32] Hutchinson was luckier than some. Joe Allgrove's Manager, for instance, accompanied him on fieldwork twice in four years: 'One learnt – or failed to learn – by trial and error.'[33]

Estate work also varied enormously. Virgin land had to be felled, burned and cleared before planting; where the rubber was mature (after seven years' growth) tapping and processing were the main tasks. But maintenance and improvement work went on constantly. 'We were terracing, weeding, [doing] pest and disease work and path making with the Tamils,' wrote Hutchinson after his transfer to the Sepang division of Lothian Estate, Selangor. The eradication of invasive lalang grass, though a thankless job, was a necessity. But the new challenge suited him. It was 'a real [rubber] planting district. I had about 20 Chinese budding and tending the Nurseries. Then a mile or more away was Bute Division where the jungle had just been felled, and Chinese, having burnt it were clearing it, ready for the hole digging and planting. It was the very essence of Planting. I loved it.' 'Budding' rubber, it should be said, was a new production method which appealed to the enterprising. An alternative to using seed, it was a technique 'to bud graft common stock from the branch wood of proved high yielders'; it 'was just coming into general use in Malaya when I went out in 1927', stated Hutchinson.[34]

On his second agreement, in 1934, Hutchinson was in charge of a division of 3,300 acres in north Johore, part of an estate of 7,000 acres, which involved more responsibility. As Leopold Ainsworth had already discovered, a planter was 'called on to supervise the construction of buildings, roads and bridges and see that his factory is well and economically run. He is expected to know about cattle, and also to keep an intelligent watch over his small hospital or dressing station and the general provision store.'[35] Hutchinson's original training as an engineer now stood him in good stead. He was involved in replacing the wooden bridges over the swampland (or *tenang*) to the railway. Redraining the swamp 'was a major opus . . . most interesting work'; but 'as soon as the road and bridges had been done we did another job at the A.B. [division] water supply, building yet another reservoir and putting in a bigger and better pump and also an electric light supply'.[36]

The planter's other major task was overseeing all the workers on the estate, his little kingdom. He was responsible for 'the human relationship – the very close contact between Assistant (the S.D. or Sina Dorai or Small Master) and his "Narlakies" (headmen) that made everything worthwhile'. As a young Assistant, Hutchinson sympathized with his Indian workers, especially his store clerk, Game-leg Pillay ('as opposed to his "Cousin-brother", Pox-eye Pillay, the field conductor'):

> I got quite fond of these two Pillays and they certainly went out of their way to help and teach me. It was all a matter of how you spoke and treated them. Some people never got on with 'the kranis' [Indian clerks]. They were said to be 'rude', 'stuck-up', lazy crooks etc. But if you dealt fairly by them I found that 90% were decent chaps. They had very small sala- ries [*c.* 60 cents a day], very long hours, and a lot of responsibility. Taking it all round I liked them . . . Our labour force were all Tamils, mostly Pariahs or casteless; some 25% were rather low caste . . . But once you 'knew the rules' and didn't put the wrong caste in the next room to the pariah etc. then they all lived amicably together . . . The Tamil labourer was a great family man, a terrible gossip, and a frightful squabbler . . . You had to know your Indian labour force backwards, all their relations and enemies; you listened to their woes, married them and divorced them – the lot. As they said, 'You are our Father and our Mother', and you were too . . . it was the human element that made it worthwhile.[37]

Others echoed all that Hutchinson said about the human dimension of planting. 'On the whole estate labourers, Indians, Chinese, Malay and Javanese, were in their different way hard working and responded to an employer who spoke their own language and took some interest in their welfare. Estate management', J. S. Potter concluded, 'was to a large extent social welfare and . . . could be well rewarding in itself . . . The names and faces of my first Tamil labour force remain with me to this day,' he added proudly.[38] The only times Hutchinson's Tamil work- force gave him trouble was when they became high on toddy, which invariably sparked a drunken brawl. He hated having to don his Bombay bowler for protection and go down to the coolie huts to sort out a row in the lines, as happened about once a month. Fortunately, 'a single hard "clip" was enough to knock them out – then under the tap to cool [them] off'.[39] Otherwise the Tamil lines were peaceful places. Katharine Sim remembered them as rustic settlements, 'smelly, with the soft-eyed Indian cattle wandering about, the goats, chickens and pariah dogs. The babies were slung up in voluminous saris hanging from beams under a shelter where one woman could look after them all while their mothers laboured on the estate.'[40]

The daily round of everyday life on a rubber estate began before dawn with the preliminary muster. Attendance for the Assistant was *de rigueur* – proof that he was reliable and trustworthy. In the estate where Guy Hutchinson worked:

We were called, or called the cook, at about 5.15 a.m. . . . donned our shirt and shorts and a sweater and then went off to the Coolie Lines. It was still quite dark. The idea was that the Tappers – those that bled the rubber trees and collected the latex – got out to their 'task' of say 400 trees by dawn – they often had 3 miles to walk and, except on the coastal plain where it was dead flat, most estates were fairly, some very, hilly. Having chased off the tappers we went to the 'store' (factory) or the divisional office, and there were collecting in lines the Weeders, mostly women and children (over 11 years old) and a few old men, the Pest Gang men, who cut down and cut up fallen or diseased trees, the Road and Drainage Gang, again men, and any other odd jobs. Also a separate line of those reporting sick – or for leave – and each gang under a Kangany (headman). Meanwhile the Tappers' Kanganies were reporting and bringing with them the buckets of any of their gang who was sick or absent. First job was to fill up the vacant tappers' tasks and see that the Factory was started. By this time it was getting light. The Weeders etc. were sent off, the leave attended to . . . Then the 'sick parade' was attended to. Stomach ache and a dose of 'Mix Alba – Epsom Salts' administered. Those recently discharged from the Estate Hospital were given their medicine – quinine – spleen mixture etc. Then those really sick sent off to the Estate Hospital. The pocket checkroll was made up – this was the daywork book with every coolie's name in their Recruited Gangs – and from this the BIG Checkroll was made up and this was the official Pay Book. A wise man kept his checkrolls right up to date – the end of the month was busy enough – Big Checkroll and Full Report on all work – yields per field and per tapper all to be worked out and neatly written up and ALL to be on the Manager's table by 7.30 a.m. of 1st. Not much sleep on the last night of the month, and woe if your pocket and big checkrolls were not right up to date and properly tallied.

By this time it was 6.15–6.30, according to the time of year. There wasn't much difference in light all the year round; after all, we were only 3 degrees North of the Equator. Having spoken to and sent off our Field Conductor – usually a Malayalam from Southern India – and seen that the Factory was well and truly started, back to the lines to see that no one had been missed or had slipped back for a 'cupper', checked all the little ones were in the creche with the Ayah and chased the nippers off to school – over 5 and under 11 sent to our own school till midday . . . Then whistle up the dogs and back to the bungalow for a wash and shave and about 4 cups of tea and by 7 a.m. we were out inspecting the Tappers.

We tried to see at least 50% of our tappers every day, the whole lot if possible . . . We had to check against wounding the trees, excessive removal of bark, the cleanliness of the latex cups, the spouts that led the latex into the cups, collecting buckets etc. Usually one called up the Tapping Kangany of each field (say 50 acres) and went round with him from tree to tree and tapper to tapper, and so from field to field. There was a certain amount of low cunning as to how you arranged the work of the tappers . . . On the way round the tappers we inspected the weeders, pests, drainers etc. Only a mug would have his weeders working in a field not in tapping or not adjacent to a field in tapping that day . . . By about 9 to 9.30 most of the trees had been tapped and there was a pause before the 'horn was blown at the factory' to start collecting latex. We then nipped back home and had Breakfast – the best meal of the day I always thought. By 10.15 we were out again, seeing the weeders etc., then to the Factory (or if a large estate the collecting station) where the division's latex was measured, each man being measured for gallonage and specific gravity of his latex: by this we knew how many lbs of dry rubber he had got . . . By 12.30 all the latex should have been 'in'. Then either out to the 'outside' gangs . . . or an inspection of the packing sheds and smoke houses. And so by 2 p.m. work was over. Some assistants had to take the names in of their gangs. We only did this about twice a week: the conductor did it. This taking in of the coolies' names every day was important as it was by this that they were paid . . . however it was done it was wise to take the small (or pocket) checkroll back to your bungalow and see that it was properly entered up, and everything cross-checked before you could say you had finished for the day . . .

Except on the very small estates it was a rule that the assistants went to the Main Factory about 2.30, checked in the amount of rubber collected from their division, making sure that the Factory Bulk Figure agreed with the figure you got at your collecting station. If you didn't, the wily Factory Clerk would mark you down short and so cover any losses his end at your expense. This didn't matter so much with Day Paid tappers, but woe to you if you had Chinese on contract and your figures were short at the end of the month. When you had done this it was usual to see the Manager and see if he had any special orders etc. for the next day. And then you could go home and have tea. *It was a long day – and seldom were you finished until 4 p.m. and you had started at 5.15 a.m. But it was a fine outdoor life. You were handling people, and once proved trustworthy, very much your own boss.*[41]

Although the estate routine varied little, there were many other changes during the inter-war years. In the immediate aftermath of the Great War, 'European estate staff were built up to pre-war numbers which was usually a ratio of one to 250 acres' – a generous figure in the light of later staffing levels. One Johore planter admitted, 'we did not work particularly hard'; in addition, 'returns per tapper were, by present standards, poor'. However, a short, sharp slump in 1921–4 brought the first shock waves of hardship and unemployment, as companies made staff and pay reductions. Reorganization was necessary – principally the replacement of Chinese tappers by more docile Indian labour, the Chinese being reserved for heavier clearing and new planting. 'Kota Tinggi was an uneasy spot' at that time, Allgrove recalled. 'About 1922, one of the hard years, the runner [who carried the post to and from the mines beyond the Pelipah valley] was set on in the jungle and murdered', though the robbers gained only a few cents. 'One remembers [too] the long series of leaders [in] the *Straits Times* demanding some control of rubber production. Eventually the Stephenson Scheme was adopted . . . Estates were assessed on past results and production allowed on a reduced scale.' The planters learned 'many lessons, not least being the value of periods of rest for the rubber tree'.[42]

This rationalization steadied the industry, so that by the time Guy Hutchinson went out to Selangor in 1928 buoyancy had returned. In 1929 rubber exports from the Federated Malay States were worth over $200 million dollars. Indian immigration to the rubber estates peaked in the late 1920s. Labour troubles were rare. The Indian labour force readily accepted low wages of 30–45 cents a day in return for guaranteed work, free housing, free medicine and hospitalization; 'it was wealth compared to what they could earn in the villages of southern India . . . And we used to "bank" their money for them . . . and it is surprising the amount they sent back to India.'[43]

The improved prosperity of these years, however, came to an abrupt end with the Wall Street Crash and the Great Depression. More work and productivity was expected from each planter. The Sepang Club was forced to close in 1931. Paper chases, a cheap form of exercise and relaxation, suddenly became popular. The value of second-hand cars and car-hire charges dropped like a stone. Unable to keep up the payments on his beloved Nash, Mike Hutchinson replaced it with an old second-hand Morris Open Tourer acquired at a knock-down price. Another symptom of the Slump was the revival of some gangs of Chinese bandits – 'real "Robber Gangs" and these caused a lot of trouble'. Guy Hutchinson played safe and bought a .38 colt automatic. By 1931 he noticed 'The married planters began to be much more careful, and instead of big parties or trips to K.L. etc. quieter evenings and every weekend on the estate became much in evidence . . . Club nights dwindled, till almost everyone went home after parade.' Indeed:

> The effects of the Slump were becoming more and more visible. So many planters going home on leave did not return, and worse than that . . . Suddenly the local papers were full of reports of European planters who had been given three months' notice and at the end of this time they found themselves stranded in Malaya. They had no money . . . [and] had a job to pay their debts . . . Many tried to raise a bit extra by selling all their household goods – but there were few buyers . . . Previously on the odd occasion that this sort of thing had happened, the unfortunate man was sent home by Government as a D.B.S. (Distressed British Subject) at government expense. But what was to happen now? The numbers grew almost daily. Many, most, were unmarried and under 30–35.[44]

In April 1932 the Hutchinson brothers had to accept 'another cut in pay – making 33% in all, which meant', Guy recalled, 'that I was on approx. $220 a month – less than I had started with over four years ago!' In fact, the pay cut was a preliminary to receiving notice – hardly a surprise when the great majority of European Assistants had been paid off and sent home by the middle of the year. Even highly experienced and able Managers like Herbert of Batu Caves and Hedley Bragg of Tenang were retired – a euphemism for axed: 'so it went on everywhere . . .' Getting rid of pets was a job . . . when we left we took our Dogs to the local Police Station to be put down . . . It was all very sad . . .' But as they boarded the *Chitral* at Penang for home, it was heartwarming to see that 'Half the planters from Kedah had come to see her off . . . On board were sixty planters and only two had return tickets!'[45]

The visual evidence of the Slump in Johore was described with feeling by a civil servant returning from leave. 'A neglected allure hung over everything – empty clubs, silent roads, abandoned bungalows with weed-grown paths and broken shutters creaking in the evening breeze.'[46] Devastating, too, was the effect of redundancy on morale and self-esteem: 'it is a thousand times worse', argued one, 'for a white man in a tropical country' to be unemployed; it would 'destroy European credit and prestige'.[47] The earlier slump had produced a crop of personal tragedies, such as the suicide of Captain Lester, a planter who had fought in the Great War but then found there was neither a job nor the prospect of one. However, both government officials and the planters' organizations, such as the Incorporated Society of Planters, had a vested interest in the planters' welfare. As one senior official admitted in the detached language of the bureaucrat, 'It is quite impossible to retain a number of unemployed white men in the country in the midst of a native population.'[48] Temporary solutions were found in 1930 with the formation of a new company of the Malay States Volunteer Rifles and the revival of the European Unemployment Fund, first set up in 1921, to help unemployed planters and their families with grants and passages home. The plight of the rubber men continued to be aired in the pages of *The Planter*, with warnings about the need to restore salary levels 'when the tyranny of world depression' was past.[49] Meanwhile, in England the situation was little better, and repatriated planters, Guy Hutchinson found, were driven to 'doing the most odd assortment of jobs, taxi-driving, Stop-Me-and-Buy-One ice cream selling, driving delivery vans – anything in fact'.[50]

Much later, when the painful memories had faded, it was possible to be philosophical about the slumps of 1922 and 1932. Taking the long-term view, they were powerful levers in forcing progress on estate operation. The losers were individual Europeans and Asians, the beneficiaries the big rubber companies and agencies like Dunlop's and Guthrie's. Guy Hutchinson observed the way market forces changed Malaya's rubber industry:

> When I left Malaya in June 1932 . . . only a very few estates were still producing rubber in quantity. The native owned estates and kampongs were producing as much as they could, selling at rock bottom prices, while we, the axed planters were doing the best we could to keep our noses above water . . . the City Sharks that ran the industry from London were not idle. They appear to have had their scouts out . . . and were ready waiting to pounce. In 1932 they pounced. The victims this time were the

Asian estate owners and smallholders, anyone that had some decent land planted up in rubber in good condition and who were as near as no matter bankrupt. The City sailed in and through a few very astute local Agents started to buy up the planted rubber. What they wanted was a block of say one to 3,000 acres – or failing that a lot of small holdings . . . in lots of 100 acres each, making anything up to 4,000 and 8,000 acres. They searched diligently, silently and very effectively. I will give you an example of but one European company, 'XY'. In 1932 they had owned about 8,000 acres of mature rubber in Selangor, divided into four estates. By the end of 1934 they had acquired in Johore alone two Asian estates of approximately 3,000 acres each, a block of about 7,000 acres that had belonged to 700 different owners, all adjacent to each other, in South Johore . . . Messrs XY had in a short space of time increased their acreage three fold . . . Thousands of acres of Chinese rubber [planted since the Great War] were brought by European companies in 1934–35 . . . They then had a fine choice of planters to pick from; experienced Managers who wanted but one more agreement to be able to retire without being in penury, and Assistants of every shade of experience, all eager to return to do their rightful profession. Most of us would have come back for almost a 'song'; for my own part I signed on for four years at $300 a month.[51]

The revolution in land ownership which came about with the Slump resulted in a big increase in the number of European planters from the mid-1930s, and this in turn brought a lot of extra money and business to even the small towns. The Dunlop Rubber Company took the lead, eventually planting some 15,000 acres of rubber adjacent to the railway. Rubber was once more in demand; indeed, from the late 1930s the industry enjoyed boom conditions. These good years went a long way towards eradicating memories of the bad. J. S. Potter, who in 1937 transferred from office work in Kuala Lumpur into estate work in Negri Sembilan, found he preferred the latter: not only was it better paid with cheaper living, but he liked the independence and responsibility of a senior Assistant. On his return in 1934 Guy Hutchinson voiced unbounded enthusiasm for planting:

You can have no idea of the, well, 'Elation' is the word, that we, the ones who had 'been on the beach', felt to be back again, with a job we knew and liked. No one was going to worry, ever again about conditions. We were Planting . . . It was a simply marvellous feeling – I am sure I am not speaking for myself when I say this.[52]

Later he found himself headhunted by a rival company, but personal loyalty prevailed over financial gain. Tenang estate remained his home for what proved to be four very happy years.

Segamat, the administrative centre for north Johore, was a pleasant little town with fine shady trees and streets lined with jacarandas. It was well served by the railway, and had a very good market and a branch of the Singapore Cold Storage based at the large Chinese grocery store. In his newly built bungalow, with its own electricity plant, good water supply and excellent views, Guy Hutchinson felt he lacked nothing. By courtesy of Dunlop's, which owned most estates from Gemas to Tenang, the Europeans in the area had the benefit of two clubs, with nine-hole golf courses, sports pitches and tennis courts.

A planter on his second contract was expected to 'do his social bit . . . It will not do him any good to be thought "eccentric", or a snob, and if he clings to a hermit existence he may very easily be written off as both.'[53] Planters were as gregarious as their location permitted. On isolated estates friendships were largely confined to work colleagues – planters, the factory engineer, the estate doctor and so on. When the Malets were planting in Selangor, most of their acquaintances were planters and members of Klang Club, together with two Kuala Lumpur doctors, Dr Robert Hardie and Dr Macintosh. Guy Hutchinson's old bachelor group in Kuala Lumpur had given way to a wide network of friends around Segamat, including Hugh Bryson, the Assistant Adviser, and his wife. As he harmlessly boasted, 'I ran the [Genuang] Club as Honorary Secretary, I ran the local Johore Volunteer Engineers and I ran my little Morris 8 hp. almost to death. I "ate out" as often as I "ate in"'. But no matter what, I never missed a Muster!'[54] He also took up cricket and golf, and he joined enthusiastically in 'house-parties', where copious supplies of beer, whisky and champagne ensured there was a jovial atmosphere. Hutchinson, as much as anyone, demonstrated that the typical planter was a convivial soul.

In Singapore the planter from up-country had the image of being an unsophisticated, cheerful, gregarious cove, but inherently suspicious of Managers, Visiting Agents, Secretaries and Directors. The planter was not unique in his liking for stengahs, and the average club made its profits from hard drinkers and a fair number of steady ones. However, Somerset Maugham's assertion that the majority of rubber planters were rough and common men runs contrary to evidence, and, for cynically targeting the weakness of individuals and creating stereotypes which passed into historical myth on the strength of two short visits, he was never forgiven by the British community.[55] While honest enough to recognize some truth in aspects of Maugham's charge, Hutchinson was keen to put the record straight, wondering if the writer knew, for instance, that

> In those days the Rev. Petter used to come over from Malacca [to the Segamat district] and hold a C. of E. service once a month in the evening . . . and then the next morning an early service . . . Mrs 'Joe' Allgrove of Maur River Estate used to play the piano for the hymns and we usually had a congregation on the Thursday evening of about 15 to 20 people, and that was Club Night and Government Servants' Holiday Night too. So all Planters are 'Whisky Swillers all the time!'[56]

Rubber planting, like Janus, presented two faces. One appealed to the idealist who saw himself as a member of a profession and for whom rubber was a lifelong enterprise, if not a vocation. In this context one thinks of men like Jack le Doux, who changed career from Estate Manager for a large company to become a modest owner-planter in close touch with Asian life (and who wrote under the pseudonym of Tuan Djak); or Rupert Pease, who, Cunyngham-Brown noted, 'shared with his labour force the profits of his rubber estate down at Port Dickson; daily writing up the balance sheet on a blackboard in a manner that would have pleased Mao Tse Tung and dividing the profits equally among them all, including himself'.[57] The other was the face of capitalism, which appealed to the pragmatists and fortune-seekers. Whether they embarked on this hard, profit-conscious, market-driven career through inclination or through force of circumstance, many knew they had been sent out East 'to control their Employer's interests to the best advantage'.[58] Change is indigenous to market forces, and changes have come thick and fast in the second half of the twentieth century. Some have been for the better. 'Present day planters have more creature comforts (including "real" wives!) . . . They are technically better equipped . . . Health has improved immeasurably,' Joe Allgrove reported. But in the flux of economic life, rubber has lost out to oil palm, just as coffee, tapioca and coconuts once gave way to rubber; so the planter's work 'lies more in tree and palm care than in labour care which used to occupy so much time'.[59]

Looking back over their experiences in the inter-war period, the old hands saw special virtues in the planters of their day. Courage, integrity and honesty went with the job.

> I have heard many Ex-Servicemen say, 'I am used to handling men' etc. But they forget that they had the whole Army behind them. A Planter was quite on his own, and if he was 'made a fool of' in front of his coolies, he lost their respect for him. If he showed fear, they knew it . . . you had to show that you meant what you said.[60]

As to the lure of money, 'The reputed fortunes made were confined to the very few who formed an almost negligible proportion of the profession.'[61] In any case, planters, like every other section of the British community, were to lose out heavily during the Second World War. In this respect Guy Hutchinson was no exception, though he was remembered long after as an unselfish comrade, 'both a character and a gentleman'.[62] The same, he would have argued, was true of many planters. 'Now it is a funny thing,' he mused, thinking of the two types, educated Scots and English public-school men, who dominated the planting community of Malaya:

> For some reason they were [both] better than any other types in the Whole World at the 'handling of labour'. I don't know why, an inborn sense of justice, a fairness and determination that this should be given to all under them. They were not ashamed to take off their shirts and work, to give an example, and by and large they could be trusted not to drink to excess nor to womanise too much. There are of course exceptions to every rule . . . but on the whole the Planters were a very decent, honest, clean living and hard working lot.[63]

## 10

# *The* Mem, *the* Missee *and* *the* Tuan Kechil

'What was the poor Planter to do – stuck out in the East with no women of any kind?' fumed Guy Hutchinson, and his frustration was echoed by hundreds of heterosexual bachelors in the inter-war years.[1] 'There was very, very little female company in Kuala Lumpur. As far as I remember in that year 1931 there were only two unmarried British girls and they had already got fairly firm boyfriends,' confirmed a young police officer. 'You couldn't get a look in.'[2] The only hope came from 'the "fishing fleet" of unattached ladies [who] came regularly up from Australia to Singapore, Malaya and Ceylon. They would have friends or relations here and they would stay with them. Most of them found husbands alright!'[3]

The Great War had marked a watershed in social conventions, including attitudes to sex. Asian mistresses with Eurasian children were no longer acceptable to the European community; the social pressure on employers to employ married men was growing, although the rule that men should not marry before thirty persisted, at least in theory. (Those with private incomes could always circumvent the ban, the planter John Theophilus recalled.) 'After the big slump – from 1934 onwards – the number of European men was smaller and the number of wives greater, and the older generation's daughters were beginning to come out.'[4] Then, as the decade progressed, a visitor noticed a huge increase in the number of European women, which coincided with, and was facilitated by, modern developments like motor cars and railways, and electricity and refrigerators and radios, and also by the expansion of shipping lines such as P. & O. and Blue Funnel.[5] 'Everyone seemed to be getting married – the omens looked good,' rejoiced Hutchinson, as 'the all-male society that had centred on the local clubhouse was slowly infiltrated by the gentler manners of the English and Scottish shires'.[6]

By 1931 women accounted for 28 per cent of Malaya's European population – some 5,000, together with about 2,500 children, almost half of them resident in Singapore. By the end of 1940 the figures had increased to about 8,500 women and around 4,300 children.[7] Whereas many of the older generations of immigrants remained unmarried, the new generation had partners who tended to be from similar commercial, technical or professional backgrounds to their own. They came from the middle-class suburbs around London or Manchester, Liverpool or Glasgow, or the industrial towns of northern England and Scotland. Wives had known their husbands from schooldays, as neighbours or family acquaintances, members of the same church, tennis club or social set. Thomas and Ethel Barnes both came from the Clapham district of London. E. Milroy Dickson of the Singapore Harbour Board had known his wife, Barbara, since childhood, as both families had lived in Brigham, near Cockermouth. While on home leave, Fred Snell, a quantity surveyor with Singapore Municipality, met his wife, Peggie, in Radlett, Hertfordshire, where she was a journalist. Kathleen King was a secretary at Vickers Armstrong's shipbuilding works in Barrow-in-Furness when she met her future husband, Bill Price, a naval architect in the drawing office there. Of the generation of women whose marriage hopes had been blighted by the Great War or by post-war slump, some were probably beguiled by descriptions of Eastern life: 'all the "best" clubs, golden nights in palatial hotels, shopping by motorcar'. 'Well, the dear girl has no doubt been living modestly at Home,' quipped a male journalist patronizingly, 'not a bit averse to washing a window or lighting a fire', until an exchange of letters with a bachelor in Malaya turned her into a 'dizzy optimist'.[8] And so the new Malayan wives, the *mems*, became the envy of 'aunts and uncles who . . . never left Brixton or Paisley' – though they were anathema to the old colonials as symbols of 'lower-middle-class suburbia, generaled by a small coterie of determined, hard-faced females who might have done better to remain in Surbiton'.[9]

Under the conditions of service for both officials and unofficials, marriage was delayed until the second agreement or term of service. Some couples seized on the opportunity to marry during the future husband's first home leave, but others felt financially constrained to wait and endure inevitable separation.[10] Since 1928 Hutchinson had kept in touch with a Scots girl from his home town of Bo'ness and

> For my part anyway I was quite serious in my idea that if things had been good – pay, prospects etc., that I would have tried hard to get engaged during my home leave. But I now [1930] saw that this was hopeless, and I finally wrote to her explaining that my future was dim in the extreme and that she was, from then on, not to take me seriously.[11]

Occasionally engagements were whirlwind affairs, but generally they were long, and husbands and wives tended to be mature by the time they married. Only nineteen when she met Bill Price in 1925, Kathleen King was twenty-five and he was forty-one at their marriage. Facing possible redundancy in the era of disarmament, he left England in 1926 to take a post as Assistant Manager at Sungei Nyok Dockyard, Province Wellesley. She followed him out in 1932 at the start of his second agreement. William Price of Penang (no relation to the above) married at the age of forty while on leave in England. In 1908 he had joined his brother as a rubber planter, but in 1910 he changed career. Returning to Malaya in 1919, he rejoined his old firm, Whiteaway Laidlaw, and had risen to be Assistant Manager of the Penang branch when he married Mabel in 1929. Thomas Barnes, who joined Dunlop's around the time of the Great War, waited fifteen years to marry. 'My mother, whom he had long known in England,' wrote his son, 'sailed out to Malaya to join him in 1929', when both were in their mid-thirties.[12] Guy Hutchinson's courtship of his future wife was also protracted, and he was in his middle thirties when he proposed. Although she 'gave me a lot of "heart throbs"', he admitted, 'I had said nothing, nor written anything, to Jessie about getting married. I did not think that a fair way to go about things.' Instead, he left it until his next home leave to '"go All Out" on the "Personal Relations" line'.[13]

Sometimes prolonged separation played havoc with relationships, and shipboard romances were a feature of the sultry run east of Suez. Guy Hutchinson knew of one planter who 'got married to a girl he only met first on leave. He sailed for Singapore with her on a P. & O. When they got there she informed him that "she was going on to Hong Kong with "that bloke", another passenger, so poor old C.K. went ashore and . . . started divorce proceedings.'[14] Arriving at Penang in 1928, Alex

Cullen watched an eager fiancé dash prematurely up the gangway, pursued by a harbour policeman, in the rush to embrace his bride-to-be: a rash gesture which carried a $400 fine! And in another incident on Penang wharf a wife threw herself into the arms of a man she mistook as her husband, to the wry amusement of the watching crowd. But, despite these occasional mishaps, an increasing number of brides-to-be travelled out unchaperoned in the inter-war years, to be married within a day or two of landing.

Outside the metropolis, European weddings added some spice to social life. Frequently the occasion would be organized by a *mem*, a married acquaintance of the husband, often the wife of a senior colleague in his company or department, who gave the bride away. Thomas and Ethel Barnes were married in Malacca on 18 June 1929 in Christ Church, the old rose-coloured Dutch church built in 1753. Their wedding had been arranged by the wife of the head of Dunlop's, Malacca, Mrs Wiseman, whose daughter was bridesmaid. In Singapore the favoured venue was St Andrew's Cathedral, where, for instance, Fred and Peggie Snell were married in March 1931, and their friends the Cannells in April 1932, while William Vowler recalled that his parents, aunts and uncles were all married there. All the European residents of Butterworth were invited to the marriage of Kathleen King and Bill Price, which was conducted by the Revd F. T. Loader at St Mark's Anglican Church in March 1932. The matron-of-honour, Dolly Black, wife of a Harbour Board official, had organized the wedding and lent her spacious home for the reception. All the bridegroom had to do was to book the honeymoon at Fraser's Hill. A decade before, Roger Barrett's parents, rubber planters near Sungei Patani, had been married in the same little church, which served the scattered European families in Province Wellesley and south Kedah. Since Kedah was an Unfederated Malay State, there was no Christian Marriage Enactment to allow Europeans to marry in Alor Star, but the Regent of Kedah ordered an Enactment to be passed for Wilfrid and Agnes Davison. 'I was married from the Residency,' Mrs Davison recalled,

> and the Acting British Adviser, Mr. A C. Baker, and Mrs Baker, made our wedding a very happy and memorable occasion. All Government Offices were closed, both Europeans and Malays attended, and the quaint little church was filled to overflowing. After a wonderful reception there was a noisy departure with Chinese crackers etc. and when

the Residency car, with all sorts of old tins and boots etc., tied to it, passed through the town, the Malays thought the *Orang Puteh* had gone mad.[15]

The suggestion that all colonial wives were immersed in a frivolous social whirl, oblivious to social problems, was a simplification of reality, although there was inevitably more understanding of social needs among the core of professional women – doctors, nurses, teachers, missionaries – who worked among Asian women and children. Staff of the Young Women's Christian Association, such as Gertrude Owen, were active in social welfare. Mrs Ferguson-Davie, a medical doctor and wife of the Bishop of Singapore, had started the medical mission which became St Andrew's Hospital. Mrs Helen Band was highly regarded not simply for her philanthropic work in Singapore, but for the all-pervading support she gave to the ministry of her husband, the Revd Stephen Band, who was head of the Presbyterian community in Malaya.

The demand for the services of British doctors and nursing sisters to train and work alongside Asian nurses was unremitting. Although most European *mems* did not work in the 1930s, an experienced theatre sister such as Syliva Cannell was encouraged to leave her children in the care of their *amah* while she worked part-time in Singapore. Medical staff were well respected in the community they served: caring characters like 'Houghie', an Australian nursing sister, who had been sent in 1937 to start a children's welfare scheme in the kampongs around Segamat, or Elizabeth Darville, whose 'decision to go to Malaya was prompted largely by my longing to do pioneer work', and who started up maternity and child welfare work from scratch in 1927 on Penang Island.[16] After Dr Lowson of the Colonial Medical Service was posted to Johore Bahru, his wife, Dr Winifred Lowson, mother of four, ran the children's ward in Johore Hospital and also the women's and children's clinic with Dr Margaret Smallwood.

However, medicine and the mission were not the only fields in which women of initiative were to be found. 'By the 1920s there were a number of well-established English schools in Malaya that attracted a small group of teachers with high standards of devotion to their calling.'[17] Among them were Alice Doughty and her sister, who worked in Malacca, Alice teaching in English and her sister in Malay. Another dedicated teacher, and head of the Pudu English School, was Josephine

Foss, who began by establishing a new school on the site of 'a discarded tin mine, full of large holes, huge tree trunks and with plenty of squatters in residence!'[18] She also became involved in training Malay teachers, advising the Malay girls schools and helping on literacy courses for Malay women. Ada Weinman was a notable music teacher for almost sixty years from the 1920s. Her gift was to inspire the lesser stars, the local music and theatre enthusiasts. 'She was like the Pied Piper, standing four-square in the doorway of her little school, welcoming small boys and girls, Malays, Chinese, Indians and Europeans alike, all armed with books, sheet music and recorders. Soon the sounds of music raised the roof.'[19] Lillian Newton launched a successful children's dancing school in Singapore during the 1920s. In 1939 her most talented pupil, Pahang-born Sally Gilmour, danced on the London stage with the Ballet Rambert. With her flair and family connections with music and amateur theatricals, Lillian Newton stamped her individual style and enthusiasm on her pupils. Her friend and sister-in-law, Miss Griffith-Jones, continued the Newton tradition at her school in the Cameron Highlands. The craze for dancing and fancy dress spread wildly in the 1930s, encouraged by the success of child film stars like Shirley Temple. Penang's popular children's dancing school drew its pupils not only from the island but from Province Wellesley, presenting colourful displays to enthusiastic parents. Even in depths of rural Selangor the daughters of a rubber planter were taken to dancing classes in a nearby bungalow, where in pink frocks they performed 'a loathsome number called Basket of Flowers to the tune of *Tea for Two* ground out of an old gramophone'.[20]

'Idleness, the bane of so many women in Eastern countries, need never be known in Malaya' was a message to which some women certainly responded. 'True, the household tasks of the average *Mem* are few, but . . . there are many outside interests – Girl Guides and various classes, to enumerate only two – which are crying out for help and for support.'[21] Guiding, first introduced in 1916 among pupils of the Methodist Girls' School, Kuala Lumpur, had spread to Singapore and Penang after the Great War. In the 1920s companies were formed in Province Wellesley, Ipoh, Taiping, Telok Anson, Batu Gajah, Tapah, Malacca, Seremban and Klang. The Girl Guide's promise of community service harmonized with the prevailing climate of internationalism and Empire, and consequently the movement received financial support from the governments in Malaya. Many different nationalities participated; Guides and Brownies included Chinese, Indians, Eurasians, Ceylonese, Japanese and Europeans, and all worked in co-operation in the spirit of the Guide laws. However, with the support of the Sultans of Selangor, Johore and Kedah, vernacular Guiding began in the 1930s; in 1931 all-Malay Brownie packs were formed in Kuala Lumpur and Seremban by Mrs L. A. Thomas. Similar all-Malay initiatives were started by Dr M. G. Brodie in Kedah and by Mrs Marsh in Singapore, and later in the 1930s a Chinese vernacular company and a Tamil Brownie pack were established in Kuala Lumpur. The success of Guiding in Malaya rested on the commitment of a band of British officers, from Captains to Commissioners, and when the movement celebrated its twenty-first anniversary in 1938 the contribution of individuals was duly recognized.

Gardening was a popular interest for a section of *mems* who enthused over the miraculous profusion of colourful shrubs and flowers. Katharine Sim was amazed to find 'The sunflowers grew 4" each day' and zinnias took only three weeks from seed to budding flowers. She tended her garden nearly every evening. Visiting other gardens to gather seeds and cuttings, she came across a Scottish planter's wife who 'in two years made a wonderful garden out of nothing'.[22] However, for the less industrious, ease and entertainment were on offer in Singapore and Penang. There, 'The butterfly can enjoy her weekly *thé dansant* at the Club, her frequent tennis tournaments, her golf, her bridge and her Mah Jong. There is usually an amateur dramatic society, where she can display her gifts . . . and there may be a musical society.'[23] Satirists found easy targets in Singapore: 'the charming young thing who is all frills and flounces', the 'wicked young person of the dance floor', who 'likes to be thought just a little naughty and daring, or "advanced"', or the sportswoman who 'dresses for golf better than she plays it . . . disdains the underhand serve at tennis . . . She plays an aggressive game of bridge and knows how to score the honours. She smokes of course. And she can put away a whisky-soda with relish.'[24]

In all her varieties, the *mem* was a leading figure in the social scene, as a local writer testified:

On Saturday mornings it is the mems who predominate in Raffles Place: the wives of the men from England. There are fat mems and thin mems

. . . mems towing roaring children; smart mems . . . the considerably less affluent-looking mems of serving soldiers; smiling mems and dour mems . . . flashy mems from England's industrial suburbs . . . mems who are younger than they look and mems who look as old as they are . . . empty-headed mems, intelligent mems, thoughtless mems, bridge-playing, mah-jong playing, useless mems, hard-working mems, parasitical mems, hard-drinking . . . common mems . . . mems with three servants and to whom the novelty of the situation has never quite faded; missionary mems, both dismal and jolly . . . mems, mems, mems.[25]

In practice, there was strong social pressure on these women to be sociable. European houses in the Straits Settlements tended to be large and airy, with extensive verandahs and generous gardens – perfect settings for parties. Wives joined their husbands at the club, and weekends often revolved around games of golf or a day at the swimming club; happy memories of these times still linger. The Malets were much involved in amateur dramatics at the Klang Club, and their friends in Kedah and Selangor were also keen on cricket, so that when Mrs Malet's brother Jock Sandeman played she acted as official scorer. 'Peter' Watkins was typical of countless *mems* whose favourite forms of relaxation were tennis, bridge and mah-jong, which suddenly became fashionable in the 1920s. A child of the time recalls, 'I loved the clatter of the tiles and the picturesque designs of the three suits, including bamboos and circles, as well as the "fancy hand" tiles of the four winds and red and green dragons and the blank tiles called "soaps".'[26] A more unusual leisure activity was riding, which was one of the Rawcliffes' pleasures. For Doris Barrett of the planting community in south Kedah, leisure focused on both home entertaining and the Sungei Patani Club, where she and her husband, Malcolm, enjoyed playing games of all sorts. Such people were the life and soul of the British community. Their lifestyles were plainly far removed from the tales of colonial excess, the dipsomania and adultery portrayed by some journalists and visiting celebrities 'for whom bottles and larders were opened, and whom hosts and servants danced eager and unending attendance . . . *We didn't live that way*,' protested an indignant Singaporean.[27]

As for life up-country, even in the 1930s it took courage and common sense to live in an isolated tropical settlement with little or no company and few distractions. Posted to 'a very remote district', Kuala Selangor, in the mid-1930s, a police officer felt that, although his wife was resilient,

> It really wasn't very fair on a new bride to be sent . . . where there wasn't a single other government officer who was married . . . The house was . . . by modern standards very very crude, there was no electricity, no proper sanitation . . . For a young woman straight out from England the sanitation was pretty awful, what we called the thunderbox, and it was a very lonely life for her.[28]

Many planters' wives faced similar problems, as did even the wives of Malayan civil servants. In 1937 John Peel (later Sir John) considered himself fortunate to be appointed District Officer of the new hill station at Cameron Highlands, but the official residence was 'a wooden hut with a tin roof and the office was attached . . . There were two rooms, no running water or sanitation . . . all very primitive [and] there was a hole through the wall to use the telephone in both places, the office and bungalow.'[29] Here the Peels lived with their first baby. Yet traditional attitudes towards a colonial wife's role – to support her husband wherever he went – persisted through the 1930s. Her reward would come when ultimately they retired comfortably home to the British Isles. Meanwhile, there was a moral obligation on the *mem* to recreate the atmosphere of England in a foreign dwelling.

Some women had difficulty, Katharine Sim suspected, 'shut away in themselves perhaps because they try to live in one place with their hearts in another – in England'.[30] The practical ones did their best. 'Fresh from England, the *mem* invariably tries to make the place look "less bare" by putting up curtains and hangings', or by introducing familiar touches such as home-made cushions and lampshades, one of them wrote.[31] Advice was always forthcoming from the senior *mems*. Treasured cushions increased the chance of prickly heat, and, in view of the high humidity and the ravages of the mason bee,

> Simple *rotan* furniture is favoured in Malaya; it is light and cool and easily replaced, and it can be made to look very dainty if painted with bright paint . . . Pictures are a care, and need constant attention . . . The same may be said of carpets, although bright rugs, which are brought from India . . . lend a touch of colour to rooms, and are easily taken up and shaken.

Advice was also offered on choosing a comfortable, *cool* house at a reasonable rent, and about hiring servants. 'Tamil servants are generally cheaper than Malays and Chinese, and many of them are good for general duties. But the experienced *Mem* and the *Tuan* who is careful about his clothes will prefer a Chinese or a Malay.'[32]

Household hints for *mems* appeared routinely in print. In the slump years the emphasis was on economical housekeeping, such as how to double the life of a bath towel, how to revamp frocks using the skirt of one and the bodice of another, how to curry casseroled rabbit or make macaroni cheese or prawn and green pea wiggle to serve on buttered toast; most of all, how 'to avoid Cold Storage as much as possible, except for a few cheap and good dishes such as breast of veal . . . or neck of lamb'.[33] A refrigerator was a necessity by the 1930s, and budget-conscious housewives liked to keep a grip on the food buying to reduce the cook's overheads, his commission from the market stall-holders and his bicycle or rickshaw allowance of perhaps $5 a month. The kitchen, however, was Cookie's domain. 'The new *Mem* . . . is usually in the hands of her cook,' observed Mrs Gun Munro, before advising her to 'inspect the food when it is bought . . . If at any time it is found unsatisfactory, she can deduct the price from the cook's allowance.'[34] But even mature *mems* were happy to keep out of the kitchen. (A bizarre proof of their dependency is that some European women cooked for the first time in the wartime emergency of 1941–2.)

For a young British woman fresh from England, with little experience of the world and no knowledge of Malay, learning to manage a 'cookie', 'boy', *amah* and the other male household servants was sometimes a daunting task. To her surprise, Mabel Price discovered that she was paying her *kebun* for flowers which he stole from a nearby cemetery, but 'petty theft by the servants was taken for granted and not resented'.[35] Advice on such matters was usually on hand:

> Newcomers would do well to beware of the houseboy who is ready to accept a small wage [under $30 a month]: either he will be found hopelessly incompetent or else he will make up the deficit by 'pickings' and other devious means . . . it might [also] be well to warn new arrivals . . . to carry out irregular but fairly frequent inspections [of the servants' quarters] to ensure cleanliness and sanitation above all things. Also to keep a reasonable check on the amount of electricity used . . . Some would never turn off the switch from one month's end to another.[36]

It was vital to learn some basic Malay for communication (even Chinese and Indian servants spoke pidgin Malay). Many new wives must have just muddled through, but Peggie Snell in Singapore acquired a useful dictionary entitled *Malay for Mems*. If an employee showed particular skills (and the Sims' 'boy', Ah Seng, was a dab hand at turning table napkins into rabbit's ears or water lilies, boats or spires), it was important to know how to thank and praise him. All in all, however, the new *mem* faced a steep learning curve in the matter of language. To someone just out from England it was bewildering to be greeted with 'what was practically gibberish to her!'

> 'Will you have your *mandi* now and a *pahit* after?' . . . Why not say bath and a drink? . . . A typical sentence would run something like this: 'Oh yes, old so-and-so, he's living in the P.W.D. bungalow at T.A. His Mem has been rather *sakit* (ill) lately', or 'The D.O. from K.K. came in for *pahits* before tiffin yesterday', or 'My amah is quite *gila* (mad); she sent my black dress to the *dhobi* (laundry)', or 'You should always put *ayer busok* ( Jeyes Fluid) in the *jamban* (lavatory) . . .' People were extremely kind, but they had not the slightest idea how odd this kind of talk sounded to newcomers.[37]

Once the *mem* adjusted to social protocol, she still had to become acclimatized to living in a perpetual Turkish bath. This called for physical and mental adjustment, as a Singapore housewife implied.

> Life, for the women, means sitting in the house, alone, all through the long hot morning. Lying down for a rest, sleeping if you are lucky, reading something light perhaps, and too weary to do anything, too hot to make the attempt. Half of you lying, resting, when you do not want to rest, and the other half, like a disgruntled grasshopper . . . conscious of the long expanse, stretching away in front of you . . . How to fill the days, how to make life profitable and satisfying, how to adjust yourself to a climate from which there is no escape, no let up, no time ahead when it will be cooler, more bearable. It is the monotony, partly, that gets on your nerves.[38]

The effect of the tropics on the nervous system was taken very seriously in the inter-war period. Health and education became public issues. In 1929 a prominent Federal Councillor protested, 'If you strip the ladies of their lip-stick and their face powder, who do you get? You see women entirely worn out. You see their health breaking up . . .'[39]

Some respite in the form of weekends by the sea or trips to hill stations was needed both for anaemic-looking wives and for leggy children fighting prickly heat and other ailments. Parents were also anxious about the effect of lassitude on their children's learning. In their early years children were often taught by their mother or by a neighbour. The Barnes boys had lessons with the daughters of Mrs Nankivell, a trained teacher and wife of a Public Works Department engineer near Malacca. Until she was eight, Ray Soper learned at home.

> My mother taught us for a couple of years using the P.N.E.U. [Parents' National Education Union] Correspondence course which came out from England. We had school in the mornings, myself and Momoy Low from next door. We put the small table and chairs in the carport and also a blackboard. We made models of wigwams and used plasticine. How I struggled with 'Songs the Letters Sing' (a phonetic reading system), and why Australia, though entirely surrounded by water, was a continent and not an island! When I did master reading, I went on to a reading series with Dick, Jane and Rover the dog. Some of the books had stories in them such as Henny Penny.[40]

As the result of constant contact with their *amahs*, toddlers learned to speak pidgin Malay even before they were fluent in English. Mothers sometimes had to take in hand the learning of correct speech. John and Peter Kelley were taught to read English (and also to speak it) by their mother, using a little Malayan primer illustrated with scenes of Malay life.[41] A hotchpotch of comics and books – *Chick's Own Paper, Pip, Squeak and Wilfred's Annual, Mother Goose's Nursery Rhymes* – or old copies of *Punch* and the *Straits Times* gave reading practice to a rubber planter's family; science consisted of watching fauna in the garden. 'Our education suffered dreadfully. Occasionally Mother had a vague dab at it.'[42]

All arrangements undoubtedly had drawbacks, and, with inter-ruptions for leave, few children enjoyed much continuity in their early education. Planters were warned, 'Parents who can afford the great expense have, as soon as possible after the infant stage has been passed, to send their children Home to school. The separation is a cruel thing . . . It is one of the tragedies of life in the East for Europeans.'[43] One option was to attend local mixed-race mission schools. In 1929 Robert Oliver, whose father was in the Post and Telegraphs Department, went at the age of five to St Mary's School in Kuala Lumpur. 'Another little boy and I were the only whites in the class. All the rest were Chinese and Malays. Like most primary schools at that time it was run by a religious order.'[44] The actress Dulcie Gray was also a pupil at St Mary's for two terms, during which she passed her School Certificate. Dulcie was the only European girl there, but 'I made special friends with a Chinese girl, the daughter of Sir Chu Kia Peng [*sic*], and went to her magnificent home in Kuala Lumpur. A beautiful Indian girl called Jaya was another friend.'[45] However, some parents found the mission schools unsatisfactory. The Barneses of Malacca and the Prices of Penang withdrew their sons from Catholic convents run by French nuns. There were additionally private schools about which little is now known, but Derick Cullen attended Tomlinson Hall School, Singapore, run by his Aunt Molly. After four years' schooling in England a planter's son attended a small school in Penang run by the Revd Greer, with half a dozen other European children. Some British parents preferred a boarding school at Kaban Djahe in Sumatra, which was run by a husband-and-wife team, the Cooksons, both teachers. Among the British pupils were the children of medical doctors, and the school was also popular with Americans working in the oil industry.

After 1939 a fair number of English children from Malaya and Singapore were sent to private schools in Australia, and their adventures in transit on Blue Funnel's little ships *Centaur*, *Gorgon* and *Charon* make a fascinating story. However, the establishment of private schools in the Malayan hill stations during the 1930s greatly improved educational prospects. The first was St Margaret's Church of England School at Fraser's Hill, which Jette Rawcliffe and her sister Sheila attended, and where Dulcie Gray's sister, Rosamund Savage-Bailey, was a teacher. A low white-washed bungalow with a red corrugated-iron roof, overlooking the jungle treetops, it was, as Dulcie recalled, 'ugly to look at and ordinary, but it was set in paradise'.[46] There were twenty-six pupils there, mostly boarders, aged from four to fourteen, and the teachers found themselves acting as nursemaids and housemothers too. A successful Brownie pack, which the Savage-Baileys helped to run, was started in 1932. In the mid-1930s Rosamund moved on to Cameron Highlands and St Margaret's was bought by a kindly and determined Scotswoman, and when Christopher Watkins, aged six, was sent there it had become known as Mrs Davidson's School.

When the Cameron Highlands were developed in the early 1930s the choice became wider. The Catholic Church had shown an early interest in acquiring land in the Highlands, and with wealthy backers a convent boarding school – an attractive building in Flemish style, the Pensionnat Notre Dame – was built on the lower plateau at Tanah Rata. Open to children of both sexes and all denominations, its numbers increased from twenty-seven in 1935 to 300 by 1940. The official opening on 1 May 1935 was attended by the English planter Henry Malet and his wife, whose daughters, Susan and Jennifer, were among the initial intake. Meanwhile another boarding school had been established on the higher plateau of the Cameron Highlands. The school's founder, Miss Anne Griffith-Jones, came from an old colonial family and had experience of running a nursery school at Tanglin Club in Singapore. Known universally as 'Miss Griff', she possessed a restless energy and great efficiency. Inevitably there was some rivalry between the two institutions. In their brown-and-gold uniforms, Miss Griff's pupils were easily distinguished from the convent children, who wore blue and grey, and the two groups were nicknamed the 'Blue Beetles' and the 'Yellow Cockroaches'.

The new Tanglin School employed Froebel-trained teachers from England and, with a hundred boarding pupils, soon acquired a good reputation, although its single-storeyed wooden buildings were low-cost compared with those of the convent. Maureen Fairchild, whose father, the Executive Engineer for Pahang, had been responsible for overseeing the construction of both schools, was one of the first pupils. Tanglin claimed that 'children are educated up to the age of thirteen and are prepared for common entrance examination, so that they can pass directly into public schools in England. The fees are $300 per term.'[47] Music tuition was an extra, and one pupil remembers:

> I used to have riding lessons in a clearing in the jungle; we went down a path with long steps, past trees festooned with orchids and venus fly traps; there were many different brightly coloured butterflies. A similar path led down to an area where we each had a tiny garden; the best gardens were those in the tree roots.[48]

The pupils also went on a Sunday-morning walk along jungle trails. The liberal curriculum but traditional Anglican ethos appealed to Protestant parents. Teachers such as Miss Delaney, Miss Furze and Miss Grey were much respected, as was the athletic Miss Raine, whose coaching stimulated William Vowler's cricket skills: 'She taught me how to play with a straight bat,' he recalled. Miss Griff herself was held in universal awe, and 'always spoken of with respectful affection by my parents', Gordon Snell remembers.[49]

However, going to boarding school, whether in Malaya, Sumatra, Australia or England, could prove traumatic to little ones. Separation from family, friends, servants and beloved pets was hard to bear, underlining the transience and insecurity of colonial life. Susan Malet was only four years old when she was sent to the Cameron Highlands, her sister Jennifer six. Boys as young as five and six were taken back to school in England and Scotland. Some were stoical about it: 'I suppose I was upset, briefly, when my parents left me at boarding school at the age of seven but I had been brought up always knowing it would happen.'[50] Others later in life recognized the emotional damage; at the time they wept repeatedly or stifled the loneliness and learned not to get too close to anyone.

The development of the hill stations did not eliminate all problems. Health hazards remained, and the Cameron Highlands schools were temporarily closed in 1941 when infantile paralysis struck a number of children. Down on the plains it was still possible to catch malaria or dengue fever from mosquitoes (as Kathleen Price found to her cost). The monsoon rains and fierce 'sumatra' storms regularly caused flooding in streets and homes, after which everything – clothes, shoes, books, furnishings – had to be dried and aired. Occasionally, as in the Great Pahang Flood of Christmas 1926 – when large parts of the state were submerged under 163 feet of water and one man remembered how he 'sailed over Kuantan, sailed over Pahang, sailed over Malaya!'[51] – there was serious damage and dislocation. That, however, was exceptional.

In jungle areas, danger still lurked. In 1934–5, when the Watkins family was stationed at Kuala Lipis, Pahang, they lived on the edge of town. Christopher Watkins recalled how as a four-year-old he

> would often hear tigers in the garden at night and find their spoor the next day. My mother was worried that they would catch the dogs or, worse, chase them into the house. She had strong iron mesh made from quarter inch material, put on all the windows. In those days we often saw tigers in the car headlights when we were driving after dusk.[52]

In Malacca, too, sometimes the Barnes family were advised not to visit friends on rubber estates, after some estate workers had been killed by a tiger. Most families had their 'snake' stories and tales of lucky escapes from kraits and cobras. Even in the relative safety of Singapore, Christopher Cannell remembered 'an incident of a huge black spider in the dining room when I was quickly ushered out' and 'a lot of fuss because they found a cobra on the driveway'.[53] In Malacca the Barnes boys received constant warnings about snakes, but it came as a surprise when 'One hot, heavily overcast afternoon . . . a large cobra came into the house. It mounted the coconut matting covered stairs, and coiled itself up outside the door of the bedroom which Ken and I shared.' The yell of 'Ular! Ular!' brought Father on the scene, bearing a niblick: 'the result was one mangled and very dead cobra and a triumphant pater familias'. When a spot of snake's blood fell on Geoffrey's foot, 'I recall the thrill of doubt: could cobra's blood poison me?'[54]

At Fraser's Hill, Christopher Watkins had a close shave with a potentially poisonous Mata Hari or Sealingwax Snake. 'I remember running down the path one day and nearly stepping on a very bright, beautiful snake . . . For most of its length it was a bright metallic blue but about nine inches at each end were vermilion.'[55] It was also called the Two-headed Snake, because 'when alarmed it raised its head about 3″ high and also its tail, and so to an enemy presented a puzzle: which end was its head? which way would it go?'[56] It was customary to pickle snakes in *samsu* (rice spirit) – the Chinese believed in the medicinal properties of cobras, for instance – and for Christopher Watkins the pharmacy at Fraser's Hill 'was a fascinating place . . . It had shelves full of specimens in jars of methylated spirits or formaldehyde. I remember a human embryo about six inches long, a huge bullfrog and any number of snakes.'[57]

Parents usually took care to shield their children from undesirable or lurid sights (such as cases of *latah* or scenes of self-immolation associated with the religious festival Thaipusam). Surrounded as they were by exotica, the European children of Malaya faced surreal situations with a mixture of awe, fear and phlegm. A former boarder in the Cameron Highlands, Anthony Pybus, remembered 'the whole school going to look at a tiger in a wheelbarrow after it had been shot for marauding livestock'.[58] At Tengkil, in the wilds of Johore, four-year-old John Edington saw 'the body of one of my father's horses lying on its side with its tongue hanging out', and 'a large black boar lying in its own blood which was being licked up by the local pie-dogs'. More horrendous was the sight at Lingui tin mine of 'a Chinese man carrying the head of his wife by the hair which he had cut off and was reporting . . . to my father together with the gruesome exhibit. Anyway, the poor fellow was duly convicted and hanged.'[59] For another child, an incident at a fair on Fraser's Hill struck a deep chord.

> One of the acts was a wandering magician; an Indian, perhaps a Tamil. He was fully dressed. He called another Indian, almost certainly his henchman, out of the crowd. This one was wearing only a loincloth. The magician took out a small doll and broke it. Inside was a ball of string about the size of a golf ball which he made his henchman swallow. The string was multicoloured with the colours continually changing along its length. The henchman disappeared into the crowd but was hauled back some time later. He put on a great show of terror when he saw that the magician was holding a dramatically large, sharp pointed knife, but eventually he had to submit to having the skin of his stomach nicked in the area of the appendix. You could see everything that happened very easily because he was wearing so little. The magician then proceeded to pull out yards of string through the wall of the man's stomach as he stood there. I remember vividly the colour of the string changing as it emerged, and the way the man's skin was drawn outwards as it resisted the passage of the string. It may have been a case of hypnosis but it was the most dramatic conjuring trick I have ever seen.[60]

It was not unknown for small children to feel frightened by this kind of situation. Many years before, Lillian Newton had been terrified by the tricks of an Indian juggler and snake charmer, and five-year-old Margaret Price always avoided looking at the Tamil *kebun* because his mouth flowed red with betel nut.

The relationship between the servants and the children was inevitably quite different from that of the servants with *Mem* or *Tuan*. A boy was referred to by the servants as either *Tuan Kechil* or *Kechil Tuan*, literally Little Lord, but the word *Kechil* was frequently corrupted into 'Kechy' or 'Kichy'. A girl was called simply *Missee* – little miss. Young children generally admired and looked up to a kind servant. 'Cookie was my favourite,' one recalled. 'He was a small, spare man with cropped hair, all pepper and salt, and sinewy arms' and 'a gummy toothless grin', and when he rested in the hammock 'there was a look on his face as peaceful as a lotus pool'.[61] He also made excellent battered *ikan merah* (fish) and crisp prawn fritters and potato straws for *Missee*. The Watkins's Chinese cook produced models out of mashed potato to please Christopher. 'The snake curled round a rock was a relatively tame example but the motor car was a *pièce de résistance*.'[62] Geoffrey Barnes relished Ah Fong's special sherry trifle, fish cakes and 'delicious bacon and onion omelettes'.[63] William Vowler remembers to this day the names of the family servants: his *amah* was Ah Sui, Josephine was the wash *amah*, 'Lightning' the 'boy', Ah Cheng the cook and Ismael the *syce*. Occasional bouts of domestic discord in the servants' quarters (as between cook and *amah*, husband and wife) puzzled these children, who felt loyalty to both. 'I remember nothing but kindness from [the servants] but Amah and Syce were the only ones I was at all close to,' admitted Gordon Snell. Syce's special attraction was as driver of their Vauxhall car – 'which had those whitewalled tyres and a "dicky seat" and the registration number 4187'.[64] Margaret Price also remembered the Malay *syce* who taught her to count in Malay.

Strong bonds of affection and familiarity were formed in babyhood. Gordon Snell's *amah* in Singapore was 'a Malayan woman of whom I was very fond and I remember tearful tantrums when we were leaving and I would be separated from her'.[65] The Cullen family felt much affection for their *amah*, who was 'very loving and close'. 'There was an annual giving of presents', which Derick Cullen remembered, 'usually money from us, awful ties from her, but my mother was very attached to her.'[66] Geoffrey Barnes's experience was shared by many born in Malaya:

From birth I was put in the care of our Chinese amah whom I knew simply as 'Amah' . . . She was probably in her thirties at the time. She had a plain, kindly face, long shining black hair, which she always fastened decorously in a bun at the back of her head, and wore the traditional amah's uniform of white tunic and black trousers. Amah was our frequent companion, nurse and mentor. She bathed and dressed us, supervised our meals at the small separate table . . . in the dining room, took us for walks in the garden and along the dusty, red, laterite roads . . . She often accompanied us to birthday parties or on outings with our parents.[67]

Many *amahs* prided themselves on their sewing and laundering skills, and spent hours pressing out creases and making shantung or lawn dresses for *Missee*, with deep bands of coloured embroidery across the bodice. Relationships were forged in the many hours a child spent in Amah's company. The Sopers' Chinese *amah*, Ah Chat, a friendly soul, often took Ray and her younger brother John in their rompers and topees to paddle on Butterworth shore. They dug up *siputs* (tiny molluscs), which Amah boiled for her dinner. A minority of children might have sensed that they were privileged compared with these servants: 'I remember thinking how different our lives were and wondered how it would be to live in their one room dwelling,' said Ray Soper.[68] But more common was Gordon Snell's attitude: 'I suppose as a child I simply accepted (as the adults did) that we had a retinue of people to see to our needs.'[69] Parents *did* worry about the danger of a child 'becoming selfish, spoiled and generally objectionable'. The worst, according to Leslie Froggatt, were 'those babies who learn to shout "Boy!" during their first two years'.[70]

Childhood diets and routines were devised by the *mem* but largely implemented by Amah. Fresh milk could be a problem away from the towns, where supplies from government dairy farms or the Cold Storage were available. Up-country, families used condensed milk or one of the powdered-milk preparations, such as KLIM, which came in tall brown tins with yellow writing. Breakfast, consisting of fresh fruit, was often eaten with parents; other meals were taken separately in the nursery tradition. 'We had a paw-paw tree in the garden, and luscious papayas were a fruit I recall with mouth-watering delight,' wrote Gordon Snell; other family favourites included pineapples, mangosteens, rambutans, mangoes, custard apples, passion fruit and bananas.[71] 'The durian', on the other hand, 'you either liked or hated; as a child I hated it,' observed Roger Barrett.[72] (He was not alone; the smell, a mixture of onions and rotten eggs, was enough to make many a European retch.) The other family meal was curry tiffin on Sundays – 'generally a lavish affair', in Norman Price's recollection.[73] 'Loved it and still do,' wrote Roger Barrett, and 'I still like a good curry,' agreed Christopher Cannell.[74] According to hallowed tradition, curry *makan* was followed by *gula malacca*, a sweet tapioca goo, served with coconut milk and palm sugar – altogether an unforgettable experience.

The lack of relatives in Malaya enhanced the importance of friends and neighbours, who became in many ways as close, or closer, than blood relations. This gave rise to the convention whereby children called all adult friends 'Uncle' or 'Auntie'. Household pets helped to ward off boredom and filled the role of an extended family. 'My father was known as St Francis as he collected strays almost daily,' said Susan Malet.[75] Dogs and cats abounded in European homes – scruffy kampong creatures and mongrels of every size and colour, cherished equally with Siamese, tabbies, terriers, Dalmatians, setters, Alsatians and cocker spaniels, not to mention chicks and ducklings, budgerigars, rabbits, goldfish, and the occasional monkey, baby owl, tortoise, terrapin and mongoose. In Butterworth, Dr Low kept snakes as pets to the apprehension of the Soper family. Recollections of the inter-war years had a special place for Tufty, Sooty, Titi, Billy, Sammy, Bonzo, Ginger, Peter, Sandy, Chips, Jock, Paddy, Budu, Rufus, Buster and countless other adored companions.

A daily walk was *de rigueur* in many households (supplemented at about seven years by the bike), and exploring, climbing and playing on swings and seesaws filled many a happy hour in the garden or at the club. Swimming was especially popular. Geoffrey Barnes recounted, 'Ken and I learnt to swim [at Tanjong Kling] when we were only two or three years old.'[76] Gordon Snell confirmed, 'We children learned to swim at the earliest possible age – in fact I can't even remember learning.'[77] He and his friend Christopher Cannell from Singapore's Adam Park went regularly to Singapore Swimming Club, where Christopher had swimming and diving lessons, and even as a young child had no fear of the top board. Christopher Watkins learnt to swim in the reservoir at Kuala Lipis at four or five. Norman Price lived close enough to frequent Penang Swimming Club at Tanjong Bungah, where children's treats included 'Eskimo Pies' – chocolate-coated ice cream – and fizzy Fraser & Neave orangeade costing twenty cents a bottle in 1939. For less fortunate children who lived inland, an excursion to the beach was an occasional treat, as was a weekend up Penang Hill or at one of the main hill stations.

Fun for *Missee* and *Tuan Kechil* was a mirror image of their parents' social life. Birthdays, Christmas, Empire Day were all opportunities for children's parties and dressing up in fancy dress as favourite nursery-rhyme or fairy-tale characters. Amah would be there as escort; sometimes mothers were invited for afternoon tea in time to watch the party games or the conjuror's performance. 'One of our exciting entertainments was home movies,' Gordon Snell recalled. 'My father had an eight-millimetre camera so we could see films of ourselves running, jumping, clowning – and also cartoons: the black-and-white image of Felix the Cat is still a laughing memory from those drawing room shows.'[78] Snow White and Shirley Temple were the favourite images of the girls. The coronation on Empire Day, 12 May, 1937 was an unforgettable occasion, with hundreds of celebrations and children's parties. 'I remember the . . . parades for King George VI and Queen Elizabeth, and troops and police in white uniforms parading on the Malacca waterfront,' said Geoffrey Barnes. 'We were given various Coronation mementoes, mugs, handkerchiefs and medals with red, white and blue ribbons.'[79] 'The roundabout at Fraser's Hill was a mass of flowers,' Jette Rawcliffe remembered.[80] For Margaret Price the coronation meant a new white frilly organdie dress with a red, white and blue sash. 'I remember going over to Penang to see the fireworks, the decorations: lots of Chinese lanterns, and the bands,' said Ray Soper.[81] 'We celebrated the Coronation at the Runneymede Hotel,' Susan Malet recalled. 'We children were allowed to stay up late, which made it a very special occasion.'[82]

In reality, however, imperialism was outside a child's comprehension. As one ex-Malayan said, 'In our small lives there was little to cause us to question our role or presence' in the scheme of things.[83] In some cases, colonial privilege had no meaning until the children returned to Britain and felt the drab contrast with Malaya. 'Childhood in Singapore was very happy,' was Gordon Snell's recollection.[84] Another of that inter-war generation recalled 'the general experience of a happy, indulged childhood, really – how lucky!'[85] 'Pre-war, children had an idyllic life,' echoed a third.[86] 'A *wonderful* childhood!' This, for the British, was the irreversible blessing of Malaya. 'From my youth, the *wonderful,* carefree life on estates, the happiness of my childhood . . . Sunshine, servants, *wonderful* memories.'[87]

PART III

*The Long Retreat*
*1940–1960*

# II

# *The Unprepared Society*

Despite the façade of peace and plenty in Malaya, the 1930s were a period of increasing international tension. 'Reading about war . . . was one of the daily occupations of mankind. Talking about war and about the imminence or the chances of a general war was another,' declared *The Times*'s review of the year 1937.[1] In the East, Japanese forces had occupied Manchuria in 1931 before turning on Mongolia and China's northern frontier, while in the West in 1936 Spain had dissolved into civil strife. The Barretts, rubber planters in Kedah, left Malaya in 1936 on home leave aboard the German luxury liner *Potsdam*, calling at Barcelona, the centre of Catalan separatism, as the Spanish Civil War erupted: a curious odyssey mapping the approaching global conflict. Their six-year-old son Roger noticed and long remembered how 'this German ship already had mountings ready for guns in the event of war'.[2] That year Japan joined Germany in an Anti-Comintern Pact. In 1937, after alleged 'Red' attacks on Japanese property were blown up into a full-scale 'Incident', Japanese troops poured into China's eastern provinces, launching the Sino-Japanese War on 7 July 1937.

In Malaya, anti-Japanese feeling intensified at these events, and the Chinese community in Singapore formed an Association for the Relief of Refugees in China, presided over by the influential entrepreneur Tan Kah Kee. Yet the British response to Japan's aggression was ambivalent. The Anglo-Japanese alliance of the Great War had been allowed to lapse in 1923, and Japanese withdrawal in the 1930s from the League of Nations and from international disarmament agreements was viewed seriously by the British Cabinet. Consequently work on Malaya's airfields and defences, including the new Singapore naval base, was accelerated. However, concurrently, 'the policy of H. M. Government in the period 1935–40 [was] to abstain from any action likely to embarrass relations with Tokyo', and even when the Japanese overran the populous Chinese cities of Canton and Hankow in 1938 the colonial authorities saw Communism as more immediately threatening than the Japanese.[3] Labour problems, including strikes during January and February 1940 and an illegal May Day rally in Singapore, were regarded as evidence of Communist subversion, and were firmly dealt with; at the same time, anti-Japanese activity was suppressed.

The government's compliant attitude towards Japan was not shared by British Malayans, who tended to speak pejoratively of the Japanese.[4] The Japanese community in Malaya – over 3,000 in 1931, and at least 4,000 in 1940 – was secretive and self-contained. In the townships, the Japanese monopolized certain businesses. In addition to providing the 'Marys', who had long satisfied European lusts (before their trade was stopped by the Japanese government), the Japanese immigrants dealt 'mostly in teeth and photographs, haircuts and sukiyaki'.[5] The British community harboured racial stereotypes of the cunning yellow peril and disdain for a race which produced cheap, imitative products. Conversely, while travelling in Japan in 1921, Maurice Glover, later the editor of the *Malaya Tribune*, had observed Japanese resentment of 'all things white' and 'was often conscious of hidden antipathy and dislike'.[6] In preferring the Chinese, another Englishman in Singapore reflected the general view among Britons in the colony. He admired Chinese self-control in dealing with Japanese commercial rivals ('I know they hated the Japs') and their successful boycott of Japanese trades and goods.

> The Chinaman is an honest rogue – with him it is a battle of wits, and you have an even chance, but there's something incalculable about the Jap. He's altogether too humble and respectful considering how he hates you, and the way he bows and sucks his teeth as you approach is in every way revolting . . .
>
> After 1938 I didn't drink any more Japanese beer or fill my bowl with sukiyaki from the pan. I didn't watch the Geisha girls dance with a fan, or play at strip-tease to the tune of a mandolin. These and other pleasures, I gave up, not from any personal animosity, but because I loved the Chinese, and was indignant over the Japanese invasion of their country.[7]

With hindsight, it seems extraordinary that after Japan's onslaught on China the British government took no firm, concerted action with the other interested nations – France, the Netherlands and the United States – to negotiate a joint guarantee of their Far Eastern territories against Japanese aggression. The expansionist ambitions of imperial Japan were no secret. Singapore officials had been 'fully conscious of the threat from Japan during the Great War',[8] and Japan's grand design to dominate the South Seas, stimulated by a culture of militarism and by the decisions of the Washington Conference of 1921, had been leaked to the world in the Tanaka Memorial of 1929. The conquest of China was intended to be a prelude to the expulsion of the white colonial races from South-East Asia, India and Australasia. So again it seems paradoxical that as late as December 1939 Churchill at the Admiralty still doubted whether 'the Japanese would embark on such a mad enterprise', and early in 1940 both the Governor, Shenton Thomas, and the Foreign Office advocated that Malaya's economy should take precedence over strategic defence requirements, since the Imperial Japanese Army 'was not strong enough to go to war with the British Empire'.[9] Whitehall, it appears, ignored the evidence that Japanese penetration of Malaya's economy was both extensive and politically subversive. The penetration covered many fields, from industry and trade to propaganda and labour relations. A visiting journalist in 1935 noted 'the potential menace of Japanese conquest and the already existing menace of Japanese trade competition', which raised the spectre of a head-on clash 'if the British Empire is to survive'.[10] The British government's failure to act in the East as well as in Europe was, in the opinion of a Singapore resident, the long-term result of the uneasy union of appeasement and pacifism.

The concentration of the Japanese in certain areas, notably in the Unfederated Malay States, was a subject of public comment. Japanese holdings tended to be at key road and rail junctions, in the mining districts of Trengganu and Kelantan, and in a concessionary arc around Batu Pahat and Kota Tinggi, Johore, from which they gained a detailed knowledge of strategic sites which was later to prove critical. Already, in 1935, Bruce Lockhart had noted how 'every second day, a Japanese steamer goes out from Batu Pahat carrying away from under our very noses the ore which Japan lacks in her own country, and which she doubtless uses for some form of naval or military armament'.[11] Japanese prospecting had also opened up a lucrative trade in manganese, bauxite and wolfram, all used in armaments production. By the late 1930s Malaya's export trade in iron ore to Japan exceeded 2 million tons per year. An English couple confirmed how this trade was allowed by the authorities to continue up to the approach of the Pacific War. In November 1940 Alfred and Nancy Wynne were holidaying in the government bungalow at Endau on the Pahang–Johore border when they were awakened by a loud noise. 'All night long motor boats were pulling strings of barges along the river carrying iron ore to a ship anchored off the bar. We met the captain, Norwegian, and the engineer, British (Welsh, Alfred thought) in Mersing and they had just arrived from Vladivostock and were taking ore to Japan.'[12]

Meanwhile several organizations, such as the Japanese Chamber of Commerce and the Commercial Museum in Singapore, served as cover for political activities. They worked in tandem with a network of Japanese companies, headed by the Nissan group and the Ishihara Sangyo Kaiun Kabushiki Kaisha (ISKKK), with its Singapore subsidiary, the Southern Godown Company, which was involved in the notorious Kaseda–Kizaki espionage case of 1934.[13] Japan operated a multifarious system of political warfare. In 1934–5 a number of prominent Malays, including members of the Johore ruling family, were invited to Japan on official visits in attempts to curry favour. Return goodwill tours of Malaya by Japanese officials served as cover for intelligence gathering. Japan's fishermen, nosing their way among the estuaries and creeks of Malaya's coastline, performed a similar function on behalf of the Japanese navy. Informants also came from the ranks of Asian labour on Japanese-controlled estates. On the eve of the Pacific War the British swooped on a secret organization called KAME, which, allied with the Malay Youth Union, had forged a fifth column among middle-class Malays in the Unfederated States of Kedah, Perlis, Kelantan and Trengganu. Information on Japanese espionage was collected by the Special Branch of the Straits Settlement Police, but, as one expert admitted, it was impossible to know how much went undetected.

Rumours of Japanese activities were commonplace as early as 1934. Secret fortifications and armaments were found sited on the Japanese-owned Pengerang Rubber Estate in Johore, uncomfortably close to the Singapore naval base. Talk of Japanese spies operating in the guise of barbers, photographers and planters circulated in European circles during the 1930s.[14] In Sitiawan, 'The local Jap barber, obsequious and kow-towing . . . built himself a little shop overlooking the aerodrome where he had a perfect view of its total lack of defence,' Katharine Sim remembered.[15] 'We were, I suppose, a little complacent,' added Leslie Froggatt, knowing that 'the Japs were there too, measuring the swamps and the jungles, the beaches and the bays, watching, working, never relaxing in their preparation for our destruction.'[16] Sometimes encounters reached the English press, but to avoid a political 'incident' most espionage agents were quietly expelled from Malaya in the pre-war years. However, Japan learned the propaganda value of the press: the Eastern News Agency was established in Singapore in October 1938, followed six months later by a Japanese-owned newspaper, the *Singapore Herald*, to counter the *Tribune*. Thanks to the benevolent censorship in the colony, this low-cost paper, aimed at the English-speaking Asian community, was able to disseminate its bogus patriotic message up to the very outbreak of hostilities, reinforced from February 1941 by propaganda broadcasts from Tokyo and Taihoku purveying false news items to sow racial discord and undermine morale.

Although the colonial authorities were aware of the importance of propaganda, it was the Axis powers who were seen as the enemy, to the advantage of Japan. 'Every new addition to the defences was boosted. Photographs and articles on troops training were commonplace,' one official later commented.[17] One random example illustrates British naivety. A copy of the *Trengganu Government Gazette* intercepted in March 1941 on its way to a Japanese investigation bureau contained full details of recent defence exercises in Trengganu. At the centre of Japan's intelligence operations, espionage and fifth-column work was the Japanese Consulate-General in Singapore, an institution which grossly abused diplomatic privilege throughout the 1930s. The British, on the other hand, had limited resources for intelligence work and it was not until 1941 that a Civil Security Officer was appointed. Yet in 1939–40 the Secretary for Defence, Malaya, knew 'there were planters, miners and prospectors, foresters and game rangers who could send word of strange things which were happening in odd places', including 'an old Malay tracker friend who brought me news of Japanese activities in the northern frontier region'.[18] In 1940 a small band of civilians, run by the Chief Game Warden, E. O. Shebbeare, was sent on unofficial forays into Thailand (as Siam had now become) to assess Japanese activity. To the bitter chagrin of this Frontier Unit, the intelligence reports they sent to Singapore were ignored, and, the Secretary for Defence having been effectively dismissed in February 1941, the Unit was disbanded.[19] While Malaya lacked a coherent counter-espionage organization it could not hope to contain the Japanese threat.

The real concern of the British in Malaya after 1937 was the deteriorating situation in Europe. The Nazi threat was starkly revealed when Hitler's forces invaded Czechoslovakia in March 1938, and after much diplomatic manoeuvring stormed Poland on 1 September 1939. Two days later, their ultimatum rejected, Great Britain and France had no alternative but to declare war. The news reached Malaya by wireless at 5.45 p.m. that Sunday, 3 September 1939. Shenton Thomas and other prominent citizens were attending evensong at St Andrew's Cathedral. Marine engineer Leslie Froggatt and his wife, May, had a special reason for remembering that evening, for they had just attended the christening of the three-month-old daughter of some Singapore friends.

We were still drinking champagne . . . when Neville Chamberlain's fateful words came over the air, 'England is now at war.' The international atmosphere had been particularly tense for some days before that, and although Britain's decision for war was not unexpected, it nevertheless shook most of us there into a feeling of realism, and our thoughts went back to England . . . England at war once again![20]

In their bungalow in Lumut, the Sims also heard the broadcast.

Sadly we went down to the estuary and sat in the Rest House garden alone. We watched the sampans and *koleks* coming in against the sunset up the brilliant coloured river. It was so beautiful and peaceful it seemed impossible to believe we were at war at last. The frangipanni petals dropped to the grass one by one and lay there, creamy white and pure; a dog barked in the village . . . *This* was the only reality; this beauty.[21]

Most Britons went though the gamut of emotions as they adjusted to the news. For some the overriding reaction was 'agonizing worry about parents at home, and our minds were full of horrific pictures of raids and gas'.[22] Yet officialdom was symbolically reassuring. The following day the *Straits Times* – the '*Tuan's* paper' – thanked God that Britain was at war, and with sublime insouciance the editorial claimed, 'At this distance from the scene of battle, with our defences perfected and Japanese participation in the struggle on the side of Germany an extremely remote possibility, Malaya has little to fear.'[23] In a broadcast on 5 September the Governor departed from the tradition of 1914–18. He appealed to the people to stay at their posts and urged Europeans not to return to Britain to enlist. Subsequently John Soper of the colonial agricultural service interpreted the situation thus:

> September 1939 found Malaya in the throes of a slump: tin output was restricted to less than half of full capacity and rubber was little better . . . With the outbreak of war, however, there came the demand for American dollars and the realisation that Malayan tin and rubber would provide the best dollar arsenal we had. Both prices and export quotas began to rise, and by 1941 the country was enjoying the biggest boom it had known for years. In the wake of the American dollar the Straits dollar began to flow freely again. Patriotism with profit, the Elysian dream of the exploiter, came true with a vengeance.[24]

While people threw themselves into work and enjoyed unparalleled prosperity there was little interest in defence: 'war had not come to Malaya for a hundred years, so why should they worry about it now?'[25] On the other hand, some in Singapore did sense that they were living in the Indian summer of colonialism:

> We could still lie in the sun as the clean white cumulus drifted by, we could still watch the lightning crack through the sky at night . . . We could still play golf at five, drink to the setting sun, and dance as the moon came up over the palms. We could still sit in a crowd at a cinema, we could watch a cricket match, and mingle with the masses of Asiatics [*sic*] who crowded the streets. We could still enjoy life without fear. And yet I know there were some amongst us who felt a certain qualm of uneasiness, that we, on the outside edge of the Empire, could enjoy still the things that England had so willingly put aside.[26]

For a while fears were lulled as the European war went through its 'phoney' phase. If anything, the suspense broke down old social inhibitions. Nancy Wynne, young and recently arrived from England, was surprised how approachable her husband's superiors were. Referring to one of the wives, she added, 'I like her very much, she is very friendly and like most people here she has no "airs". There is very little snobbery.'[27] If one event shocked the European community and brought people together it was the sinking of the *Rawalpindi* on 23 November

1939 by the German warships *Scharnhorst* and *Gneisenau*. The heroic end of this once elegant P. & O. liner was mourned in Malaya. Many knew her like an old friend on the Far East run. Meanwhile, the British sent home food parcels to relatives and friends, and a few began growing their own vegetables. 'I am going to knit for the navy,' Nancy Wynne assured her parents. 'I have finished a balaclava helmet and half a pull-over.'[28] Elsewhere, in Penang and Singapore life continued normally, with picnics, parties and subscription concerts. Again, Nancy Wynne was in cheerful form:

> We are getting a good deal of tennis . . . this is a very easy-going country . . . Singapore is a marvellous place to go . . . Mr and Mrs Emmett gave us a grand time in the big city. They took us swimming in the S[inga-pore] S[wimming] Club . . . It is a fine place and they serve excellent food. The second night we went to the Airport Hotel for dinner and ate fresh strawberries flown from Australia.[29]

It was when the tempo of the conflict in Europe changed dramatically in the early summer of 1940 that the colonial community understood the meaning of war. Until that point 'we were still preoccupied with our peace', one man admitted.[30]

> On May 10 1940, the Bishop of Singapore came to Sitiawan [in Perak] to take the Whitsun monthly services. Nearly the whole district, about 25 people, turned out for evensong . . . It was then we heard the first rumour of the invasion of Holland . . . the news stunned us . . . The 'phoney war' was over, we were all now intensely conscious of the reality: Brussels, Amsterdam, Luxembourg, so near to England . . . The heat and oppression of that terrible night weighed like lead; the threat to England was now clear; fear clutched us.[31]

But there was worse to come: in June, France fell.

That day will never be forgotten. The shock that England suffered sent out vibrating waves right to the very corners of the Empire, so that even in Malaya, so many miles away, we felt the tremors, and were afraid. Our first thought was for England, abandoned and alone, and in such deadly peril. We read of the plight of the BEF [British Expeditionary Force] in France, exposed to every kind of humiliation and defeat. We followed them in their desperate trial of Dunkirk, we watched in suspense their miraculous deliverance from what had seemed most certain death. We waited for the invasion of Britain as anxiously as if our own soil would be attacked and, with bated breath, we heard the Churchill speech of blood, toil and sweat. We suffered through the Battle of Britain, and we knew that the life of England and the colonies depended on the inde-structible courage of those 'so few'. It was agony to be so far away and so helpless.[32]

'Whose blood, sweat and tears?' asked another bemused Malayan. 'The tears we could share; but we felt more than ever conscious of our inactivity.'[33]

There was one group of European men for whom the new situation was infinitely worrying: those whose wives and children were still in Britain. There had been something of a rush home in 1939 to beat the uncertainty and settle children in boarding school, but after the fall of France this trend went into reverse. Some returned to Malaya during the Phoney War. Deck games and swimming pools gave way to the pri-ority of life jackets and lifeboat drill. But once the Mediterranean was closed to British shipping, the choice seemed stark: to face the dangers of Britain at war or to risk mines, U-boats and surface raiders on the long and dangerous voyage back East. Eric Froggatt, rising eight, left England in June 1940, travelling in the Captain's care via the Cape of Good Hope aboard the steamship *Ascanius* to join his parents in Singapore. Ken and Geoffrey Barnes travelled by the same route, leaving in July on the P. & O. ship *Viceroy of India*, their voyage always being associated with their guardian's favourite tune, 'Over the Rainbow' from *The Wizard of Oz*. William Vowler, in a party of forty children, sailed from the Clyde in Blue Funnel's *Sarpedon* in the charge of Captain Nelson and two nurses. A strict regime was enforced; the evacuees had to carry their passports and money in waist belts at all times. Henry Malet left his daughters Susan and Jennifer with friends in the safety of Mauritius in 1940, although they later moved to Cape Town with their mother.

Mabel Price decided to risk the Atlantic crossing with her two young sons. It was a brave decision, for in September the *City of Benares*, carrying ninety child evacuees to Canada, would be torpedoed with only thirteen survivors. However, in July the Prices left Liverpool on a Cunard liner, accompanied by a strange 'ghost ship' and a destroyer. Mother and son told the story. 'We sailed in convoy to Canada. Our ship suffered slight damage by a torpedo attack in the Atlantic.' 'The ship shuddered which was frightening . . . One evening about two days out to sea we noticed the destroyer was no longer with us, nor was the ghost ship, and the feeling of depression overtook the passengers. On awakening one morning we were astonished to see icebergs not far off and we realised how far north we had sailed to avoid any more trouble.' 'We travelled by rail from Montreal to Vancouver where we were met by my Father,' Norman Price recalled, 'returning across the Pacific via Auckland and Sydney.' Much to their surprise, the 'ghost ship' reappeared in Sydney harbour: it had been carrying to Australia re-calcitrant prisoners of war, who had to be held below deck. 'Whilst crossing the Tasman [Sea] it was rumoured that a German "raider" was in the area [having already sunk their sister ship], so we flew by Empire C class flying-boat to Penang.'[34]

In Malaya, fund-raising measures had already been initiated:

A Patriotic Fund devoted to war charities was started and well sup-ported: it was soon followed by a War Fund from which gifts to the Imperial Exchequer were made for conducting the war, and this again attracted considerable contributions. All through the country the women organized sewing parties and purchased the materials from their own contributions. There was a rush to subscribe to the War Loans.[35]

The Patriotic Fund received contributions from all the racial com-munities. A leading Ipoh barrister organized the Fund in Perak: John Woods sold home-made jigsaws and his own knitted goods to raise money, while his wife, Lydia, worked in a 'Wool and Sewing Depot' in the town, boasting that 'we sent home 13,000 garments in the last batch (3 weeks' work)'.[36] Nancy Wynne was another worker. 'We went to Johore Bahru where I attended a meeting of the Patriotic Fund, Women's Section . . . We are making mosquito nets for the troops in the Middle East now, besides the knitting and hospital sewing . . . I am waiting for the material to start the same here.' January 1941 saw her 'very busy sewing for the Patriotic Fund' and also helping to organize a dance at the Masonic Hall in Segamat in aid of the War Fund. 'I think we raised about $1,200 which was quite good for such a small place . . . We made 500 sandwiches ourselves and begged curry puffs, sausage rolls and pork pies . . . Mrs Kennison and myself did the decorations. We used all her pot plants, lovely maiden hair ferns and jungle ferns, and masses of red and yellow cannas.'[37] April saw the launch of Salvage Week, when 'everybody is asked to bring all the waste paper, tinfoil, empty bottles and the like . . . The paper goes to India to be repulped, the metal will be offered to U.K. and what is not wanted there will be used here, the bottles go to the General Hospital.'[38]

Yet some felt that greater efforts could have been made. The generosity of the Malayan Chinese to the Patriotic Fund (to which the rickshaw owners gave $1,000) and to their own China Relief Fund showed how the Europeans lagged behind in their giving. Instead, 'the usual dances and tournaments were held, causing an enormous amount of expenditure on petrol and drinks which seemed not quite the right approach'.[39]

> Business was good and it was easy to be 'patriotic', but there was very little, if any, 'giving till it hurts', as was witnessed by the income tax controversy . . . It must have been toward the end of 1939 that H[is] E[xcellency] first suggested the introduction of this tax: it met with a howl of opposition from every business interest in the country. All manner of arguments were brought to bear against it . . . In the Federated Malay States it was confidently stated that even if the colony accepted the tax they would not, and all the Unfederated Malay States refused to have anything to do with it. After dropping the original bombshell, H.E. went home on leave to England . . . The opposition was allowed to vent its fury, boil over, and simmer down: then on his return from leave H.E. began a policy of quiet propaganda . . . Eventually the bills authorizing the tax passed more or less smoothly through both the Colony and F.M.S. Legislatures, much to the surprise of the rank and file in the country. The rates were not high . . . And so . . . the business, rubber and tin sections of the community managed, in spite of taxation and restrictions, to make a very good thing out of the war.[40]

During 1940, unknown to the public, the British Cabinet's thinking on the defence of Malaya underwent a critical change. Earlier strategies placed Malaya second in importance to the British Isles, but in the autumn of 1940 a statement of Malaya's defence needs by the Chiefs of Staff was surreptitiously overruled by Churchill, to be replaced by a new set of priorities deriving from the War Cabinet, abetted by Whitehall, putting Malaya below the Middle East and Russia. The heavy losses of men, planes and armour in France, at Dunkirk, and in the Battle of Britain, forced a reduction of Far Eastern defences. In Malaya and Australasia this policy switch was later considered to be a shameful breach of faith. Commitments to defend the whole of the Malay peninsula with 556 first-line aircraft and twenty-six battalions of troops were reduced in October 1940 to 336 aircraft and ancillary support such as anti-aircraft and motor torpedo boats, which would be in place by the end of 1941 (any deficiency in air reinforcements to be made up with ground forces). This was a landmark decision. The policy of defending all Malaya had been abandoned in favour of all-out defence of the fortress of Singapore with 160 obsolete or obsolescent planes, the equivalent of three and a half weak divisions, no tanks and too few guns. It was, as the furious Secretary for Defence in Singapore stated, a case of a plan that would be impossible to implement, 'for the defence of an imaginary country against an imaginary enemy with imaginary resources in circumstances which were quite unimaginable'.[41] The logical responsibility for Malaya's subsequent unpreparedness clearly rested with the British government, led by Winston Churchill, who later famously admitted, 'I ought to have known. My advisers ought to have known and I ought to have been told and I ought to have asked.'[42]

In the meantime, with the coming of New Year 1941, the European civilian population faced other changes calmly. Petrol was rationed, and there were the inevitable grumbles at the club over the rising cost of living and tax increases on beer, whisky and cigarettes. The first trial blackouts had been held before the end of 1940. Unexpected difficulties hit a trial run in Perak when the Malay kampong involved was lit up by the mass light of fireflies; others complained privately of the problems of blacking out open-plan bungalows. But in Singapore 'we became accustomed to the siren. We even treated the blackout trials as fun, and got into the way of throwing what we called "Blackout parties" – soup, sandwiches and sausages rolls, eaten under a dim lamp hanging so low that only a little of the table shone under its light, and the whole of the room was in darkness.'[43] People learned to combine duty and pleasure. Singapore's cinemas were packed, as George Formby, Vivien Leigh, Deanna Durban, Anna Neagle and Gary Cooper kept audiences entertained. Alex Cullen, a Singapore surveyor and an officer in the Volunteers, attended to his normal office work and Volunteer meetings, but found time for the Scouts, sailing his yacht at the Royal Yacht Club and watching the latest films: 'I've just come from a first house at the Pavilion,' he wrote to his wife, in Australia, '"Penny Serenade" . . . We rocked with laughter for minutes on end . . . I had to wipe my eyes.'[44] As reinforcements of Australian, British and Indian troops arrived in late 1940 and early 1941 to support the resident British and Malay battalions, the sense of security increased. In Segamat, Johore, Nancy Wynne observed, 'We have seen thousands of lorries and equipment passing here lately . . . We sit on the balcony and watch them go.'[45] The Wynnes, like many British couples, were glad to do their bit by giving free hospitality to the new arrivals. The Sims were encouraged 'to see husky-looking Australians around in the towns', and remarked how Penang 'was full of soldiers, mostly Punjabis and the hotel was packed with bored-looking officers'.[46] On the other hand, 'Social life . . . was affected [for the better] by the arrival of the Indian army and some British regiments. It seemed to be a constant round of parties.'[47]

When cinema newsreels showed the bombing of London, the evidence of Britain's isolation divided opinions. 'I think we were fairly evenly divided into two camps – those who believed we should escape the war, and the others who knew we shouldn't. Most civilians had no idea how strong or how weak we were . . . Hadn't Britain spent millions of pounds building up Singapore's security?'[48] Rumours became myths. People were confused. Could the island of Singapore really be a fortress, a new, bigger and better Gibraltar? Was it true that the great guns of Singapore naval base were fixed and faced out to sea? What of the wonderful jungle aerodromes that would guarantee Malaya's defence? Were the Japanese so short-sighted and their air force so inferior, as the propagandists proclaimed, that they would not be able to fly at night? Despite some doubts, many civilians believed that to be pessimistic was unpatriotic. 'Malaya is prepared,' Nancy Wynne wrote home in March 1941 with a touch of defiance.[49] In May there was still a feeling that 'the Japs would stay on the fence', though 'everyone has his own special choice of dates for the big one, varying from about 14 days ahead to next Spring', noted Alex Cullen.[50] As late as June, 'If there was trouble here we should certainly go short of a lot of things which are imported but . . . I really don't think there will be anything here, we have certainly plenty of protection and I am sure we should be quite safe.'[51]

Then in July 1941 the prospect of a Pacific War moved closer as Japan's assets were frozen by the United States, Britain and the Netherlands. There was talk in Singapore of 'the present trouble blowing into a real do'.[52] Earlier, in 1940, the Japanese had flexed their diplomatic muscles to force the temporary closure of the Burma Road, China's lifeline to Western supplies. Further skilful manoeuvring early in 1941 had forced Vichy France to concede the occupation of Indo-China by crack Japanese troops. Japan now had an airbase a stage nearer Malaya and a naval base at Camranh Bay some 700 miles from Singapore. In the light of subsequent events, British colonials would feel betrayed by this concession, but for the moment there was no panic. In July 1941 Alex Cullen was saying, 'I don't think myself that the Jippons [*sic*] will dare try anything more for a bit, unless in desperation, which would bad enough, of course, though quite fatal to them in the long run.'[53] Unruffled, Nancy Wynne also wrote home, 'The Japanese have just occupied Indo-China which brings us much nearer but I don't worry much because we are ready for them here.'[54]

However, defence now figured more and more in conversation. The government took appropriate steps to build up food stocks, particularly rice (though sharp criticism was voiced about the siting of the stores).[55] Leslie Froggatt, returning to Singapore from an Australian business trip at the height of the general embargo on trade in essential commodities, remarked how 'Gas courses and fire drill began and first aid and emergency dressing stations were springing up . . . All our women friends flung themselves wholeheartedly into lessons on blood, bones and bandages. Bridge dates, Mah Jong and morning teas slowly slipped back, and their time was spent on lectures, parades and practices.'[56] By 1941 English women were working alongside Eurasian and Asian women in the Passive Defence Services, in First Aid and Home Nursing, and in the Medical and Transport Auxiliary Services, while the older age group of European men enlisted as ARP wardens (in charge of air-raid precautions) and auxiliary fire fighters or enrolled in the Local Defence Corps as officers and NCOs in charge of Asian volunteers undertaking guard duties at vulnerable sites like bridges and power stations. Prominent unofficials, such as G. W. Seabridge, editor of the *Straits Times*, and F. D. Bisseker, General Manager of the Eastern Smelting Company, pressed the government on civil defence. The *Tribune* urged for more action to build slit trenches and air-raid shelters to protect the urban population should war come. In some areas Passive Defence was quite inadequate. In Kedah, for example, the local defence system

was swamped out by red tape. In Province Wellesley the Resident Councillor disapproved and took good care to see that nothing was done

. . . There was considerable rivalry and bickering between the various branches, especially in the smaller places, over personnel. A more unified control would have led to much smoother working . . . In Penang the Resident Councillor again proved an obstructionist: as one example of his strange mentality he refused to sanction expenditure on fire hose, the supply of which was utterly inadequate . . . The organisation of one important service . . . was disgracefully neglected in the early stage with the result that it never really functioned smoothly: this was the air observation corps.[57]

As for the Volunteers, they had attracted a core of keen members in the 1930s from across the whole of the British community. Most of them took the business seriously, training in their spare time on an unpaid basis. There were very few of what G. J. O'Grady identified as 'slackers', and in his view the majority made first-class soldiers. At their first embodiment in August to September 1940, the Johore Volunteers were exemplary: 'Discipline was very strict . . . the standard of drill, smartness etc. was amazing . . . The Quarter-Guard would have done credit to any regular unit.'[58] But if Regulars tended to be sceptical of civilians in uniform it was understandable, for elsewhere in Malaya the training lacked credibility. It

consisted of one parade a week . . . very orthodox in nature, weapon training with one day per year on the range, tactical exercises on pre-1914 lines, a non-compulsory camp and a field day to round off the season. The Europeans were mostly trained to the Vickers gun [but] the infantry were armed with Lewis guns and rifles: we never saw a Bren gun, and not until war actually broke out did we acquire a Tommy gun or two. With conscription came some more intensive training in the form of embodiments . . . but a number of semi-key-men, myself among them, were exempted. In Kedah most of the two months [of the embodiment period] seemed to be taken up by digging trenches round Sungei Patani aerodrome and filling them in again.[59]

Others also deplored the bungling they witnessed. At Perak in 1940

The Volunteer Camp was on the Ipoh race course and the first announcements about it calmly stated that there would be a few days' gap in the middle of training so that the races could take place. But later it dawned on the authorities that this was not *quite* the thing in wartime and the races were cancelled.[60]

J. S. Potter, who had served with the Territorials in London, grew ever more cynical about the Volunteer system:

> I . . . was at once sadly disappointed with its efficiency . . . In Malaya, money was spent lavishly on buildings and appointments but was not backed up by man power or enthusiasm; nor was the best use made of limited available man power . . . and as a result I steered a middle course and performed the minimum number of requisite drills each year which the Authorities regarded necessary for efficiency.
>
> With War in Europe my second term of duty in Malaya was vastly different from my first. Indeed for me it was a period of extreme frustration. Denied war service at Home, I was 'keyed' to the estate ostensibly to maintain the flow of rubber . . . [with] service in the so called Volunteers in our spare time. In my opinion this was not a very practical way of either preparing for war or prosecuting the war effort.

His disillusion was complete after mobilization. 'One hoped that one's local knowledge, ability to speak two local languages and previous military experience would be appreciated by the Authorities and fighting services . . . But not so. I was condemned to running a few lorries in a Motor Transport Unit.'[61] And yet, with the exception of Singapore's Fortress garrison, an Indian battalion and a battalion of the Malay Regiment, Malaya's defence before 1940 depended on Volunteer battalions of the Malay States and of the Straits Settlements, and skeletal Air Force and Naval Reserve contingents who, even after compulsory service was introduced in 1940 for men between eighteen and forty-one, totalled no more than 10,000 Europeans. According to dispatches sent by General Arthur Percival, who took over as GOC, Malaya, in May 1941, there was a serious lack of trained units and insufficient experienced leadership, which would amount to a grave deficiency in the defences.

Despite the personal socializing, there was no real empathy between the armed services and the civilians. A Singapore resident recalled a tense conversation he had in 1940 with a Dunkirk veteran serving with the Royal Artillery. John Moore was 'a quiet, thoughtful sort of chap' (he did not survive the war), but on this occasion he burst out indignantly: 'Why do you Singapore people sit with your heads in the sands? . . . the ships that bring your cigarettes and Scotch expose themselves to every kind of hell for your amusement. England shakes, and you in Malaya sit in the sun tanning your hides, dicing with drinks and sucking your Esquimo Pies.'[62] A naval officer was heard to remark that Malaya was 'a slough of mental despond'; a bemused Australian officer, viewing the formal mess dress and finery of wartime Singapore, felt 'Either we were crazy or they were crazy. Either there was danger, or there was no danger.'[63] But some civilians were growing uneasy about the effectiveness of the defences. 'We don't need any more stuffed shirts. Singapore is brimming with 'em. Every shade. White, blue, grey, khaki . . . We want planes.'[64] Ridicule of the top brass became a habit. Alex Cullen wrote with feeling, 'If it weren't so pitifully futile and tragic, it would be almost amusing to see the flutter of the old school ties beginning to be somewhat frayed nowadays.'[65] The Governor, Shenton Thomas, had by now forfeited much of his earlier respect. 'I had a feeling', Leslie Froggatt observed, 'that he knew even less about the situation than I did, which could not possibly be.'[66] Even the Commander-in-Chief, Far East, was not exempt from comment. 'I saw Brooke-Popham passing by,' said a civilian heavily, 'bit nose, big topi, big moustache, in a big car.'[67] And Gordon Snell, one of many who recalled the period wrote:

> I do remember that there seemed to be no love lost between the groups of people in civilian jobs and those in the military side. My mother always recalled how at a party once when they were discussing security in Singapore, she did actually mention to a military person that all the defences were directed seaward, and couldn't an invader come by land down the Malay peninsula? The military person pooh-poohed this as an impossibility.[68]

Though servicemen might denigrate Malayan society, they were less vocal in this than a section of the press. Somerset Maugham's literary portrayals of a decadent and philistine community had been augmented by Noël Coward's aphorism about Malaya ('a first-rate country for second-rate people'). In 1937 an attack on the colonial regime by the American scholar Rupert Emerson added academic weight. Then, when the situation became grave, journalists such as the *Daily Express* war correspondent O'Dowd Gallagher turned on 'the white civilian population [who] evinced no interest in the war whatsoever' and for whom the war news simply 'gave them something exciting to chatter about' at the breakfast table.[69] The American CBS newsman Cecil Brown (who was expelled from the country early in

1942) later castigated the colony's leadership and the hedonism of British Malayans as reasons for the country's downfall. Lady Brooke-Popham allegedly accused the women of Singapore of being too busy playing golf and tennis to help with voluntary services – an accusation that was indignantly denied. Whatever the truth, all the criticism was deeply and bitterly resented in European circles. One Singapore resident tried to rationalize the mood:

> We did have a tendency to fête our visitors . . . And so they often went away full of headache and hangover, to print and publish criticisms of a way of life that was planned primarily for their amusement, and was not in any way typical . . . The nastiest jibe of all was made by a visiting journalist who charged us publicly with 'swilling' while our Rome burned. Out there, we didn't condemn them for making merry in the Café de Paris while the bombs came racing down [but] the brave face that Singapore tried to put on in spite of the growing sense of bewilderment, confusion and utter chaos . . . was condemned as foolish frivolity.[70]

Others, however, felt ashamed that the regime failed. The malaise, they believed, was deep-rooted. 'The British and the Asiatics lived their lives apart . . . and the small British community formed no more than a thin and brittle veneer,' wrote Ian Morrison, the London *Times* correspondent.[71] In European circles 'the social round . . . proceeded at the level of the least intelligent . . . This state of affairs . . . was symptomatic of the deadness of our thought.' At its root was 'the aversion to treating any members of the Asian races on a basis of equality. We would mix with them on business, on government committees, in games, at Rotary clubs, at big functions, and yet many of our clubs had rules which specially excluded them.'[72] This same mentality precluded the mass mobilization of Malaya's Asian population on a properly organized basis. 'Allies with our servants and cooks, allies with our tailors and our sewage coolies, may Heaven forbid! We'll manage this show by ourselves or perish,' a British Volunteer recalled – adding, 'My own cook implored me to get him enlisted in something; he would shoot, he said, but there was no sort of organisation which wanted him.'[73] Only after the Pacific War began did the authorities recognize the defence potential of the Chinese in particular, but by then it was a matter of 'too little too late'. One colonial servant gave his verdict:

To sum up, the invasion found the country incompletely prepared and considerably under-equipped. The population was partly apathetic (the Malays), merely existing (the Tamils) and partly 'on the make' (the Chinese and Europeans), with no uniting force to bind them into a resistant whole. The climate and social life was such as to damp initiative and discourage original thought. I had the strange feeling that the spirit of the land [was] . . . waiting to take vengeance and indeed it would seem that only some supernatural force can account for the follies and blunders which were committed.[74]

The confusion continued up to the eventual eve of hostilities. Japanese troop concentrations in Indo-China were still interpreted as bluff, while other warning signals went unchallenged. Reports in August of the night-time penetration of two strange ships up the Endau river were three weeks late in reaching the colonial authorities, and there was no apparent response to the evidence of Japanese submarine operations in Malayan coastal waters. The final evacuation from Singapore of Japanese civilians in mid-November 1941 perhaps sent critical signals (more than half the Japanese community having already left since July). By late November the intensification of diplomatic exchanges and increased activity in the Japanese armed forces finally set alarm bells ringing. On 1 December 1941 all military, naval and air personnel were ordered to return to their bases in a general mobilization. On the 2nd the battleship *Prince of Wales* and the cruiser *Repulse* arrived in Singapore to reinforce Malaya's defences and reassure the British *tuans*. However, when Japanese armed convoys were spotted in Thai coastal waters on the 6th, the Commander-in-Chief, Sir Robert Brooke-Popham, dampened 'alarmist' reports in the press. The same day the Governor told his cipher clerk in private, 'You can take it from me there will never be a Japanese bomb dropped in Singapore – there will never be a Japanese set foot in Malaya.'[75]

In the early hours of 8 December the Japanese landed on the northeast coast of Malaya and simultaneously bombed Singapore and Pearl Harbor. The final irony was that as 'Japanese bombs were falling on a perfectly illuminated Singapore . . . our preparations, precautions and general arrangements were such that the lights were still fully on at the end of the raid!'[76]

# 12

# A Campaign of Cards

During the early hours of Monday 8 December 1941 the Japanese invading forces landed from choppy seas near Kota Bharu, in the beautiful and unspoilt state of Kelantan. Their official orders were to rescue Asia from white tyranny and aggression. In no time the town's European residents 'were awake with the roar of guns and the rattle of musketry up and down the beaches six miles away. Very soon there were also the sounds of aeroplanes in the sky. At 1.05 a.m. as we paced our verandahs and looked eastwards, the awful certainty was borne in upon us that the foreboding of the past 20 years had become reality.'[1] A faint moon rose in the cloudy monsoon sky as Hudsons of the Australian Air Force attacked the landing craft, but the troops of General Yamashita's 18th Division forced their way inland through a thin line of coastal mines and pillboxes defended by a gritty battalion of Dogras of the 9th Indian Division. In Singapore the Governor, Shenton Thomas, seemed unperturbed. 'Well, I suppose you'll shove the little men off!' he allegedly told General Percival.[2]

The Volunteers of Kedah and Perak reacted very differently: 'that morning's news came as a great shock', shattering 'the carefully fostered belief that it was impossible to land a military force on the east coast, especially during the monsoon'.[3] In fact, well before dawn the Europeans of Kota Bharu had been driven to the railhead at Kuala Krai. Within hours the Japanese landed unopposed at Singora and Patani in southern Thailand, poised to bypass the sate of Perlis and make a double thrust through Kedah down the western flank of Malaya. It was a classic operation, the stuff of war games played by soldiers at both the War College of Tokyo and the Imperial Defence College, Camberley.

Seeing that it was already too late to implement Operation Matador, the contingency plan to contain the Japanese in Thailand, Malaya Command issued a warning: Japan had made 'a grievous mistake'. 'We are ready . . . our preparations are made and tested . . . We are confident. Our defences are strong and our weapons efficient.' Britain was committed 'to defend these shores, to destroy such of our enemies as may set foot on our soil'.[4] The next ten weeks would expose the futility of these assertions and the momentous deception perpetrated on the people of Malaya.[5]

More immediately, the Indian brigade group at Kota Bharu was unable to defend the airfield, which was hastily evacuated, leaving behind a working runway and stores of bombs and petrol. By one of those ironies that litter this episode, on that morning of 8 December the Straits Trading Company in Province Wellesley was due to reopen full production at its Butterworth tin-smelting works, which had been closed since the Slump of 1932. Kota Bharu changed everything: rapidly the labour force evaporated, leaving peacetime commerce in ruin. On Tuesday the 9th the main British aerodromes of northern Malaya – Alor Star, Sungei Patani and Butterworth – were badly damaged by Japanese dive-bombers, and at a stroke the Allied force of 110 aircraft in this sector was reduced to fifty. To top this, the squadrons at Kuantan were withdrawn that same day to Singapore, and Kelantan's remaining forward airfields, Gong Kedah and Machang, were abandoned on 10–11 December. In three days Britain had surrendered her air power in northern Malaya.

The consequences proved catastrophic. As reports of Japanese landings were received in Singapore, Admiral Sir Tom Phillips, Commander-in-Chief of Britain's Eastern Fleet, ordered his squadron to proceed to the Gulf of Siam. Its vulnerability was apparent too late. Though the order to reverse course had been given, the *Prince of Wales* and the *Repulse* were caught by eighty-five Japanese bombers in the South China Sea on the morning of Wednesday 10 December. Deprived of air support from the east-coast airfields, the two capital ships of Force Z were torpedoed from the air and sank with the loss of 840 men, including Admiral Phillips and Captain Leach of the *Prince of Wales*. The impact on morale throughout Malaya was immediate and devastating. People wept, struggling to come to terms with Britain's worst naval disaster of the war.[6] Churchill himself was profoundly shocked: 'As I turned over and twisted in bed the full horror of the news sank in upon me. There were no British or American capital ships in the Indian Ocean or the Pacific . . . Over this vast expanse of waters Japan was supreme.'[7]

The unfolding drama of the Malayan campaign has been recorded by dozens of those involved – regular servicemen, volunteers, journalists, civil servants, Britons, Australians and Japanese.[8] On the British side it was a chronicle of disaster, of individual resourcefulness, heroism and initiative, of struggling in vain to rise above collective inefficiency and blind muddle. In those first three days the pattern of the whole campaign was established. First, the bemused European civilian population was hurriedly transported south. (It was hit-or-miss as to whether non-Europeans were evacuated.) The British regulars, with half-trained units and totally lacking air cover and heavy armour, tried to hold their ground and counter-attack, but could not contain the steady Japanese advance supported by tanks, superior reconnaissance and fighter-bomber aircraft. Guided by local informants, the Japanese forced back the Indian and British troops repeatedly before the demolition of bridges, supplies and installations could be completed, driving their way down the well-built roads of western Malaya. Whenever they met resistance, the Japanese infantry swiftly infiltrated the surrounding jungle, outflanking the British and Allied defence lines. By exploiting their prior intelligence of Malaya's coasts, they cut behind the Allied front in surprise amphibious manoeuvres, splitting Percival's forces in pincer-attacks and cutting off pockets of troops to be mopped up later. Against these tactics, time and again the raw, demoralized forces of Malaya Command fell back to alternative defensive positions, until fresh Japanese pressure forced another withdrawal. From the battles of Jitra, Kampar, Slim River and Muar to the struggle for Johore and Singapore, the litany of dig in, fight, stand to the last round and the last man, waver, regroup, destroy communications, retreat to another defensive line was repeated the length of the peninsula.[9] To the civilian Volunteers the impotence of the military was incomprehensible. As M. C. Hay (Malayan Civil Service and Lance-Bombardier in the FMS Volunteer Force) protested, 'It was one of the features of this incredible campaign that if a handful of Japanese were reported in our rear the whole British army must perforce retire – infantry, guns, and armoured cars – often without firing a shot.'[10]

Meanwhile the war in Kedah began with a 'blitz' of airfields on 8 December. Civilians in northern Malaya were utterly bemused. Ken Hartley was only a boy; Pelham rubber estate, which his father managed, was on the Thai border. He later tried to remember what happened.

> Well, war started. Didn't mean anything to us. We didn't have a telephone. We didn't have a radio . . . Can't recall seeing a newspaper . . . I don't know how communications came about, probably by letter, and we were told to move up to Tapah – Tapah being on the main north–south route. I remember staying with my aunt who ran the Rest House there.[11]

Two planters' wives from Sungei Patani appeared on the Kedah–Perak border on the 9th: 'both were very badly shaken by the previous day's bombing. Apparently a flight of Jap planes had come over the aerodrome before any news of war had reached there, and everybody thought they were our own reinforcements until the bombs started to whistle . . . News of the fighting was very scanty . . . even so it was obvious that the land operations both in the east [in Kelantan] and west [around Jitra] were going none too well . . . the movement of the Kedah government to Kulim was not reassuring.'[12] The reality was a good deal worse. With their superior mechanized troops, the Japanese kept breaching the unfinished defences of the 11th Indian Division; and if regulars could not hold the line, there was little the Kedah Volunteers could do.[13] By 11 December British positions in both Kelantan and Jitra were effectively lost, but only after contradictory evacuation orders were issued were all Europeans finally ordered to leave Kedah on the 16th. The British Adviser, Mr J. D. Hall, felt it was his duty to remain behind, and had to be forcibly pushed into a car by other government officials. Among the planters who abandoned everything to escape were the Barretts of Kuala Muda Estate. Their home was to be destroyed in the fighting. Like many other British wives, Doris Barrett set off with her sons to drive in stages down the length of Malaya, staying with friends who would themselves in turn become part of the flood of refugees. By Tuesday the 16th, after only a week of action, the British had fallen back to the Muda river between Kedah and Province Wellesley, leaving Penang in serious danger of being outflanked.

Charles Hartley, an Agricultural Officer in the Malayan Civil Service serving as a Volunteer in the so-called Fortress Reserve at Penang, had no illusions: 'Penang was called a fortress, which it certainly wasn't.'[14] Even so, listening to the cicadas in 'the dense velvet black of the tropical night' vying with the noise of distant firing, Mabel Price, wife of the manager of Whiteaway Laidlaw, found it difficult to believe that the call summoning her husband to Georgetown's ARP station indicated a real emergency.[15] But Penang's sea defences proved irrelevant and its air defences non-existent, and the island's fate was sealed in the first three days when Japanese planes attacked Bayan Lepas airfield and Butterworth aerodrome on the mainland opposite. Left without anti-aircraft batteries or fighters, Georgetown was, in official words, 'absolutely defenceless against air attack'.[16] The critical blow came on the morning of Thursday 11 December. Fifty-three Japanese aircraft swooped over the town in waves, blasting European commercial buildings and the congested shophouse quarter; many Asians, unwitting spectators, rushed to open spaces on the seafront and *padang*, only to be machine-gunned where they stood. In two hours the fire station, the island's only fire engine, a water main, the dispensary and food shops were all wrecked. The Resident Councillor witnessed the carnage:

> Whole blocks of shophouses were a mass of flames, while dead and injured seemed to lie every few yards in the streets . . . At least 1,000 bodies were buried under the debris. The General Hospital admitted over 1,100 injured. The other aid-posts dealt with many more. *For sheer intensity of attack on a comparatively restricted area, nothing else in Malaya can be compared with it.*[17]

Hospital staff under Dr Evans and the Medical Auxiliary staff, European and non-European, including two stalwarts, Nella Macdonald and Iris Parfitt, worked unstintingly. But despite the efforts of individuals in the ARP and the depleted Fire Service, fires continued to blaze around the island for several days. Law and order collapsed; policemen, transport workers, labourers all melted into the kampongs, leaving to the rats the debris and putrefying corpses on the streets. The horror of it all, particularly the images of machine-gunned civilians, played havoc with the emotions of Renée Parrish, wife of Penang's pharmacist. After further raids on the desolate town, the Japanese concentrated their destructive fire on Penang Straits. Leaving her home in

Brown Road, Mabel Price sought the safety of Penang Hill, where many Europeans were congregating. There with her two young sons she watched 'the bombing of the harbour and the ships sinking or going round and round in circles to dodge the bombs. It was a tragic sight.'[18]

While the Japanese moved inexorably down the mainland, as many of the civilian population as could fled by car, boat or train from Province Wellesley and Penang, fearful of the consequences of capture by Japanese soldiers. A party of Eurasians from Kedah reached the Perak border by car on the 11th and were helped by the Volunteers to move on to Ipoh. A much larger body of some 600 Penang Chinese appeared down the Perak coast on the 13th, intending to find refuge with friends and relations in the fishing villages around Kuala Kurai. Meanwhile, Captain Hartley's wife, alone in Butterworth since he was in Penang, 'only just got out . . . She had two babies and had to find her own way down the peninsula.'[19] Kathleen Price and her eight-year-old daughter took temporary refuge on a rubber estate, but when the surrounding padi fields were strafed by machine-gun fire they returned to Butterworth, packed a few essentials, and boarded the train at Prai on Friday the 12th to join the Froggatts in Singapore.

The official evacuation of Penang began the following evening, when around 550 women and children crossed by ferry to Prai to catch the train. A Penang mother remembered what happened. 'Then came the word. *Secretly* the women and children were to be taken to Singapore for safety and instructions given to be on the jetty ready for evacuation at 9 o'clock in the evening.' Since its Asian crew had deserted, the ferry was manned by 'the boys of the *Prince of Wales* and the *Repulse* who had been taken out of the sea 24 hours previously'. 'We waited from 9 p.m. to 6 a.m. before we could sail and daylight was breaking which made it dangerous for us to get away. I understand the enemy was only a few miles behind us.' At Ipoh and Kuala Lumpur residents appeared on the station platform offering much-needed food and water, and 'we had a bath and refreshed at the Spotted Dog Club before boarding the train for Singapore'.[20] In Segamat, Nancy Wynne also did her bit for those fleeing from up-country. 'We have had people staying every other night, coming at all times for a bed or a meal. Several of them have lost everything except what they stand up in and others have lost their beautiful houses in Penang . . . I have a lady staying with me now whose husband is "missing believed killed" and who was living in what is now enemy territory.'[21] The last train from Prai left on the night of 15–16 December. By the time they boarded it, Charles and Violet Samuel, a senior Penang lawyer and his wife, had already lost most of their luggage in the journey from Penang Hill. It was a traumatic departure for a middle-aged couple, and their leaving marked 'a terrible break with the past'.[22]

That same night Province Wellesley was cleared on military orders. After dark, Bill Price of Sungei Nyok Dockyard and Straits Steamship engineer Bobby Moffatt drove off from Butterworth. They travelled mainly at night to avoid being dive-bombed, navigating with a hand-torch in the blackout all the way to Singapore. H. B. Hall, Manager of the Straits Trading Company's Butterworth works, escaped in the nick of time without being able to demolish anything in the smelting complex. On the 16th, by military order, Penang's remaining European civilians and military personnel were packed aboard one of the old Bagan Luar ferries and the Straits Steamship's little SS *Pangkor* to make for Singapore. So within nine days British rule in the Crown's oldest Malayan territories came to an abrupt end.

The Penang episode sparked a wave of public recrimination. Not only had the scorched-earth policy been botched, allowing loads of oil, petrol, tin, rubber and rice to fall into enemy hands, but critically the wireless station had been left in working order. In no time Penang Radio was taunting, 'Hello, Singapore, how do you like our bombing?' There followed a flow of disinformation and propaganda aimed at sowing disunity and undermining morale. One official remembered hearing shortly after 'that Tunku Abdul Rahman, the District Officer of Kulim [in south Kedah] . . . broadcast from Penang. His speech was anti-British.'[23] Equally serious was the authorities' failure to scuttle the armada of small craft and self-propelled boats scattered in and around the harbour, which proved invaluable to the Japanese in their seaborne operations along Malaya's west coast during the next month.

But the issue which outraged many people was the racial discrimination implicit in the evacuation, which was apparently condoned by Duff Cooper, Churchill's transient Special Adviser in Singapore.[24] Since there was neither time nor means to organize a mass evacuation of Asian civilians, some 500 Asian Volunteers stayed behind to face the Japanese. 'The British, so it was universally held amongst Asiatics, had ratted out of Penang, had thought of saving no skins but their own, and left the

Asiatics to their fate at the hands of the Japs, as if they didn't give a damn what happened to them,' noted Ian Morrison of *The Times*.[25] Official renunciation of responsibility reinforced the private guilt which many British Malayans felt in the coming weeks and months. As Kenneth Brundle, an architect with the Public Works Department, admitted, 'This sudden order to pack up and leave without a word to our Asian staff threw me into utter confusion as it did many others. There were mixed feelings of hope, defeat and nausea.'[26] However, he had the satisfaction of helping his Chief Draughtsman, a Eurasian, to leave Johore Bahru with his family, thus saving their lives.

Leslie Froggatt afterwards wrote with feeling:

> I betrayed my Malay gardener. He cut my hedges, watered my flowers, cut and rolled my tennis lawn, and brushed up the leaves that blew down from the trees. I betrayed my round fat amah, who liked me, and amused me with her funny ways. I betrayed my Hockien cook, who had a wife and four lovely children, whom he kept beautifully dressed at all times on the money he earned from me. I betrayed 'Old Faithful', our No. 2 Boy, who knew no word of English or Malay and padded round the house silently in bare feet, always working cheerfully. I betrayed the caddie who carried my bag, searched for my ball, and always backed my game with a sporting bet. I betrayed all the little helpless babies with their almond eyes and soft black shining heads. From the college student to the Tamil coolie who swept the street, I betrayed them all.[27]

Muriel Reilly also felt ashamed. As the danger grew, 'Our Malay Syce was so good . . . It still hurts to think how the white race "let down" hundreds of similarly faithful servants who trusted in us, and looked to us for protection from the hated Japs.'[28] Tom Kitching, Singapore's Chief Surveyor, did not want to be accused of leaving the sinking ship. 'There is great argument, should all Europeans leave? I say no. Most people say yes.'[29] In his Pahang fastness, Vincent Baker also knew he could never abandon his workers. The European staff had been drafted elsewhere as Pahang Volunteers, but to Cheng Kan, his foreman, as to the rest at the Sungei Lembing tin mine, 'the idea of the *Tuan Besar* deserting them was unthinkable'.[30]

The Penang débâcle, meanwhile, resulted in withdrawal to the line of the Krian river. Perak was the next battleground. From the border with Province Wellesley 'the stream of southward traffic was as intense as ever: convoy after convoy of troops, guns and material moving in an endless line'. John Soper, who lived nearby at Parit Buntar, braced himself for 'the blow of leaving all our household and personal possessions to the mercy of looters, the army and the Japs: furniture, silver, books, bedding, typewriter, electrolux, pictures, wedding presents, radio, all the treasures collected during thirteen years of married life'.[31] Everyone had cherished belongings. Penang's Chief Surveyor, Aylward, 'lost everything, of course, including his tiger trophies, which cuts him more than anything else does'.[32] Typically, Kathleen Price of Butterworth and Ethel Barnes of Malacca never saw their precious china, silver or crystal again. The Vowlers were remarkably lucky that their silver sporting trophies were saved, thanks initially to their devoted household servants, but Tom Kitching felt the blow of losing his collection, especially the silver cup presented to him by the Sultan for winning the Royal Trengganu Golf Club competition, and his first 'pot' for the long jump at Peterhouse Sports.[33]

Another distressing moment for many British civilians came when they parted with much-loved pets. It was small consolation that the Soper mongrel dog had a habit of getting in the way of a ball, so 'the odds are that he was killed by the first shell that landed'.[34] The Barretts and the Prices lost their golden cocker spaniels, Leslie Froggatt his aviaries of prize budgerigars and tropical birds, and Katharine Sim her pedigree Siamese cats. Knowing her two bull mastiffs, Brandy and Brutus, could not possibly accompany her, Nona Baker reluctantly had them destroyed. At the end Muriel Reilly and her husband took the same heartbreaking decision to have their six racehorses shot:

> we weren't going to leave then to the Japs to use as beasts of burden . . . They were our pets . . . They knew my voice and would 'talk' to me whenever I came to see them. Another thing that hurt more than I can tell. I had a most lovely dog – a Kangaroo Hound . . . he was almost human. I called in a Veterinary Surgeon and had my 'Bluey' put to sleep . . . it took three hours and I sat beside my lovely 'Bluey' until he at last stopped breathing.[35]

Meanwhile, the speed with which the Japanese persistently forced the British back down the peninsula baffled those who knew Malaya. Soper agreed with Tom Kitching's assessment. 'I should have thought there was no better line to hold them than Taiping–Port Weld, only ten miles of it, with mangrove swamps and the sea on the west, and steep jungle-clad hills running up to 4,500 feet on the east. Yet this was apparently given up without a thought.'[36] This was not quite true: withdrawal was forced by the threat which was even then developing from the townships of Kroh and Grik.[37] Japanese air supremacy was another factor. On 17 December central Ipoh was bombed, and the next day Taiping in a raid reminiscent of that on Penang the week before: 'Because of the large number of civilians in town and the crowded nature of the market and its surroundings, casualties were heavy. Fires broke out and were fanned by a wind,' the Resident recalled.[38] Four days later, on a dismally wet Sunday, the civilian evacuation of Taiping was completed.

Soper, with the Volunteers at Ipoh, heard with disbelief the news of the army's withdrawal across the Perak river: 'we reckoned that this river would be a formidable obstacle, and might indeed prove the turning point of the campaign'. The Perak Volunteers, however, were soon on the move again, this time to Kampar, some twenty-five miles away, where Soper's company, stationed in the Anglo-Chinese school, were ordered to prepare defensive positions. It was Christmas 1941.

> I shall never forget that Xmas morning: it dawned cool and fair, the mist still clinging to the hills behind us, and with the dawn we set off on our mission of destruction [demolition] . . . It was a strange Xmas dinner: seven of us seated round a table improvised from school desks . . . a marvellous assortment of tin mugs, mess tins, enamel plates and ill matched cutlery, the whole scene lit by a solitary hurricane lamp. We had caught a turkey that morning but it . . . had to be eked out with bully beef rissoles and tinned vegetables. This was followed by a good tinned plum pudding with which we found some brandy to burn, then followed the port, chocolates and a sing song . . . in such surroundings and conditions the old Xmas carols seemed rather incongruous. On me they had a very morbid effect, bringing back memories of the year before with happy children's voices singing them in a peaceful, contented home.[39]

Elsewhere in the Far East the picture was even darker. Kuching, in Sarawak, was overrun by the Japanese on Christmas Eve, and on Christmas Day Hong Kong had surrendered. In central Malaya there were still hopes of containing the enemy, if not indefinitely, at least until reinforcements arrived. On Boxing Day 'the military authorities announced that they were going to make a stand North of Kampar and hoped to hold the line for six months'.[40] Other misleading stories reached Singapore that British troops had 'inflicted terrific slaughter on the Japs in Perak – "wave after wave mown down"'.[41] But that same day the old capital of Selangor was the focus of a well-targeted raid, raising serious alarms about fifth-column activity. The local bank manager recorded, '26th December was Klang's Waterloo for from that day it ceased to exist as an organized community.'[42] There was no halting Japanese progress: Ipoh fell on 27 December, Kuala Lumpur was repeatedly bombed. 'In the Kinta valley the first really serious attempt at some sort of scored earth policy was begun. Estate rubber factories, stores and smoke houses were systematically fired by the local defence forces, and tin mining machinery was blown up by contingents of Royal Engineers. In Kuala Lumpur some of the large stores and godowns were also blown.' As someone whose peacetime career was in agriculture, John Soper was appalled by the impact of huge fires all around: 'it seemed stark madness thus to consign to the cosmos the hard won fruits of a bounteous earth'.[43]

In eastern Malaya the story was similar. As the Japanese were thought to be approaching and since no evacuation orders had been received in Trengganu, the civilians of Kuala Trengganu decided to take matters into their own hands. On 11 December a group of sixteen – members of the Malayan Civil Service, Police, Customs, Education and Public Works, with Dr Cecily Williams, two other women and two Malay policemen – embarked on a phenomenally difficult 120-mile journey. They travelled by car, motorboat, flat-bottomed boat, raft and cattle truck, their route taking them by the headwaters of the Tembeling river across jungle terrain of the central mountain range in monsoon conditions. Finally in the evening of the 18th they reached Kuala Lipis, the capital of Pahang and a railway junction, which promised to be a stage nearer safety. Shortly after, on 29 December, Vincent Baker was ordered by the British Resident at Kuala Lipis to flood the massive Pahang Consolidated mine at Sungei Lembing. As he dumped the tin and fuel-oil stocks and stopped the pumps, he gazed at the complete disintegration of his life's work.

But it was not simply careers and lives that were in jeopardy, but seemingly civilization itself. The full facts about Japanese atrocities, of the bayoneting and beheading of prisoners, wounded soldiers and civilians, did not emerge for some time, but there began to trickle through stories of the indiscriminate rape and killing of Chinese, of a British planter and his wife being hanged by soldiers on a tree in the garden in front of their servants, and of the establishment of an execution ground at Telok Sisek.[44] In much of the Malayan peninsula the British presence ceased, colonial communities evaporated.

The Volunteer system was another casualty of the swift enemy advance. As one by one the Malay States fell, according to the terms of their embodiment the Volunteers were disbanded to give way to the regular forces. Many Volunteers, it may be remembered, had held responsible positions in pre-war Malaya, as well as being university-educated, and among some of them disillusionment over the conduct of the war set in rapidly. M. C. Hay, a contemporary of Alan Morkill in the Malayan Civil Service, who was with a Light Battery unit from mid-December when his civilian job ceased, was soon convinced that 'the authorities never meant to make any serious use of us': his battery's morale was undermined when a week later regular troops took over their guns, leaving the Perak Volunteers with 'ancient weapons'.[45] Kenneth Brundle, who had joined a machine-gun company of the Straits Settlements Volunteers, felt strongly that Malaya Command never exploited the Volunteers' potential, their facility in Asian languages, their knowledge of terrain and the local population, but instead set them to dig ARP trenches and perform other secondary tasks. As a result, 'Sadly, the Volunteer Forces up and down the length of Malaya were prevented from making a proper contribution to the campaign.'[46]

There were, of course, individual exceptions, but there is no adequate survey of the various tasks undertaken by British Malayans in uniform, nor of the sacrifices they made.[47] After his fleeting command of a company of Penang Volunteers, Charles Hartley joined 'Dalforce', a formation of Chinese irregulars which was hastily organized in Singapore by a former Director of Criminal Intelligence, Kuala Lumpur, Colonel J. Dalley. But it was typical of the Heath Robinson nature of Singapore's defence that Hartley's unit had 'fourteen different kinds of rifle scrounged from all over Singapore', and his priority was to teach his inexperienced Volunteers from scratch how to use them.[48] Disbanded Volunteers undertook high-risk missions because of their intimate knowledge of the countryside. Four men of the former Drains and Irrigation Department – Wilson, Pelton, Cubitt and Wynne (the last Nancy Wynne's husband) – were willing to try their hand at commando raids behind the lines, but ended as prisoners of war in the notorious Pudu Gaol, Kuala Lumpur.[49] Douglas Broadhurst, another Volunteer, formerly in the police and based at Sungei Patani and Butterworth, served as liaison officer with the 12th Brigade, which saw heated action in the northern and central sectors. He found himself behind enemy lines. Major Barrett, ex-planter and former second in command of the Kedah Volunteers, spent the rest of the campaign as a liaison and intelligence officer attached to the 11th Indian Division, moving between the divisional headquarters and Singapore. There was inevitably a good deal of haphazard promotion and some resentment over the way commissions were granted, especially in the Indian regiments: 'Some did a wangle . . . they became "two-or-three pippers" in the S.S.V.F. [Straits Settlements Volunteer Force],' observed Sapper Guy Hutchinson – the peacetime Assistant Estate Manager – 'we called them "Robinson's Commissions" as that was where we reckoned they bought their pips.'[50]

However, these irritations made no difference to the effort put in by Volunteers, nor did they affect the mounting crisis as the New Year approached.[51] Singapore had enjoyed a phoney peace since its first blitz, but now, as if to warn Malaya Command that the campaign was moving up a gear, Japanese planes appeared out of a starry, moonlit tropical sky to usher in the New Year with bombs. 'I was foaming with rage at them,' observed a helpless Muriel Reilly.[52] At the same time the Indian brigade holding Kuantan (and its airfield) withdrew too late into west Pahang, suffering heavy casualties. The threat from west-coast infiltration was also serious, and FMS Volunteers Hay and Soper found themselves involved. Hay, now attached to the 73rd Royal Artillery, was moved to Kuala Selangor: 'We heard that a Jap convoy was approaching the mouth of the river at Kuala Selangor'; in the subsequent barrage, several boats were hit. Then 'our officers, who of course knew the country, told the Regulars that the party repulsed at Kuala Selangor would probably try to land at Sabak Bernam. No notice was taken of this, and that is exactly what they did. The landing was unopposed. Meanwhile there had been another landing at Telok Anson.'[53]

As the situation changed and casualties increased, many Volunteers found themselves being redeployed. Soper, now Company Sergeant Major with a mobile light-arms patrol, was south of Port Dickson when there was 'a brand new "flap" . . . Not only had the Japs landed a force up the Bernam river, and so threatened the flank of the Slim River and Tanjong Malim positions, but they had also got in at Port Swettenham still further South, and were threatening Kuala Lumpur from the West.'[54] It was known that, with their good road systems, the states of Selangor and Negri Sembilan would be difficult to hold. Also, 'Malacca has no defences, and no troops,' a civil servant's wife casually told Tom Kitching, 'in fact nothing to stop the Japanese walking in at their own sweet will.'[55] The Barnes family did not wait to find out the truth of this: they shut their home and left on 6 January. In that first disastrous week of 1942 the battles of Kampar and Slim River sealed the fate of central and eastern Malaya. 'Slim River was one of the few places where we had the Japs trapped,' Norman Bewick protested. 'It's the coastal plain, you might say. They couldn't run *that* way because of the mountains, and they couldn't run *that* way because of the sea, and we had them really tied up there; but they got through finally by our withdrawal, withdrawal, withdrawal . . . They didn't come down the main road, they came down the jungle.'[56]

Last-minute efforts were made to deny the enemy soft supplies: 'We are not going to defend K.L. and in pursuance of the "scorched earth" policy X helped to destroy 51,000,000 cigarettes, $50,000 worth of whisky, 800 tons of meat in the Cold Storage,' Tom Kitching recorded.[57] However, the 11th Indian Division was decimated at Slim River and sent reeling; the survivors fell back 125 miles to Johore, leaving Kuala Lumpur, the federal capital, to be taken by the Japanese on 11 December without a shot being fired.[58]

The next stand was to be along the line from Muar to Gemas or Segamat on the western flank. Tom Kitching had doubts about its efficacy. Although 'it should be possible: the Muar river is a big obstacle anywhere near its mouth . . . there's always this "infiltration" bogey . . . they can infiltrate anywhere, through jungle, rubber, through anything. What I fail to understand is why infiltration should all be on the one side. Why can't we infiltrate in the reverse direction?'[59] The trend, however, was irreversible, despite a build-up of reinforcements and the assurances of the Australian commander, Gordon Bennett, that his men were itching to get at the enemy. By 18 January the word in Singapore was that 'the Australian Imperial Forces are fighting at Gemas; the Japs have crossed the Muar River *at Muar*! It seems incredible . . .' By the 24th the line had moved again: 'Official, we are holding the Japs at points north of Kluang and Mersing and at Batu Pahat'; and 'the Japs were fussed then, really fussed'. But two days later 'We are out of Batu Pahat . . . Jap vessels observed off Endau – why don't we bomb them?' On the 28th, 'We are now fighting at Rengit, south of Senggarang and Ayer Hitam . . .'[60] Kitching was unaware of a desperate sea evacuation, spread over the nights of 26–8 January, by the gunboats *Dragonfly* and *Scorpion* and a cluster of small craft from Singapore manned by Volunteers of the Naval Reserve, who picked up 2,700 British and Indian troops from the mangrove swamps south of Batu Pahat. In truth, the Japanese had cut through Johore 'like a knife through cheese'.[61]

On the night of 27–8 January, Lance-Bombardier M. C. Hay slept on the grass in front of the State Palace at Johore Bahru, where he had once been Acting General Adviser Johore. Until recently the traffic had been two-way, creating huge congestion in the town as reinforcements pushed north past lines of southbound ambulances and carloads of civilian refugees in search of friendly hospitality. Together they created – in Sjovald Cunyngham-Brown's phrase – the atmosphere of some insane tea-party. Hay's unit crossed to Singapore on the morning of the 28th. He was genuinely puzzled about the Allied retreat in which he had taken part. 'We have retired over fifty miles from a strong position, which we had been told to hold at all costs, without having seen an enemy or fired more than one shot. We retired in perfect safety. The whole army with the exception . . . of one brigade passed the bottleneck of the causeway without air attack . . . with what object?'[62] Hay was lucky: there were, in fact, formations of lost men, stragglers, wounded, ambush survivors, scattered throughout Johore, some of whom never made it back. Kitching's diary recorded, 'Thursday, Jan. 29th. Johore Bahru has been evacuated and blitzed . . .'[63]

That evening Lieutenant Soper found himself retreating across the Johore Causeway for the second time in a fortnight.[64] After Guy Hutchinson's Johore Volunteer Engineers had prepared the key demolition targets around Kota Tinggi, Australian troops blew the communications on the night of 30–1 January. Hutchinson's men were among the last Volunteers to cross the Causeway, and they were surprised how easy it was. 'We . . . prepared to fight our way to Singapore . . . All we saw was one Red Cap who waved us over.'[65] 'Saturday, 31 January: The Naval Base is evacuated . . . So much for all the millions spent on it . . . We expect the causeway to be blown up at any moment now,' Tom Kitching wrote.[66] By day 'A Jap observation balloon was up in Johore having a good look over Singapore Island';[67] at dusk, constant artillery fire boomed in a blood-red sky. Years later a war correspondent relived the emotion of those last hours:

> I saw the Argylls coming back across the Causeway by moonlight, leading their wounded. I don't know how many of them got out of it. Perhaps one tenth of them. One man was just able to keep the 'Flowers of the Forest' on the bagpipes. Coming through the moonlight in the last stage of the battle . . .[68]

That battle for mainland Malaya was over, but the battle for Singapore was about to begin.[69]

# 13

## An Inexcusable Betrayal

From the start of hostilities the residents of Singapore had been buoyed by a mood of false optimism. One of Shenton Thomas's closest office staff, Mrs Muriel Reilly, insisted that 'the Governor had repeatedly assured me Singapore would *not* fall'; and she believed him.[1] To the European community there was still an air of unreality about events on the peninsula. In mid-January, Alex Cullen, a municipal surveyor, watching 'an eagle soaring majestically and unconcerned away high in the sky', took comfort from the sight. Remarkably, nature was undisturbed. 'In the garden the golden orioles and kingfishers flash and wheel in their glorious colour.'[2]

Thanks to Percival's conviction that to fortify the shores on the Johore Straits would somehow undermine morale, the north side of the island had no defences. When Churchill finally learned of this dire news on 19 January, he was horrified and issued a ten-point action plan requiring the whole male population to be conscripted for defence work. He warned his Chiefs of Staff in Whitehall that 'this will be one of the greatest scandals that could possibly be exposed'.[3] It was little wonder that the planter Guy Hutchinson was stunned when, immediately after he and his weary section of engineers had crossed from Johore, they were ordered to start setting up barbed-wire entanglements along the beaches facing the Scudai river. 'I nearly wept,' he said. 'We had expected a rest – and we were told the Island was a fortress!'[4] Though they carried out the task to order, the machine-gun posts intended to punctuate the barbed wire were never built. Others were equally shocked. When the Australian Prime Minister learned that events might force a withdrawal from Singapore, he sent Churchill a stern warning of the strategic implications if this 'central fortress in the system of the Empire' were to be allowed to fall: it would be seen throughout the Southern Hemisphere as 'an inexcusable betrayal'.[5]

In the second half of January the raids on the island had intensified, the naval base and the aerodromes of Seletar, Sembawang and Tengah receiving the heaviest pasting. In Muriel Reilly's words, 'for weeks there had been huge oil fires burning and the whole of Singapore was covered by a pall of black smoke. I would awaken up at night almost choking.'[6] Tom Kitching kept a tally of the casualties resulting from the indiscriminate bombing of the town – 150 on the 17th, 50 killed, 150 injured on the 20th, 304 killed, 625 injured on the 21st; 383 killed on the 25th; rising by February to around 2,000 casualties a day – yet despite these figures he felt assured that 'the civilian morale in Singapore is magnificent. Asiatics of every race are doing their duty most nobly', while European civilians laboured equally beside them in the air-raid, fire and medical services.[7] However, the civil-defence problem was exacerbated by the acute congestion in the built-up areas. Singapore's population had mushroomed to over a million with the influx of thousands of refugees of all races from the mainland. In addition to the whole rank and file of the defending army, all the top brass of the armed services, civil servants from the Malay Straits, Penang and Malacca, members of the specialist services, planters from all over the peninsula, and the whole tin-mining and commercial community, most with wives and families, were now packed into the island. 'They came across the Johore Causeway like the children of Israel crossing the Red Sea into an already crowded Singapore,' remarked the architect Kenneth Brundle.[8]

The government, however, was dilatory about evacuating women, children and elderly civilians.[9] In 1940 and 1941 a number of European wives, among them Marjorie Soper, Dorothy Cullen, Peggie Snell, Sylvia Cannell, Edith Warin and Ursula Holttum, had chosen to move to Australia, mainly to settle their children into school. When May Froggatt and Kathleen Price decided to make for Perth in December 1941, a number of their acquaintances felt it was premature to leave their husbands, so that there were still berths available to Australia to the end of the year.[10] But the movement of non-European wives was hampered by red tape: it was not until the situation appeared critical that the Australian government, for instance, relaxed immigration restrictions.

Meanwhile, one group of women had been singled out for compulsory evacuation and were treated with unnecessary officiousness by the authorities. When the refugee train from Penang reached Singapore, typewritten notices were handed out to passengers, indicating a government order. Women without children were required to remain in Singapore; women with children – 'non-effectives', to use the bureaucratic language, who included Mabel Price and her sons – were kept locked inside the train for at least three hours, receiving refreshments from the hands of agitated friends through the carriage windows until they were driven by officials to the wharf and herded on to an old Eastern & Australian steamship, the *Nellore*, bound for Java. According to a subsequent report, 'There was no appeal. None of the women knew anyone in Batavia: they had, for themselves and their babies, only the money and the clothes that they could take in their suitcases, and some of them had lost their suitcases at the embarkation at Penang.'[11] As a concession, each woman was allowed to notify her husband by telegram that they were leaving for an unknown destination. The bewildered Price family were confined daily to the hold as far as Batavia. At dusk Mabel took her two sons above, and they 'slept on the deck right beside my lifeboat, the one allotted if misfortune befell us. It wasn't comfortable sleeping on a hard, draughty deck but I felt we had a better chance of rescue should we have been torpedoed.'[12] From Batavia they were shipped on to Australia.

As the Japanese continued to advance down the peninsula in January 1942 the trickle of escapees became a flood. The Barnes, Pallister and Webb families were among those who left aboard the Blue Funnel ship *Charon* on 8 January 1942. For Geoffrey and Ken Barnes, due back at their Australian school in February, the war put a question mark over everything: 'We had no idea what the future had in store or when we should be together again. Mother, bless her, was wonderfully self-possessed and calm. Many were not; and tearful, agitated wives, fretful children and strained faces were to be seen everywhere along the rail facing the dockside as the ship slowly drew away.'[13] The *Charon* reached Fremantle on 18 January after an uneventful voyage, but schoolboy Derek Allton, returning to Western Australia on the SS *Orion*, packed with women and children, recalled the dread of air and sea attack. 'Some are still "swithering", not knowing whether it is safer on the sea or the land,' Alex Cullen observed in Singapore.[14] Those who had been in Australia for some time and had been keeping abreast of events by letter and radio found the news profoundly depressing. 'I imagined that a great stand would be made when they [the Japanese] got down to the Straits of Johore, and that a great battle would be fought for the city,' asserted Ursula Holttum, wife of the Director of Singapore's Botanical Gardens, knowing that her husband was trapped there.[15]

By the end of January 7,000 European women and children had left Singapore (more than twice the number of Indian and Chinese), many hoping to get back to England or at least to India.[16] Among the last ships to take the westward route via Colombo and the Cape of Good Hope were four converted troopships which had arrived on 28 January with 12,000 soldiers. Two days later, amid constant alerts and with the docks ablaze, 'an indescribable scrum' of passengers boarded the *Duchess of Bedford* and the *Empress of Japan*. The *Empress* sailed in the rainy hours of darkness, carrying 1,221 evacuees, some of whom have already figured in these pages: Katharine Sim, Joan Kitching, the nineteen-year-old daughter of Tom and Nora Kitching, Guy Hutchinson's wife, Jessie, and their baby daughter, Mrs Edington, wife of the Johore tin-mine Manager, Nancy Madoc and her son David, Valerie Walker and her mother and sister, from Kampar Estate near Ipoh, Phyllis Benton and her young son from Negri Sembilan, and the Vowler family of Batang Malaka Estate. Eventually the liner reached England safely by way of South Africa.[17] Five days later her sister ship, the *Empress of Asia*, bringing last-minute reinforcements into Singapore, met a different fate. Already bedevilled by rumbles of mutiny, the troopship was dive-bombed in a ferocious Japanese air attack off Pasir Panjang on the island's south coast. It was a major emergency, and Lieutenant Cunyngham-Brown, Malayan Civil Service and Volunteer Naval Reserve, would never forget that day, spent 'hauling soldiers out of the sea – some of them without a stitch of clothing – and landing them at Collyer Quay'.[18] In the rush to save the survivors, their kit together with essential equipment for the British 18th Division was lost, and with the burning wreck of the *Empress* went the hope of escape for 2,000 of Singapore's trapped civilians.

Yet, despite the intensifying air raids and the boom and stench of demolition at the naval base, the first few days of February seemed strangely uneventful to those who had battled their way down the peninsula.[19] 'Nothing happens,' recorded Bombardier Oppenheim, the former Ipoh accountant, on Saturday the 7th: 'A few raids . . . P.T. – reading – arguing – drinking . . .'[20] Troops were encamped haphazardly wherever there were defensible positions with some space and shelter from rains. Periodically they were subjected to intense shelling, and one close pounding brought home to John Soper 'that dreadful experience of stark terror'.[21] But in his last letter to his wife Alex Cullen was bullish: 'It will take a whole lot more than the enemy has been able to do so far.'[22] After a peaceful night, Sunday 8 February dawned fair; 'it seems incredible', thought Tom Kitching, 'that 15 miles away 100,000 men are waiting to kill each other, armed with every inconceivable engine of destruction'.[23] In the afternoon, the Japanese artillery began to soften up the north-west sector of the island. By evening a major bombardment was under way – a prelude to invasion. 'Hell breaks loose. Shells, shells and more shells all night long,' wrote Bombardier Oppenheim summarily.[24]

Having gained a foothold on the island of Pulau Ubin in the eastern sector of the Johore Straits, the Japanese launched their main assault near Sungei Kranji, in the north-west. A breakdown in communication meant the British defence plan to highlight 'the killing area' with search-lights failed; and between dark and daylight 23,000 Japanese troops landed, to begin skilfully infiltrating between the Allied sectors. In twenty-four hours Tengah aerodrome was in enemy hands. Soon after the RAF ground staff abandoned Seletar, the north-eastern airfield. Yet, after wandering round Seletar to locate some guns on Monday the 9th, Bombardier Oppenheim, with surreal timing, was granted a day's leave to have his hair cut at Robinson's, where everything was normal: 'the place is full of folk having elevenses'.[25] Tom Kitching, meanwhile, was mulling over demands for his subscriptions for Singapore Golf Club and Swimming Club while shells whistled overhead, noting drily that 'they should cut down the sub when you get absolutely nix for it!'[26]

It seemed incomprehensible that the Australian, Indian and British brigades defending the northern front would be driven back in three days from Bukit Panjang to Bukit Timah, the last line of defence, but such was the effect of a totally confused Command issuing unrealistic orders. Eyewitnesses noted Australian soldiers looting, throwing away their guns, hot-footing it to the city centre or the harbour.[27] Hutchinson of the Johore Volunteer Engineers spoke from the heart: 'We were very cold, very dirty and very depressed – everyone was running away and leaving us, and we hadn't even seen a Jap.'[28] The city itself was clogged with bomb debris and aimless human traffic. All the hospitals had been shelled and were overflowing with casualties; St Andrew's Cathedral, a temporary dressing station, was crammed with wounded. Yet, to Tom Kitching's disgust, everywhere there were soldiers doing absolutely nothing. By Tuesday 10 February Malaya Command knew the situation was irredeemable, but they ignored a Japanese invitation to capitulate. Churchill was still urging the 18th Division to fight to the last man and make its name in history.[29] Governor Shenton Thomas resorted to the obvious piety – 'We are all in the hands of God . . .' This 'exceeded all others for its sheer fatuity' remarked Morrison of *The Times*.[30] The next day, the 11th, after telling General Percival that the Army must fight to the bitter end, the Supreme Commander of the Allied forces, General Wavell, flew out of the beleaguered island.

The option to stay or to go was not open to everyone – certainly not to the bewildered Asian and Eurasian population, nor to many of the European civilians in uniform, the infirm, the over-fifties and the old hands who had lived in Malaya since before the Great War. For the likes of old 'Abang' Braddon, now an octogenarian, and the survivors of the pioneer generation, T. E. Edmet, who came out in 1898, F. W. Douglas, there since 1895, R. H. Young, doyen of Malayan surveyors, approaching ninety, who first arrived in 1875, and H. W. H. Stephens, who founded the Cold Storage and the Royal Yacht Club and was now ninety-one, there was little point in running away. And there were a number of other pre-1914 veterans not many years younger, such as E. N. T. Cumming, Jack le Doux, Edwin Brown, Dugan Hampshire, Captain Barton, Captain Ramsay, and the elderly Archdeacon Graham-White and his wife, a sweet, frail lady, for whom home and duty lay for ever in Malaya. On the other hand, members of the press corps were advised to leave on the 11th, the day on which the transmitters of the Malayan Broadcasting Corporation were destroyed and Wavell ordered the final evacuation of naval and air-force staff to the Dutch East Indies.

Two days later that order to leave was extended to key service and civilian personnel, including the two naval and air-force supremos, the peacetime head of the Public Works Department, the newly appointed Colonial Secretary, Hugh Fraser, Brigadier Paris of 12th Brigade, Charles Moses, head of the Australian Broadcasting Company, and the

Australian commander, Major-General Gordon Bennett (the latter leaving in controversial circumstances, without General Percival's prior knowledge).[31] Another group who left on the night of the 11th were the Singapore Harbour Board staff, who managed to avoid the minefields and reach Batavia in the old Penang ferry. However, not all European officials who were given the green light to leave did so; some still refused to abandon their posts and accepted the consequences. Dr Philip Bloom and his American wife, Freddy, an auxiliary nurse, who were married during an air raid on 6 February, decided to stay as a matter of conscience. Constance Sleep, who worked in the Blood Transfusion Service, decided that to leave when the demand for blood was ever more urgent would be to desert the very people she was there to serve.[32] Tom Kitching also stayed, though, like countless others, he was now without a home, having been forced out of his beautiful residence in Mount Rosie Road by the approaching bombardment.

Thursday 12 February was a day of wild rumour, indicative of the febrile atmosphere that prevailed. As a precaution, the Governor ordered the removal of all alcoholic spirits, to calm the soldiery. In the evening Kitching went down to the Singapore Club. It was packed out with new arrivals for what proved to be a grand reunion of old friends on an historic evening:

> the last stengahs are being quaffed prior to the destruction of stocks. They have over 200 cases of whisky alone, which must be got rid of . . . The Club of course is absolutely filled to capacity with refugee members from up-country and Singapore members washed out of hearth and home by the ever-advancing wave of the hordes of Nippon: all the fossils of Malaya are there, paleozoic (Abang [Braddon]), mesozoic (E. N. T. [Cumming]) and cainozoic (me). All the boys have disappeared, except one faithful retainer, dumping out stengahs behind the Bar, with Broadbent, the Club Steward perspiringly assisting. And what stengahs! You still go through the formality of signing for them . . . but you can have 'em any strength you like, it matters not, one, two, three, four fingers, take what you want, the rest will be down the drains and into the Singapore River before noon tomorrow.[33]

It was an astounding scene, enacted on a day when law and order had disintegrated, Government House was subjected to heavy shelling, and the Japanese 5th Division was advancing from the Bukit Timah Road towards the outskirts of Singapore town, now ringed by fires.

In the next few hours orders went out to destroy the oil tanks on Pulau Bukum and sabotage Singapore's strategic reserves. Thick black smoke filled the entire sky, turning day into night; paradoxically, it was visible 120 miles away. Down at the docks the mood was one of *sauve qui peut*. Armed and drunken deserters forcibly boarded the *Empire Star*, a cargo ship designed to take sixteen passengers but now crammed with 2,154 servicemen and nurses, preparing to leave under naval escort.[34] Loading also on the 12th were the ill-fated *Vyner Brooke*, once the pride of the Straits Steamship Company's Kuching run, taking on service people, women and children, and sixty-four Australian nursing sisters, and the *Chiang Bee* with Robert Scott on board – as Director of the Far Eastern Bureau of the Ministry of Information he knew he would be a wanted man.

There were still an estimated fifty vessels in Singapore waters – though some were scuttled in these last hours to deny the enemy – when the call came on Friday the 13th for the final evacuation.[35] The order was to move under cover of darkness and to lie low under camouflage by day. A group of Straits Steamship and Mansfield's staff were told to take out two of the Company's remaining 75-tonners, *Rantau* and *Relau*, with Chief Marine Superintendent Baddeley and his assistant, Captain Chamberlin, in command. Joining Captain Baddeley on the *Rantau* were Singapore's Chief Pilot, Captain McAlister, the Superintendent Engineer Les Froggatt and Bill Price, who had supervised both boats' construction. In the heat of Singapore's Dunkirk no records were made of this flotilla, but among the little ships were the *Chiang Tay*, the *Tien Kwang*, the *Kwang Wu*, the *Mata Hari* (a coaster used to plying the Malacca Straits between Singapore and Belawan, now full of women, children and Harbour Board officials), the *Hung Jao* (a customs boat from the Yangtse, carrying sixty officers from Military Headquarters at Fort Canning) and a fast naval patrol launch, the *Fairmile* (which would take a complement of forty servicemen, including Rear-Admiral Spooner and Air Vice-Marshal Pulford).

Throughout that day, Friday the 13th, nearly a thousand civilians – men, women and children – waited to embark in glaring heat at the water's edge. At one point Japanese planes roared over dropping bombs; the crowd flattened, a great human wave lying upon each other. Afterwards the survivors picked themselves up from among the dead and wounded to continue with the waiting game. Then, Sjovald Cunyngham-Brown remembered:

> A distant sniper from the roof of some high building was sending an occasional spray into them with a 'rat-tat-tat-tat' . . . [But] he was certainly not destroying the morale of the waiting crowd. Gramophones were playing – I shall never forget 'Violons dans la nuit' as long as I live – and babies were being fed.[36]

The captain of the *Kuala* took on some 600 passengers. Half were women and children; the rest were RAF personnel, Volunteers such as Naval Reservist and former customs officer Sub-Lieutenant Stuart Sim, doctors and nurses like Dr Margaret Thompson and Nora Kitching, and most of the Public Works Department, including the popular G. J. O'Grady and Major Nunn and his wife. With them, too, were members of the Hartley family, who had made the long trek down from Kuala Ketua on the Thai border. They had been trying in vain to get passports for some time when, suddenly, 13 February seemed to be their lucky day. Clutching pass forms, they headed for the docks. Thirteen-year-old Ken recalled how he and his brother Gordon got past the trooper armed with a tommy gun, and with their mother, grandmother, aunt and crippled uncle boarded the *Kuala*. 'My father didn't even try; he knew where he stood. A couple of my brothers were there to see us off . . . that was the last we saw of the men of the family . . . We looked back and could see Singapore. It was just flames.'[37]

In the sweltering heat and darkness of that Black Friday, the motley flotilla headed out to sea. Bringing up the rear of the armada was the little *Kedah*, beloved by countless Europeans whom it had taken on many happy trips to race meetings in Penang before the war. The *Kedah*, converted to a naval auxiliary vessel, had been bombed on entering the harbour, was shelled at the wharf, and would be repeatedly bombed again at sea by as many as eighty-five enemy planes – 'the most fearsome five hours I have ever experienced . . . I was absolutely petrified', admitted Mrs Muriel Reilly, the Governor's cipher officer. But *Kedah* defied the odds, dodging enemy ships to reach Tanjong Priok, the port of Batavia, largely due to the cool skill of Captain Sinclair.[38] Blue Funnel's steamship *Gorgon*, which had left on the 10th, and the cargo ship *Empire Star*, which formed the advance guard of the mass evacuation, also endured the full onslaught of Japanese dive-bombing, the latter receiving three direct hits before she limped into Batavia, and thence to Fremantle. In the capable hands of Captain Marriott, the *Gorgon* withstood being bombed and machine-gunned and also miraculously reached Western Australia.

However, in the disorganized evacuation, the Singapore authorities took no account of the warning from Allied intelligence in Java that Vice-Admiral Ozawa's squadron had sailed on 10 February to cover the Japanese attack on southern Sumatra and Java and was steaming towards the Banka Straits. In contrast, the British ships, patched up and grossly overcrowded, could make only slow progress. In the menacingly clear dawn of 14 February a number were visibly strung out across the Riau–Linggi archipelago. They were caught in mid-morning by forty Japanese planes, which deployed a relentless hail of bombs and bullets, and in the next five hours eleven boats were destroyed. The *Kwang Wu*, lying off Pompong Island, sank in five minutes. The *Chiang Bee* was caught by an enemy destroyer, and, although a group led by Robert Scott left by lifeboat to try to parley with the Japanese captain, their approach was ignored and the ship was blow up. Cunyngham-Brown on the *Hung Jao* stopped to save some badly wounded men from the *Chiang Bee*. Firing the single gun on the foredeck was a prominent planter and cricketer from Negri Sembilan; with the ship listing sharply, he went down with it, the gun still blazing. The sole survivor from the *Chiang Tay*, which blew up around 11 a.m. in the same attack, was another well-known planter, Puckridge, from Damansara Estate near Klang.[39]

Meanwhile, the *Kuala* had also been caught off Pompong Island. At 9 a.m. a spotter plane flew by. Ken Hartley saw it, and 'I got a ringing clip across the ear for creating panic,' he recalled. But by eleven the Japanese were there in force, and the boy watched the horror unfold.

> They flew really low, and you could see the bomb bays opening . . . One of the bombs went straight down through the bridge to the engine room. The boilers exploded, which blew the Lewis gun off the bridge and wounded the Captain very severely. It was pandemonium. My mother took her life-belt off, tied it on me and shoved me over the side. I can only remember being terrified. I bobbed along and lost contact with everyone. So far as I knew, I was the only one alive – and then the second wave of aircraft were back. I remember those fantastic waves, twenty or thirty feet high, immediately after the bomb had exploded.

There was a massive wall of water, and shrapnel whizzing through it . . .
At some stage I lost consciousness.[40]

Another survivor recalled the scene as men, women and children
fought for their lives.

> Between the islands and the phosphorescent sea floated boats and rafts
> laden with people; and here and there, upheld by his life belt, the lone
> swimmer was striving to make land. All around the rafts and the swim-
> mers were dismembered limbs, dead fish and wreckage drifting with the
> currents; below, in all probability, were the sharks; and above at inter-
> vals the winged machines of death.[41]

After the morning's crushing attack the little *Kuala* continued to
burn until she sank under a canopy of black smoke at 4.30 p.m. Some
of her survivors were later picked up from Pompong and other nearby
islands by native craft or passing boats. On the second night a Chinese-
owned launch, the *Tanjong Pinang*, commanded by a young New
Zealand Volunteer Reservist, was diverted to Pompong to collect the
priority evacuees – 180 women and children and twenty wounded –
who braved a stretch of jagged rocks in pitch tropical darkness to reach
the ship. It is thought that Nora Kitching was among them, a mother
of three, who had worked tirelessly at the General Hospital and was
the last of the Survey Department's wives to leave Singapore. Probably,
too, this was the ship which took Mrs Hartley: 'Gordon told me that
Mother played hell trying to stay behind but she was forced on board
with the rest of the party.'[42] Their respite was tragically brief. The next
night, caught like a trapped hare in the glaring beam of a searchlight,
the *Tanjong Pinang* was slammed by shells. There was a massive explosion, and instantly 'the ship was a ghastly shambles of mutilated
bodies'. As she went down, 'the cries and screams of the wounded, the
helpless and the dying were quite terrible', a survivor recalled.[43] Almost
all were lost, including Nora Kitching, Violet Samuel of Penang, and,
it would seem, Mrs Hartley, the planter's wife and mother of Gordon
and Ken.[44]

As massed Japanese warships and aircraft homed in on the natural
passage of the Banka Straits – 'Bomb Alley' as it came to be known –
the chances of survival for those fleeing Singapore fast diminished. In
an attempt to escape from a formation of Japanese cruisers, the
*Fairmile*, with Rear-Admiral Spooner and Air Vice-Marshal Pulford

aboard, ran aground on Sempang, an inhospitable, malarial island some twenty miles from Banka. Helplessly shipwrecked, their prospects of survival rapidly decreased. Half the forty-two-strong party died, including the two senior British commanders. Meanwhile, on Saturday the 14th the *Vyner Brooke* was approaching the Banka Straits when nine enemy dive-bombers scored several direct hits. The ship was soon ablaze, her lifeboats smashed; she sank in forty minutes, leaving the wounded to drown and the survivors to swim for the Banka shore. By nightfall they had dragged themselves on to a beach near Muntok and set up a rough camp. Here they were discovered by a Japanese patrol on Monday the 16th. The sexes were separated. Officers and men were blindfolded and taken round a small headland where they were bayoneted to death. Twenty-one nurses were made to walk into the sea and machine-gunned. The atrocity might never have become known but for the testimony of two survivors, a stoker from the *Prince of Wales* and an Australian nursing sister.[45] At much the same time the *Mata Hari* was fortunate to escape the fate of the *Tanjong Pinang*. Having survived several air attacks, she was lit by searchlight and ordered to surrender and unload her passengers on Banka Island.

The Straits Steamship boats *Rantau* and *Relau* were also saved from destruction by a twist of fate. Captain Chamberlain recalled that on Monday the 16th

> as daylight came we saw a large cruiser which signalled us to stop immediately, and as the light got better we found ourselves in the midst of a large Japanese convoy of vessels . . . bound for the occupation of Palembang [in southern Sumatra]. We were off the northern tip of Banka Island. We considered the scuttling of Relau but we had so many sick and wounded on board that it was decided against.[46]

Taken prisoner by a boarding party, the *Relau's* crew were disembarked on Muntok's long finger of a jetty, where they met up with their comrades from the *Rantau*, who had had the same experience. 'We got as far as Banka. I remember we woke up in the morning to find ourselves under the guns of a Jap cruiser,' Bill Price recalled. 'They'd have blown us out of the water but they were too close. So they sent a boarding party instead. There was nothing to be done but to take it on the chin.'[47] They were followed into Muntok some hours later by a third former Straits ship, the minesweeper HMS *Tapah*.

Out of the whole flotilla which left Singapore between 11 and 14 February, only six emerged unscathed in the region of Banka Island, to be captured on 16 or 17 February. In this desperate coda to the battle of Singapore, some 3,000 people had died at sea and the vast majority of the little ships that carried them lay at the bottom of the ocean.

On land, too, lives were snuffed out. The Indian army base hospital at Tyersall Park was hit on 11 February and almost 200 soldiers in the wooden huts were burned to death in the ensuing firestorm. As the Japanese net closed ever tighter around Singapore's perimeter, pressing on the west around Mount Faber, another of the many atrocities of the war occurred. On Saturday the 14th ('St. Valentine's Day! What a mockery!' wrote Tom Kitching, on hearing that 12,000 people had been killed the day before)[48] enemy shells exploded an ammunition dump at Alexandra Barracks. The Japanese believed they had been fired on from the site, so they overran the Barracks and the adjacent Military Hospital. There they proceeded to bayonet or shoot patients and medical staff, doctors and orderlies, in cold blood.[49]

Though he had been urged by Wavell to continue the fight to the limit of human endurance, Percival foresaw the possibility of mass reprisals against the civilian population in the event of prolonged resistance and the risk of raging epidemics with the imminent loss of water supplies. With no let-up in the bombing, machine-gunning and shelling, the General consulted his key defence advisers and senior commanders and reluctantly concluded that the only humane course was to negotiate a ceasefire. A deputation led by the Colonial Secretary was rejected out of hand by the Japanese. They insisted that the British High Commander should come in person to their General Headquarters in the former Ford Works at Bukit Timah. The unique picture of British officers, led by General Percival, bearing a white flag alongside the Union Jack as they marched to surrender to a triumphant General Yamashita and his staff appeared in newspapers around the world. It was Sunday 15 February – a day which marked Britain's worst military capitulation on record: some 130,000 British and Commonwealth troops were now prisoners.[50] Tom Kitching summed up the universal feeling: 'from whatever angle you look at this débâcle . . . the manner of the fall of Singapore provides the blackest page in the History of the British Empire'.[51]

A ceasefire was agreed for 8.30 p.m. 'Then came that unbelievable silence – unheralded and uncanny. It was heavenly in its relief, but ominous in its foreboding', wrote G. H. Wade of the Medical Auxiliary Service.[52] 'That Sunday of capitulation I wept some bitter tears,' wrote Constance Sleep.[53] 'So the "Fortress" of Singapore has fallen in one week! It all seems like a dream,' wrote an incredulous Tom Kitching.[54] Bitter disbelief swept over some of the keenest Volunteers. When the message came from his superior officer, 'At first I didn't quite catch what he had said and thought it was the enemy who had surrendered,' was Bombardier Hay's first reaction.[55] 'I was absolutely shocked; had never dreamt of surrender,' Guy Hutchinson admitted. It was his job to tell his section. 'I started to weep and told Pendrigh [his second in command] to tell the chaps while I went off to pull myself together.'[56] John Soper similarly found it impossible to face his platoon: 'I broke down completely with tears in my eyes and my voice just refusing to produce a sound of any description.'[57]

Malaya Command gave out in a circular to all troops that shortage of stores and ammunition had forced the surrender. Seething anger might have overtaken shock had they known the truth. Some Britons began to suspect it the next day, seeing 'a most extraordinary situation. British troops all over the place. Fully armed . . . And yet we have surrendered. And the number of Jap troops to be seen is absolutely negligible.'[58] Ironically, in his last letter to his wife Lieutenant Alex Cullen had posed a hypothesis: 'I'm wondering if they [the Japanese] have the stuff to do it. It seems quite possible that their comparatively meagre resources are strained to the limit . . . *Or is that wishful thinking?*'[59] The same thought struck Bombardier Hay. At the time of the surrender, 'They could only have a small force on the island and it seemed quite possible that they had been outflanked.'[60] Neither he nor Cullen nor Percival knew of Yamashita's anxiety that Japan's shock troops might be overstretched. 'My attack on Singapore was a bluff,' the Japanese commander wrote in his diary – 'a bluff that worked . . . I was very frightened all the time that the British would discover our numerical weakness and lack of supplies and force me into disastrous street fighting.'[61] He had gambled on the British propensity to misjudge the situation – and won.

In the hiatus after the ceasefire some men made their getaway to the harbour. Even at this late hour a few made their way by boat to Sumatra and ultimately to Ceylon. As the darkness deepened, an unnatural calm reigned, 'but most of us were overtired and too keyed up to sleep well', wrote Soper.[62] '11 p.m. . . . I lock my room', recorded Kitching, 'and sleep in the main survey office on four aspirins and a stiff stengah.'[63] Somehow Wade and his medical colleagues found something to celebrate. 'That night we had steak and kidney pudding, Xmas pudding and strawberries and cream all out of a tin for our "Surrender Dinner"', followed the next morning by pork sausages, macaroni and haggis for their 'Internment Breakfast'.[64] They could not have known that these would be their last square meals for three and a half years.

Why did Britain lose Malaya? Why did Singapore fall? Those who paid for the disaster with their freedom were driven by a need to know, and, as soon as the news of the capitulation circulated, 'Around the imaginary camp fires there then began the first of an interminable series of recriminations, trying to place the blame for our failure.'[65] As one man bitterly protested, 15 February was 'the disastrous day that took all the prizes of life away from us'.[66] As if to pre-empt a flood of criticism against the military, two days after Singapore fell General Wavell asserted that 'The trouble goes a long way back: the climate, the atmosphere of the country (the whole of Malaya has been asleep for at least 200 years) . . .'[67] However, this teleological argument had no appeal. The handling of the campaign did not reflect well on senior officers of the armed forces, who stood accused of defeatism, lack of co-ordination, complete chaos at headquarters, and a lack of leadership and foresight. Answers were called for to assuage 'the feelings of those who suffered in the darkness of what they considered to be incompetence'.

Why were our two capital ships, 'Prince of Wales' and 'Repulse' . . . allowed to go outside the zone of our air defence even after the accuracy of Jap bombing had been amply demonstrated? Why were 18th Division ever brought into a battle which had already been lost? Was it mere pig-headedness on the part of somebody in the War House? or was it done on incorrect information supplied by Malaya Command? . . . Why were there no heavy up-to-date A.A. [anti-aircraft] guns to defend such an important fortress? Why was no determined effort made to study, counter and prepare our fresh troops against Jap tactics, especially as regards noise? . . . Why, after wasting valuable troops by sending them to Singapore was the Navy's offer to evacuate a large number of them refused? Was it because Command were incapable of organising such a withdrawal?[68]

General Percival's official explanation for the surrender – shortage of stores and ammunition – cut little ice. 'He might have added total lack of air support and a non-existent Navy,' noted prisoner of war Captain Henry Malet, and the fact that 'the 18th Division which arrived a few days before the end were totally untried troops pitchforked into a pretty chaotic muddle and were only trained for desert warfare. The last 4,000 Australian reinforcements had had 3 weeks' training and had never even fired their rifles in practice!'[69] Inevitably, people cast about for stones to throw, and the most vulnerable figure was General Percival, the commander on the spot. After his eventual release at the end of the war his military career was over, and his reputation has never been fully rehabilitated.[70]

So far as prisoner of war John Soper was concerned, the General and his staff officers were responsible for 'an incompetent and unimaginative command, incapable of rising above red tape and a military orthodoxy based on out-of-date ideas' so that defeat was inevitable. To illustrate this point, it was

> a day or two after the landing on Singapore island when things were extremely critical that an order came round about dress. It had been noticed that some of the troops, both officers and O.R.s [other ranks], were going about slackly and dirtily dressed: this must cease forthwith, and correct dress must at all times be worn. Slovenly habits would have a bad effect on the civilian population. *Even at a time of crisis it was impossible to overcome the ingrained belief, so assiduously cultivated in the army, that the outward appearance of a thing is the only part that matters.*

It was this failure of perception that inhibited proper jungle training, the use of amphibious attacks (of the kind carried out once, in late December 1941 by a mixed naval group on the Perak coast, code name Roseforce), and the exploitation of other guerrilla tactics; it was this absence of imagination that had prevented the British from maximizing the services of the Chinese against the Japanese in Malaya. Those Chinese Communists who were enlisted as irregulars in Dalforce fought with the utmost tenacity and heroism, but 'in Singapore alone their strength could easily have been trebled and the up-country potentialities were entirely untapped'.[71]

This was no maverick view. It was shared by Major Spencer Chapman, who spent the rest of the war with the Chinese guerrillas and agreed with the Chinese judgement that, if the Governor and the GOC had implemented a scheme put to them in August 1941 by the Special Operations Executive for Asian stay-behind-parties under British officers, the Japanese advance could have been delayed until the 18th Division and RAF reinforcements were deployed. As for the controversial commander of the Australian Imperial Forces, remarkably, news reached the prisoners in Singapore that, in the search for scapegoats, 'Feeling in Australia ran very high against General Gordon Bennett, who escaped with his staff before the end. In other words, he was nearly lynched.'[72] According to the evidence of a British Volunteer in the same escape party, the General's nerve cracked on the flight from Singapore.[73] He was the second senior commander for whom the strain had proved too much – Air Vice-Marshal Pulford being the other.[74] Inside the confines of the military headquarters at Fort Canning and Government House, the debilitating personality clashes between the leading figures – Brooke-Popham, Duff Cooper, Wavell, Shenton Thomas and Colonial Secretary Stanley Jones – and the absurd transience of their responsibilities, had undermined cohesive command.[75] The leaders encapsulated the mistrust between civilians, who felt they belonged in Malaya, and the servicemen who had been arbitrarily posted there. Even in the most desperate of situations – on Pompong Island, for instance, after the sinking of the *Kuala* – the hostility between RAF Squadron Leader Farwell and Group Captain Nunn of the Straits Settlements Volunteer Air Force exposed the intense dislike felt by the civilian group of survivors towards the regular services. Civilian Kenneth Brundle, who was there, explains:

> These extreme feelings were symptomatic of the times. Everybody wanted someone to blame for the Malayan campaign fiasco. The first hate was against the Australians because so many of them appeared to be drunken deserters during the late days of February, and secondly the R.A.F. because it was believed that most of their aircraft had been destroyed on the ground with little effort made to get them airborne. Also it was known that when they retreated from their airfields, they failed to destroy aircraft under repair and left their maintenance tools on the ground. (I actually saw this at a Singapore airfield.) Apportioning blame became a prime pastime on the island . . . The survivors were desperate.[76]

The British press had meanwhile added fuel to the fire by denigrating both civilians and service commanders for failing to harness the support of the Malay people. This accusation aroused deep indignation in Europeans like Tom Kitching, who wrote angrily in his diary:

> The home papers are furious about Malaya, but the height of absurdity is reached by the 'Daily Express' which says 'Whisky-swilling planters and military birds of passage forgot that the Malay has the makings of the finest soldier in the East' . . . Ye Gods! Even for the 'Daily Express' this is the utterest of utter tripe. The Malay Police have ratted all over the place, the Volunteers have refused to fight.[77]

It was true that by the New Year of 1942 the Malay Volunteer platoons had disbanded en masse, but those who knew the Malay people well did not necessarily blame them for this action.[78] It has since become obvious that the Malayan disaster was the responsibility of the Europeans, not the Asian races.

This is probably the only point of common agreement. For the rest, the debate continues even after fifty years or more. Duff Cooper's charge against the Malayan Civil Service – that it 'failed lamentably in making adequate preparations for War' – was repeated with relish in the 1990s by the military historian Corelli Barnett, who vilified the Service as 'a handful of imperial rulers in white duck or khaki drill whose minds (with rare exceptions) were ossified by the arrogance of race and empire and hierarchical snobberies of colonial society, and whose energies had been unsprung by long service in damp heat, by a social round lubricated by an excess of gin-slings and stengahs'.[79]

Since then, Peter Elphick and Michael Smith have introduced a new inflection to the debate by demonstrating how the treachery of an army officer – turned mole – helped to precipitate the initial loss of airpower in northern Malaya.[80]

However, British Malayans continued to believe, with some justice, that their civil government was repeatedly hamstrung by Whitehall in its efforts to meet the demands of war, and that the loss of Malaya and Singapore was the responsibility of the armed services and the result of decisions made at home in Britain. The consequence was a deep legacy of bitterness. In the words of Constance Sleep, 'We who remained in Malaya must feel bitter about it until the end of our lives – we still feel that Malaya and we who remained in it were sacrificed.'[81] And Leslie Froggatt asserted, 'London has never experienced, and will never understand, the reactions of the European in the Far East when the Japs came in . . . and above all, that bitter sense of betrayal.'[82] A Volunteer prisoner, Captain Malet, tried to rationalize the situation: 'we know we were sacrificed for Libya and the European fronts, and rightly, too, probably, but it is a bit hard on the likes of us who lived in the country'.[83] To Malet's fellow Malayans (for he himself did not survive his ordeal), it was galling to have to live with the knowledge that in the eyes of the British government around 18,000 British and Allied civilians were expendable – used 'like the instalments of hire purchase to keep an Empire'.[84]

# 14

# *Terrible Forfeits*

In seventy days the Japanese 25th Army had swept the British from Malaya – a month faster than General Yamashita, 'the Tiger of Malaya', had predicted – and had laid the foundation of a Greater East Asia New Order. In a vain effort to stem the Japanese tide, a joint American, British, Dutch and Australian Command (ABDACOM) had been set up on 10 January 1942 under General Wavell, but ten days after Singapore fell this Allied directorate was dissolved, on the irrefutable grounds that there was nothing left to command.

As if to reinforce this point, on 27–8 February a makeshift Allied fleet was badly mauled in the battle of the Java Sea, enabling the Japanese to proceed with their invasion of Java. Meanwhile, the Japanese 15th Army had pushed from Thailand into Burma, forcing British troops into an unparalleled retreat of 1,000 miles to Assam. Rangoon fell on 8 March – the very day on which the Dutch colonial authorities surrendered the Dutch East Indies unconditionally to Japan. Then in Easter Week Vice-Admiral Nogumo's powerful fleet entered the Indian Ocean to threaten Ceylon. In the bombing of Colombo the cruisers *Cornwall* and *Dorsetshire* were sunk, and a few days later the carrier *Hermes*. The remnants of Britain's Eastern Fleet were forced back to Bombay and Mombasa, there to face prolonged inactivity. In the interim, American resistance in the Pacific collapsed, and by May 1942 Japan's conquest of the Philippines was complete. In six months Japanese forces had occupied empires stretching from Rabaul in New Britain to Rangoon – a massive region containing 88 per cent of the world's rubber, 54 per cent of its tin and 90 million people. Churchill had expected that there would be 'terrible forfeits in the East' if Japanese arms went unchecked, but not the true cost, the terminal decline of British authority in the Orient and a horrendous price paid in human terms.[1]

When Singapore fell, there remained a residual European presence on the peninsula. 'Small groups of British and Allied troops and civilians, including a number of former planters, tin-mine managers and district officers, still moved in a kind of twilight freedom around the jungle fringes.'[2] Some had decided to remain in expectation of a British counter-offensive. Men like John Creer, a thirty-five year-old Manxman and District Officer at Kuala Trengganu, the Game Wardens T. R. Hubback and E. O. Shebbeare, and Pat Noone, a brilliant young anthropologist, commissioned in the Argyll and Sutherland Highlanders and an expert on the Sakai aborigines, all had invaluable knowledge of the people and terrain. With a band of experienced rubber and tin executives, they had the potential to form an embryonic guerrilla movement. This included the Glaswegian Bob Chrystal, General Manager of Guthrie's Kamuning Estate, near Kuala Kangsar, his Assistant Boris Hembry and neighbour William Robinson, experienced planters Bill Harvey, Frank Vanrennan, Ronald Graham, Maurice Cotterill and James Hislop, and mining engineers Pat Garden and Brian Tyson, the latter assistant to Pahang Consolidated's Manager, Vincent Baker, who refused to leave Sungei Lembing. A few Britons had stayed at their posts for humanitarian reasons. Dr Evans, Medical Officer at Penang General Hospital, and Dr Gordon Ryrie, Superintendent of the Sungei Buloh Leper Colony near Kuala Lumpur, had decided to brave the Japanese for the sake of their patients. Meanwhile, somewhere in Kedah or north Perak were survivors of the European mining community in southern Thailand who had trekked south in December 1941 after narrowly missing death in a Japanese massacre of Europeans inside a bungalow on the Betong road. There were in addition dozens of servicemen scattered through the jungle, casualties of the swiftly moving battle front, lost, wounded or left for dead by Japanese executioners.[3] Finally, a nucleus of irregulars had infiltrated the mainland, supported by Chinese volunteers, many of them Communists released from prison, who after the Japanese invasion had been hurriedly trained at 101 Special Training School in Singapore to act as 'stay-behind parties'. Their task was to disrupt the enemy's advance.

Early in 1942 the planter turned Defence Security Officer John

Theophilus was busy preparing the ground for these 'behind the lines' guerrillas. He turned to the only help available. In a mission to leave a dump of provisions for a stay-behind party high up in central Johore,

> I had a British forest officer and I had ninety kerosene tins full of ammu- nition, rice, foodstuffs – all to be put on top of this mountain. I had only one lorry and one car, so I said to someone I could trust, 'I want to see the head Communist in Kluang' – this was January '42 . . . he came along. I said, 'One man, one tin.' 'O.K.,' he said. 'Eight o'clock tomor- row morning, on the outskirts of Kluang, I'll have a hundred Chinese, and they will take the stuff and dump it at the top.' Well, I managed to get two or three other chaps with cars. I had about a dozen Communists in my car. The lorry was piled with bodies on top of the stuff, and the Forest Officer took them up to the top and I waited down below. When they came down, I said to this head Communist, 'How much do you want?' – not that I had much money. 'Nothing!' he said. 'It's against the Japanese.' Then he took all the men back to Kluang, and that's the last we saw of them. I also put in two loads of food and receiving sets for some Dutch officers and N.C.O.s and Javanese pirates, one up the Johore river and one at Kota Tinggi.[4]

Another officer involved in the Training School was Spencer Chapman, who became leader of No. 1 Guerrilla Group. He was joined at different times by two members of the School, a New Zealander, Frank Quayle, and an ex-army demolition instructor, John Sartin. In the next three and a half years they all faced formidable difficulties as they operated in the jungles of Perak, Pahang, Kelantan and Selangor. In addition to evading capture, finding secure sites, maintaining supplies of food and munitions, and surviving in isolation in impen- etrable, poisonous vegetation, they had to adapt to the competing presence of Chinese Communist guerrilla bands and those supporting Chiang Kai-shek's rival Kuomintang or National People's Party. But all that lay ahead: little had been activated in February 1942 when Singapore – or Syonan, as the Japanese now called it – lay under a canopy of smoke from smouldering fires, its streets scarred with corpses and the flotsam and jetsam of war.

The logistics of organizing the imprisonment of Allied soldiers and civilians taxed the conquerors, and at first there was little outward sign of the promised new order. A number of lucky Europeans – civil engi- neers, technicians, fire officers, clergy, ordered to keep essential services going – continued to enjoy a certain degree of freedom, but on Monday 16 February the former rubber planter Captain Harry Malet of the Federated Malay States Volunteer Force had his first encounter with the reality of capitulation. 'Outside Brigade H.Q. was a sandbag barricade with a notice printed in English stating that anyone found disobeying or disregarding orders given by Japanese soldiers would be "shot to death" by order of the Imperial Nipponese Army.'[5] As Adjutant to Colonel W. M. James of 'James Force', he accompanied his CO to Fort Canning for a conference to agree arrangements to move the British prisoners of war.[6]

> A huge Jap flag was floating from the top storey windows of the Cathay building which was being used by them as General HQ. [In Fort Canning] I saw quite a number of Malayan Civil Service . . . all looking very lost . . . Among them was Hugh Fraser, Federal Secretary [*sic*] . . . He had been ordered to muster on the Padang on the following morning . . . together with all other civilians. At the Conference . . . we learnt that all European and Australian Forces would be sent to Changi Cantonments . . . Indian and Malay troops were to go to Farrer Park for subsequent dispersal.[7]

At 7.30 a.m. the next day James Force set off on the fourteen-mile march through comfortable Chinese and Eurasian districts to Changi, once home to the Royal Artillery and the Gordon Highlanders. In Captain Malet's words,

> we were actually the first troops to march out of Singapore to 'prison', and as Adjutant I marched beside Col. James at the head of the column and so became actually . . . the first man of the 30,000 British troops to march into captivity – a somewhat doubtful distinction! . . . Here every house, or so it seemed, hung out the Jap 'poached egg' flag and all looked at us in a sort of dumb, sullen way, but not unkindly. Malays we passed en route were inclined to snigger and jeer and also the unpleasant type of Southern Indian shopkeeper. Tamil coolies were plainly horrified and many salaamed as we passed. One Chinese stepped off the footpath into the street and said quite clearly to us, 'Keep your chins up' and 'Good luck'. We marched out entirely without guards and actually saw few Jap soldiers . . . about midday we arrived and parked ourselves at Kitchener Barracks B. Block . . . My feet were almost raw.[8]

John Soper, ever a practical man, had changed his socks during the hourly halt, to prevent feeling footsore. Bringing up the rear of his column, he found they were scheduled to start in the worst of the midday sun, and marching through the damaged village of Payar Lebar, they passed a charred body curled up in the back of a burnt-out car. It was evening before he and two fellow officers finally staggered the last mile to their billets in India Lines, stripped off their kit, and lay down on the grass to breathe in the cool air, which for once was untainted by death or excreta.

Earlier that day, at 10.30 a.m., over 2,000 European civilians had assembled, as ordered, on the grass at Singapore Cricket Club. Harold Cheeseman of the Education Service sensed a viciousness in their captors' mood. 'We were . . . harangued bitterly, passionately, contemptuously on the utter and permanent defeat of the white races.'[9] Tom Kitching's memory was of intense heat, a fearful thirst and interminable delays. His chivalrous instinct bridled at the way 500 women and children (including the wives of senior personnel) were forced to undergo such treatment during the hottest part of the day; despite promises of transport, many of the women had to walk the five miles to internment at the Sea View Hotel, Tanjong Katong. Kitching's eventual destination, with about 600 others, was a large Muslim compound with houses at Karikal, 'absolutely bare, dirty, everything smashed to atoms, very little water, no sanitation, no light . . . nothing to sleep on of course, and no food, only a trickle of lukewarm water to drink'. As gnawing hunger intruded into fitful sleep, he reflected ruefully on the end of a Shrove Tuesday without the traditional pancakes.[10]

Tanjong Katong was a brief interlude which ended on 6 March with official notification that 'the Japanese army is going to accommodate all civilians of enemy nature in Changi Prison', twelve miles from Singapore town. 'Well, I never thought I'd be in gaol,' thought Kitching as he prepared to sleep on sacking over concrete with a sandbag pillow. There were four lorries for the aged and infirm among the 2,000 male internees, and separate motor transport for sick and pregnant women, the elderly and children under twelve. 'The others will walk' was the order.[11] To protect themselves from the scorching sun, the women scrounged every kind of headgear imaginable, from newspaper, cardboard boxes and towels to lampshades and men's hats. This column of 400 women entered Changi legend. The march started with an unexpected glimpse of Japanese *bushido* and ended with a bold display of bravado, as Harry Malet explained:

As they stepped out of the Hotel drive into the roadway they were met by a jeering crowd of Asiatics, mostly Malays. The Jap Guard promptly turned the column back into the Hotel grounds and proceeded to clear the street, chiefly by means of piles of metal ready at the roadside, kept for road repairs! This was a friendly gesture and much appreciated. No more trouble was experienced except at one point where more Malays had gathered by the roadside to have a good laugh at the 'Mems' and children, now being herded to the common gaol like 'Orang jahat' [wicked people]. The Jap soldiers set about them and beat them unmercifully – teaching them a lesson in manners. At the end of this exhausting march, in the heat of the afternoon, the women and children swung into the gaol courtyard through the huge doors, singing at the tops of their voices, 'There'll always be an England' – and if that isn't splendid, I'd like to know what is.[12]

The men on the other side of the walls cheered themselves hoarse.

The Asian races in Malaya reacted in different ways to the collapse of British power. The Japanese anticipated that the 45,000 defeated Indian troops would be a soft target. They were immediately separated from their British officers and were harangued by Indian nationalists to enlist in the Indian National Army and fight to free India from British rule. Whether inspired by a desire for independence or by an instinct for self-preservation, some 20,000 followed this advice. The remainder, who mistrusted the Japanese, were incarcerated in inhuman conditions at Seletar Camp. In their ranks were Muslims who feared a Hindu-dominated Indian National Army and those who had witnessed Japanese executions of wounded and captured soldiers.[13] The Gurkhas held out to a man against the nationalist propaganda, and suffered outrageously: their senior officers were clubbed, starved, tortured and killed. Indian civilians also endured harsh treatment. A merchant recalled his frightening brush with the *Kempeitai*, the military secret police, at the house of a neighbour and local headmaster, Mr Krishnan. The Japanese officer

> turned at me furiously, and he took out his sword and put it on the table and said, 'You are going to be killed today! You are hiding a lot of petrol; you are helping the British!' In the meantime, Mr Krishnan explained, in the little Japanese he had learnt, that we were naturally happy with him as we were his subjects, but . . . he was looking for an excuse to take me, so he said, 'Petrol?' I said, 'Anything you want, I can give you', so

he took the petrol and left me. That was the first time I knew what it was to fear death . . . If Mr Krishnan hadn't come in, I think I would have been slaughtered.[14]

The British languishing in Changi had little time for the conscripts to the Indian National Army – 'mostly composed of ex-Bengali bullock cart drivers, jagas, milk wallahs and cattle herds', one Volunteer remarked heavily. 'Scruffy looking lot and terrified looking too. They must know what's coming to them when this show is over!'[15] The anti-British speeches of Indian nationalists Mahatma Gandhi and Chandra Bose aroused British indignation. Referring to the prominent Singapore Indian lawyer C. S. Goho, an exasperated internee asked, 'Could there be a finer example of biting the hand that fed you? He was up at Cambridge with me in the same college. He takes all he can. He comes to Malaya, he makes a very comfortable living and a small fortune and now . . . !'[16]

Some of the Sikhs and Punjabis employed by the Japanese as watchmen or prison guards were plainly antagonistic to the British, relishing their power, but others showed kindness and respect.[17] One Sikh who refused orders to beat captives was badly beaten up himself and went to the internees' hospital for dressings, but the Japanese immediately tore them off. Meanwhile thousands of Tamil estate coolies were drafted into the Indian National Army or later press-ganged as slaves on the Thailand–Burma railway, where they ended as starving scarecrows, many left to die in charnel houses thrown up in cholera-ridden clearings. Punishment for attempted escape was instant death – a risk that one young Tamil, K. P. Cherian of Kajang, felt was worth taking when he jumped from a Japanese lorry crammed with coolies and fled into the jungle in the hope of surviving until the day the British returned to Malaya.[18]

With their policy of divide and rule, the Japanese treated the Malay people more tolerantly, to gain their tacit co-operation. The Malay Regiment was a patent exception: having won their spurs fighting tenaciously in the battle for Singapore, over 100 Malay officers and men were executed for refusing to disown allegiance to the British Crown.[19] Among the remaining Malay officers the old bonds held firm.[20] Survivors from the *Kuala* testified to the courage of Tunku Mohamed Mohaidin, a Federal Councillor and high-born civil servant, in helping those stranded on the islands and Pompong: 'this Malay was indeed a hero in his self-imposed task of organising rescue missions'.[21] But the price for the Malay people was high. Tunku Jamil of Negri Sembilan, who was lucky to escape being shot as a British spy, admitted, 'I lost everything in the Japanese Occupation.'[22]

Since the British had allowed Malaya to become a battlefield, the Malay peasantry were not surprisingly unconcerned about the fate of Britons caught behind enemy lines. Indifference was interpreted as disloyalty, and reports of Malay treachery circulated in Changi, brought in by new prisoners: 'the Kedah Malays were rotten. They were told by the people in Kelantan and Upper Perak not to trust any Malays lower down the river: "they'd sell anybody to the Japanese for a dollar, tuan!"'[23] The Malays' attitude was '*Apa boleh buat sudah untong nasib?*': 'What can one do when Fate takes control?'[24] The Lancastrian Tom Kitching observed cryptically, 'they can't do owt about it', so 'their attitude is entirely "wait and see"'.[25] Among civil servants who knew the Malay people there was sympathy, but also shame and regret at the British government's failure to protect them. In his farewell message to the British community in Changi on his transfer to Japan, Shenton Thomas asked, 'when the time comes, do what you can for the people of Malaya'.[26]

In the meantime Japanese terror methods tested the loyalties of the local races: 'Posters in the villages printed in Malay and Chinese promised instant death to anyone seen speaking to a European.'[27] In Ipoh a newly married Chinese intellectual, Foo Eng Keng, had to watch while his stationery shop was looted by the passing Japanese. 'I lost everything,' he said simply, but nevertheless, like Tunku Jamil, he was pleased to find himself still alive. With barely enough to live on, he resorted to black marketeering, despite the agony of being caught. 'Every time any small crime was committed, everyone . . . had to go to an open space and stand in the hot sun – it was what you would call mass punishment!'[28] Yet Asians and Eurasians still risked their lives by giving food and shelter to Europeans.[29] The trauma and uncertainty of war turned the Eurasians into 'a distrusted, unhappy community, ill at ease with the new regime'.[30]

Chinese looters had been active in the twilight of British occupation, but their community paid the highest price for the capitulation, particularly those suspected of being Communist. Thousands of Chinese were covertly massacred, drowned, decapitated, tortured to death or machine-gunned in the first week alone. The Japanese admitted to killing 5,000, but estimates of between 40,000 and 100,000 circulated later, including a putative 20,000 beheaded up-country. Among the first victims were a group of sixty to eighty Chinese irregulars machine-gunned at Changi Spit, evidence coming from the Straits Settlements Volunteers who were ordered to bury the bodies. Atrocities were regularly flaunted, the heads of executed Chinese and Malays being displayed on spiked railings in public places. In view of this, the exceptional courage of the Christian Chinese, exemplified by Elizabeth Choy, a young teacher tortured for smuggling food and blankets to sick British internees in Changi, deserves the highest recognition.[31]

Changi cantonment, meanwhile, was home for thousands of Allied men and women, segregated by race, sex and civilian/military status into their own sections or camps. Subject to a body of rules laid down by the Japanese, discipline and organization were handled in the internee camps by camp representatives, and in the military camps by senior officers following military procedure.[32]

Little has been said hitherto about the tensions created by the behaviour of the officer corps in Changi, but in fact some of the Volunteer prisoners were bitterly critical. Norman Bewick, a sugar planter who became Private Secretary to the Sultan of Pahang, had been badly wounded (officially 'killed in action'), a more honourable status in Japanese eyes than surrender. He was treated with respect by his captors, but regarded the British officers as 'scum': 'they had surrendered while they could still fight. We suffered more from our senior officers than we ever suffered from the Japs,' he asserted.[33] In the secrecy of his diary, Lieutenant Soper also berated the quality of the military leadership, describing his superior officer as 'a most despicable character, ill-educated, pig-headed, smarmy and extremely selfish; besides that he is dishonest in his distribution of the stores'. As a result, theft and pilfering were rampant, from the highest to the lowest circles, as if imprisonment had 'thrown into the limelight the inherent self-seeking and greed which seem to be the main factor in the make-up of most characters'. A man of inherent spirituality, Soper was also scathing of the church parades as unnecessary physical punishment for the rank and file and gratuitous ego trips for the officer corps.[34]

Prisoners looked hopefully to the Church for comfort, and occasionally they found it. On his transfer to Singapore, Padre Duckworth, who 'did a very fine job under awful conditions' at Pudu Prison camp in Kuala Lumpur, gave a series of evening sermons which were 'very popular with the troops'.[35] But the missionary teacher Josephine Foss, who was for a time Superintendent of the Women's Camp, observed that 'The Ministers of Religion have not shown up so well.'[36] Leslie Froggatt, a civilian in the military camp, was more explicit:

The forced confinement of so many thousands of men deprived of their liberty . . . meant an immense upheaval in senses of value. Things which before the war were necessities – for instance, a new razor blade weekly, decent soap, a clean towel, changed clothing etc – were now luxuries impossible to obtain. Every man had to adjust himself radically to this different scale of living and values, and here it was that the Church should have played an important part in the delicate task of adjustment.

But the Church missed the opportunity. It was not through lack of Padres and Chaplains – it was not through lack of facilities, nor was it through lack of assistance from the Japanese, who, strangely enough, showed themselves remarkably accommodating in the matter of religion. Church services were extremely well attended and with every prisoner eager for spiritual comfort and guidance to help redress their mental balance surprisingly little effort was made by the Church authorities to take advantage of the circumstances so exceptionally in their favour. There were, of course, individual chaplains who strived hard to meet this need but in the main – especially by example – the Church failed lamentably. In some instances there were cases of extreme selfishness shown by Padres and this attitude did much to destroy the seeds of renascence of spiritual belief amongst the prisoners.[37]

Froggatt made no mention of the Bishop of Singapore, who alienated some Changi internees by exploiting his privileged situation and arrogating to the clerics a personal supply of tinned food.[38] On the other hand, he singled out the four Australian YMCA delegates for their compassionate work in the hospital wards so 'when the tale is told the Y.M.C.A. can be justly proud that its reputation was in such capable and enthusiastic hands'.[39]

However, the picture was not uniformly dark. Shared misfortune produced a certain camaraderie among the prisoners. 'Quarrels were rare and of short duration, with no malice felt afterwards and idiosyncrasies were borne with sympathy and humour . . . In the early days of imprisonment the novelty of the new life had something to recommend it'; without alcohol and tobacco, 'hard drinking old topers, middle-aged men and even younger ones, [were] all losing waist lines and looking clear eyed and clear skinned'; also, sea bathing was unrestricted at first and 'the sea shore looked more like Ramsgate or Southend on a Bank Holiday than a P.O.W. camp'.[40] Despite the gross and demoralizing overcrowding (ten times as many prisoners living in the space of pre-war days), there was still a certain optimism that the war would be over in six months or so.

However, the buoyancy was intermingled with apprehension. The urge to degrade Europeans who had surrendered, the insistence on their bowing to Japanese personnel, beatings for trivial misdemeanours without exception, and the propaganda value attached to the indignity of defeat quickly created disillusion among the prisoners. In the first month, 'We were turned out on two occasions to line the roads for Jap High Command officers,' wrote Harry Malet, observing how smart the officers appeared in their well-cut riding breeches and double-handed swords. The top brass drove in armed convoy, followed by lorries with mounted machine guns. 'The news reel cinematographer also was very much in evidence and took shots of us as he passed in a specially built car.'[41] Within weeks there was a restless impatience for release, followed by apathy, as men joked about the possibility of 'never getting off the Island'.[42] That prediction might be true for some, but in August 1942 the Japanese transferred all senior officials and officers above the rank of colonel, including General Percival, to Japan, in a calculated manoeuvre which deprived the bulk of Allied troops of experienced leadership. Nevertheless, conditions for the internees, though grim, were bearable for the first year, except for the elderly. The failure to repatriate them aroused deep indignation. 'Injustifiable homicide amounting to murder' was Tom Kitching's judgement on hearing that R. H. Young had died at the age of ninety; eighty-three-year-old 'Abang' Braddon and ninety-one-year-old H. W. H. Stevens had already gone.[43]

Kitching, a conscientious recorder of camp statistics, claimed that twenty-four nationalities were represented in Changi Gaol, with the total numbers fluctuating in excess of 3,000 and including French, Dutch, Danes, Norwegians, Eurasians and Jews. In the women's camp the single largest group were wives and housewives, with some sixty children and babies. They were accompanied by a contingent of nurses, a handful of doctors, some missionaries and teachers, and a small

number of elderly or infirm ladies. To keep the children under control
an open-air school was started, and they were taught in age groups of
mixed nationality.[44] On the whole the male internees were professional
people – intelligent, well educated and skilled, resolved to make the best
of the situation.[45] Their first priority was to set up basic medical services
and camp amenities (including a library of 5,000 books salvaged from
homes and collections in Singapore). Despite a lack of space, football,
cricket, badminton, hockey and volleyball matches were played before
enthusiastic spectators, and there was an insatiable demand for mental
stimulus in the form of books, lectures, talks, debates, quizzes, bridge
and chess. The Australian concert party drew universal praise among
prisoners, while 'the energy of 10,000 Britons camped up in Changi
burst out in a thousand different directions – courses on every subject
and language, societies for every hobby and sport, theatres for everything
from Shakespeare to *Journey's End*, classical concerts and light music'.[46]
Harry Malet, gave a taste of the exuberance of the early months:

> Amateur talent is abounding. We put up an excellent show here in W
> block, built a stage with canvas back cloths, curtains and all, in the
> garden . . . Bill Riches sang, 'As you're strolling down Changi High
> Street', all local songs and topical stuff . . . Russell Weight played his
> squeeze box and also did all the piano accompaniment . . . Our Southern
> Area permanent theatrical party is established in the old Changi village
> outdoor cinema; the stage and orchestra being covered and the enclo-
> sure holding 600 men. This party is composed of mostly ex-professional
> actors, musicians, etc. and with local talent added, they have . . . so far
> put on three vaudeville shows. They have a Christmas pantomime
> coming into rehearsal shortly.[47]

Classical music was equally in demand, and John Soper recalled a
symphony concert held in March 1943, 'a magnificent effort . . .
They played a lovely piano concerto from Schumann, the pianist a
professional, Rennison by name.' Confinement, however, produced
frustration. As Lieutenant Soper also remarked: 'Never have we had
so much leisure, never, I hope, shall we be so powerless to make full
use of it.'[48]

Morale was vital for survival. A joke at Japanese expense was a tonic.

> One small example of this sense of humour that kept us going; Jim
> Swanton (the Daily Telegraph Cricket Correspondent and Broadcaster)

and myself and some others were trying to prepare a cricket pitch out of mud for a Christmas Day cricket match when we were approached by a suspicious looking Japanese who seemed intent on wishing to interfere with our labours and wanted to know what we were doing. 'Preparing for a religious festival,' promptly replied Jim Swanton. 'Cricket is religion in England you know.' 'O.K., O.K.,' said the Japanese, who at that period had some respect for religion, and walked off much to our relief and amusement.[49]

However, on 15 March 1942 Tom Kitching recorded, 'We have our first suicide today. There will be more if conditions are not improved.' In May a young police officer lost his reason and was committed to a mental hospital, but died a week later.[50] In another case death was attributed to 'simply not having the will to live or help himself, constantly brooding on his troubles, a mass of self-pity'.[51] Malnutrition brought bouts of depression. Although he was involved in vital life-saving work, Soper became introverted and nursed wild compulsions.

May 17th 1942. I don't seem to be doing anything really worthwhile here . . . What I've been doing as my major job these last fifteen years is not of much value . . .
7th February 1943. It has been a mentally disturbed week. I think I've successfully conquered the idea that I am going to die here which came very strongly some days ago, but I have a sort of general feeling of unrest which may even exhibit itself in some rash attempt to escape. For two or three days I've been toying with the idea of working down to Australia by sampan . . .
21st February 1943. Felt very bad yesterday, mentally and physically . . . Am I a fool to keep harping on escape? It means almost certain death if caught, but it often seems that a swift death would be better than this slow suffocation.[52]

The trauma suffered by married prisoners in the Far East is a neglected subject, hidden in the pages of diaries and undelivered letters touching on intimate physical details and a gnawing sense of loss. 'I need somewhere to put down my thoughts and feelings as if you were here to talk to and discuss things with . . . to make life more liveable,' scribbled John Soper in a flimsy exercise book; 'after the capitulation I willed and telepathised you with all the intensity I could muster to let you know I was safe, and I am quite sure I got through to you . . . Every night I try to send you, by will power and prayer, strength and encouragement.'[53] Alex Cullen cherished a photo of his wife Dorothy in her 'snappy little hat'. He wrote, 'I'm very conscious of you . . . my own to love, my own to hold in my arms again if God is kind . . . All the days we have had together make a wonderful story . . . I know you will not fail me . . . Dearest, whatever happens, you must remember that I did think of you like that.'[54] Now and then emotion spilled over, as in this soliloquy of an interned planter to his wife:

> How long, how long . . . mio? This waiting is a wearying business . . .
> If, by the remotest chance, it should not go well, then . . . my dearest,
> you will know that my heart is full of love for you and that my only wish
> will be for your well-being . . . Last night I dreamed of you . . . such a
> lovely dream, and today I feel quite happy and confident. We are really
> very close together. I wonder if you feel the same?[55]

Dreams helped Tom Kitching to cope with his anguish about his wife's fate: 'Nora comes to me in a dream this night. We have a long, intimate talk. I feel sure she is all right.' He was sustained by mental evocations – Nora in conversational flow, Nora throwing a dinner party, Nora and Tom together on a repatriation ship – although she had died in the *Kuala* tragedy before his internment.[56] Thinking of his wife, John Soper found solace: 'at the early morning service you seemed to be kneeling next to me at the altar rail' and at Christmas 'you came and stood beside me, very real and very near, so distinct that you must have been willing it'.[57] Dorothy and Alex Cullen shared a commitment to the Presbyterian Church; his 'deeply Christian spirit' – the words of Fr Gerard Bourke, the Redemptorist priest who prayed with him – bolstered his faith in his wife's courage and devotion.[58] Harry Malet found comfort from attending Benediction in camp with his brother-in-law, Hugh Sandeman. He 'loved this as I could imagine Jo and the kids going to the very same service six hours later'.[59] But the Japanese policy of withholding mail increased prisoners' worries. 'If only they knew we were safe and well, it would make all the difference,' Malet grumbled. 'The uncertainty of everything must be pretty deadly and I know Jo worries herself sick and cannot show it in front of the kids. Please God the Japs will allow us to write or send our casualty lists home to the War Office via a neutral country.'[60]

As their imprisonment dragged on, many husbands felt the nagging fear of infidelity, as physical weakness destroyed their self-esteem. A diary entry records 'A long discussion the other night on what attitude we should take if upon return we found that our wives had been unfaithful.' John Soper pondered: 'Sometimes I wonder whether it might be better if I don't come through, then a very much better, idealised me would go on living in your heart, but if I come back to you, disillusionment will come with me.' His anxiety was transferred to his wife's state of mind: 'Spiritually and mentally you must be going through a bad time. It might even be better for your present peace of mind if I were dead and gone . . . But as it is you must be alternating spells of worrying about me with unfulfilled longings and frantic prayers for the ending of this ghastly war which keeps us apart.'[61]

Family men speculated as to whether their wives could cope alone with family responsibilities away from home. In his diary of letters, the rubber planter Pat Warin begged his wife, 'please don't despair . . . I fear that it is going to be very difficult . . . You have a big task to take care of J. and A. and I'm sure you will succeed, and my love will be with you always, always.'[62] As if answering her husband (though events prevented her from posting the letter), Dorothy Cullen insisted, 'Don't worry about us . . . for your sake and the children's I will be strong. I won't give way to despondency and despair. I'll try and make a happy home for the children and please God some day we'll be together again.'[63]

With hindsight, stress levels among the refugee women from Malaya were probably greater than anyone realized, and anecdotal evidence suggests that a fair number of these women died relatively young. Although emotions were seldom openly discussed, they were privately recorded. 'I have gone down into the depths . . .' wrote Dorothy Cullen, 'a black darkness where one feels the waters are going to close above one's head.'[64] In addition to worries over husbands captured or posted missing, there were concerns for relatives in war-torn Britain and for brothers and sons fighting at the front. For those in Australia there were also misunderstandings with their hosts over the conduct of the Malayan campaign.[65] The British refugees felt vulnerable, facing indefinite separation, possible widowhood and financial constraints. 'After all, what were we?' asked one. 'No home and no country . . .'[66] Mabel Price had a small reserve of £200 in the Bank of New South Wales, but otherwise had to manage on £4 10s (£4.50) a week from the Lord Mayor of London's Fund. With rent of 30s (£1.50) a week, she was allowed to do 'menial tasks to augment the allowance':

I found myself a position as a 'char lady' to a lady living in a flat close by
. . . My little charring job went well until I was asked to clean the lava-
tory pan. That I refused to do, so I started to sew with a machine I had
bought cheaply . . . Then I got another job to clean a flat occupied by
American servicemen . . . This I did, expecting some continuity of work.
It was very dirty. As soon as I cleaned up the mess, I was promptly given
the sack . . . I was being used.[67]

There were many adjustments to be made. Some British refugees
found it hard to share cramped accommodation and to do without
refrigerators or air conditioning. 'The dry, burning heat was much
more trying than Malaya. There we never had dust or grit and our huge
trees were vast and shady, and our houses open to the moist air. I was
homesick for Malaya,' confessed Ursula Holttum. Her Australian
neighbours were curious 'to see what crazy kind of an English woman
I could be'.[68] In Fremantle Mrs Price felt:

> we were received with mixed feelings by the Australians, who only knew
> us to have servants to work for us, while they had to struggle in the olden
> times to make a home and find work. I remember on arrival being told
> 'Jack was as good as his master in this country' . . . A tough lot the
> Australians, living in a tough country.[69]

In time the newcomers adjusted to their new environment, and
many Malayan children received great kindness and an excellent education in Australian schools.[70] Living in close communication, the
wives gave each other moral support. 'My mother and others in her situation in Geelong gave us children a marvellous and rich childhood,
concealing what must have been a constant anguish and anxiety about
what was happening to their husbands and relatives,' Gordon Snell of
Singapore remembered.[71] When the Japanese bombing of Darwin
posed a direct threat to Australia, young Malayans accepted it as part of
a never-ending adventure. 'I remember being amused when the Jap
invasion panic hit Western Australia in 1942,' said Derek Allton. 'We
were given picks and shovels and frantically urged to dig zig-zag
trenches' in the school grounds, and 'we practised air raid drill flat on
our faces in the corridors'.[72] The threat receded after the American
fleet's two costly victories in the Coral Sea and at the battle of Midway
in May and June, which in retrospect marked the turning point in the
Pacific War.[73] Meanwhile British families listened in to the plaintive

tinkling of 'Home, Sweet Home' as Tokyo Radio broadcast names of prisoners in enemy hands, and rejoiced at the arrival of an occasional postcard via the International Red Cross. The prisoners' messages were stereotyped and out of date, but there was no denying the thrill when one husband beat the Japanese censor with the curious message 'Continuing Healthy And Not Getting Ill', revealing that he was in Changi.[74]

By 1943 conditions in Changi were deteriorating. The interminable diet of rice, supplemented by black-market purchases and some camp-grown produce, preyed on minds and bodies (and incidentally reduced the sexual drive). The prisoners became obsessed with the minutiae of their diet and with 'feasts' to celebrate birthdays, wedding anniversaries and other occasions. 'I am loath to admit', wrote Pat Warin to his wife, 'that my thoughts were very often, and are, concerned with food, but it is difficult to think otherwise when one is hungry.'[75] Stealing became acceptable, as 'the stomach overrides all morality'.[76] Other ranks suffered much more than officers: 'One sees some ghastly specimens of walking skeletons about the place,' Harry Malet observed.[77] Rations and rumours dominated conversation. Rumours that internees would be repatriated circulated like wildfire, but were always dashed.

The separation of 173 internees from their wives was a hardship never shared by Japanese nationals imprisoned in India. (But, with ingenuity, the internees found a way for them to meet each other once every six or seven weeks, to exchange a glance and a hurriedly whispered word over a bin of garbage.) More culpable was the Japanese strategy of raiding Red Cross supplies, depriving prisoners and internees of essential medicines, so that hundreds – diabetics, for example – died untreated. 'The Nipponese are a curious mixture of savagery and elements of decency,' wrote Tom Kitching: the result was total unpredictability.[78] The first Camp Commandant, Major Kito, was, in Harold Cheeseman's words, 'a beast of a man whose appearance was a reflection of his bestial brutality'.[79] Even Lieutenant Asahi – a moderate man, reputedly a Christian – could not prevent face-slapping and punching. But in April 1943 a new and sinister figure, Tominaga, took charge of discipline. He imposed a regime of calculated deprivation and ill-treatment. Touring the camp one evening, a Japanese officer indulged in a mass assault on twenty-two men and four women.[80]

In September 1942 there was a major confrontation. The Japanese required all military prisoners of war to sign a form undertaking never to attempt escape. They met with mass refusal. In retaliation, the prisoners were marched to Selerang Barracks, where over 15,000 were crammed into an area built for 2,000. That same day four British soldiers who had escaped and been recaptured were executed by firing squad before the British area commander. After three days without proper food, shelter and sanitation, amid a growing threat of epidemics, the senior officer accepted the 'order' to sign, taking personal responsibility for his men. The British saw it as a moral victory. 'The spirit of the troops throughout, though it sounds hackeneyed, was magnificent,' said one participant.[81]

For the internees the testing time came a year later. This crisis was triggered by a daring Allied commando raid on Japanese shipping in Singapore harbour. On 10 October 1943 the *Kempeitai* descended on the gaol to seize individuals they believed had conveyed vital intelligence to the commandos. From dawn to dusk the internees were kept outside in the sun without food or drink while an intense search went on for a radio transmitter and other damning evidence. Starting that day of the notorious Double Tenth and continuing through 1944, some fifty-seven civilians were arrested and taken to various interrogation centres in Singapore. They were held in cramped cages under barbarous conditions, deprived of food, sleep, movement, speech, privacy and medicine, and underwent mental and physical torture. Many of the men were middle-aged or prominent figures such as Leonard Wilson, Bishop of Singapore, Hugh Fraser, Acting Colonial Secretary, and Robert Scott, Director of Information and survivor from the *Chiang Bee*. Three women were also seized – an American-born journalist, Mrs Freddy Bloom, her friend, Dr Cecily Williams, a gifted and dedicated doctor, and the latter's successor as Commandant in the Women's Camp, Mrs Dorothy Dixon. Although they were spared the physical inquisition, they were subject to gross humiliation and mental torture. Fifteen men died; one, J. S. Long, Assistant Commissioner of Police, was executed.[82] In the meantime all remaining privileges in Changi were cancelled, the diet was drastically reduced, and draconian orders were constantly issued. 'So the war goes on,' wrote Tom Kitching cryptically. But his health was fast deteriorating. The last entry in his diary, on 1 April 1944, records, 'We thought the "Double Tenth" inquisition was over, but today they take three more, I am told, including Rendle and Ker.'[83] The third was Penseler, once Manager of the Raub gold mine in Pahang. All of them, and Tom Kitching himself, died in Japanese hands in the course of that year.

Throughout 1942 news of atrocities against the Singapore Chinese and of deaths and executions up-country were brought by prisoners' working parties or those transferred from other gaols, such as Penang Gaol and Pudu Gaol, Kuala Lumpur. Reports also percolated into Changi of failed escapes, and the disastrous events at sea around Black Friday emerged from prisoners transferred from camps in the Dutch East Indies. Scraps of news were seized on eagerly, kindling hopes that loved ones might be free; twenty-seven husbands in Changi awaited news of their wives aboard the *Kuala*. Dozens of evacuees, including a few of the *Kuala*'s passengers (G. J. O'Grady was one), did make it by the only viable routes along Sumatra's Indragiri or Djambi rivers and over the highlands to the west coast. Most of the parties who arrived at Padang-Emmahaven before 6 March, including 1,600 British soldiers, eventually reached Colombo by boat. Safety eluded hundreds more, however. The Penang lawyer Charles Samuel, who had been on the *Kuala*, reached Padang on 7 March but waited in vain for a passage to safety. Cunyngham-Brown, volunteer Naval Reservist and former Labour Controller in Johore, arrived too late and was eventually captured, as were his colleagues Lieutenant Robin Henman, and Sub-Lieutenant Stuart Sim, the erstwhile customs officer at Lamut. The Dutch ship *Rooseboom*, which had left Padang on 26 February with over 500 people on board, was well on course to Ceylon when she was torpedoed by a Japanese submarine in the Indian Ocean. All but four passengers went down with the ship or suffered a lingering death adrift in a single lifeboat. The dead included Brigadier Paris, commander of the 11th Indian Division, Major Nunn, head of the Public Works Department, and his wife, and Mrs Savage-Bailey, mother of the actress Dulcie Gray.

The fate of the Straits Steamship–Mansfield's party captured off Banka Island on 16 February was decided at Muntok. Les Froggatt recounted:

Members of the Services, civilian men, women and children – about 1,500 in all – were herded together in the Jail and in the coolie quarters of the Tin Mining Co. at Muntok, the men being sent on working parties to the aerodromes and seaplane anchorage almost immediately. A little badly cooked rice and extremely weak tea was all the food available for the first five days and on Saturday morning various members of the crews were ordered on board to take the captured ships back to Singapore where they arrived at the Naval Base on Friday, 27 February, the escort comprising 32 Japanese men o'war, including battleships and heavy cruisers . . . Those who remained behind at Muntok were later transferred to camps near Palembang in Sumatra where food conditions were appalling, and the death rate extremely high.[84]

Starvation, malnutrition and disease would be the common experience of all the civilians who fled from Malaya only to be caught in Sumatran waters. Interned in various camps around Palembang, Padang, Lobok Linggau or Banka Island, they faced worse conditions than their compatriots in Changi, where there were at least permanent buildings, water and sanitation.[85] Those past their prime had little hope of survival: Charles Samuel, aged sixty-one, who fought against aching worries about his wife's fate aboard the *Tanjong Pinang*, died of pellagra in Padang Gaol in December 1944. He had fought hard; his diary entry for the 233rd day of internment noted, 'I must *not* let myself go "down hill".'[86] Conditions at Banka – known as 'Dead Man's Island', because of the prevalence of the severe, recurrent Banka Fever – took a progressive death toll among young women, including nursing sisters, in their twenties and thirties. Almost a third of British women and around a half of the men died in Palembang and Muntok camps, many, tragically, towards the end of their internment.

Even so, these civilians fared better than the Malayan Volunteers, who, although military prisoners of war, found themselves drafted as slave labour to various parts of Japan's Co-Prosperity Sphere. Few of those transferred to Borneo were to survive. Captains Chamberlin and Baddeley, captured off Banka Island, were sent to Japan for interrogation as suspected naval intelligence officers. After a spell in Ofuna, a special *Kempeitai* camp, during deepest winter, they spent two years labouring in the Mitsubishi shipyards and Honshu steel mills. Others were drafted into Japan's carbide factories or to Formosa or Korea. Cunyngham-Brown and his companions, following a series of bizarre and poignant adventures redolent of fiction, were sent as lumberjacks to the Manchurian Railway Company at Pekan Baru on the east coast of Sumatra, where they met up with Katharine Sim's husband, Stuart, among the dwindling band of slaves. Only those at the peak of their physical stamina and with experience of living in the East had a hope of survival. Driven beyond endurance, starved, disease-ridden and dehumanized, three-quarters of these in Pekan Baru died in eighteen months – almost 3,000 out of a workforce of 3,800.

By comparison, Leslie Froggatt's group, repatriated from Muntok to Singapore, were fortunate. 'During the next 14 months we were engaged in work at the Naval Base, operating from there to Johore, Penggarang and Keppel Harbour, at the end of which time native crews were employed and the P.O.W.s were all congregated on a depot ship which was moored off the main pier at the Naval Base.' Some also worked as coolies at the nearby Seletar airfield, which had suffered in the Japanese shelling of Singapore. It was gruelling labour for middle-aged Britons:

> There were about 100 in all and daily working parties were sent ashore to undertake all kinds of jobs varying from digging drains, cleaning latrines, salvaging and breaking up boats which had been sunk or scuttled during the attack on Singapore, making roads and every kind of arduous, humiliating and objectionable task that could be found. Food was scarce and beatings frequent. One by one our members fell sick, no medical facilities were available, and when we reached an extremely low state of health, we were transferred to the British Camp Hospital at Selerang, Changi.[87]

Already a flow of hospital cases had returned to Changi from other work camps around Singapore, particularly Blakang Mati (now Sentosa). From May 1942 rumours mounted of more distant transfers: there were hints of rest camps in the Cameron Highlands for convalescence, but also talk of Bangkok and a railway project. Harry Malet grew anxious:

> June 26th [1942]. Bob Hardie left with an up country working party today. I shall miss him . . . I wish I knew their destination. Guesses range from K.L. to Thailand. Some fifty went from F.M.S.V.F. which pretty well clears us out . . .
>
> July 17th. A party of 2,200 (750 from S. area) to go – all colonels upward; B party of Lt. Colonels and below to O.R.s – 1,100 (800 from S. area).
>
> August 6th. The Japan party is said to be due to leave on the 11th or 12th and the rest of Changi moves to Bangkok soon afterwards to a camp

already prepared for 10,000. I do not like this idea as I feel we may be dumped in some fearful fever-ridden hole . . .

August 17th [referring to a further party about to go overseas] . . . Please God the same fate as that which is said to have befallen the second overseas Aussie party (to Rangoon) won't be theirs. That ship was sunk by an American submarine and 1,500 Aussies were drowned like rats in a trap.[88]

Captain Malet's fears were fully justified. Allied submarine activity in the Malacca Straits accelerated the construction of the railway from Bangkok to Rangoon. The route ran from Bampong to Kanchanburi, past the Mekon river and skirting the high mountains above the valley of the river Kwai to the Three Pagodas Pass into Burma, serviced by a chain of primitive work camps. 'The line is an amazing feat, running on shelves cut out of rock faces, over bridges made entirely of timber except for cement foundations, and through the wildest and hilliest country,' wrote one prisoner.[89] But the cost was a saga of perverse cruelty, suffering and death, of endurance and superhuman achievement by slave gangs who lost one human life for every sleeper of its 400-mile length. 'If you should hear stories of ill-treatment which you would be inclined to disbelieve as being far-fetched, think again and believe them,' begged John Soper, who was with the last of the doomed F Force to leave for Thailand; 'nobody can invent things worse than actually happened.'[90]

Forced into long night marches through pitch-black monsoon jungle until they arrived at the highest reaches of the Kwai, the white coolies of F Force then slaved to clear the ground from the railhead, while H Force followed up, laying the track. Isolated from normal human contact, they were driven without mercy and ravaged by cholera, transformed into hollow-eyed, emaciated human wrecks. The Japanese put European POW deaths on the Thailand–Burma railway at 13,000, but that figure rose to 20,000 as the evacuation of the sick and dying navvies began, while the death rate in the Asian workforce may have exceeded 200,000.[91] The causes were 'starvation, climate, hardship, accidents, occasionally personal violence, neglect, poor physique, despair, neurosis and disease', as bodies were plagued by fever, malaria, dysentery, cholera, beri-beri, pellagra, ulcers, gangrene, scurvy and skin parasites.[92] In June 1943 both Harry Malet and Alex Cullen died from amoebic dysentery at a notorious mud and jungle clearing above Tarsao known as Kanyu, along with many other Volunteers. Malaria, dysentery and cholera killed a tenth of the camp in four weeks, as the torrential monsoon rains were at their height. Letters telling of her husband's death, written to Dorothy Cullen after the war by fellow Kanyu prisoners, her brother, Robin Band, and the Catholic priest Fr Bourke, tactfully concealed the truth: that it was a malignant place, shrouded in 'a dim, grim sense of foreboding'. Malet's diary, which ended in April 1943, came into Dr Robert Hardie's hands; Cullen's few possessions – fountain pen, scissors, pocketbook – were also salvaged. His compassionate nurse and friend David Waters survived only two more months.[93] On the completion of the railway in October 1943 the remnants of F and H Force returned piecemeal to Changi. They could move only in slow, painful stages – a weak, scarred, bandaged, 'bedraggled, ragamuffin, pitiful crowd'.[94] Some units were reshipped to Japan; others were directed to base camps at Chungkai, Kachanburi or Nakhon Nyok, and remained in Thailand until 1945.

In 1944 changes occurred in Changi. On 1 May the internees were transferred to a pre-war British service camp at Sime Road. 'The sense of comparative freedom is a wonderful mental tonic,' remarked internee Pat Warin: there were timber huts, room to grow vegetables, and the promise of better conditions from the officer in charge, Major-General Saito.[95] Changi Gaol was then filled with 7,000 military prisoners, including the survivors of F and H Force, employed on light duties, while the able-bodied were deployed on heavy construction work building Changi Aerodrome. The prisoners were plagued by deficiency diseases – the result of cuts in rice, tea and palm-oil rations, a shortage of drugs, and hyperinflation in the black-market economy of Singapore. Despite the relative humanity of Commanding Officer Takahashi, beatings and deaths continued daily. Yet a new-found camaraderie gripped Changi, enlivened by concerts, theatrical performances at the prison playhouse, and illicit daily news bulletins on the progress of the war from the BBC, which proclaimed the advent of D-Day and sweeping Allied successes in Europe. Among the heroes of the war, it was universally agreed, were Volunteers who at the risk of torture and death ran successful radio operations. The brothers Max and Donald Webber, for example, operated in Thailand, giving over 700 news bulletins to camp inmates. 'It would be hard to overestimate the importance of these regular listenings to the BBC in maintaining and boosting the morale of all of us,' wrote Robin Band.[96]

In 1944 growing air and naval strength began to turn the war in the East decisively in the Allies' favour. Changi men felt a certain satisfaction when the Allies bombed the Burma–Thailand railway and destroyed a Japanese troop train and an ammunition train, and on 5 November there was great excitement when American Superfortress bombers attacked Singapore harbour. Allied planes were also making reconnaissance flights over the peninsula, to begin shortly the dropping of supplies and personnel to the Chinese resistance groups of the Malayan People's Anti-Japanese Army. With Japanese power concentrated in the towns and on the western plain, covert operations were limited to occasional ambushes of troops in transit. In 1943 and 1944 the Japanese struck back with concerted attacks on the jungle plantations supplying the resistance with food. Urban Chinese then took even greater risks in supporting the guerrillas.[97]

Meanwhile the British stay-behind officers had suffered mixed fortunes. A number were captured or died from disease in the jungle. When in 1942 their attempted escape from Pudu Gaol failed, Ronald Graham, Bill Harvey and Frank Vanrennan had been beheaded at Cheras Cemetery, Kuala Lumpur, after digging their own graves: 'the horror of that final scene haunts me to this day', wrote Cecil Lee, a fellow prisoner and friend.[98] One remarkable woman, Nona Baker, who shared her brother Vincent's jungle ordeal until his death in spring 1944, survived in Pahang by co-operating with a Chinese Communist guerrilla unit, helping to prepare leaflets in English and teaching English songs. In June 1942 Bob Chrystal had become instructor in jungle warfare to a group of young Communists, the No. 5 Independent Anti-Japanese Regiment, based in upper Perak. Among them was an intelligent Chinese youth named Chin Peng. Driven by idealism, Pat Noone also co-operated with the Chinese Communists, inducing Sakai tribesmen to work as spies and couriers against the Japanese. However, Noone, Chrystal and his jungle companion John Creer grew disenchanted with the Communists' tactics and their anti-British propaganda. Creer and Chrystal were forced into an eerie, itinerant existence, spending alternatively months on their own or together, or with Temiar aborigines and the Kuomintang in Perak and Kelantan.

Maurice Cotterill and Bryan Tyson had joined a Communist company in north Johore, where Spencer Chapman visited them on New Year's Day 1943. Chapman was a pragmatist and accepted the need to work with the Communists, but he moved between the guerrilla groups in Pahang, Negri Sembilan and Perak. At Christmas 1943 he linked up near Tapah with two intelligence officers who had escaped from Malaya in 1942 but had returned by submarine in August to take over covert warfare in Malaya: John Davis, a Chinese-speaking officer of the Straits Settlements Police, and civil servant Richard Broome of the Chinese Protectorate. The two men made a perfect team, in Spencer Chapman's judgement. Davis – determined, stocky and immensely strong – was the head of Force 136, the Far Eastern branch of the Special Operations Executive, based in Ceylon.

Their initial priority was to establish wireless communication between South-East Asia Command (SEAC) and the anti-Japanese forces in the interior, to facilitate intelligence gathering. But 1944 proved a frustrating year. The cumulative effect of lack of food, medicine and technical equipment was exacerbated by the capture in Perak of key Chinese agents; one, Lim Bo Seng, a fiercely anti-Japanese member of Force 136, died under torture. In October two former planters, Major Paddy Martin of Sungei Papan and his estate-deputy Captain Browning, who had also escaped in 1942 but enlisted for special operations, were betrayed to the Japanese and ambushed in Johore: Martin was killed. Spencer Chapman had a lucky escape in Perak. However, as SEAC's plans to reoccupy Malay took shape, intelligence information became crucial. From the end of 1944 submarine patrols were stepped up in the Malacca Straits to land and retrieve British and Asian agents.

As head of Force 136 in Malaya, John Davis worked to forge a political understanding with the Communist leadership through Chin Peng of the Malayan People's Anti-Japanese Army in Perak. In return for Allied air drops of arms and supplies British liaison officers would prepare some 3,500 Chinese guerrillas for organized resistance. From January 1945 Force 136 parties of British, Malay, Chinese and Gurkhas were dropped in various parts of the country. Chrystal and Creer linked up with Major Peter Dobree, a Malay-speaker of the Agriculture Department, who with two officers had parachuted into upper Perak in late 1944. Early in 1945 other Force 136 officers moved into Kedah:

Major G. A. Hasler was to liaise with a Malay guerrilla group (where he was joined in June–July 1945 by two nephews of Tunku Abdul Rahman in Force 136). Ex-Johore planter and ex-Dalforce officer Major James Hislop, who had been involved in submarine and surface-craft operations, parachuted blind into Kedah, and Tunku Mohamed Mohaidin of the Malay Regiment was sent into Kelantan to prepare for the anticipated British reoccupation. Two planes left Calcutta with another party targeting Selangor. Their mission was to supply and train Chinese guerrillas in anticipation of the coming Allied invasion, when they would be ordered into action. One plane – carrying James Robertson, a former tea planter, Douglas Broadhurst, of Province Wellesley police, and two Chinese agents – missed the dropping zone, and the party spent a hazardous seven months, twice repelling attacks by the pro-Japanese Indian National Army.

From early 1945 Changi buzzed with rumour. Conditions for both sides were deteriorating. 'Towards the end we did not have enough food, neither did the Japs . . . a lot of the chaps were going blind from malnutrition.'[99] When Red Cross supplies were confiscated, pessimists forecast, 'We are to face 5–6 months of starvation culminating in a massacre . . . Singapore can't be attacked till August at the earliest, Nips are really putting the defences in order.'[100] Apprehension grew as 'Things here are very muddled but moving fast . . . They are obviously getting us split up into smaller units so that we are less dangerous . . . parties are being rapidly organized into 600s – looks like train loads! Speculation, rumour, order and counter-order are rife.'[101] After the news of Germany's surrender and the fall of Rangoon in early May, hopes and fears see-sawed more wildly, with confused reports of Allied landings and peace moves. By June, relief was not expected before September; in July there were 'rumours of a move to Penang before fighting starts, which Nips say is August', then 'Nips clearing civil population off the island and very busy on earth works.'[102] Malaya was evidently one of Japan's defence strongholds.

Sinister evidence was also growing that the Japanese planned a bloody confrontation with the Allied liberating forces in which the remaining prisoners of war would be wiped out. In Thailand, prisoners picked up from Japanese papers 'the probability of our total liquidation about August 21st'.[103] In Sumatra, Cunyngham-Brown took a grim view of his prospects:

Reinforcements of Japanese arrived and we were all suddenly ordered to dig pits thirty feet long, seven feet wide and six feet deep; a work which was undertaken and completed under strict guard of an exceptionally unpleasant squad of Korean soldiers. When we saw the machine-gun positions being arranged, we realized what these pits were for. They were our graves.[104]

Then the end came with a miraculous and unimaginable *coup de théâtre*. 'It was like the sunlight coming from half a dozen suns instead of one . . . and right through the centre was this column going up . . . We watched it forming a mushroom shape.'[105] The witness of the phenomenal explosion at Nagasaki was a British prisoner of war, and among the many factory workers who shared the experience was Malayan planter H. S. MacDonald, who had already cheated death three times.[106] The news was instantly broadcast around the globe. After five days of unendurable strain, the wife of a British prisoner could hardly contain her relief: 'What a week of world shaking events – the Atomic Bomb – the entry of Russia into the War and then – Peace.'[107] In fact the bombs that landed on Hiroshima and Nagasaki on 6 and 9 August were celebrated as a sign of divine intervention, saving not just the slaves of Sumatra's Pekan Baru but hundreds of thousands of other Allied prisoners, soldiers and Asian civilians throughout the East. In Singapore the internees at Sime Road heard the news from an outside working party, who had themselves heard it from a resourceful Eurasian cyclist:

> as this Eurasian slowly pedalled past he sang a little song to himself without taking his eyes off the road. The words of his song were: 'The Japanese have surrendered. The Japanese have surrendered.' The cyclist went on but soon returned and overtook the working party, still singing the same song. The Sikh guard escorting the party suspected nothing. This news ran through the camp like wildfire.[108]

Changi was instantly rife with speculation, but without official confirmation the prisoners were uncertain of Japanese reactions and were warned against indulging in triumphalism. The suspense made it 'a very trying nervy week'.[109] This was a common experience. When the Japanese surrender was confirmed, at Tamuang Camp in Thailand Dr Hardie noticed that 'after such long suppression of hopes and fears . . . one just felt rather numb, rather shaky and rather inclined to sob'.[110]

Then, in Changi, the elation became irrepressible as suddenly Red Cross cigarettes and food supplies appeared. Spirits ran high and 'we really began to feel free', crowed John Soper.[111] Anticipating the coming reunion with his wife and children, Pat Warin was jubilant. 'Not very long surely. What a great and glorious time that is going to be. Oh! the thought of our meeting is almost too sweet to bear.'[112]

Joy was invariably tinged with sadness, for friends who had not survived and for their wives and children who had yet to face the truth. The Ipoh barrister John Woods felt only heartfelt gratitude and humility. 'I have been one of the lucky ones and have come through safe, sane, sound and whole . . . Even if I have lost everything I had in the world . . . I have something far better . . . the realisation that my material possessions were of no consequence whatsoever and that real happiness is possible in complete poverty.'[113] To some ascetic souls the Changi episode had been emotionally liberating, offering solace and fulfilment. 'To lose one's property, to suffer privation and experience cruelty does not do one any harm, rather good, providing one is not permanently maimed . . .', reflected J. S. Potter; 'the experience of captivity taught me a sense of values.'[114] These were minority views: most men longed for the comforts of civilized life; most preferred to look forward rather than back. And for survivors of the Malayan tragedy the prospect of peace was the most precious prize. 'The biggest thing of all, of course, is that the mad war is all over.'[115]

# 15

# *False Dawn*

The legacy of the war and the Japanese occupation gradually worked itself out in the next fifteen years. The events of 1941–5 had shown that no great power was invincible. The British presence had been benign and just, but sadly impotent in a military crisis. All the same, the relieved people of Singapore gave the returning British a tumultuous reception, lining the streets, cheering and waving flags. Driving north from the island in September 1945, a former internee, John Woods, observed how in Johore

> people did not take much notice of us beyond staring. But when we got to Negri [Sembilan] and Selangor the fun started. Not only in the towns and villages but all the way along the road the kiddies ran out and the grown-ups too, cheering like mad and making the thumbs-up sign and waving . . . It was really a wonderful feeling. The whole thing was so spontaneous and genuine.

And at every town, kampong and estate, 'arcs de triomphe' lined the route to Ipoh.[1] The Japanese, on the other hand, were feared and hated, and, in token revenge, locals defaced their monuments celebrating the victory in 1942.

Jim Winchester, a child in Malaya in the 1930s, returned as a planter in 1948. He recalled the pockmarked bridge and shophouses at Slim River, where bullets had flown in the vicious battle of 1941. During the 1950s Christina Browne heard stories of Japanese atrocities from the Indian community in Selangor, and in the estate office at Sungei Way, where Tom Kerr was Estate Manager from 1947, he found 'two school jotters with, it seemed, dozens of Indian names. These were of labourers sent to Siam and never heard of again, I was told.'[2] A shipping assistant identified 'old posts near the Chartered Bank, Klang, upon which the Japanese hung the heads of local people when they had been executed by sword'.[3] Even after independence, Edward Read, a marketing manager in Singapore, recalled how in 1958 Chinese and Malay taxi drivers recoiled when he gave his address as 26 Oxley Rise, a Japanese interrogation centre whence few had ever emerged.[4] John Anderson, whose distinguished career in the plantation industry began in 1951, noticed the war debris at Petaling, where the railway repair works had been located:

> Visual evidence of the Japanese occupation was abundant . . . There were the railway traces, well ballasted, which made excellent estate roads, excavations into the low hillsides in which locomotives sheltered from air attack; unserviceable Japanese arms, grenade casings and ammunition littered the ground. There were also large amounts of Japanese 'banana' money lying about, and all this some five to six years after the re-occupation . . . A rather grand entrance to these railway works had been reduced to two badly leaning brick pillars. On Seaport Estate there were still Japanese drugs in the dispensary. At Sungei Senarut Estate in Batu Anam the manager's bungalow had formed part of the Gemas Line; there were six Japanese war graves in the garden and a greater number of Australian dead . . . There was a great deal of hearsay evidence of paranormal activity related to this.[5]

As for the inmates of Changi, when asked if she hated the Japanese, Freddy Bloom replied 'No', since they did not have a monopoly on evil.[6] 'I never felt vindictive towards the Japanese on the basis that two wrongs do not make a right,' admitted J. S. Potter, 'but some of my fellow planters felt more strongly on the subject.'[7]

The cataclysmic ending of the Pacific War had a strange consequence. Victory had been achieved, but the victorious Allied troops were nowhere to be seen. Instead, Malaya was in the grip of a power vacuum. The British could be counted in mere hundreds (apart from the defenceless prisoner population). Force 136 officers, supported by technical experts and other ranks, British, Malay, Chinese and Gurkhas, a total of 380 men, had landed in the final months of the war. Their allies in the Malayan People's Anti-Japanese Army were 7,000 strong, but together they were no match for a Japanese occupying force estimated as high as 130,000. Undismayed, however, as news of the surrender percolated into the jungle the MPAJA began to emerge from their hideouts, eager to take over, although in Kelantan and upper Perak their political rivals of the Kuomintang (KMT) still had a residual hold. The peace proved at best uneasy. At worst, anarchy threatened as Chinese guerrillas thirsted for revenge on suspected collaborators.

From the British standpoint, Force 136 was there to maintain stability until the arrival of a large military force and a new administration. Shortly before the dropping of the A-bombs, its officers received a covert warning to lie low and refrain from offensive action. On 17 August they were notified of the ceasefire by wireless and were instructed, via John Davis, to ensure that the capitulation terms were observed. Preparatory to measures to bring them under control, the Japanese were to concentrate at surrender points in the main towns and the MPAJA would remain outside.

In the charged atmosphere of political hiatus, individual British officers of Force 136 acted with considerable courage and sang-froid. Having survived a traumatic existence throughout the war, John Creer was determined to reassert a British presence in Kelantan. Despite his emaciated condition, accompanied by KMT supporters he walked into Kota Bharu, the town where the Japanese had first landed, and took it over in the wake of their departure. At the same time, early September, Spencer Chapman, who had parachuted back into Pahang at the end of August, entered Raub and the capital, Kuala Lipis, accompanied by his liaison officer, Major Leonard. They were the first Britons to be seen in the area since the Japanese invasion. Chapman then went on to Kuantan, where he welcomed the indomitable Nona Baker, who finally waved goodbye to her Communist colleagues in the MPAJA.[8]

In upper Perak, meanwhile, Major Dobree, with Bob Chrystal and a KMT group, had already taken control of the township of Grik after a tense and potentially dangerous six days which ended on 22 August when the Japanese followed orders to withdraw to Taiping and Ipoh. Dobree went on to Kuala Kangsar (where he was soon installed in the Sultan of Perak's palace), leaving Chrystal and his KMT guerrillas to hold Grik. Chrystal's nerve was promptly tested again when a band of 200 Communist guerrillas approached the town. While he averted violence in Grik by powerful persuasion, he was powerless to prevent the shooting of Malay villagers and threats of anti-Chinese rioting by Malay peasants in the area. But from Singapore up to Pahang, a wave of bloodthirsty reprisals was under way. Communist lynch mobs seized suspected collaborators, spawning reprisals such as the slaughter by Malays of forty Chinese villagers – mostly women and children – in Negri Sembilan. These acts continued over several months. 'Each act of vengeance was like a pebble dropped in a pond,' declared John Gullick, creating 'widening ripples of fear and hate'.[9]

A confrontation in August between Japanese and Force 136 troops highlighted the fragility of the peace. After Japan's capitulation, on the 15th two Force 136 units based north of Rawang in Selangor emerged from the jungle and headed for Serendah. The first, led by John Davis (who had walked down the spine of Malaya from Perak in early August) and including Douglas Broadhurst, Group Commander for Selangor, and a Gurkha platoon, stationed themselves in the Serendah Boys' Home. The second, under Major Philip Thompson-Walker with Flight Lieutenant James Robertson and a group of Chinese Communists, were billeted in the police station. Shortly after, in the anarchic mood of the time, a cohort of Chinese guerrillas shot up a convoy of Japanese soldiers on their way to surrender twenty miles away at Tanjong Malim. Enraged, the Japanese took their revenge, directing a company of troops from Rawang on an all-out attack on Thompson-Walker's men, killing their sentry. Jimmy Robertson recounted in low-key style what happened on this first and last military clash between British and Japanese troops since 1942:

> We were in the police station. It was a wooden building. There was lots and lots of small-arms fire, and hand grenades were being thrown from the other side of the road. I suppose I thought I'd better put a stop to it, so I nipped out to the front. There was a defence point in front of the police station at the side of the road, so I nipped across into this thing. I bawled in Malay at the Jap officers and tried to tell them that the war was over. Eventually the fighting died down. Their officers came across into my defence point with a couple of soldiers, and I was taken prisoner. This brought Major Thompson-Walker out to the defence point. Just then John Davis, who had heard all the shooting, came marching down the road with the Gurkhas, waving a Union Jack. He was furious. He persuaded one of the officers to go to Kuala Lumpur and make contact with the powers that be. There was no more hostility after that. I suppose the shooting lasted half, maybe three-quarters, of an hour.[10]

From the Boys' Home a quarter of a mile away, John Davis had, indeed heard 'the shemozzle'. 'The important thing was not to have a confrontation,' he affirmed, forcing the British to intervene in a Japanese–Chinese shoot-out. Ordering the Gurkhas to carry their guns over their shoulders, indicating they were not about to fire, and in company with the local Communist commander, Davis pushed the Jap sentries aside.

> We bluffed it up, and it worked. We soon got Robertson out, and then we tried to settle the fuss with the Japanese commander. It went on for quite a while, and he had the local O.C.P.D. as interpreter, but ultimately it all quietened down. We phoned the Jap headquarters in K.L. and told them to send a lorry for us. And then Dougie Broadhurst and I and the Chinese Communist leader, we went into K.L., and the beautifully kept lawyer's house which the Japanese officer had used became our headquarters.[11]

The seizure of key points by Force 136 was planned as a prelude to Operation Zipper, the reoccupation of Malaya. Intelligence about conditions in the camps and instability in the kampongs indicated the need for urgent action, and there was understandable impatience when America's supremo, General MacArthur, insisted there should be no landings until after the principal peace-signing ceremony in Tokyo Bay on 2 September. Britain's second in command in the Pacific, Admiral Walker, sailed for Penang on 15 August but was forced to kick his heels until the 28th, when he finally arrived to begin the vital task of clearing the Malacca Straits of mines. Penang's surrender was duly received on 2 September aboard the *Nelson*, after which the Royal Marines occupied the island. Singapore's turn came on the 5th, when Lieutenant-General Itagaki and Vice-Admiral Fukudome boarded the *Sussex* to sign the island's surrender, and afterwards the men of the 5th Indian Division marched in triumph from the Empire Dock to the Cathay Building.

The retaking of the mainland began on 9 September, when British troops landed unopposed at Morib beach, the first of several points on the Selangor coast. They entered the federal capital of Kuala Lumpur on 13 September. With his long experience as a marine pilot in Malaya, Captain Harry Rawcliffe of Force 136 piloted the first ship into Port Swettenham after the surrender.[12] Japan's humiliation was already complete when on 12 September Admiral Lord Louis Mountbatten received from Itagaki the general surrender of all Japanese forces in South-East

Asia. 'As I speak there are 100,000 men ashore,' declared Mountbatten from the steps of Singapore's Municipal Building, and, as if to signify that Britain was reclaiming her imperial birthright, a Union Jack which had been hidden inside Changi since the fall of Singapore was hoisted to the strains of 'God Save the King'.[13] In Kuala Lumpur the final act came with the victory parade in October.

Given the circumstances of Japan's defeat and Britain's restoration, it is small wonder that two interpretations of history were to emerge. 'To this day, it is the Chinese belief that it was they, and not the British, who reconquered the country' asserted Norman Bewick, a man dedicated to Malaya, who saw in this Communist conviction the seeds of the later Emergency. Among the general lawlessness, 'the only organised force was the Malayan People's Anti-Japanese Army'. The British returned, but they did not reconquer Malaya. In December 1945 'the MPAJA were just told to disband, hand in their arms and collect three hundred dollars apiece in payment; but they said, "Oh! to hell with you!" and went back into the jungle.'[14] John Davis, who was much involved in the process of restoring British authority, saw things differently. The British, he argued, retrieved 80 per cent of the arms supplied in the war to the Chinese Communists, together with 3,000 additional weapons which were handed in by unattached guerrillas.

However it was fortunate that British control was not put fully to the test, for there seems no doubt that had the local Japanese command decided to oppose Operation Zipper the result would have been mayhem, since the British were working from inaccurate second-grade maps of the Selangor coast.[15] Naval officers discovered too late that the terrain was unsuitable for an amphibious landing, and gullies were soon littered with 'drowned' vehicles. An officer in the Sappers and Miners charged with making captured airfields quickly operational told how their landing zone

> was reported to be a wide, sandy beach . . . and we went forward but the heavy machinery needed for airport repair had to be unloaded. The tide was coming in over my entire heavy vehicles and lorries – the sand was 8–10 inches deep and under that was thick mud, and as the vehicles landed they punched holes through the sand and got bogged down. It was just as well the Japs were not fighting. But we were not operational the same day as we had planned.[16]

In the view of K. A. Brundle, a former PWD official in the new British Military Administration, signs were that 'the old lethargy crept back into military organisation'.[17]

The organization Recovery of Allied Prisoners of War and Internees was another target for criticism: 'exasperation at the slowness of events has sent several people, mostly officers, a bit queer in the head, and there's one case of attempted suicide,' John Soper noted.[18] After a month languishing in Singapore, men bitingly referred to RAPWI as 'Retain All Prisoners of War Indefinitely'. At Sime Road, frustrated internees also waited through September. 'Events are beginning to move at last, but slowly, even now . . . We have not heard definite arrangements regarding our repatriation,' one of them complained. Unfavourable comparisons were drawn with American efficiency. 'Still nothing has happened regarding our repatriation . . . About 40 American internees were whisked away yesterday . . . Events seem to move very slowly now.'[19] The YWCA, meanwhile, flew in from India and pipped the Army to the post by commandeering Raffles Hotel for the women and children internees. Anne Langlands recalled their plight – 'some of them just literally draped in rags' – before she and her co-workers set about raiding local bazaars, making clothes, and loading trucks of soft bread baked by the Navy to replace rock-hard Army-issue biscuits.[20]

At the death camps, only the unexpected appearance of Lady Mountbatten, unblinking at the stench and the sight of jungle ulcers and skeletons in loincloths, gave waiting prisoners some special comfort and cheer. Her humanity contrasted with the treatment meted out under RAPWI to Whiteaway Laidlaw's Manager William Price. Prevented from returning to Penang, he was hustled on board a ship for the UK, as his wife records:

Five ships left Singapore with the prisoners, my husband being on the fifth and slowest. Those on board were mostly Civil Servants and men of good rank in that service. What happened to cause the Captain to punish the men I don't know but I do know he punished all of them by stopping their allowance of beer and chocolate. This to men who had been starving for years. Someone in authority went ashore at Colombo and contacted London. Result, rations were restored and the Captain was removed at Port Said and replaced by another. He was treating them as he would men in the army.[21]

Freddy Bloom was similarly disillusioned. Repatriated on the *Monowai* with several hundred men and a few women, they were all emaciated, tense and 'fed up with the way they were being treated'. The unsympathetic attitude of the officers and crew meant 'it was not a happy ship'.[22] On the *Tamaroa*, 'the rough food' was Pat Warin's only criticism. However, on reaching Fremantle that was forgotten:

> The welcome we . . . received was just marvellous. Crowds lined the wharf and a band struck up as we pulled alongside . . . Red X workers gave us warm clothing – all very well organised. Refreshments were also provided. The kindness of everyone was overwhelming . . . Arriving in Perth . . . we were again received with every kindness and telegrams were immediately despatched to our loved ones. Exchange of greetings and news completed, we were supplied with a very good tiffin . . . We then strolled down some of the main streets. The people and the shops were literally dazzling. I feel like weeping for joy. I shall never forget the day.[23]

In a Britain suffering acute shortages and rationing, there was far less sympathy for colonials who had lost everything. It was Norman Bewick's view that this hard-nosed indifference came from anti-colonialism at the top, in Britain's new Labour administration:

> The government at home couldn't have cared less. They'd won the war with Germany and that was all there was to it . . . We were just humbug, you know, the prisoners of war from the Far East. All the flag waving and all that sort of ballyhoo, they'd washed themselves of that. When we got home, there was nothing except the Mayor of Bootle and the Mayor of Liverpool to welcome us![24]

On an individual level, insensitive behaviour usually sprang from thoughtlessness or embarrassment rather than callousness. After his father's release, Gordon Snell and his parents were asked out for a meal and were given rice pudding as a special treat! Bewick remembered how 'you became rather an exhibit – "Oh! you must meet my brother, back from the Japanese" – and this sort of thing'.[25]

Others had problems with the British Military Administration, which ran Malaya for eight months until 1 April 1946. Sjovald Cunyngham-Brown, fresh from the death camp at Pekan Baru, resented being spoken to in baby talk and being offered 'nauseating pity'. His reception by the BMA's Chief Civil Affairs Officer in Singapore, Brigadier Patrick McKerron, was singularly inept: 'We don't need you chaps around here . . .' he was told. 'Everything is new nowadays you know, and you have a lot of things to catch up with. We are doing very well without you people.'[26] Fortunately for Cunyngham-Brown he found a sympathetic administrator (a contemporary in the Malayan Civil Service) who was glad to use him in Johore.

Though far from fit, a few ex-prisoners – Colonel W. M. James, and his second-in-command, Major Arbuthnott, for instance – insisted on staying to help with the repatriation of Tamil labourers from Thailand. Captain Mervyn Sheppard received permission to spend October rounding up *Kempeitai* in the Riau Islands, where, as it happened, he unearthed all the mess silver of the Royal Scots and the Argyll and Sutherland Regiments, stolen by the secret police, and extracted information to compile a list of the interrogators and interpreters involved in the Double Tenth episode. On his release from Sime Road, Dr Winchester delayed a family reunion in Australia to start the reorganization of the administrative, technical and medical operations at Singapore General Hospital, of which he subsequently became Chief Medical Officer.

Some internees were reluctant to leave Malaya. Mrs Edith Rattray, owner of the Green Cow Tavern (where visiting parents of Tanglin pupils used to stay before the war), defied official protests to return to Cameron Highlands. In 1943 the Japanese had turned the hill station into a rest camp for their troops. Like the Pensionnat Notre Dame, which had been declared Japanese property and transformed into a hospital, her hotel had been stripped of its contents, but it was still standing and Mrs Rattray set about re-establishing her business; the convent sisters were instructed to reopen their school, too. James Anderson, an elderly Scotsman, said, 'Well, I wish to go back to Trengganu and see what property I have lost and what I've got to do. Then I'll go back to England . . . And I didn't go home till the May of '46.'[27] Instead of going back to Ireland, John Woods was determined to restart his law business in Ipoh and he set up a merger to create the firm Maxwell, Kenion, Cowdy & Jones. He had to secure a BMA pass to return to Perak, and holed up at a RAPWI transit camp in Singapore before sailing home to Europe in March 1946.

Norman Bewick, meanwhile, also had difficulty with red tape – particularly with the BMA and the civil servants sent from London to deal with war damage claims – and he had the added problem of being officially listed dead on the casualty lists. He found he owned nothing. His demands were as incomprehensible to the government officer as the concepts of clothing coupons and plastic collars were to him. When he set about picking up the threads of his old life at Pekan – as the much-admired Secretary to the Sultan of Pahang – one irritation followed another.

> I got things cracking, and then this fellow, a Colonel Dobson of the British Military Administration, came round to me and said, 'Who the hell do you think you are? You're interfering with my Administration; I'm in charge of this District!' I said, 'You may be on paper, but I am in person – is that clear?' Then he came with more and more abuses, so I went to H.H. and said, 'Have him removed, Tunku. Have him removed!' And he was gone from there in twenty four hours! He was an objectionable type. The people the BMA sent out here, having been clerks in a railway station or something, and suddenly they were colonels, thought they were important. It was one of the problems of the BMA that the Sultans didn't like them.[28]

This was not an isolated case. There is ample evidence of the unpopularity of the untried post-war administrators – civilians with military titles – among the pre-war generation. The mistrust was compounded in May 1946 when 258 seasoned men of the Parachute Regiment mutinied at Muar Camp in protest at their conditions (receiving heavy sentences which were later quashed on technical grounds). The sentiments of J. S. Potter of Guthrie's would have resonated with many returning civilians whose personal possessions had been looted by British servicemen. 'Post-war Malaya was another disillusionment', he wrote:

> The British Military Administration was in power and it was a great shock to find corruption rife at all levels . . . One of the reasons for fighting the war was surely to prevent corruption. I suppose British morals had declined in the long war years of restrictions and shortages. We, however, who had lost everything we owned in the war did not take kindly to our fellow countrymen filching what was not theirs. It was noticeable that the Japanese had taken care of property meticulously; those of us who had left valuables in the Bank generally got them back. Anything that the B.M.A. could lay their hands on was not seen again.[29]

By comparison, the loyalty of Asian domestic servants to their former employers was remarkable. Ali, the Kitchings' *syce*, who had looked after their Morris car throughout the occupation, approached the

31. Fraser's Hill, Pahang: a view of the centre of Fraser's Hill, overlooking the golf course (*front*). On the far left is the Government Dairy, next to the Post Office (*centre left*), and across the junction (*right*) the well-known public house, the Maxwell Arms, masking the labour quarters at its rear. The 'cottages' in the centre were occupied by forest or police officers

32. Singapore Golf Club, 1931: despite the heat and humidity, golf was widely popular in Malaya from the pioneering days. After playing a round, a foursome of members relax over drinks

33. Leslie Froggatt, Superintendent Engineer, Straits Steamship Co., Singapore, 1934–48, and a well-known figure in the shipping world: he escaped from Singapore in February 1942 but was captured at sea and spent the rest of the war as a POW in Changi

34. Guy Hutchinson: a rubber planter, he started in 1928 in Selangor but in 1934 was moved to Tenang in Johore. A keen member of the Johore Volunteer Engineers, he was captured at the fall of Singapore. Hutchinson was highly regarded by fellow POWs on the Thailand-Burma railway. After the war he returned to planting, serving under his old friend Stan Nias at the Fraser Estate, Johore, until he himself became Manager

35. Tom Kitching: he joined the Colonial Service from Cambridge in 1913. His career in the Survey Department covered years at Seremban, Kuala Lumpur, Trengganu, Kulim, Kedah and Malacca, before he became Chief Surveyor, Singapore, in 1938. In 1942 his wife Nora died in the Tanjong Pinang disaster; Kitching was interned in Changi where he died in 1944

36. J.R.P. Soper: a Cambridge graduate, he became an agricultural officer in the Colonial Service and worked in East Africa before moving to Province Wellesley in 1936. He also served in Kedah and Perak, fought as a Volunteer and, like Hutchinson, was sent to Thailand as a POW, where he almost died. He was working in Kuala Lumpur when the Emergency broke out in 1948 but left Malaya soon after

37. Industrial transport in the inter-war years: this curious trolley was the only mechanism for transporting both bags of tin and people from the Lingui tin mine in Johore to the landing-stage on the Lingui river. From there both were taken by sampan to Kota Tinggi. In the 1920s a compressed air pump was tried but eventually a petrol engine was fitted

38. Tapping rubber in Johore: John Edington oversees the tapping of an old rubber tree on the Kulai Young Estate, South Johore

39. British Volunteers in peacetime: members of the Singapore battalion of the Straits Settlements Volunteer Force at camp in Singapore, *c.* 1933

40. Women and Babies' Clinic, 1938: Asian midwives and European doctors at the clinic at Johore General Hospital. Seated (*left*) is Dr Margaret Smallwood (remembered also for her work with internees in Singapore, 1942–5) and (*right*) Dr Winifred Lowson

41. Evacuation in the last days at Singapore, 1942: amid chaotic scenes at the quayside, women and children board a transport ship shortly before the Japanese onslaught on Singapore

42. The surrender of Singapore, 15 February 1942: under an armed Japanese escort, British staff officers, headed by General Percival (*far right*), march to surrender to the Japanese commander, General Yamashita

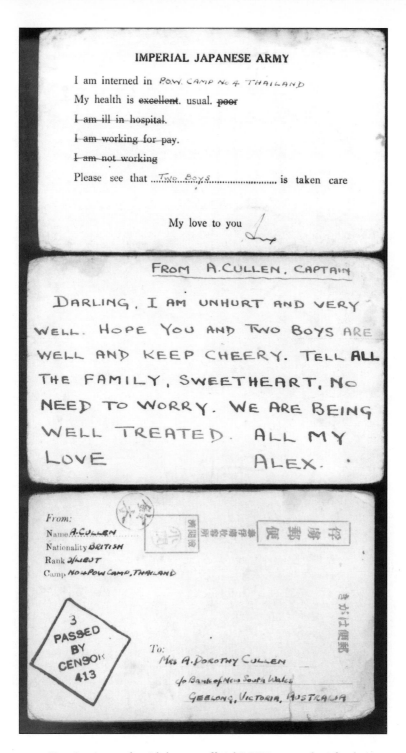

**IMPERIAL JAPANESE ARMY**

I am interned in P.O.W. CAMP N° 4 THAILAND

My health is ~~excellent~~. usual. ~~poor~~

~~I am ill in hospital.~~

~~I am working for pay.~~

~~I am not working~~

Please see that ...Two Boys................... is taken care

My love to you

FROM A. CULLEN, CAPTAIN

DARLING, I AM UNHURT AND VERY WELL. HOPE YOU AND TWO BOYS ARE WELL AND KEEP CHEERY. TELL **ALL** THE FAMILY, SWEETHEART, NO NEED TO WORRY. WE ARE BEING WELL TREATED. ALL MY LOVE ALEX.

From:

Name A. CULLEN
Nationality BRITISH
Rank 2/LIEUT
Camp No 4 POW CAMP, THAILAND

3 PASSED BY CENSOR 413

To:
Mrs A. DOROTHY CULLEN
c/o Bank of New South Wales
GEELONG, VICTORIA, AUSTRALIA

43. Keeping in touch with home: official POW postcards. After being captured in Singapore, Captain Alex Cullen was sent to work on the Thailand–Burma railway, from where he sent these standard, censored cards to his family in Australia. Despite their brevity and random distribution, postcards were a source of great moral support to wives and families

44. A prison cell in Changi camp: one of a series, this drawing of the inside of a POW cell in 'D' block was brought back to Scotland by a survivor, A.G. Donn, though the identity of the artist is uncertain

45. Selerang Barracks, Changi: part of the Changi complex, the barracks were the scene of a notorious incident in 1942 when over 15,000 POWs were herded into a space formerly occupied by 2,000 men, without adequate shelter, food or sanitation. This photograph, taken secretly, was smuggled out of the camp

46. Victory Parade, Kuala Lumpur, 1945: after the Japanese surrender and the British reoccupation of Malaya, celebrations of victory were held in major towns. In October at Kuala Lumpur the GOC Malaya took the salute at the march-past of Allied infantry. The ceremony was held before the Government Secretariat buildings, across the road from the Padang

47. Members of Parliament see the Emergency at first hand, 1950: at the height of the Communist Emergency visiting MPs A.T. Lennox-Boyd (*right*) and A. Vere Harvey (*left*) are 'fitted' with bandoliers at the police post, Bukit Putus. Later, as Colonial Secretary (1954–9), Lennox-Boyd was prominent in facilitating Malayan Independence

48. Inspecting a prototype New Village in Jelebu, Negri Sembilan: in August 1950 the High Commissioner, Sir Henry Gurney (*left*), visited the new village of Titi to see for himself the work done by Charles Howe, the District Officer (*second left*). Accompanying them were Dato Jelebu Shahahmudin Ismail, H.P. Bryson (British Adviser, Negri Sembilan) and their escort

49. General Templer meeting Malay security personnel, 1952: as the pro-active Director of Operations, he knew the importance of security and self-help. Here (*left*) he inspects a Malay unit of the Home Guard, who played an important security role

50. British Malayans in the Emergency, *c.* 1953: a group of friends who were in the front line in Johore. *Left to right:* Jimmy Hislop, planter, wartime hero of Force 136 and Gurkha commander in Ferret Force; John Edington, planter and ex-Royal Scots Fusiliers; Herbert MacDonald, veteran of the infamous Thailand-Burma railway and senior assistant on the Kulai Young Estate; Ian Campbell, subaltern in the Black Watch who died leading a patrol of the Suffolk Regiment against CTs in Kuala Selangor; and Captain (later Colonel) Gordon MacDonald of the Gurkhas and Ferret Force

51. Colonel John Davis, CBE, DSO: Davis was in the pre-war police service (1930–40) and spent two years in China. In 1943 he returned from India by submarine as head of Force 136 to organize anti-Japanese intelligence in Malaya. After the war he transferred to the MCS, organized Ferret Force and played a vital role in the Emergency years through his special knowledge of Chinese and of the Communist leader, Chin Peng

52. The struggle for the hearts and minds of villagers, 1950: C.L. Lewis (*left*), a Schools Inspector and also Inspector of the Home Guard, offering comfort to the inhabitants of a remote kampong between Rembau and Sri Menanti, who had been visited by terrorists a few days earlier

53. Social life in Penang, 1952: by now social life for Europeans in Penang had returned to pre-war patterns. Here Miss P.L., a young resident, enjoys the pleasures of the Penang Swimming Club as she poses decorously at the edge of the children's pool

54. New Year's Eve, 1947: the Froggatt family and friends celebrate the approach of the New Year in traditional style at Raffles Hotel, Singapore

55. A garden party in Seremban, Negri Sembilan, 1950: across a tea table of tunkus and prominent Malays, including the Dato Bandar of Sungei Ujong (*centre*), discussion flows between Hugh Bryson, British Adviser, Negri Sembilan (*left*), and H.H. Tunku Abdul Rahman (*right*), the future Prime Minister of Malaysia

56. A special event in Malacca: a celebration service in the Cheng Hoon Teng Temple, Malacca, on the occasion of the coronation of Queen Elizabeth II in June 1953

57. For service to the Empire: a fortnight before Malayan Independence,
Guy Madoc, Director of Intelligence, Malaya, receives the CBE at King's House,
Kuala Lumpur, from Sir Donald MacGillivray, the last High Commissioner of the
British era

58. Celebrating Independence, Penang, August 1957: the Duke and Duchess of Gloucester, representing the Queen, with Prince William (*left*), mingle with the guests at a final garden party in Penang

59. A gathering of Chieftains: in 1984 the Scottish community celebrated the centenary of the Selangor St Andrew's Society, symbolizing the enduring strength of Scottish tradition in the former British Empire

authorities to return it to the family, since both Kitching parents were dead. The Winchester family's cook and gardener were waiting on their return in 1946, as were the Rawcliffe's cook in Port Swettenham and the Barretts' servants in Sungei Patani. Returning in May 1948, Ursula Holttum was touched by the sight of familiar faces. 'Even our old syce Bakri, very small and gnome-like now, pops up in the driver's seat and grins most pleasantly at me.' Then, at the house,

> there was Ah Joon, out on the step to meet me, really pleased to see me again, smiling all over his face, and showing a great many gold teeth. I am truly glad to see him; he is an old and trusted friend. I engaged him over ten years ago, without any other character or reference than . . . that I liked his face.[30]

The Cullens' *amah*, Ho Ah Yee, wrote to the family several times from Singapore after 1946, and even sent them a food parcel from Singapore for Christmas 1948. The concern of the Cullens' Chinese friends was touching: 'The terrible experiences of this war, especially the death of Tuan in Siam must have caused much unhappiness to you but we must let the dead past bury the past . . . We send you sincere greetings for Christmas and the New Year, and hope to see you in Singapore in the near future.'[31]

Malaya had too many memories for widows like Dorothy Cullen; she made a new life for herself in England. But the need to work brought many of the pre-war generation back East, and for some it was an emotional experience. From Singapore docks 'we drove away, through the familiar streets, all shabby, some ramshackle, some scarred and pitted by bombing, but all teeming with life', Ursula Holttum wrote. And at the sight of her old home beside the Botanical Gardens,

> They were so many [impressions], so fleeting, so charged with joy, with astonishment . . . So much is there that I never dreamed of seeing again. After all, the house was not looted, and although shelled, not very greatly damaged . . . It was somehow touching to see the same old covers on armchairs and couch, with the faint design of soft brown leaves all over them . . . that I chose so long ago, and to think that they have survived so many and so strange tenants, in this house which is now ours again. How many people came back to their houses, to find nothing left.

Seeing everything shabby and dirty, Mrs Holttum spring-cleaned each morning, 'red in the face, dripping with perspiration, my clothes sticking to me', consoling herself that it was 'marvellous to have any furniture left to polish. Three small blackwood tables, bought long ago, are still here . . . and the beautiful Chinese cabinet, carved all over with celestial dragons, has stood in its old place, ever since I went away in 1940.'[32]

The Holttums were fortunate that their home had escaped the predatory eyes of the military. Daphne Davidson, a tin miner's wife, remembered that 'when we came [in 1948] the reputation of the BMA was absolutely frightful'.[33] But there was another reason for the authorities' unpopularity, particularly with the Malays: the nature of Malaya's new constitutional arrangements. It had been announced in October 1945 that Singapore would remain a colony with its own government. The nine Malay States, with the territories of Penang and Malacca, were to merge in a Malayan Union. The creation under the British Crown of this unitary state, which was to supersede the BMA from 1 April 1946, alienated the Sultans and galvanized the Malay people in an unprecedented way. In protest, the United Malay Nationalist Organization was formed under the aristocratic Dato Onn bin Ja'afar, Johore's Chief Minister. Datuk Puan Halimahton, an early activist among Malay women, explained:

> I was involved in UMNO since its inception in 1946. I fought tooth and nail against Malayan Union. That was the beginning of it; that was the time when everybody knew that something was wrong. According to that Constitution, our Rulers were to become sort of figureheads, only concerned with the Adat, the religion; and the tradition of the Malays . . . There was that feeling, Why? Why? Why? I managed to call everybody in Rembau – thirty thousand of them – they filled up the courthouse padang – to give them a talk about what had brought us all together . . . people were saying, 'this is *our* country! Why should our masters want to disorganise it? No! No! No! That's how UMNO was formed![34]

The Malays resented the loss of the Sultans' traditional sovereignty and the privileged status of their community. Chinese and Indian shopkeepers and small businessmen also responded coolly, even though the new constitution promised democratic self-government and equal rights for all races under the British Crown. Lack of consultation was another source of grievance, and in an unprecedented show of displeasure the Sultans boycotted the inauguration ceremony of Sir Edward

Gent as first Governor of the Union. As the implications of the Sultans' action dawned, the Colonial Office was impelled to go back to the drawing board and consult the rulers and UMNO. The outcome was the constitution of the Federation of Malaya, headed by a British High Commissioner and based broadly on the old blueprint of the Federated States. This came into effect on 1 February 1948.[35]

The first two years after the war were necessarily a period of reconstruction. The economy of Malaya had been the first casualty under the Japanese. Food – especially rice – was in desperately short supply. In 1946 the ration was a quarter of a labourer's normal needs, and until 1948 Asian workers endured hardship and malnutrition of a kind they had not known before the war. Basic social services, anti-malaria precautions, hospitals, clinics and schools had to be restored. Among the pre-war doctors who came back were the Lowsons of Johore: Dr Winifred Lowson returned from Geelong to reopen the Women and Children's Clinic with the help of her old team of Asian nurses and midwives. After nearly four years of neglect, a programme of repair to the country's infrastructure of docks, bridges, telegraphs, roads and rail lines was imperative, against a background of shortages of essential goods, spare parts and equipment. As a small reminder of how inconvenient it was in 1945 for people in Penang and Bukit Mertajam, Brian Stewart, a captain in the Black Watch, noted that 'the train journey from Singapore to Butterworth took four days of slow motion'.[36]

Britain's post-war shortages were paralleled in Malaya. Accommodation, cars and electrical equipment, both industrial and domestic, were difficult to obtain, and salaries did not meet the inflated costs. European firms in Malaya, large and small, had obviously ceased all business during the occupation. Private schools had been forced to close, and as an internee in Singapore the headmistress of Tanglin, Miss Griffith-Jones, lost her livelihood. However, the demand for schools for European children revived after the war, and 'Miss Griff' returned to reopen hers. While visiting Cameron Highlands in 1948, Marjorie Soper wrote to tell her daughter that, 'It really looks much the same as pre-war only more crowded, but the beds and cupboards are the same ... There are 170 children at Tanglin now – 130 in the big school, which is surely more than you had, isn't it?'[37]

Large companies faced a major rebuilding challenge. Every director of Boustead & Co., for instance, had been interned in Singapore, and most companies had suffered gravely from loss of personnel and assets and the end of production. Guthrie's had lost its General Manager, 'Jiddy' Dawson, in the evacuation of Singapore.[38] Many of the Straits Trading Company's senior and able executives had died from their wartime experiences. Demolition by retreating British troops in 1942 had ruined the Pulau Brani site, while the Butterworth plant, which had been used by Mitsubishi, had to be rebuilt. Sir John Bagnall's successor as Managing Director, Sir Ewen Fergusson, confessed, 'we had no office, no housing, no records, no transport, and worst of all, no smelter'. Plant belonging to the company's subsidiaries had been similarly destroyed, but negotiations over the company's claim to the British government for damages of $10 million were to drag on for ten years, during which Straits Trading had to find its own salvation. For a year or two life in post-war Malaya was 'harsh and uncomfortable', but by 1948 the company was beginning to turn the corner.[39]

The disruption of tin smelting was paralleled in 1945 by the deplorable situation in tin mining, particularly the condition of the country's 126 dredges. Having extracted large quantities of ore, the Japanese left the sites in chaos. In 1946 production was a mere 8,500 tons of tin, but an all-out effort with the help of the Mines Department more than trebled that figure in 1947, promising a continuing upward trend. At Pahang Consolidated's mine at Sungei Lembing, six key European staff had lost their lives and the company office with its plans and records had been destroyed, making it extremely difficult to recall the workings in detail.[40]

Much the same occurred at Sungei Nyok Dockyard. The Eurasian Manager, H. E. Ward, who had remained at his post in 1941, had been killed by Chinese bandits during the war. Forced by the Japanese to continue construction work in 1942–3, the Chinese workmen were treated with gross brutality. When he took over the management in 1946, Bill Price found 'the enemy had removed all records, both clerical and technical. Losing all drawing office records was a big loss since it is extremely difficult to carry on a drawing office without plans of previous ships built for guidance. Further, most of the foremen and quite a number of the more senior men had disappeared.'[41] In these circumstances the completion of 'the last and the best of the 75-tonners', *Renong*, was much delayed, but on 23 June 1948 she was finally launched, watched by crowds who included the machine-shop foreman, Chin Ah Teck, who had worked at Sungi Nyok for forty-one years.

Labour shortages and disruptions affected the whole of the economy. Although rubber suffered less physical damage than other industries, labour problems and replanting needed to be tackled urgently. The Tamil labour force had been decimated after the mass deportations to Thailand, in some cases planters' bungalows had been destroyed, and land was overrun by lalang, requiring labour-intensive rehabilitation.[42] Even in 1954 there was still evidence of neglect on the older estates. According to John Edington of Tebrau Rubber Estates, it was 'all work and no play'. Even so, competition from synthetic rubber kept prices low, and 'it wasn't until the Korean war [1950–3] had started, together with the devaluation of the £1 by a Labour Government in the UK, that funds from profits made became available to pay shareholders a dividend and acquire funds for replanting'.[43] Thus 1951 was a record trading year for Singapore in both rubber and tin.

Well before this, however, planters and miners had become caught up in a new conflict: a protracted guerrilla war euphemistically called the Emergency. War veterans such as John Davis, John Creer and Bob Chrystal, who had lived among the Chinese Communists in 1942–5, knew that the ultimate goal of the Party was a Communist Republic of Malaya.[44] Five years of economic chaos had produced a bedrock of sympathy for Communism among Chinese smallholders and squatters eking out an existence along the jungle fringes. And the British government laid up trouble in store by its determined policy of introducing trade unions into colonial territories, leaving estate managers to handle racial disputes and demands for pay and conditions that were often difficult to meet. In 1947 the furore over the Malayan Union gave opportunities for demonstrations, racial rivalries, rising crime, trade-union provocation and 300 strikes. Peaceful subversion, however, was not enough to give the Communists control of Malaya. The turning point came in early 1948, when Malaya's Communists, in conjunction with those elsewhere in South-East Asia, were ordered on to the offensive at the international Communist Youth Conference at Calcutta. Consequently, under Chin Peng, the new Secretary-General, and Lau Yew, head of the Military Committee, the Malayan Communist Party (MCP) turned to a strategy of violence, intimidation, sabotage and raids. Lau Yew formed the Malayan People's Anti-British Army (which included old comrades of the MPAJA and was renamed the Malayan Races' Liberation Army in 1949, to widen its appeal), while a civilian army of half a million Chinese villagers and squatters, known as the Min Yuen, supplied the necessary food, money, information and recruits – willingly or under coercion.

Against this backcloth, in October 1947 a Johore planter named A. E. Nicholson was robbed and killed. The attack came as no surprise to John Dalley, head of the pan-Malayan Political Intelligence Bureau. For some while he had told his friend Hugh Bryson of the MCS (whose Singapore house he was sharing) of political and criminal developments and the Governor's reluctance to take firm action. Dalley left Bryson in no doubt that 'serious trouble was coming to Malaya from Communist, or Communist-inspired, organizations'.[45] After Nicholson's murder John Theophilus, the rubber planter, received a visit from Dalley, an old friend from Dalforce days. They talked into the small hours.

> He told me, 'Tomorrow I'm going down to Johore Bharu', where the Governor, MacDonald, and all the heads of the Services and the ambassadors of the area were having a meeting. He said, 'John, I've written a treatise. There is going to be a great deal of trouble in the country, and I am sure they will not believe me' – which, of course, roughly turned out to be true; and, having told the truth, poor old Dalley was sacked about a year later. It was June '48 when the nonsense really started. He foresaw exactly what subsequently happened: that the Communists would endeavour to take over the country![46]

After Bryson was moved to Kuala Lumpur as Deputy Chief Secretary in May 1948, he accepted that senior police officers – Dalley included – were being blamed unfairly for deficiencies in anti-terrorist precautions. He was present at meetings 'at which representatives of the planting and mining communities pressed Gent for firm action to protect the men and women living in isolation on mines and estates from attacks by armed gangs . . . but official help was given very unwillingly'.[47] The planter Dato James Crawford blamed the colonial government for aggravating the situation by having insisted on the introduction of trade unions on estates, observing how the Communists manipulated the unionized workforce – resident Tamil labourers in particular – to resist change. In May 1948 when John Edington arrived in south Johore as an Assistant on Kulai Young Estate, he found it a remote and dangerous place, and there were suspicious developments afoot:

> there had been considerable activity at night, both in the labour lines and on the estate road below the hill where the bungalow stood. Comings and goings of unknown people; all very sinister and unnerving to say the least, as the only weapon available to my senior assistant and I was an old Dutch carbine minus its bolt which rendered the weapon totally useless. So it was with considerable relief to us both when a detachment for 'B' Coy, 1/10 Bn. Gurkha Rifles arrived to set up their headquarters on the estate.[48]

On the day of their arrival the terrorist war began.

The Emergency, by common consensus, is reckoned to have started on 16 June 1948 in Sungei Siput, a mining township north of Ipoh, an area familiar to the Communist leader Chin Peng. Dato Crawford, who later took over the main estate involved, recalled what happened:

> There had been a strike of Chinese tappers throughout Siput, but they had all been settled except those under Allison on Singai Siput [*sic*] and Walker on Elphil Estate. Then the local leader of the CTs [Communist terrorists] jumped the gun, and they shot Allison and Christian, who was only a youngster, just twenty-one. They tied their hands behind their backs and walked them up to the bungalow and shot them on the verandah; and Walker was sitting in the Elphil office, and one chap came up to the door and said, 'Tabek, Tuan!' (Greetings!) – and shot him in the back.[49]

The terrorists set fire to buildings on Allison's estate, leaving the labour force wailing in shock. Dr Reid Tweedie, the local doctor, with Boris Hembry, Manager of Kamuning Estate, drove past the estate entrance, noticed a policeman on guard, and immediately offered their services, but it was too late.[50]

The High Commissioner, Sir Edward Gent, had no choice but to declare a state of emergency in Perak and Johore, which was quickly extended to the other states. When the news reached Britain there was panic talk in the press. Eleven days after the Sungei Siput incident John Soper tried to calm the worries of his daughter, who was at school in England:

> You seem to have got the wrong idea of things out here. There has been no rising . . .

> For the last year or two they [the Communists] have been stirring up trouble by strikes . . . But these tactics haven't been working as well or as quickly as they expected, and they have now threatened to kill every European, every policeman and everybody who supports Chiang Kai Shek. The police have rounded up quite a few and have probably put quite a lot of spokes in this wheel, so they are now all out in the jungles again, striking here and there, but no all-out offensive yet; we may be able to stop it before it happens, and are getting well organized for it. The next month is critical; if nothing big happens before mid-August, then I don't think it ever will.[51]

On this occasion his confidence was misplaced. The Communists replied by extending their terror attacks. In Pahang, a gang of forty fired the police station at Jerantut, burned a family alive, and viciously extorted food and money from labourers on an estate near Kuala Lipis. At Voules Estate, Johore, a Chinese headman was severely mutilated; at Senai Estate another was peppered with bullets. In a well-organized strike, five groups of guerrillas, probably totalling eighty men, converged on Malaya's only coal mine at Batu Arang, Selangor, on 13 July. Before the terrorists withdrew, five men were selected and killed, machinery was sabotaged, the police post was overrun, and the Kuala Lumpur train was hijacked when it stopped at the nearby station. In August tin-mine staff in the Kinta valley became targets. A gang ambushed the General Manager of Meru Tin Mines, Ian Ogilvie, who died in a hail of bullets. A week later the Welsh dredge master of Tronoh Mines, Baden Powell Wills, was attacked, along with a young Scot, James Ritchie. A Sten-gun fusillade killed Wills, and the wounded Ritchie was lucky to escape. A rush of other vicious incidents forced the government to outlaw the MCP, but its objective was already apparent: to undermine the economy by breaking machinery, cutting communications, attacking rubber trees and estate buildings, and targeting European managers and government officials, especially the police, the majority of whom were Malays. In this context, the murder in December 1948 of Alan Blake, who ran the Serendah Boys' Home, seemed an act of gratuitous violence.

In reply to the attacks the Security forces – soldiers and police – were boosted by the formation of a Special Constabulary, and later by a part-time Home Guard. Meanwhile, at the suggestion of John Davis and others, former 'Chindit' fighters and Force 136 men were brought back to lead special patrols of British, Malay and Gurkha troops, supported by Dayak trackers brought over from Borneo. 'Ferret Force' began to scour the jungle for the terrorists, and quickly proved their worth when the Communist military commander Lau Yew was killed with other CTs in a July encounter near Kajang led by Police Superintendent 'Two-Gun' Bill Stafford, a veteran of fifteen parachute drops into Burma. Planter James Hislop, whose unorthodox military career had started in Dalforce, was given command as Lieutenant-Colonel of 4 Ferret Force, to operate in Johore. His Force 136 experience and knowledge of the jungle and of Communist procedures were invaluable in achieving results. The Johore drive exposed twelve terrorist camps with substantial supplies and arms. Twenty-seven Communist terrorists were killed, and Hislop was mentioned in dispatches. But the Ferret Force initiative proved politically sensitive, and after four months it was discontinued.

However, in another controversial decision, the federal government imported several hundred ex-Palestine police, headed by Colonel Nicol Gray. The move demoralized the Civil Service and the Malayan police, although to a planter like John Edington the newcomers' knowledge of anti-terrorist methods made them invaluable colleagues in training the Special Constables.[52] With two of the Palestine sergeants, Bob Graver and Jock Sutherland, Edington trained young Malays from surrounding kampongs. 'Drill, weapon training, fieldcraft and even barrack-room inspections became the order of the day. We dug slits-trenches or weapon pits, using them for the regular duties of stand-to at dawn and stand-down at sunset, such being the likeliest hours for an attack by terrorists.'[53]

Ferret Force had demonstrated the kind of tactics needed in special anti-terrorist jungle operations. The Malay Regiment also included officers and men trained in jungle warfare; among them was Hussein, a decorated officer who had joined as an eighteen-year-old in 1935 and had fought the Japanese in Singapore. His loyalty had been recognized in 1945 when he was chosen to march in the victory parade in London. Three years later his battalion was involved in anti-terrorist operations, tracking down bandits in the Temengor region of northern Perak.

I was with the First Battalion, and my platoon was sent forward to contact them at about six o'clock in the morning, in the fasting month. We had contacted them on the top of a hill. There were about three hundred and seven of them and my platoon was only about twenty-five; but, of those Bandits, only eighty of them were armed. The rest were just followers. We captured one. He told everything to my Company Commander. That is how I came to know how many there were.

I have contacted many Bandits; I have killed two or three also. It's hand to hand; but very rare. I seldom used tracks. I used a compass bearing to move about in the jungle. If you use the track you may be seen, get ambushed – booby-traps – all sorts of things. I went with a parang [machete] very quietly. We crawled through undergrowth, no noise; we used the parang especially on thorns and creepers. You cut them, otherwise they tear off your shirt. There are leeches, too, especially on wet weather days. We had a type of ointment called DDT. We needed it for scrub typhus; and before we went out they used to give us twenty-four hours' warning of it, to get our jungle boots ready, and we would rub in the ointment so the insects wouldn't bite. We had our field dressing bundles; we had medical orderlies and our wireless group was also following us.

Fighting the CT's in the jungle, I just gave out the orders. I cannot go too far forward because if I got killed then all will be complicated. So I have to dominate the area, where I can be in command. Number One, check in front. Number Three, to the left. Observe the target, and if you can see the target, then fire. But in the jungle it is very hard to see; you only can hear. Use your ears and brain: those two. Ears and brain. Once you hear a stick go click! you think: has it been broken by animals or by humans? Then the brainwork begins. You have to freeze and wait ten or fifteen minutes. Wait and see what will happen. Don't be hasty. In the jungle there is no need for hasty command or hasty movement.[54]

Infantry operations of this kind tended to last only one or two weeks. As the Emergency continued with no end in sight, another special force, the Malayan Scouts, was established in 1950 to undertake much more prolonged operations in the jungle. Later the Scouts were to become part of the 22nd Special Air Service Regiment. But in a guerrilla war the civilians were also in the front line, as James Hislop found when he was forced to make a desperate dash from his bungalow as it was being attacked by a large force of terrorists.

In 1948 John Edington and his proprietor's Visiting Agent, Dato H. E. Mackenzie, had a close shave while travelling by car to Kulai:

We were accompanied by two special constables who were both seated on my right at the back. He [Dato Mackenzie] drove himself with his driver sitting in front of me. We were just approaching the estate entrance at speed when we were fired on from our left. I could see figures moving, up on the forward slope of rising ground about 150 yards away. I struck my sten gun out of the open window, emptying a full magazine at them. By that time we were through the ambush and the road ahead was clear, and thanks to the very skilful driving we soon reached the main tar road near Kulai, and thence to the police station to make our report. From the spent cartridges recovered it was shown that automatic weapons including a bren gun had been used, although the CTs only hit the car three times . . . Fortunately no obstruction had been placed across the road such as a felled tree.

On a second occasion, in 1950, terrorists from the 5th Independent Platoon laid an ambush for Edington as he took his regular morning jeep ride to Division 2 of the estate. He was saved by a lucky change of itinerary that day, but a police vehicle with a number of special constables and wives was caught in crossfire.[55]

'The CTs went for miners and planters because they had guns. We were easy sitting targets,' said miner's wife Daphne Davidson. She came out to Rawang, Selangor, in December 1948, and four days later 'we had this very big first ambush . . . There was a platoon of Scots Guards, and they were all under twenty-one!' It appeared they were National Servicemen, quite unprepared for what they had to face, and 'they didn't know one end of a gun from the other!' It was a tough, wearying existence for wives. Rawang had a tin dredge and a power and railway station but

no church, no doctor, nothing. There was just a dresser with a dressing-post . . . Planters, in particular, were very isolated; miners were mainly in camps, but the CTs got them on the roads, or going to their places of work. We weren't supposed to go anywhere without armoured cars, but we reckoned we were safer if we just nipped out when we thought of it instead of going in a convoy.[56]

Donald Macpherson was a planter on Rasa Estate, Kuala Kubu Bharu, Selangor, in 1949–51. It was his friend James Robertson of Force 136 who had dropped by parachute in 1945 just south of Rawang, 'so we always had a laugh. He trained the Commy terrorists, who had so many goes at me and who killed the Assistant Manager before me in 1948. I've always said he made a poor job of training, as they were b—— bad

shots!'[57] The terrorists also took risks carrying out forays into Rawang.
Daphne Davidson again:

> One Sunday we heard a lot of shooting and we went out on our veran-
> dah and saw this chap leap out at the back of the coffee shop and run
> across the tin tailings, and he was shot down by the police. They were
> always doing this. They'd come into a little shop on the edge of the town,
> and they'd sit among the people and hear information; or they'd hold up
> the proprietor, snatch tins of food, and then nip back into the jungle.[58]

Despite – or because of – their willingness to take risks, the terrorists scored successes. Donald Macpherson pointed out that in two years
at Rasa, 'we had numerous lorries burned, our special constables killed
and my driver was burned by Communists. Our Chinese linesite and
our estate office were burned down. In one week we were attacked at
night three times. Rasa estate was considered a most unhealthy spot by
Army and Police, possibly the worst estate in 1949–50 for incidents.'[59]

James Robertson took over Sungei Tekal rubber estate, near the town
of Kuala Krau, after the previous Manager had been shot; at the time,
Pahang had become a focus for Malay recruitment for the Malayan
Races' Liberation Army, starting with a spectacular attack on the little
railway town by 300 Communists. Such was the level of danger
Robertson faced that ninety Special Constables, a platoon of British
troops and five European police sergeants were needed to guard him
and his Assistant, the estate headquarters, the rubber and palm-oil
factories and the living quarters.

Tom Kerr was Assistant Manager at Sungei Way, Selangor. He rated
his a reasonably quiet area – only two murders were committed on his
estate around the end of 1948 or early 1949: they happened 'at the
Chinese tappers' latex collection when two terrorists appeared and cut
the throats of the Chinese conductor and kepala [headman]'. Extortion
and intimidation had become routine. In 1950, as Kerr was about to
take over as Acting Manager, 'the Chinese tappers returned to the
factory and said terrorists had appeared and told them to go on strike
or die'.[60]

The planters had to meet impossible CT threats resolutely, as John
Anderson found in 1951 when facing a demand to raise his workers' pay
to $7 – a three- to fourfold increase – within ten days. But, when he
found a pair of CTs in the rubber lecturing his tappers on the benefits

of Communism, one of his Special Constables 'charged forward, shouting a suitable Koranic war cry, firing rapidly from the hip', and the two men rapidly disappeared.[61]

In a war in which the battlefields were lonely estate roads, dark rows of rubber, ugly mining camps and the ubiquitous rainforest, planters, miners, police, officials and their wives – and thousands of innocent and defenceless Asian villagers – found that their daily routine was fashioned by the Emergency. But the Europeans adjusted to siege conditions, surrounded by barbed wire, floodlights and armoured vehicles, and guarded twenty-four hours a day in their bungalows by dogs or constables. They learned to vary schedules and never to divulge their routes and venues. Curfews were in operation from 3 p.m. to 6 a.m. away from main roads and from 7 p.m. to 6 a.m. elsewhere. Although planters were issued with passes, 'To venture out socially in a remote area required a lot of courage and determination, particularly at night,' said Jim Winchester.[62] In fact, there was very little social life or chance for relaxation in the early part of the Emergency. John Edington recalled infrequent trade-union meetings of the Incorporated Society of Planters in the Johore Civil Service Club; otherwise, going to Kuala Lumpur for the AGM and 'a rumbustious weekend' was a rare highlight.[63] There was a general view that the planters as a group were 'really incredibly brave': ninety-nine of them were killed in the Emergency.[64]

Meanwhile, people in the towns were largely unaffected by the conflict. Life in Singapore in 1948 was very vibrant, John Loch recalled. He was in his early twenties and a member of the Special Constabulary: 'I was a marine policeman and one used to go out patrolling the Straits of Singapore . . . I never knew what we were trying to stop – it was quite a lark – and we used to leap on to junks and inspect them.' Even as Assistant District Officer, Parit, in 1949, taking due care on the road between Parit and Ipoh, his riverine district of Malay kampongs, padi and rubber was largely exempt from terrorist activity. 'One was aware of the Emergency but not concerned with it.'[65]

Shrugging off occasional incidents which occurred in places like Balit Pulau, Europeans in Penang found the pleasures of life had in no way diminished.[66] Not so for those up-country in the front line. The casualty figures may not have seemed high compared with a conventional war: 886 civilians and security forces killed or wounded in 1948, some 500 civilians killed or 'missing' in 1949, rising to 646 civilians murdered,

409 wounded and 106 'missing' in 1950. However, behind the figures were unpalatable facts and personal tragedies. The Cameron Highlands, long a popular area with the British, became a focus for terrorist activity, and, as the Communists kept up their operations, women and children were no longer safe. In 1951 there was clearly no improvement in the trend. The Lucys, a British planting couple with twin baby boys, whose estate was a mere half a dozen miles outside Kuala Lumpur along the Betong road, endured twenty-five attacks within the space of a fortnight. It was a sign that 'things were floundering', as one MCS officer put it with typical understatement.[67]

Sir Edward Gent's two unhappy years in office had ended sadly with his death in a plane crash in July 1948. His successor was Sir Henry Gurney, a man well equipped to deal with terrorism from his experience as Chief Secretary of the British administration in Palestine. But progress was slow, and in January 1950 British Malayans were mortified when Prime Minister Clement Attlee officially recognized the Communist regime of Mao Tse-tung in China. With the perception growing in Malaya that Britain was losing the Malayan War, in April 1950 General Sir Harold Briggs came out as Director of Operations to co-ordinate the offensive against the Communists. Though both he and Gurney had a sound grasp of the situation, neither felt satisfied with their achievements when within the space of a month in 1951 fate dealt a double blow. Ill health forced Briggs to resign in November 1951, but not before Gurney himself was the victim of a terrorist ambush. Sir Henry, his wife and his secretary were being driven up to Fraser's Hill for the weekend. Jim Winchester would not forget that October day in 1951.

> We often went to Fraser's Hill, where our Company had a holiday bungalow, on local leave. [But] I was driving from a posting on a rubber estate in Selangor [Batang Berjuntai] to another in Pahang [Kuala Lipis]. It was, therefore, just a coincidence that I caught up with the tail end of the convoy as it was attacked. I didn't know Sir Henry was in the convoy (or indeed that there was any sort of military movement) but opinion seemed fairly certain that the CTs did. The ambush occurred somewhere between Kuala Kubu and the Gap.

In fact, the thirty-eight-man unit of the 11th Regiment of the MRLA, Pahang, was expecting to seize a convoy of military arms. Instead, they saw a Rolls-Royce with escorting vehicles, and when they started shooting Sir Henry stepped from the car into the line of fire to save Lady Gurney. He was killed instantly. 'I was turned back by police in the last A.P.C. [armoured personnel carrier]', said Jim Winchester, 'and spent the night at the Kuala Kubu Rest House, reading the story in the Straits Times the next morning, by which time the road had been re-opened and I was able to complete my journey.'[68]

The murder of the British High Commissioner, the Queen's representative, in broad daylight horrified all races in Malaya. The security forces responded swiftly against the little village of Tras near Fraser's Hill, burning it to the ground. A young Volunteer Red Cross worker, Pearl Cox, recalled:

> There had been a fair amount of Communist activity in that area, so the Army were made to round up every single person, every man, woman and child in that village, and they were all pushed off to Perak! I can remember driving through the place and not a single soul lived there. Everybody had been taken out. Every one of them was a Chinese. It was a very, very harsh thing to do.[69]

Gurney's death had pinpointed the problem facing every government where the enemy are terrorist guerrillas: how to defend the vulnerable majority against a ruthlessly determined minority. The postwar promise of a stable and successful Malaya was balanced on a knife edge. Some decided to leave the country, feeling that the promise was no more than an illusion. By the end of 1951 the need for strong direction had never been more urgent.

# 16

# *The Battle for Hearts and Minds*

Three men personified the British presence in Malaya during its final phase: a political impresario, an administrator and a soldier. The first of these, Malcolm MacDonald, served as Governor-General of Malaya and Singapore from 1946 to 1948 and as Commissioner-General for South-East Asia from 1948 to 1955. The son of Britain's first Labour Prime Minister, he was an unconventional, unstuffy influential politician, though in co-ordinating policy from his Johore residence of Bukit Serene he was sometimes at odds with Colonial Service opinion. 'He had an exceptional memory,' a member of the Malayan Civil Service remembered, and was 'A natty little man who dressed rather loudly' and sat in his Rolls-Royce 'like an orchid in one of those cellophane packets'.[1] In 1947 MacDonald had identified Communism as 'Enemy No. 1' in Malaya, and consequently won the respect of the planting community in the early days of the Emergency. 'The vital part played by the Commissioner-General cannot be over-estimated,' wrote the Johore planter John Edington. 'In the interest of the economy, his priority was the protection of the estates and mines with their personnel against banditry', leading to the introduction of Special Constables.[2]

The second man was Donald MacGillivray, last of the High Commissioners, an industrious administrator and 'a gentle approachable personality . . . who believed that faith and commitment should underlie one's life'. According to a Malayan colleague, he 'did not see himself especially talented in spite of a lengthy and very distinguished career in H.M. Colonial Service', and he never had the easy relationship with the future Malay Prime Minister, Tunku Abdul Rahman, which the British Colonial Secretary Alan Lennox-Boyd enjoyed. But

MacGillivray was to oversee an accelerated timetable to independence, after serving as Deputy High Commissioner in the crucial years from 1952 to 1954, when 'he was a perfect foil to General Sir Gerald Templer'.[3] And so to the third figure: it was without doubt General Templer who countered the Communist insurgency, galvanized British morale, and steadied Malaya's multiracial community in preparation for a new political future.

Templer arrived in Malaya in February 1952, charged with the joint responsibilities of High Commissioner and Director of Operations, and carrying the hopes of Britain's newly elected Tory government under Winston Churchill. In Malaya his appointment was greeted with caution – not everyone, including Malcolm MacDonald, rejoiced at the prospect of a soldier heading the civil government – but, as Templer threw himself into his self-appointed task of getting to know the people of Malaya, his stock rose. The upswing in British morale was palpable, said an administrator who transferred to Malaya on the heels of Templer. John Loch, a member of the General's planning staff, was one of many to be won over by his charismatic leadership. In appearance, he noted, Templer

> looked rather like Charles II – if you have seen the effigy of Charles II at Westminster Abbey – fairly short, wiry, and he had a little pencilled moustache . . . and the moment he talked his eyes lit up . . . You felt the whole time you were under his gaze . . . He was one of those leaders who attracted younger army officers who later most of them became generals in turn . . . You gave him all you could, partly out of loyalty to him. He was a very, very great man . . . He was legendary.[4]

This praise was echoed by a young Chinese Affairs officer: 'Dynamic, enthusiastic, energetic, and for someone in my position a hero, who was always open to ideas from junior officers like myself . . . Templer was a charismatic leader who helped to break down social barriers between the races in our complicated plural society.'[5]

Within a short time the commercial world as well as the Civil Service was reassured by Templer's capacity to make and implement decisions. The planter John Anderson, who arrived in 1951 to work initially on two estates outside the capital, Kuala Lumpur, remembered him with enthusiasm. 'He was a breath of fresh air to the planting community and a much needed boost to morale at a difficult time. I thought he did a great job.'[6] This view was also shared by J. S. Potter, Chairman of his District Planters Association in Negri Sembilan:

> I remember being present and hearing General Templer speak when he addressed Planting Representatives for the first time in Kuala Lumpur. I was at once impressed. Here was a man at least who knew what he wanted to do and how to do it. Later I formed one of the first Estate Home Guards for him . . . encouraging . . . the common people to take some active part in the war against the C.T.s instead of being passive lookers on . . . General Templer . . . paid us a visit one evening with Gen. Sir Hugh Stockwell (G.O.C. Malaya Command) and others . . . [His] visit was greatly appreciated and everyone on the estate had an opportunity of airing his views, asking questions and meeting him face to face. No previous High Commissioner had taken the trouble to do this before
> . . .

Here was a man 'who got off his office chair', ended Potter approvingly.[7]

Templer was also given to straight-talking and strong language, devoid of rhetoric. His admirers considered him to be enormously likeable, but Loch conceded that 'some people didn't like him . . . Although open to argument, he could be incredibly rude to people if he didn't agree with them. He sent them packing.'[8] To the astonishment of Kuala Lumpur's European community, he criticized their mindset almost as sternly as he tongue-lashed the recalcitrant townsfolk of Tanjong Malim.[9] Among those who came under his scrutiny was the Malayan Civil Service, which included men of the pre-war generation. (Some, it was said, had never fully recovered from their experiences during the Japanese occupation.) Templer described the British Advisers, for instance, as 'an uninspiring lot', but Mervyn Sheppard, ex-prisoner and now Adviser in Negri Sembilan, was one who felt energized by his dynamism.[10] To the average District Officer, however, a visit from Templer could be 'quite an ordeal: you'd wonder if he'd agree and like what you were doing, and if he didn't you were probably out'.[11] Although he was promoted with Templer's approval, Guy Madoc, the extremely able head of the Special Branch, found him disconcerting. Recalling his appointment as Director of Intelligence, Madoc recounted that when offered the job he had asked for forty-eight hours to consider it. Templer agreed, but replied, 'Remember that I don't take "no" from anyone.' Nevertheless, Madoc took his time before accepting.[12] Templer's severest critic was Victor Purcell, a Cambridge academic and former civil servant who had retired from the Malayan scene.[13] Having observed him at close hand, Tom Morgan considered Templer to be 'naturally autocratic', and, echoing this, Hugh Humphrey, a pre-war District Officer and post-war Secretary for Defence, concluded, 'he was ruthless – very ruthless indeed'.[14]

Templer's overriding aim was to restore law and order and bring peace to the Federation. 'If you pull it off,' Churchill told him, 'it will be a great feat.'[15] First came an action plan to clarify priorities and select his team to devise and implement strategies. There were changes at the top: among those who left were the Chief Secretary, the Deputy Director of Operations and the GOC in Malaya, General Robert Urquhart, the hero of Arnhem. In Templer's judgement, the people of Malaya needed to know that the Communist Emergency was not simply a problem for British imperialism but a formidable obstacle to a free, independent Malayan nation. The sooner peace was restored and the various ethnic communities learned to live in harmony, the quicker independence would come. In the last analysis, Templer is alleged to have said, 'the answer lies not in pouring more troops into the jungle, but in the hearts and minds of the people'. This aphorism encapsulated the General's legacy to Malaya, though it fell to his successor and to the political wisdom of the Malay, Chinese and Indian leaders to harness the people's trust and confidence to forge a free, democratic, multi-racial state.

Templer's arrival followed a volte-face in Communist strategy. In October 1951 Chin Peng had produced a new directive, prohibiting terror tactics against the Asian population – slashing rubber trees, killing for identity cards, machine-gunning villages and burning buses – and abandoning attempts to seize control of 'liberated areas' with units of battalion strength. Instead, the guerrillas retreated deep into the jungle, emerging to launch sudden attacks on the European 'imperialists' and their security forces. In November 1951, for instance, two senior planters and their escort of ten Malay Special Constables had been ambushed, leaving only one survivor from the attack, a badly wounded policeman. Then in March 1952 the water pipeline to the township of Tanjong Malim was cut by the CTs for the umpteenth time. A repair party, led by the Assistant District Officer, Michael Codner, and a police escort, was ambushed two miles outside the town by some forty guerrillas. Fourteen men were killed, including the ADO, his Executive

Engineer, a Public Works technical assistant and five policemen. This incident caused a massive outcry. Codner was a hero of the Second World War, having won the MC for his part in the 'Wooden Horse' escape from a German prison camp. The ambush also brought a fierce response from Templer, who imposed collective punishment on the townspeople for abetting the attackers. But, more significantly, it high-lighted the urgency of winning over an alienated population, which now became a major priority.

Looking back over events, the Secretary for Defence conceded that 'We struggled through this Emergency with the most extraordinary methods.'[16] One group with whom the British authorities had to deal were the aborigines who lived in the high rainforests and the coastal swamps of states like Perak. The tea planter Bill Fairlie, who was famil-iar with the Sakai, found them to be 'marvellous little people', and, though shy and unsophisticated, they were honest, truthful and happy. They handled the blowpipe with deadly accuracy, and could become first-class shots with a rifle.[17] In the dark years of the war, with British connivance, they had been recruited to help MPAJA guerrillas against the Japanese; and in 1949 some were suspected of collaborating with the Communists.

From his involvement in Force 136 and Ferret Force, the planter James Hislop knew the potential of the aborigines as intelligence sources, but also that they needed to be weaned from the Chinese con-nection. In March 1950 he was appointed to recruit a new body, the Perak Aboriginal Areas Constabulary (PAAC), officered by Europeans and manned mainly by Malays. Their task was to search for and befriend tribes such as the Negritoes, Temiar and Semai. One of the officers he recruited in 1951 was another Scots planter, Donald Macpherson, whose career had been badly disrupted by CT attacks. PAAC lasted longer than Ferret Force, despite being opposed by the regular police force. However, in 1952 its covert operations were revealed to the Communists through their screen of aboriginal support-ers, and, after three of Macpherson's fellow officers and a number of tribal headmen were killed in the jungle, PAAC was disbanded and the Malays were absorbed into the Police Jungle Company. Hislop, however, had drawn attention to the aboriginal issue. He set a prece-dent by building jungle forts for the protective custody of aborigines – a tactic adopted by the security forces in the area south of the Thai border.[18] Under Templer, an Adviser of Aborigines was appointed and village headmen were entertained at King's House in Kuala Lumpur by General and Lady Templer. The logical conclusion of these initiatives to win the hearts of Malaya's *orang asli* was the formation of an all-aboriginal fighting force – the Senoi Pra'aq – which eliminated a record number of guerrillas in 1959.

Another successful tactic, in Hugh Humphrey's view, was a policy used against Communists before the Japanese War, of deporting Chinese and Indians suspected of collusion with the enemy. The former Secretary for Defence later revealed 'a story that can now be told but was kept under wraps for a long, long time'. It was a saga of official involvement in bribery and corruption and in a cloak-and-dagger operation to ship some 35,000 Chinese back to China under the Norwegian flag in the years 1948–51. He told how it was necessary to reassure an alarmed Norwegian ship's Captain, whose Chief Officer had been clapped into prison by the Chinese authorities, that Britain's man in Hong Kong would arrange to buy his way out. Greasing the Captain's palm with a hefty package of dollar notes – it happened to be Christmas Day – Humphrey told him, on behalf of the British government, how 'we'd very much appreciate it if they could continue', even though 'it was costing as much to send a deportee to Swatow as it was to send a European First Class to London'.[19]

Templer inherited a blueprint to tackle the insurgency called the Briggs Plan, devised in 1950 by the previous Director of Operations. After a slow beginning, the security forces had been increased by 1951 to a peak of 67,000 police, 300,000 Home Guards and twenty-three infantry battalions, to confront a maximum of 8,000 guerrillas. Co-operation between the administration, police and military was maintained by a system of Central, State and District War Executive Committees. 'They all worked together and all activities were very well planned and co-ordinated at each level,' recalled Dermot Barton, District Officer in Alor Gajah in 1953. As the intelligence war heated up in 1954 to eradicate CT units deep in the jungle, the membership of the War Executive Committees was broadened to include certain civilian representatives.

The Guthrie's planter J. S. Potter was initially a member of his District Committee in Negri Sembilan before serving the planting and European interests on the main state bodies, including the State War

Executive Committee, but had reservations about the DWECs and SWECs. 'Representing community interests, co-operating with the Government and helping to protect the lives of my fellow planters took a lot of reconciliation and compromise! In fact I became one of W. S. Gilbert's "apologetic statesmen of a compromising kind" whom Koko had on his list. Under the stress of the times tempers could become frayed.' It was a subcommittee (from which unofficials were excluded) which did 'the real business', but, he went on, 'unofficials were expected to provide information for the Security Forces to bring the enemy to battle. So keen were the Government to get kills that it was even suggested at one meeting from the chair that planters should be used as decoys almost to attract the enemy. My feelings on this can be well imagined!' However, Potter did admit that 'on SWEC I got to know intimately many senior Officers as we thrashed our problems out at weekly meetings. The army certainly worked hard at their task and on the whole co-operated wonderfully well with us.'[20]

The enlistment by the government and police of planters like Donald Macpherson was another sign of the times. With his incomparable knowledge of the country, Macpherson was given numerous gazetted ranks, such as Honorary Superintendent of Police in Perak and Honorary Inspector in Negri Sembilan, Selangor and Johore, and honorary roles as Game Warden and Inspector of Smallholdings in several states, and made many friends in these circles. The doyen of planters, Dato James Crawford, was the recipient of the Colonial Police Medal for his intelligence work in Perak during the Emergency. However, Guy Madoc knew that 'the spearhead of the Special Branch intelligence effort was not the European but the Asian inspector', for these Chinese and Malay officers were both highly intelligent and able to absorb their special training and the skills of disguise and infiltration.[21]

In the 1950s the symbiotic civilian and military objectives in the Briggs Plan focused on communications and the severing of the umbilical cord between the terrorists and the Min Yuen. One essential was to cut off supplies of food which the squatters on the jungle fringes had been forced to contribute to the terrorists. Guy Madoc revealed the security forces' tactics:

> We were able quite deliberately to enforce food control all round the perimeter of the Communist districts, but we would choose one or two

places, and weaken the controls accidentally on purpose . . . we allowed a certain amount of food to trickle out on the fringe. We called that the honeypot. And then when the Communists had really begun to get a bit careless, we put in ambushes.[22]

Successful ambushes weakened terrorist morale and, short of food, they began to surrender in growing numbers.

Potter, however, put his finger on the key strategy. 'One of the biggest achievements of the Emergency was the resettlement of some half a million scattered squatters . . . into compact villages where the amenities of Government could easily reach them,' he remarked.[23] To convey the new spirit behind the government rural housing estates, the term 'Resettlement Area' was replaced under Templer by 'New Village'. From his vantage point as Secretary for Chinese Affairs, Brian Stewart saw that 'The New Village was an important battleground in the campaign for Hearts and Minds.'[24] The prototype had been conceived in Negri Sembilan by a resourceful young District Officer, whom Hugh Bryson, the British Adviser, felt ought to have had more credit for his pioneering work.

Negri Sembilan was the first State to construct a 'New Village'. This was the scheme for bringing small-holders, mainly Chinese, in from isolated areas where they were liable to pressure from guerrillas, to whom they supplied – willingly or under threat of death – food and information, and to concentrate them in an easily protected area. When I arrived in Seremban in 1949, Charles Howe, District Officer, Jelebu, had started working on a plan for the area around a Chinese mining centre at Titi. I paid an early visit there . . . The shopkeepers in the village were frightened, surly and unwilling to talk to any Government official, and my attempts to open conversation with the Chinese who sold me a packet of cigarettes and a cup of coffee were a dismal failure. The scheme took many months to complete . . . When the job was finished there were three protected areas, including Titi village, and no small-holders residing outside the perimeter fences, though they went out each day to work on their land. When I made a second visit, the Chinese of Titi were a completely changed lot, ready to chat, smile and joke. I took Sir Henry Gurney, High Commissioner, there in 1950 and we travelled without any escort.[25]

The proponents of the New Villages believed that a secure environment could create a sense of community and isolate the Communist terrorists, but at first the process was hampered by financial and man-power problems, and by the end of 1950 only 12,000 people had been moved. 'It was not easy to persuade the farmer resettled miles from his farm on the jungle fringe, that he was better off than he had been living on his farm at the mercy of the Communist terrorists . . . The farmer was gravely inconvenienced,' admitted Brian Stewart, 'but so was the Communist terrorist movement, which now had to struggle to keep supplies flowing to their jungle camp.'[26] Pearl Cox, painted a similarly honest picture of the lot of Chinese rubber-tappers and tin-miners.

> So few people knew about the New Villages, why they were there, and how they were created. The original idea was that each village should eventually be an ordinary village, but some were so isolated and in such horrible places – like tin tailings where it would be very difficult to do anything with the land – that they became a community cut off from everybody else, and with barbed wire around them. The workers were allowed to go out rubber-tapping in the morning, but they had to be back in at night, under guard, and they had no contact really with the real world at all . . . Of course, the reason they were put there in the first place was that they were like nomads, people who didn't really belong anywhere.[27]

In such areas it was small wonder that a disorientated people would be troublesome. To Pearl Cox 'One of the worst villages I ever went to was north of Sungei Siput. I thought it was an absolutely ghastly place. Those children grew up in a strange, segregated environment, and now [in the 1950s] they are causing all sorts of problems.'[28] Bad resettlement was often due to bad co-ordination between government services, but Communist accusations that the villages were concentration camps were roundly denied by the British. In Perak a group of villagers were sufficiently grateful to the army unit in charge of their resettlement as to name their new home Kampong Coldstream!

The rehoused squatters needed protection and practical help, and suitable officers were seconded by the government; for instance, Ted Browne, Assistant Manager of the Rubber Research Institute Experimental Station, was brought in to resettle Chinese jungle squat-ters into the New Villages of Sungei Buloh and Subang, in Selangor. Daphne Davidson, wife of the local mine Manager, found herself involved in the Rawang area:

Special officers were asked to establish these Villages. They were go-ahead chaps, all ex-patriates. They would go out with the Police, find these people and round them up. Of course it was a sad business; they had to leave their homes, and they didn't like that very much. They were brought into the Villages and set down in brand new houses. There was probably very little land to grow anything, and they were behind barbed wire . . . There were patrols all round them at night; their own people set up a sort of Home Guard . . . They weren't guaranteed work, but I think most of them found something. A saw-mill was set up; and, of course, later the Cement Works was a help.

We used to go down and see to the children. We would go round the Village and collect up anybody that we thought needed medical attention, and send them to the doctor, either in K.L. or Kuala Kubu; and then later we got one of the Kuala Kubu doctors to come and visit Rawang once a week. There was also this Baby Clinic that I managed to set up with a few people. It was a sort of post-natal clinic. It was a thing we did entirely on our own, and it was later taken over by the Welfare Department.[29]

After 1952 the New Village programme accelerated under Templer. Most of Brian Stewart's career in the Malayan Civil Service during the 1950s was as Secretary for Chinese Affairs in Malacca and latterly in Penang. He was acutely conscious of the sensitive political nature of his work in providing a bridge between the Chinese community and the government – especially in Malacca, where his predecessor and his assistant had been ambushed while leaving a New Village. 'We tried hard to provide decent accommodation, better schools than they had before, playing fields, entertainment, shops and clinics . . . So my job had major elements of town planning, social welfare, education in the rural areas. In the "city" of Malacca the job was to get to know the leaders of the Chinese community.'[30]

It was very gratifying to twenty-seven-year-old Stewart that Gerald Templer backed his Malacca activities warmly, enabling him to set in motion the 'White Area' policy. In particular, the General co-operated

in a series of Civics courses which I inaugurated in Malacca for rural leaders from all our Districts. They came to town for a week or so and at the end of their lectures were taken by bus to King's House in Kuala Lumpur, where Lady Templer gave then tea! This may not sound very dramatic, but it was a major event in the life of a villager from Malacca, and it is difficult to conceive of a civil servant–High Commissioner allowing a junior officer to exploit King's House in this fashion! The Psychological Warfare effect was incalculable, and the General was an Intelligence expert and aficianado and so saw the point immediately. Others would have worried about setting precedents.

In the event, by September 1953 it was possible 'to "declare a victory" in Central Malacca, announce the Emergency had been won . . . due to the energetic co-operation of the Chinese community, and therefore the draconian Emergency measures such as resettlements, food control, and curfews would not be imposed on Central District. The experiment worked!'[31]

Stewart showed that, where social welfare was taken seriously, a district could return to normal and be designated 'white'. Observing the way the people set up their own committees, started schools, raised funds and brought in teachers finally convinced Pearl Cox that the New Villages idea worked. But she saw how vital it was that the soil was good, so that inhabitants could grow vegetables and settle down:

> In Pahang, Charles Corry, who was the British Adviser . . . was very keen that a certain New Village that was created there would become, and remain a proper Village. He gave them good land, and they grew bananas, and they are still there now. They were given a chance; and this allowed them later on to mingle more easily with the town, and the local Malays too.
>
> Another good example of the same thing can be seen along the road to Bentong. There is a very big valley before you get to Genting Highlands. It is like a little bit of Switzerland, all neat market gardening. Now that was originally a New Village. It was put in a place which was well-protected and with good land, and it has remained part of the country's agricultural system. If more thought had been put into the scheme, every New Village would have been like that.[32]

In addition,

> The British Red Cross were asked to do the Nursing and Medical side. Each New Village had a nurse who lived there. When they first started they had one nurse assigned, and one Welfare Officer. The two girls lived in a little house in the New Village, they had an amah, a landrover and a driver. They did a tremendous job. They didn't only run the clinics; they also took part in the village work and tried to help the schools too. This is where I came in. We were trying to get schools to do Red Cross

work and Health work and to make the children feel more a part of the community. I would run competitions and we would get the New Village schools to come up to our competition centre. There they met more people, mixed up with the Malays and other groups. This was terribly important.[33]

That was also the view of Margaret Wheatley, a teacher who answered Gerald Templer's appeal for Red Cross and St John's Ambulance volunteers to come to Malaya. She worked from 1953 to 1955 in the field of health education, first in Kuala Lumpur and then in Johore, and was involved in various initiatives, including the setting up of a blood bank. But her primary job was to train local people on health matters – especially the young, who were easy to motivate. Since her Malay was limited, older children in local schools happily acted as interpreters. Even the Communist terrorists respected the neutrality and beneficial nature of the Red Cross, as they did the Women's Institutes, which were non-political and non-sectarian.

The Women's Institutes were the brainchild of Lady Templer, a response to her husband's urging that she should take the initiative in involving the women of Malaya in public life. If Malaya was to develop into a successful and confident nation, Templer saw that it needed a cultivated middle class with leisure. One of his decisions on arrival was that there ought to be a National Museum in the capital: 'hardly the sort of thing you'd expect of a general coming out to win a war', observed the administrator, John Loch. But Templer was 'very conscious of the aesthetic side of life', and he encouraged the formation of the Arts Council in Kuala Lumpur, which introduced symphony concerts and exhibitions, for which he and Lady Templer took responsibility for entertaining visiting international celebrities.[34]

Both of the Templers saw the development of Women's Institutes as a valuable social-welfare measure: a way of fostering a sense of communality among women of all the races, a route to raising their educational and cultural awareness. There was also another benefit, which Margaret Graham, one of the professional WI organizers sent out from England in 1953, addressed in a speech she gave in Kelantan early in 1955: 'the organization and structure of the movement is democratic throughout and as such it provides a useful training for the understanding of democracy which is so necessary for a country approaching self-government'.[35] Mrs Barton (née Graham) recalled that 'Lady T. was very forceful . . . She had enormous energy and very considerable vision', and she saw the potential of Women's Institutes for the 'hearts and minds' programme.[36] She used her drive and her unique position in Malaya to gain access to all levels of society; she had no compunction in weaning European women away from their bridge parties to become involved, or in approaching members of the Malay royal families for their help, since they were the natural patrons of traditional Malay craftsmanship.[37] 'In one or two of the states – Kelantan and Negri – where there was a very well-educated, go-ahead ruling family, they were very much more able and willing to see what was needed, and to set about seeing it was done.'[38]

The example of Kelantan's Arts and Crafts Department had already encouraged Margot Massie, wife of the Legal Adviser, Trengganu, to launch a similar venture to stimulate traditional crafts there. In 1949 a workshop was opened in Kuala Trengganu with a small shop attached. Its success was proved when in October 1950 the workers won the commission to produce a new mace for the Supreme Court in Penang, designed by Mrs Massie herself. She also found that the female members of the royal family, and Mrs Aminah Kameruddin, the wife of the Mentri Besar (Prime Minister), were keen for her to teach them knitting and tatting, while she in return gained useful practice in speaking Malay.

By 1953 there were 220 Women's Institutes grouped into forty-five districts, and they were operating in Malay kampongs as well as the predominantly Chinese New Villages. After travelling all over the Federation in her official capacity as organizer – on one occasion, from Kuala Lipis to Kuala Krai in a strange little railway vehicle known as the Wickham Trolley – Margaret Graham was able to take stock. The skills of the membership varied considerably: 'Some were expert in traditional crafts, some were uneducated and unskilled, some were highly sophisticated and very capable.'[39] However, the opening of so many institutes on a countrywide basis – a policy which had been initiated by Margaret Herbertson in 1952 and developed by her successor, Viola Williams – introduced ordinary Chinese, Malay and Tamil women to a variety of activities – sewing, dressmaking and knitting classes, arts and crafts, cookery and elementary home economics. 'Knitting was very, very popular,' said Mrs Daphne Loch, then based in Kuala Lumpur. And 'we used to teach cooking – how to make biscuits, which they loved. They have a passion for sweet things, and one had no moulds, but lids of cigarette tins were a perfect size.' (She discovered, too, from entertaining the village headmen and police with her husband, John, that a favourite drink was cherryade with condensed milk!)[40]

Margaret Graham even found that the tricky process of communication could bring unexpected benefits in spontaneous co-operation. For example,

> I went to a New Village in the middle of Johore – I was doing a demo in patchwork. I was speaking English and there was a Chinese who could make herself understood to the Chinese and also to some of the Malays and also there was an Indian who could understand either a bit of what I was saying or a bit of what the other was saying. It was a complete mixed community and we had about four languages going. Fortunately, demonstrating patchwork doesn't require a great deal of talk![41]

The Girl Guide movement set itself similar social objectives to the Women's Institutes, according to Margaret Mackenzie, wife of a senior planter in Johore and District Commissioner for the Guides in that state in 1948. She recalled how 'guiding brought girls out of their homes – and girls there were not allowed out of their homes much'.[42]

The enthusiastic involvement of European women in voluntary and in paid professional work suggested that the 1950s generation had a more developed sense of social responsibility than their pre-war counterparts. 'It was gradually growing, but it was given a kick start by Lady T.,' in Mrs Barton's opinion.[43] Most of these women saw their role as temporary: they were preparing Asians to take over for themselves. The Women's Institutes were merely one outlet for voluntary work. An English woman who worked with abandoned blind children at St Nicholas' Home in Penang recalled how much the Home relied on voluntary helpers during the time of the Emergency. 'There were a lot of Army people out there, and so the wives gave us all sorts of help. Some taught English, some taught music, some did PE – any of the skills they could offer.'[44] Margot Massie, who learned to speak Malay from scratch but became fluent, took classes in Malay for wives newly arrived from the UK, teaching them also about Malay customs and culture. In addition to helping Lady Templer with the Women's Institutes, Daphne Loch became involved in starting baby clinics for Asian families. In

1955, a planter's wife, Deirdre Edington, was asked by the Officer Superintending the Police Circle to help with clinics in the resettled villages in Johore.

> This meant travelling in an armoured vehicle with escorts, and when we arrived at the villages we weighed babies, gave them milk (because every tin was searched), and so we saw that they were all quite well and we also attended to the schoolchildren's heads. Later in 1956–57 in Johore Bahru they started TB clinics, because it was a rampant disease at that time. I helped Dr Elizabeth Comber (Han Su Yin) with her clinics, and then a rehabilitation centre was set up to give these people employment.[45]

Among the new generation of British women to arrive after 1945 were more qualified women and graduates, nurses and teachers, whose professional expertise was invaluable in Malaya. Mrs Kerr-Petersen, a physiotherapist who came out to Malaya with her husband in 1947, found her skills were much in demand. She did voluntary work at Kuala Lumpur Hospital and in Malacca, until she was eventually pressed to take a full-time job at the Malacca General Hospital. Her first priorities in Malacca were the little children hit by a polio epidemic, and she set about 'begging and borrowing' for the urgently-needed equipment to treat these young victims.[46] Mary Anderson of the Queen Elizabeth Overseas Nursing Service arrived in February 1947. She started and finished her fifteen-year career across six Malay states in the General Hospital, Johore Bahru, where she began as a Sister and ended as Matron, latterly the only European on the medical staff.

After working in the New Villages in the West, Pearl Cox volunteered to go to the backward east coast, where the Malays still 'led a very, very simple life . . . In '53 the road up to the east coast was just a mud road. It was either dusty or thick, thick mud!' Against a background of social and economic deprivation, she tried to prepare the Malays for change. She recruited locals to work with the Red Cross, hoping that through this experience they would imbibe the idea of community service and take responsibility for welfare. As she said, 'We were trying to get the idea of self-help over to the people':

> I went to the schools, and ran all the occupational therapy in the hospitals; and I got the local people to start forming their own committees – trying to help the women, and the people generally, to take part in their

own welfare . . . We went round all the little village schools, which were literally four posts and a bit of atap roof, and a few benches and a sand floor. The children would trot off there every day, but if it rained they didn't go to school because the roof leaked![47]

The Red Cross held weekly clinics for women and children in the kampongs, where one of the common diseases was yaws. 'Their little fingers would be stuck together with these sores!' Pearl Cox found. 'Their legs were stuck together! Oh, it was really horrible trying to clean them up! They nearly all had worms too.' And

> We had a leper ward in the General Hospital in Kuala Trengganu. I got them doing occupational therapy. The children would go and pick the bamboo and clean it up so that the lepers could make baskets. It was a simple arrangement, but it was a beginning, I think, to give them the idea that they should help themselves and each other . . . The leper ward had three or four doctors, mostly Europeans.[48]

The problems in rural Kedah were equally severe. As Marian Gent wrote, 'The volunteers could do little more than scratch the surface of a daunting social problem, but by their example they may have laid the foundations of an enlightened attitude towards health care and self-help.'[49]

The Emergency, meanwhile, had taught both British conscripts and British civilians to be resourceful and resilient. The young matured quickly. Many of the patrols sent into the jungle on search-and-kill operations were led by National Service Second Lieutenants, who 'served there with commendable bravery and tenacity in arduous conditions'.[50] Civilian Norman Price was in his teens when he 'learnt to fly at the Penang Flying Club and this eventually led to a career as a professional airline pilot with BOAC. During the bandit troubles, I carried out pay-drops (supplying money by air) to tin mines and rubber plantations. I also joined the Malayan Auxiliary Police to "do my bit" during the Emergency in the early 1950s.'[51] Jim Winchester, a young planter in Selangor, Pahang and Perak during the Emergency, admitted that, as civilian and security-force casualties dropped to under 200 in 1955, people tended to get a bit blasé, even though

> There was always an element of risk on the road until about the middle-to-late 1950s, particularly away from the towns and main arteries . . . I solved the problem by learning to fly and did as much of my official

travelling as I could that way, as most estates built their own air strips. Pay rolls and other important matters were also delivered and dealt with by air. As more and more areas were declared 'white', armed escorts for Europeans on estates and mines were allowed to run down.[52]

Until independence, however, the risk of an isolated attack remained. Muar, Johore, had a notorious reputation, and Craigielea Estate, where veteran planters Harper Ball and Simpson had been murdered in 1948, was the scene of a desperate last attack in May 1957, as Assistant Robert Duffton recalled:

Eight terrorists had been lying in an ambush position by the Estate roadway. The twenty two men in the group had been rotating the positions between them for some three days. It was thought that as there had been no incidents for some time the [Communist] hierarchy had instructed that something be carried out in the area to maintain their status. The road was used by police vehicles supplying linesite posts, army vehicles moving out or army patrols moving into the jungle. It just happened that I stopped right on the ambush point to inspect some replanting work and an opportunity arose for them to make the headlines . . . I was shot at, at some thirty yards' range but managed to get away into a swamp. A boy beside me got shot in the arm and two wheels of the tractor were punctured. The Estate Manager drove along the road unaware I had been shot at, and he actually drew the pursuers off me. He also escaped into a nearby swamp but his bodyguard was injured. Finally, another assistant, who heard the initial shooting, came to investigate, and fortunately the terrorists decided it was time to quit and withdrew, saving the Manager who was struck in the swamp. As far as I know it was the last ambush of an expatriate in the Emergency.[53]

The experience of civilians in the main towns varied, depending on their proximity to a 'black' or 'white' area. Taiping, for instance, was on the border between two such areas, and there were Communist units operating within striking distance, an Englishman teaching at the King Edward VII School recalled. He and two doctors with whom he shared a house were always wary: 'when we came home at night we always came up the back stairs, through the back door and we didn't turn the light on . . . since you would have been silhouetted against the door and someone might have had a shot at you from the jungle which was only about 100 yards away. There was always a risk until 1960.'[54] In the late 1950s, at the northern exit from Taiping, the main road to Butterworth carried a large sign indicating 'You are leaving the British protected zone', and troops always carried side arms. However, life in Kuala Lumpur was unrestricted after 1955, although the Bartons, who enjoyed Sunday walks, had a disconcerting experience while out with friends climbing a prominent rock known as the Tiger's Tooth. Dermot Barton explained, 'We were all dressed in jungle green and I was in front of the party on the way back and came round the corner and suddenly found myself looking down rifle barrels – a very frightening moment.' In fact they had been spotted by a policeman, who had sent out a patrol to investigate: 'they were going to shoot first if we were CTs'.[55] Penang remained a 'black' area – surprisingly, perhaps, as an English resident observed, 'we didn't get a lot of terrorist activity on the island . . . [but] It was always a bit tense when we went over on the mainland.' On the other hand, 'we did have one spell when it wasn't safe and we had a curfew'. This created practical problems for the staff of the St Nicholas' Home who had to pick up the blind children by school bus. 'We were told if we were challenged, "*Stop!*"' In the long run, 'when you're living with it, you say, oh, another bus burnt down upon the road the other day, but you sort of take it in your stride'.[56]

In the towns, social life maintained many of the pre-war traditions. In Taiping 'there was a club to which of course you were bound to belong. The New Club was almost 100 per cent European, and if you were a government servant you entered automatically. It offered all sorts of things: tennis, dramatics, Scottish dancing, celebrations for St George's Day and St Patrick's Day – ways in which Europeans tried to pretend they weren't too far from home. Bridge Club in the evening, mah-jong – that was terribly well supported.'[57] In Penang, too, 'the big social occasions of St George's, St Patrick's and St Andrew's nights were celebrated with formal dinners held at the E & O Hotel', Norman Price recalled. As an adolescent, he found interests in model aircraft and motorcycles, but he could not avoid the disadvantage that had always dogged young men in Malaya:

A small community in a colonial setting had severe restriction for an adolescent youth becoming sexually aware. A young girl might get a distorted view of her own popularity and the severity of competition for a boy might lead to complexes. There was very little social integration between ANY of the various racial groups that might otherwise redress the situation.[58]

Curiously, in the culture of a Malay state like Kedah this problem had never assumed the same magnitude for Englishmen in their twenties. 'As a bachelor, most of my girl friends were Asian,' one remarked, although he married an English girl with a similar Malayan background to his own.[59] But a young oil executive, Edward Morris, who worked at various times in Singapore, Kuala Lumpur, Ipoh and Penang from 1952 to 1958, was very conscious of the disproportionate number of young European men to young European women. However, in many businesses company policy remained unyielding on the matter of liaisons with Asian women, and an offending employee would be swiftly removed from the scene.

Although post-war life in Singapore (and to some degree in Penang) was dogged by strikes and student unrest, John Loch found it offered him 'a wonderful social life and a wonderful introduction to the Far East'.[60] Even the Emergency did not disrupt the habit of taking local leave. Except when there were terrorist scares, the hill stations remained popular. Those who liked the sea chose Pangkor Island or Port Dickson. Penang and Singapore, even trips to Australia, also had their appeal. Weekends brought the prospect of relaxing or getting together with friends. Susan Tanner (née Malet), who joined the Colonial Nursing Service in 1956, still pictures the great crowd of men and wives at Singapore Cricket Club, gathering for Saturday lunch after work ended, and how she relished the delicious *ikan molet*! To Jeremy Darby, a young bachelor and commercial executive who came out in 1952, Singapore provided endless fun:

> We lived the life of Riley. We were looked after by servants. We had a nice garden. It was easy to get into clubs – Tanglin, Singapore Yacht Club . . . It was a very leisurely life. We knocked off at five o'clock. No overtime . . . Every Saturday night we were dancing at Tanglin Club or the Swimming Club or somewhere, always in black tie, of course – we even wore black tie to go to the cinema in those days in Singapore.

In 1957 Mr and Mrs Darby were in Kuala Lumpur, still 'living a life of great splendour' in a beautiful house.[61]

For Jonathan Coates, memories of childhood in 1950s Kuala Lumpur were equally idyllic. 'One remembers the sunshine, one remembers lots of parties, for grown-ups and children, everyone joining in. One remembers picnics and barbecues. School was fun. One little school I went to was called Mrs Heinz's School, simply because a lady called Mrs Heinz ran it.'[62] As a child in 1950s Taiping, Peter Rowe had vivid memories of an annual treat. There were Auster aircraft at the garrison camp where his father was Education Officer, and every Christmas they watched as a soldier dressed as Father Christmas would parachute from an Auster into the camp with a sack of presents, one for each child.

Since the start of the Emergency there had been changes in the provision of private education for British children. The Pensionnat Notre Dame became a convalescent hospital for British soldiers and the school was transferred to temporary buildings. But British parents as a whole were reluctant to send their children up to Cameron Highlands, and Tanglin School ceased to function. However, in 1952 an idea first considered in the 1920s for a school for planters' children was revived, and in 1955 Uplands School opened on Penang Hill with an intake of fifty-two pupils. The number rose quickly to 120 and remained at a steady 100 for a good many years. At the same time the regular pre-war Blue Funnel service to Western Australia was back in business. The *Gorgon* and the *Charon* became very familiar to sons and daughters from Malaya, whose parents, instead of exiling them to Britain, sent them to Australian boarding schools so they could return for school holidays.

In the Federation, the large Army presence helped to sustain colonial traditions. Jim Winchester, planting in Pahang in 1951–3 while the Emergency was in full swing, remembered 'a company of Gurkhas, commanded by two British officers, camped astride the road from the Gap down to Raub, miles from anywhere. I called in once, just on dark, on my way back to Kuala Lipis from K.L., to find that, even in such an out-going place, the officers dressed for dinner in white monkey jackets, dress trousers and black ties. Very British.'[63] The senior managers in the British community were keen to maintain good public relations with the Army. Mrs Loch accepted 'one did quite a lot of entertaining of the officers from the regiments – our job was to lay on Christmas parties and so on.'[64] Working on the State War Executive Committee with military officers, J. S. Potter was won over from his initial scepticism. 'I appreciated the Guest nights at the various messes: particularly 13/18 Hussars and 1/7 Gurkhas and 17 Division. Hospitality which we always tried to return in full measure.'[65] In the Far East the regiments zealously preserved their rituals of guest nights and dining-in nights, and proudly displayed the regimental silver.

Officers' privileges extended to the young Second Lieutenant on jungle patrol boasting how 'I enjoyed the magic carpet of S55 choppers taking us out of the filth and swamp to a Mess dining-in night.' Yet there was still an entrenched attitude to class, which manifested itself in the social distinction between commissioned and non-commissioned officers; to the anger of one Royal Army Service Corps corporal, 'the British planters and their families adopted a superior attitude towards us'.[66] Perhaps memories of the BMA's disastrous public relations persuaded the Army to separate the ordinary British soldier from the English community. But with democracy now the common credo, inevitably there was resentment. As the intelligent National Servicemen from home observed for the first time institutions like Robinson's (the Harrods of Kuala Lumpur) or the Padang in Singapore, where cricket was played with the solemnity of Lord's, he was bound to conclude that 'The post-war British colonial caste still had a good conceit of itself.'[67]

If there was any consolation, it was that young civilians were also smarting in the 1950s from out-of-date conventions. A new Harrison & Crosfield's executive knew he 'was generally regarded by the older bank managers and colonials as "one of those ghastly new first tour assistants"'! While playing rugby for Klang Club, he discovered the drawbacks of its famous long bar. 'We youngsters were not permitted to drink at the right hand end of the bar as this was "reserved" for higher government British colonials together with senior commercial managers.'[68] Time, however, was with the democrats, who rejected some of the old ways. Geraldine Kaye, teacher and writer, and her husband, an academic at the University of Malaya, decided not to join the Tanglin Club. 'We had strong feelings that there ought not to be an exclusive European club and that, if there was, we didn't want to belong to it. But we did belong to the Singapore Swimming Club . . . We used to socialize with other European and Chinese people there . . . we used to have square dances for students.' Their circle of friends included an Indian family down the road and two Eurasian families, and a great many Australians and New Zealanders on the University staff. An exclusive colonial society 'wouldn't have been our sort of scene', Geraldine Kaye admitted. 'We were pro-independence.'[69]

They were not alone in being relaxed about the future. The social scene was changing. The old-style European community in Malaya was turning into a new-style Commonwealth one, partly because 'there were a number of different Commonwealth nations represented in the military establishment. Britain, Australia, Fiji and, I think, New Zealand all contributed either army, air force or naval detachments,' Jim Winchester recalled.[70] 'When I returned in 1950,' observed Roger Barrett, a salesman with Malayan Tobacco Distributors, 'Independence was only a matter of "when". All races had mixed in Kedah, pre-war and post-war, and perhaps the only difference was we were less patronising than our forebears . . . The races generally mixed much more after the war.'[71] Up-country British managers drew their friends from all sectors of local society, which included many Asians. There was no discernible racial antagonism in this mixed community. The predominance of aristocratic, paternal leaders was reassuring: Tunku Abdul Rahman, successor to Dato Onn at the helm of UMNO; Sir Cheng Lock Tan, elder statesman of the Malayan Chinese Association: the Sultans themselves. Those British who had dealings with the Tunku spoke of him with respect and warmth. (Post-war rumours that he had collaborated with the Japanese were dismissed.)[72] 'A wonderful human being . . . one of the most charming men I have ever worked with – a delight' was the verdict of one civil servant who kept in touch with him until his death.[73] And 'a remarkable man . . . he had incredible intuition. A very, very friendly man' was the opinion of another.[74] As to Sir Cheng Lock Tan, a British officer in Chinese affairs who worked with him in Malacca found him 'a benign old gentleman'.[75]

Although the principle was accepted, the timetable for independence was still unclear when the coronation of Queen Elizabeth took place in 1953. In Penang it 'was a wonderful time, because all the groups had their own celebrations – the Buddhists, the Hindus . . . of all of them . . . there were all sorts of high jinks,' a teacher at the Blind Home remembered. In the afternoon, the children at St Nicholas' Home held their own garden party, and later they were invited to a colour film about the coronation. Despite their disability, 'they just soaked up the atmosphere and they could hear the cheering and what was happening in London. They were thrilled to have been there.' Meanwhile, on Coronation Evening, the staff were invited to 'a big "do" at the Residency. We had a real ball. The shops ran out of long gloves for the ladies. It was a real dressy affair.'[76] In Negri Sembilan, J. S. Potter 'was amazed at the great local enthusiasm. Mr Sheppard, the British Adviser, went to great trouble in staging an elaborate and most successful

Pageant at the residency.'[77] In the federal capital there was 'an enormous military parade on the Padang. And there was a very big celebration of local culture in the Lake Gardens, with Chinese dragon dances and fireworks . . . people of all races entered into it,' Dermot Barton recalled.[78] In Malacca the priests and trustees of the ancient Cheng Hoon Teng Temple held a special service of celebration.

In the event, the coronation proved to be the last great old-style celebration of colonial Malaya. In the next two years events moved rapidly. The insurgency was brought under control with growing support from the air for military operations, the stepping up of psychological warfare, and the 'white areas' policy. Political innovation had started under Sir Henry Gurney, but a series of constitutional changes had to be implemented in preparation for the taking over of the administration by the Malay leadership; for, as a former civil servant put it, 'Once the Emergency was effectively over . . . the next thing was Independence' – *Merdeka.*[79] Mechanisms were introduced to prepare the country for self-government through elections to councils, the promotion of only Asians in the Civil Service, and a policy of steady 'Malayanization' to replace British personnel by local people. In the Federation the Malays benefited, while in Singapore, where concurrent advances towards self-government were under way, it was the Chinese and Indians who rose to political and administrative prominence.

Singapore had escaped the terrors of the Emergency, but the island's politics were affected by labour troubles and sectional interests. In 1950 the Malay populace were incensed over the Maria Hertogh case,[80] and the anti-European rioting left eighteen dead and almost 200 injured. The change from full colonial rule began with the Rendel Commission in 1953, which in 1954 recommended moving towards self-government, the first elections to the Legislative Assembly to be held in 1955. The Chief Minister, David Marshall of the majority Labour Party, secured British agreement in 1956 on the principle of full self-government. Meanwhile, avoiding the party divisions of Singapore's political scene, the prominent Malayan political leaders, Tunku Abdul Rahman and Dato Abdul Razak, with Colonel H. S. Lee and V. T. Sambanthan, shrewdly came together in a co-operative Alliance between UMNO, the Malayan Chinese Association (MCA) and the Malayan Indian Congress (MIC). Their platform of self-government secured them the local elections in 1954, and the Alliance then swept to victory in the first elections for the Legislative Council held in 1955. Their triumph brought to power as Chief Minister Tunku Abdul Rahman – a man dedicated to the end of British rule and the defeat of Communism.

To achieve the latter, the Tunku responded to peace feelers from Chin Peng, who was ensconced with a rump of supporters inside neighbouring Thailand. He offered the Communist leader an amnesty, and in late December 1955 the two men met in the English School at the Kedah town of Baling. It was a tense but carefully prepared meeting, to which Chin Peng was conducted by an Englishman who knew him better than almost anyone in Malaya, John Davis, wartime head of Force 136. It was no secret that the Communists had lost the war, but observers feared that Chin Peng would charm the Tunku into making political concessions. In fact, though Chin Peng was an impressive adversary, the Chief Minister was too astute.[81] He realized that his country could never coexist with Communism, so the historic meeting proved abortive and the struggle against Communism went on. But the Baling talks proved a turning point. Aware that Britain had little to gain from clinging to her imperial role, the British government – and Colonial Secretary Alan Lennox-Boyd in particular – intimated that the continuation of the Emergency need not delay *Merdeka*. With Whitehall's blessing, a constitutional commission would recommend a new constitution for Malaya. The outcome was a parliamentary democracy in the form of a Federation of Malaya presided over by a sovereign Paramount Ruler, chosen from the Malay rulers for five years. Independence Day was set for 31 August 1957.[82]

In Singapore, where the timetable for self-government was already set, the test for the expatriate community came when the anti-Communist Labour Party was superseded by Lee Kuan Yew's left-wing People's Action Party. PAP had an anti-British agenda and drew on Communist support. In the mid-1950s there is no doubt that Lee Kuan Yew caused considerable apprehension in the expatriate community. In 1957 'I remember people saying how awful it was that the PAP . . . were going to get in, and a number of business houses in Singapore moved to Kuala Lumpur because they reckoned there was no future under Lee Kuan Yew,' said a professional soldier who served for ten years in Malaya.[83] The die was cast, however. After capturing Singapore City Council in 1958, PAP won a majority in the Legislative Assembly at the 1959 elections, becoming the party of government. Lee Kuan Yew was the Prime Minister to lead Singapore into its new self-governing regime. A consummate politician, he mollified the British community by his brand of progressive nationalism. 'He was incredibly intelligent, he had great vision and was determined to see through what he believed was right for Singapore; and the proof of the pudding has been in the results,' was the verdict of one English businessman there.[84] As to those firms which had moved to Kuala Lumpur, 'within two or three years they were flooding back'.[85] By 1960 the Singapore government was ready to break with its Communist supporters, seeing its future interests in a merger with the Federation of Malaya, which would provide a common market and long-term political stability.

In the meantime, the independence process in Malaya moved with clockwork inevitability. It was a confusing time for the British. Some welcomed independence; others accepted it reluctantly, as Malayanization brought an end to their careers. There were many farewells to be said and painful adjustments to be made by returning expatriates. One admitted, 'it was difficult to find a new job in the U.K.: it was depressing to find that we were not welcome!'[86] Some colonial servants, such as nurses, were able to work out their contracts. Experienced British police and intelligence officers, such as Sir Claude Fenner and Guy Madoc, were too valuable to dispense with at independence. Madoc admitted that 'The Tunku wanted us to stay on, and we were very happy to stay on.'[87] A few officials had already decided to remain in Malaya, Mervyn Sheppard and Sjovald Cunyngham-Brown among them.

'My Chinese friends were appalled that the British were going,' said one official. He elaborated the point. 'The M.C.A. seemed to me to be less than enthusiastic about the prospect of the British "referees" leaving the ring to a Malay government.'[88] Nevertheless, the departing British could not be certain of the private attitudes of the Malays, Indians and minority Asian groups towards them. British prestige had been shattered in 1941–2. During the public disorder aroused by the Maria Hertogh trial in 1950 it was rumoured that the lives of Europeans were in serious danger from disillusioned Malays, though this threat never materialized. A Perak planter noted that in the 1955 elections 'the local Malayan Indian Congress campaigned among estate workers saying, "Vote for us and we will throw the white man out of Malaya"'.[89] On the other hand, businessman Jeremy Darby insisted, 'There was never any question in

Singapore or Malaysia of "Whites go home, we don't want you".'[90] This may have been wishful thinking, for an experienced planter confirmed that while the Emergency lasted 'Political activity on estates was officially discouraged from the highest level. To have been otherwise could have created very volatile situations within these closed communities.'[91]

Anticipating anti-British violence on Independence Day, a senior administrator quietly briefed planters in Muar on the precautions they should take. They planned to withdraw to a hilltop bungalow 'with good fields of fire. We had a very considerable armoury of semi-automatic weapons and an enormous stock of ammunition, and two armoured Landrovers at our disposal.'[92] On the day it was all unnecessary.

> Just before Merdeka Day it was announced that whilst there would be suitable ceremonies and celebrations in Kuala Lumpur, celebrations in other parts of the country . . . would be restricted to a reading of a proclamation by District Officers and a flag-raising ceremony at District Offices. Other celebrations would follow, area by area, in a sequence defined by the availability of security forces to provide fully adequate cover. Thus the day itself was to be a normal working day on the estate, and that is what it was. My bungalow was well stocked with food and water . . . but apart from that the European staff went about their work as usual, carrying arms only as the individual's personal daily practice in view of the Emergency. There was just a steady day's work and, being the last day of the month, all the routine of declarations of rubber harvested and palm oil processed and preparations for calculating the pay of the workers. *Not a shot nor a shout, but quiet satisfaction of a good day's work done, and so ended British rule in Malaya.*[93]

Others were caught up in various kinds of celebration. From Muar Police Station, Robert Duffton watched fireworks over the river. On his estate in Negri Sembilan, Donald Macpherson and his colleagues had a huge bonfire of army residue from the nearby camp, which was being moved, and there was a public party with *ronggeng* girls in Bahau town. Schools celebrated the day with sports, concerts and dances. At Sungei Buloh in Selangor, Christina Browne recalls, 'the estate was gaily decorated and there was a Sports Day with prizes for all', while the leprosarium, known as Valley of Hope, held a competition for the best decorated ward.[94] In Penang, Britain's oldest colonial possession, there was an unexpected outpouring of emotion:

343

The Deputy High Commissioner . . . let it be known unofficially that he hoped that most of the British residents in Penang would actually attend the lowering of the flag on the eve of Independence, and so we all turned up for that. But to our utter and complete amazement when we got down to the Padang on the waterfront . . . there must have been 100,000 people there – Chinese, Malays, Indians, everybody you can think – many of them in tears, crying profusely before British rule had come to an end. Despite all the great things ahead of Malaysia, they were really desperately sad to see Britain's rule of Malaya go. It was a very moving occasion . . .[95]

The principal celebrations took place by right in the new Merdeka Stadium in the capital before an ecstatic crowd. Planter Jim Winchester summed up the situation as the British saw it. 'Much pomp and circumstance and good will in Kuala Lumpur. A feeling that it was time to let go and that the country has been well served by Britain, and was being left well endowed and in good hands.'[96]

Though the era of British political influence was over, *Merdeka* did not mark the end of the British presence. Under the Anglo-Malayan Defence Pact, the Director of Operations, General Sir James Cassels, led a force of British, Commonwealth and Malayan troops in the final operations to prise the remaining insurgents out of their jungle lairs. By the end of 1958 it was estimated that only 250 soldiers of the MRLA were left in Malaya, and, after his party's re-election in 1959, Tunku Abdul Rahman felt the time was ripe for peace. Chin Peng's admission of military defeat in a directive to his supporters enabled the Malayan government to raise the restrictions on the last 'black' areas, with the exception of the Thai border. The end of the Emergency was declared on 31 July 1960. From the British perspective, this marked the end of a long and turbulent saga that had begun when, at the end of 1941, with British military power collapsing, groups of young Chinese Communists, belatedly released from gaol, had volunteered to infiltrate the mainland and harry the Japanese in their advance down Malaya, the cornerstone of the British Empire in the Far East. After the transfer of political power to the Malaysian people in 1957, Britain's last commitment, the conclusion of the Communist episode, was now effectively honoured.

# Postscript

'When I first sailed for Malaya', a former Guthrie's Manager remarked, reflecting on life in 1934, 'it was indeed a severance with Home for five years, with mails taking three weeks, no air mails and a long journey into the unknown. When I left in 1957 air mails arrived almost daily, London was thirty-six hours away by air and in touch by telephone, wireless receiving sets for local and overseas services were available . . . Quite a change in twenty-five years.'[1] From the opening of the Suez Canal in 1869, improvements in transport and communication had been crucial to the development of Malaya's economy. Then, as the twentieth century progressed, the country was caught up in a momentum of accelerating general change. Finally, in the 1960s, the country was politically reshaped, despite internal criticism and external hostility. In 1963 a single democratic Federation of Great Malaysia was created in a merger of the Federation of Malaya, Singapore and the Borneo territories of Sarawak and Sabah. Two years later, however, the Chinese-dominated island of Singapore seceded from the Federation to become an independent, sovereign state. Once these political structures were in place, in 1965 Malaysia and Singapore were set for prosperity and evolution into two of the dynamic 'Tiger economies' of the Pacific during the 1980s.

Life for Malaya's British residents changed only gradually. There were still many familiar faces around in the 1960s. On a return trip in 1967 Guy Madoc was pleased to find 'one of my Special Branch officers still working happily away in Special Branch in an extremely important post in the complete confidence of Malays who had been his juniors, but who were now his seniors, and the whole thing still working very much on the same lines that we had laid down'.[2] In view of Britain's continuing role in defence and security, until 1971 British and Commonwealth servicemen and their families were a permanent part of the social scene, just as British managers, traders, planters and professional experts remained while Malaysians prepared themselves to take over the country's economy. 'Such things as the carriage of identity cards and the requirement to obtain re-entry permits on passports were minor irritations,' a planter-turned-shipping-agent recalled.[3] A Dunlop's planter felt he was among friends when 'locally you were well known by police and government officials'; or as another put it, 'We swam with the tide and were not adversely affected.'[4] Well-connected managers with a good track record had no apparent difficulty in remaining in post into the 1980s, and even achieved promotion.[5]

Outside the plantation industry, too, there were opportunities in Malaya for forward-looking British companies and enterprising young men with business acumen. It was after *Merdeka* that a young executive sent out by J. & P. Coats, a Glasgow company, set up a marketing and sales operation covering the whole of Malaya, taking over from Boustead's in Kuala Lumpur and Harper Gilfillan in Singapore. 'I suppose I was looked upon as a young "whippersnapper" who had arrived to take away the agency, by the then Senior Management of the Trading Houses, many of whom were of an age with my father,' he remarked. However, he saw the new political situation as a challenge:

> By 1959 we were very conscious that the 'new' commercial/industrial expats needed a forum which would be recognized by the Authorities and supported by the High Commission, hence the forerunner to the British Trade Association. The members met once a month taking it in turns to host the meeting where the agenda was a combination of business and socialising, which somehow led to my election as Chairman of this august body of males, many of whom I can still clearly visualise as the representatives from Ben Line, BOAC, Blue Funnel, Commercial Union, Liptons, Wiggins Teape, Dunlop, to name but a few.[6]

In the years of economic transition the Trade Association gave British firms a much needed line of communication to the Department of Trade in London, but technical knowhow and political skills were crucial for a successful career in a post-colonial world. After his colonial service had ended with *Merdeka*, Brian Stewart found his way back in 1965 through the Diplomatic Service. 'I was lucky', he admitted, 'that my Chinese languages attracted the FCO [Foreign and Commonwealth Office] to offer me a job – where, of course, one started again at the bottom (though Second Secretary was a far cry from a Grade II post in Penang!).' As Counsellor in the British High Commission in Kuala Lumpur at the time of the Confrontation with Indonesia (1963–6), he came into contact with officials of the Malay Foreign Office, and with police and service officers. Later he became involved in rubber-plantation interests, succeeding Sir Claude Fenner as the planters' representative, which again brought him in touch with relevant Malaysian government bodies.[7] Mark Gent was another who forged a successful career in post-independence Malaysia – as Chairman of Guthrie's Malaysian Group from 1969 to 1977, before succeeding Eric Griffiths-Jones as Chairman in London.

In the course of the 1960s, however, the policy of Malayanization began increasingly to affect business ownership and personnel, as the Malaysian government set up state ventures and bought out European-owned companies. Tin was the first industry to change to Malayan ownership. Already in the 1950s retiring British shareholders in the Straits Trading Company sold large quantities of stock in Straits Tin to Malayan Chinese, and, to reflect the new Asian interest, Chinese and Malay Directors were appointed to the board between 1954 and 1962.[8] The year 1961 was to prove a record one for the company, with profits of over $5 million. The land-rich plantation industry was next to be taken over. 'As the years went on employment came under greater and ever greater scrutiny and to be employed as an expatriate it was necessary to show that you had something special to offer,' John Anderson observed.[9] 'We knew we would all have to go,' said John Edington; meanwhile, 'freedom of action was much reduced'.[10] 'There were no real prospects for Europeans after Merdeka,' was the sad conclusion of another Manager, of thirty years' standing.[11]

> I think that had it not been for the Brunei rebellion and Confrontation . . . during the 1960s, Malayanization in commerce and industry would have been further accelerated. Elements from within the cabinet, headed by Tun Abdul Razak, the Deputy Prime Minister, who also chaired the cabinet committee on Malayanization, seemed keen to see the last of us. It was generally known that, unlike the Prime Minister, Tengku Abdul Rahman, Tun Abdul Razak was a bit anti-British.[12]

As Chairman of the Incorporated Society of Planters in 1964, 1965 and 1967, Edington, who made that observation, knew a number of ministers personally, and he held on to his position in planting until 1971, by which time, he judged, 'almost 90% of British planters had already left the country. This coincided with the date set earlier for Britain's pull-out from South-East Asia'. He himself

> was Malayanised some 19 months after the sale of Tebrau Estate to the Johore Government [1969]. Dato Abdullah bin Mohamed, the Cambridge-educated State Secretary, whom I had known for many years and who had conducted the sale on behalf of his Government, invited me to remain on as manager on a permanent basis. He was keen on continuity of management and wanted no disruption. I was glad to accept, especially as we were involved in replanting old rubber with oil palms and also in the throes of installing a new factory unit for the manufacture of crumb rubber. After some months questions were asked in the locally-owned plantation company. This proved to be something of an embarrassment to Dato Abdullah's successor as the new State Secretary and I was duly given the required six month notice which give me time to consider my future in another country.[13]

Ironically, Malayanization in the planting industry went ahead so fast that by 1972 the Malaysian government had become concerned:

> so many expatriate planters had left the country and there was a lack of experience among the newcomers, so that the rules on Malayanisation were immediately relaxed. Natural wastage then became the criterion which enabled the remaining British planters to complete their careers. In effect a number were permitted a further extension of two years allowing them to retire at 57 instead of 55.[14]

Some experienced expatriates moved on to other parts of Malaysia, such as Borneo, where change moved more slowly, or to former colonies to complete their careers.[15] Meanwhile all the remaining British companies were vulnerable: Guthrie's, for example, fell to a stock-exchange takeover in 1981. Finally, the last generation of Britons to arrive in Malaya were affected. A Scottish executive who started in 1955 as a twenty-one-year-old shipping assistant in Harrison & Crosfield had his post Malayanized in 1984 after many years in commodity marketing and a decade spent in training local people. Satisfied that he had completed his task, he was aware that most of his British friends had already left.

During the 1970s and 1980s, the British civilians in Malaysia were mainly consultants and advisers whose world view was radically different from that of earlier generations. A certain cultural friction was inevitable, as a senior planter explained:

> Towards the end of my years in Malaysia there were very few of the 'old hands' still at it in the planting business. The expatriate community was made up of people on short, two or three year, contracts. They were largely young, expert in some particular field and not deeply into the country and its people. There was not a high incidence of competent command of the Malay language, as at one time was the rule. So life and prospects changed to reflect this. Latterly the new expatriates were living in communities of their own, taking every opportunity to visit all the places of interest during their brief sojourn. The 'old hands' were still in their established clubs as a very small minority amongst a majority of Malaysian members, perhaps the more senior members of the Malaysian community. In this way perhaps there was still a degree of influence exerted. There was not a lot of contact between the 'old hands', who tended to have greater contacts with Malaysians, and the short term expatriates.[16]

On the other hand, the British community had never been completely homogeneous, and one new commercial man found himself unimpressed by the 'old hands' and the diplomats. 'I did not like many of the British attitudes towards Malays, Chinese and Indians, and later was uneasy with members of the British High Commission, who made no effort to learn Malay or how the local folk "ticked".'[17]

Hindsight tended to mellow British views on the changes in Malayan society. Though some were concerned about new undercurrents of racial intolerance to the detriment of the Chinese and Indians, there was a genuine desire to see Malaysia succeed.[18] No country could have generated more affection and nostalgia; nowhere was there more sadness at leaving or a greater sense that life might never be quite the same again. When asked for their impressions, expatriates from various backgrounds expressed very similar views: 'Malaya is a beautiful country with a largely friendly population', 'A wonderful country to live and work in', 'A great country with kind, hospitable, friendly people much missed', 'A country of great potential riches, of great beauty, possessed of an outstanding people', 'The lifestyle, the friendliness of the people, the weather, the attractiveness of the countryside away from the populated areas and the general atmosphere of stability', 'I loved the country and the people I worked with.'[19]

Mrs Kerr-Paterson wanted her children 'to remember Malaya as we loved it – the *rural* type of Malaya', not the later 'Americanized type' with skyscrapers.[20] A pre-war resident, Cecil Lee, paid homage to 'its great stretches of jungle-clad hills, its pungent-scented coastline with coconut palms bordering the long sandy beaches, the serpentine rivers past little Malay kampongs . . . the rice fields and plantations of rubber, coconut and oil palms'.[21] Agnes Davison recalled 'so many happy memories – of moonlight trips down the Kedah River with all the bushes sparkling with myriads of fireflies; of evening parties on the lawn at the Residency . . . of the brilliant ceremonies at Malay weddings, of Indian fire-walking; of wonderful sunsets at Langkawi, and countless others'.[22] Many cherished specific images: a bed of cannas and a casuarina tree against the distant brightness of the sand and sea, or dawn breaking over the Straits of Johore – 'a shawl of ripe peach gossamer, the richest, boldest, rosiest fragment in my childhood kaleidoscope' – while the train rumbled over the Causeway towards Singapore.[23] In his farewell broadcast to the people of Singapore in 1949, Bishop Wilson spoke from the heart: 'Last night I saw again what is for me the fairest sight in all the Far East, the lovely view from Penang Hill, of islands, sea and distant peak; last night I watched the light of the setting sun on the waters of MacRitchie Reservoir and saw most vividly, "the long low splendour of the level lake".'[24]

Much of Malay tradition related to water, as one might expect of a race of fishermen. For Margot Massie it was encapsulated in the celebrations for the coronation of the Sultan of Trengganu in 1949, at which she was an honoured guest. The Royal Fish Drive on the Trengganu river climaxed when the armada of little boats converged with spears and nets upon the stunned fish 'in a bubble of excitement and friendly rivalry'.[25] This special event highlighted the Malays' respect for royalty, their natural good humour and the sportsman's love of the chase, while the cordiality between the Sultan and his British guests was cemented at the Coronation Ball the night before, when everyone joined hands to sing 'Auld Lang Syne'. If Mrs Massie remembered Malaya for its rare celebrations caught on ciné or a modest Brownie box camera, Katharine Sim cherished its appeal to the senses, the overwhelming pungency of everyday smells – 'the heady wafts of pigeon orchid; the sweet cloying scent of the frangipani flowers; the spicy smoke of joss sticks . . . the delicious tang of wood fires and the fragrant, hungry smell of curry cooking'.[26]

A National Serviceman was intrigued by the colonial architecture of Kuala Lumpur, finding it the most beautiful city he had ever seen. Among some old Malayan hands, the trees of the rainforests, with their majestic proportions, aroused more admiration: as if in a cathedral, man was truly cut down to size. And for Tristan Russell there was something awesome in Malaya's mountain views:

> On almost any clear day from Cameron's you can see Ipoh . . . you can see Taiping and the islands, Pangkor and Pangkor Laut. Of course, looking east, it's much further from the sea, but on very, very clear days you seem to be able to see forever . . . and just at the very furthest distance you may see a silvery gleam, which I think is the South China Sea.[27]

On a lesser scale, a planter sketched an emotional vignette: 'Beating Retreat on a village padang at dusk by the Malayan Police Band. Colour, spectacle, British tradition adapted to Malayan requirements.'[28] At the end of his long police service, many scenes stood out for René Onraet:

> The golden rain of angsena trees. Blue distances from Fraser's Hill. Being awakened by the scent of pigeon orchids, miniature fairy-white birds spreading their wings in the moonlight. Swimming in phosphorescent water. Quiet evenings at home . . . Wonderful days out shooting. Polo . . . Happy parties in the pleasant open rooms of spacious, airy houses. All our happy life . . .[29]

And it was the happy life which many British expatriates remember when they look back: not war, imprisonment, hardship, danger or tropical disease, though over decades those scourges filled the Christian cemeteries on Penang and Singapore, in Taiping, Tapah and Kuala Lumpur, and at God's Little Acre in Batu Gajah. Here and there, too, were the isolated graves of Britons who would not leave, like Oliver Holt, who came out to Malaya in the 1930s, survived imprisonment and a spell on the Burma–Thailand railway, and settled on the east coast, where he died 'much loved by the local people'.[30] Another who saw Malaya as his final home was the barrister John Woods. After the war he built himself a fine house in Ipoh with wide views eastward to the mountains, to the Cameron Highlands where he intended to retire. 'He loved the country, the people and the climate,' wrote a friend.[31] Mrs Savage-Bailey also loved the East, and bought a plot in the Highlands for her retirement, so her daughter Dulcie Gray recalled. Penang was another place where the British felt comfortable. In 1950 William and Mabel Price of Whiteaways bought a small property to the north of Georgetown. The Rawcliffes of Port Swettenham built two bungalows in Penang: one for renting; the other, at Batu Ferringhi, for their retirement. After twenty-seven years out East, 'I was more at home in Malaysia than in the U.K.,' an experienced General Manager of plantations revealed – a not uncommon emotion.[32] Hugh Bryson left in 1950 after nearly thirty years, feeling 'that I was leaving many old friends – in fact for a time I was almost a stranger in England, I had lost so much touch with the country and with the friends of my younger days'.[33] More commonly, however, in the end expatriates felt they had no choice but to return to Europe: 'having enjoyed our sojourn there the time had come to move on'.[34]

As time lends perspective to the European colonial record, British Malayans are for the most part confident that their contribution will be seen as constructive and humane. Malaysia belongs to the Commonwealth and to the family of common-law nations. Features such as appeal to the Privy Council in London and the use of the English language for court proceedings (until the mid-1990s) indicated a subtle British influence.[35] The timing of *Merdeka* and the manner of disengagement indicated British respect for the Malayan people.

In his final reflections recorded in 1961, one of the 'old hands' probably spoke for a majority of Britons who were attracted from their homeland to work overseas:

> One often asks oneself would one do it all over again? Would one spend nearly a quarter of a century and the best part of one's life abroad in the tropics? . . . Given the same sort of conditions again I am sure it was the correct thing to do and I'm glad I did it.
>
> Recently I met an ex-Malayan neighbour who had lived over thirty-five years in the country, and he said to me, 'When I look round the world today I feel proud to have served in Malaya and call myself a Malayan.' I feel exactly the same. Independence was granted and accepted in a logical and friendly way. Few multi-racial countries in the world can claim greater harmony than Malaya. Few countries in the

world have emerged from colonialism in such a prosperous and peaceful way.[36]

This final judgement – tacit testimony to Malaysia's inspired leadership in its emergent years, as well as to the British contribution – accords with Tunku Abdul Rahman's courteous observation made in the twilight of his life, that 'Whether we look East or West, we shall always be friends with England.'[37]

# Glossary

**adat**   custom or customary law
*alor*   pool, channel
*amah*   Chinese maidservant or nursemaid
**attap**   nipa palm thatch
*ayah*   Indian or Malaysian nursemaid

*bahru, bharu*   new
*baju*   Malay jacket or long-sleeved shirt
*batu*   stone
**boy**   male servant, houseboy
*bukit*   hill

**CT**   Communist terrorist

**Dato**   title of respect conferred by a Sultan, elder or grandfather
*dhobi*   washman, laundryman
**gharry**   small horse-drawn vehicle
**GOC**   General Officer Commanding
**godown**   warehouse
*gula malacca*   sweet pudding of tapioca, coconut milk and treacle

*ikan molet*   'pretty fish': baked fish dish with spices and coconut
**istana**   palace of a Sultan

**kampong**   village, rural settlement
*kebun*   gardener
*Kempeitai*   Japanese military secret police
**Kling**   person from Kalinga or of south-Indian origin (the term later politically incorrect)
**kongsi**   Chinese coolie lines
*kota*   fort, fortified town

354

# Glossary

**kris**  Malay curved dagger
*kuala*  river mouth, estuary

**lalang**  coarse tropical grass
*latah*  a strange behavioural condition, now rare

**maidan**  open space, playing field
*makan*  food, meal, dinner
*mem*  European woman (especially a married or mature woman)
**Mentri Besar**  Chief Executive or Prime Minister

*Merdeka*  freedom, hence independence
*Missee*  European girl or unmarried young woman

*negri*  state, hence Negri Sembilan or Nine States

*orang asli*  'original people' – the aboriginal tribes of the Malay peninsula
*orang puteh*  white men
*padang*  parada ground, playing fields or grassy open space
**padi**  rice, rice field, area growing rice
*pagar*  enclosure, artificially enclosed area of water (usually the sea)
*pahits*  cocktails (literally 'bitter')
*penghulu*  Malay headman or village leader
*pulau*  island

**raja**  ruler, member of a Malay ruling family
*ronggeng*  communal Malay dance

*sarong*  wrapover skirt worn by Malay men and women
**Sepoy**  Indian soldier, originally in East India Company service, as involved in the Indian Mutiny of 1857
**stengah**  a half measure of whisky, usually mixed with one half soda
**Sumatra**  a sudden storm with fierce winds, blowing across the Straits of Malacca from Sumatra
*sungei*  river
*syce*  driver, groom, chauffeur

*tanjong*  cape, headland
**tiffin**  lunch
**topee**  helmet
*tuan*  honorific title: sir, lord, master, European man
*Tuan Besar*  great gentleman, big shot, senior European, boss of a firm or company
*tuan kechil*  assistant, junior, European boy

*tukan ayer*   water carrier

**Tunku**   title of a member of a Malay ruling house, prince

*ulu*   up-country, remote area, up-river area, often indicating jungle

**Yang di-Pertuan Besar**   title of the Sultan of Negri Sembilan, first among equals, head of state

# Notes

*Note:* full details of all sources cited in short-title form are given in the Bibliography. Short titles given without quotation marks or italics are those of unpublished sources.

### INTRODUCTION

1. Potter, 'Reminiscences of Malaya,' p. 1.
2. Nash, *Collected Verse*, pp. 193–4.
3. Sim, *Malayan Landscape*, p. 142.

### I: THE MEETING OF TWO WORLDS

1. Bird, *Golden Chersonese*, pp. 109, 125, 130, 150, 256.
2. Ibid., pp. 249, 273, 275.
3. Ibid., p. 271.
4. Swettenham, *British Malaya*, p. 113.
5. 'This is emphatically "The dark Peninsula",' wrote Isabella Bird (p. 362), 'though both Protestants and Romanists have made attempts to win the Malays to Christianity. It may be that the relentless crusade waged by the Portuguese against Islamism has made the opposition to the Cross more sullen and bigoted than it would otherwise have been.'
6. Ibid., pp. 215, 275, 271.
7. Heussler, *British Rule in Malaya*, p. 83. See also Swettenham and Gates, *Watercolours and Sketches of Malaya*.
8. Swettenham, 'The Real Malay', in *Stories and Sketches*, p. 16.
9. Clifford, 'The East Coast', from *In Court and Kampong* (1897), in *Stories*, p. 11.
10. Mahmud bin Mat, Features of Malay Life, pp. 1–2.
11. E. Innes, *Chersonese with the Gilding Off*, Vol. 1, p. 3; Bird, *Golden Chersonese*, p. 216.
12. E. Innes, *Chersonese with the Gilding Off*, Vol. 1, p. 45; Bird, *Golden Chersonese*, pp. 203, 230, 233, 296–7.
13. Clifford, 'The Fate of Leh the Strolling Player', from *Studies in Brown Humanity* (1898), in *Stories*, p. 153.

14. E. Innes, *Chersonese with the Gilding Off*, Vol. 1, pp. 41, 61.
15. Ibid., Vol. 1, pp. 3, 42, 38–40.
16. Mahmud bin Mat, Features of Malay Life, p. 2.
17. Hillier, Malacca Memories, p. 90.
18. Swettenham, 'The Real Malay', in *Stories and Sketches*, pp. 16–17.
19. Clifford, 'Among the Fisher Folk', from *In Court and Kampong*, in *Stories*, p. 190.
20. E. Innes, *Chersonese with the Gilding Off*, Vol. 2, p. 249; Clifford, 'The East Coast', from *In Court and Kampong*, in *Stories*, pp. 14–15.
21. E. Innes, *Chersonese with the Gilding Off*, Vol. 1, pp. 89–90, 101; Vol. 2, p. 15.
22. Ibid., Vol. 1, pp. 62, 79, 101–2, 106–7, 187–9, 213.
23. Bird, *Golden Chersonese*, pp. 171, 299, 300, 313–14.
24. Gullick, *Malaya*, p. 14.
25. Bird, *Golden Chersonese*, pp. 137–8, 140.
26. Ibid., p. 312.
27. Clifford, 'On Malayan Rivers', from *Studies in Brown Humanity*, in *Stories*, p. 170.
28. For more details on this subject see Purcell, *The Chinese in Malaya*.
29. Bird, *Golden Chersonese*, p. 279; T. H. Reid, 'The Miracle of Malaya', p. 40.
30. Bird, *Golden Chersonese*, pp. 280, 282. Her remark about the absence of Malays was confirmed by C. D. Bowen in 1886: 'One hardly sees a real Malay here, they are all Chinese, Klings, Tamils etc.', Bowen, 'British Malaya as it was', p. 897.
31. Bird, *Golden Chersonese*, p. 352.
32. E. Innes, *Chersonese with the Gilding Off*, Vol. 2, p. 128.
33. Bird, *Golden Chersonese*, p. 220.
34. Swettenham, *British Malaya*, p. 127; Wright and Cartwright, *Twentieth Century Impressions*, p. 107.
35. E. Innes, *Chersonese with the Gilding Off*, Vol. 2, p. 128, Vol. 1, p. 8.
36. Singam, *A Hundred Years of Ceylonese*, p. 27; E. Innes, *Chersonese with the Gilding Off*, Vol. 1, pp. 4, 34, 222.
37. Stark, Jelebu Memories.
38. Clifford, 'Umat', from *Studies in Brown Humanity*, 'Up country', from *In Court and Kampong*, in *Stories*, pp. 161, 201–4, 206.
39. Bird, *Golden Chersonese*, pp. 162–3.
40. E. Innes, *Chersonese with the Gilding Off*, Vol. 1, p. 189, Vol. 2, p. 69; Harrison, 'Last of "the Creepers"', p. 345.
41. Bird, *Golden Chersonese*, p. 243.
42. E. Innes, *Chersonese with the Gilding Off*, Vol. 1, p. 144.
43. Ibid., Vol. 1, pp. 36–7, Vol. 2, pp. 36–7.
44. Bird, *Golden Chersonese*, p. 185.
45. E. Innes, *Chersonese with the Gilding Off*, Vol. 2, pp. 25–6, 64, 71.
46. Bird, *Golden Chersonese*, p. 290; E. Innes, *Chersonese with the Gilding Off*, Vol. 2, p. 133.
47. Bowen, 'British Malaya as it was', p. 904.
48. Bird, *Golden Chersonese*, pp. 310–11, 343, 350.
49. Morkill, Malay Memories, pp. 8–9.
50. Swettenham, *British Malaya*, pp. 180–2.

51. E. Innes, *Chersonese with the Gilding Off*, Vol. 2, p. 176.

52. Bird, *Golden Chersonese*, pp. 115, 119, 255, 256–7.

53. Ibid., p. 113.

54. Turnbull, *History of Singapore*, pp. 47, 54–5.

55. Bird, *Golden Chersonese*, p. 255.

56. Bowen, 'British Malaya as it was', p. 898.

57. Heussler, *British Rule in Malaya*, p. 17.

58. Bowen, 'British Malaya as it was', p. 909.

59. E. A. Brown, *Indiscreet Memories*, p. 14; E. Innes, *Chersonese with the Gilding Off*, Vol. 1, p. 97.

60. E. A. Brown, *Indiscreet Memories*, p. 14.

61. Bowen, 'British Malaya as it was', p. 902.

62. One example of local commemoration of the Diamond Jubilee was the erection of the Victoria Memorial Clock Tower in Penang. Donated by a local Chinese millionaire, Chea Chen Eok, at a cost of $35,000, its Moorish-styled dome crowned a white tower, sixty feet high – one foot for each year of Queen Victoria's reign.

63. Bird, *Golden Chersonese*, p. 347.

64. Quoted in Heussler, *British Rule in Malaya*, p. 15.

65. Bird, *Golden Chersonese*, p. 140.

66. Bowen, 'British Malaya as it was', pp. 900–1.

67. Bird, *Golden Chersonese*, pp. 140, 255.

68. E. Innes, *Chersonese with the Gilding Off*, Vol. 1, pp. 89, 187.

69. Bowen, 'British Malaya as it was', p. 898.

70. Bird, *Golden Chersonese*, pp. 140, 279.

71. Bowen, 'British Malaya as it was', p. 899.

72. Bird, *Golden Chersonese*, p. 271.

73. Kendall, '*Dearest Mother*', p. 111.

74. Bird, *Golden Chersonese*, pp. 94–5, 103, 105.

75. Lockhart, *Return to Malaya*, p. 112.

76. Andaya and Andaya, *History of Malaysia*, p. 156.

77. Bird, *Golden Chersonese*, pp. 255–6.

## 2: PIONEERS AND PROGRESS

1. These were terms used by contemporaries: boxwallahs = men in business and commerce; officewallahs = those with desk jobs; junglewallahs = those who worked up-country in out-stations; competition-wallahs = Civil Service cadets selected by examination.

2. Gent, The Jungle in Retreat, p. 24.

3. Kendall, '*Dearest Mother*', pp. 99–100.

4. For example, the French consul, the Comte de Jouffroy d'Abbans, was an active figure in Singapore; the Comte de Bondy Riario, his successor at the turn of the century, befriended Russians, English and Irish Catholic families; while the German consul served Austrians and Hungarians in addition to German businessmen.

5. Bird, *Golden Chersonese*, pp. 110, 112.

6. Ibid., pp. 203, 224, 290.

7. Mugliston, 'Penang 1904–1908', p. 116.

8. Bird, *Golden Chersonese*, p. 222.

9. T. H. Reid, 'The Miracle of Malaya', p. 40.

10. Beauclerk, *The Mimosa and the Mango* p. 35.

11. Ibid., pp. 35–6.

12. Ibid., p. 37; Wright and Cartwright, *Twentieth Century Impressions*, p. 369.

13. Kendall, '*Dearest Mother*', pp. 103–4.

14. Ella Christie, Malaya in 1904, p. 2.

15. Newton, More Exquisite When Past, ch. 12, p. 2; Blain, *Home is the Sailor*, pp. 197–8.

16. Singam, *A Hundred Years of Ceylonese*, p. 7.

17. Mugliston, 'Singapore 1908–1927', p. 7.

18. Makepeace, Brooke and Braddell, *One Hundred Years of Singapore*, Vol. 1, p. 581; E. Innes, *Chersonese with the Gilding Off*, Vol. 1, p. 129.

19. A creeper was an unsalaried trainee, and therefore usually came from a comfortable background, though he would usually expect to be taken on as a paid Assistant in due course.

20. Blain, *Home is the Sailor*, pp. 197–8.

21. Lockhart, *Return to Malaya*, pp. 160, 214–15.

22. Butcher, *The British in Malaya*, p. 39; Hutchinson, Junior Assistant, p. 3; Lockhart, *Return to Malaya*, p. 199.

23. Ainsworth, *Confessions of a Planter*, pp. 44, 50, 52.

24. Harrison, 'Last of "the Creepers"', p. 345.

25. Stark, Jelebu Memories, pp. 4, 7–8; Lockhart, *Return to Malaya*, p. 221.

26. Lea A. Williams, 'Immigrants and Social Change', radio talk, cited in Singam, *A Hundred Years of Ceylonese*, p. 46.

27. Makepeace, Brooke and Braddell, *One Hundred Years of Singapore*, Vol. 2, p. 538.

28. Peach, Recollections of 35 Years, p. 1.

29. Hillier, Malacca Memories, pp. 4, 5.

30. Harrison, 'Last of "the Creepers"', p. 344.

31. Ainsworth, *Confessions of a Planter*, p. 14.

32. Ibid., pp. 36–7.

33. Ibid., pp. 93, 99, 122, 135, 150, 182–3.

34. Newton, More Exquisite When Past, ch. 3, p. 9; Wright and Cartwright, *Twentieth Century Impressions*, p. 644; Makepeace, Brooke and Braddell, *One Hundred Years of Singapore*, Vol. 2, pp. 538–9.

35. Hutchinson, Junior Assistant, p. 2.

36. Howard Newton is also commemorated in the modern Mass Rapid Transport system of Singapore.

37. Gent, The Jungle in Retreat, pp. 29–30.

38. Ibid., pp. 25–6.

39. Ibid., p. 33.

40. Ibid., pp. 33–7.

41. I am grateful to Ray Forsyth for drawing my attention to the career of her great-uncle, which is also mentioned in the autobiography of Robert Munro's youngest brother, Air-

Vice Marshal Sir David Munro, *It Passed Too Quickly*, p. 15; Wright and Cartwright, *Twentieth Century Impressions*, p. 492.

42. Lockhart, *Return to Malaya*, p. 83.
43. Bowen, 'British Malaya as it was', p. 897. Bowen was a District Officer from 1862 to 1919.
44. J. A. S. Edington, letter to the author, 22 April 1999.
45. E. Innes, *Chersonese with the Gilding Off*, Vol. 2, pp. 212–13; Bence-Jones, *The Catholic Families*, pp. 227–8.
46. Bird, *Golden Chersonese*, p. 275.
47. Ibid., p. 218.
48. Morkill, Malay Memories, p. 17.
49. Blain, *Home is the Sailor*, p. 73.
50. Bird, *Golden Chersonese*, pp. 357–8.
51. Lockhart, *Return to Malaya*, pp. 159–60, 209.
52. Hutchinson, Junior Assistant, p. 3.
53. Winstedt, *Start from Alif*, p. 18.
54. E. Innes, *Chersonese with the Gilding Off*, Vol. 1, p. 129. 'Tuan Hinnes' would be equivalent to 'Mr Hinnes, Sir'.
55. Hillier, Malacca Memories, pp. 64–5.
56. See Thomson, *Glimpses into Malayan Lands*, pp. 269–79, for a character sketch of Butterworth.
57. Bird, *Golden Chersonese*, p. 217; E. Innes, *Chersonese with the Gilding Off*, Vol. 1, p. 263.
58. J. R. Innes, 'Old Malayan Memories', p. 82.
59. Bird, *Golden Chersonese*, pp. 172, 248.
60. Ibid., pp. 323, 347.
61. Bowen, 'British Malaya as it was', p. 909.
62. Bird, *Golden Chersonese*, p. 187.
63. Bowen, 'British Malaya as it was', p. 901.
64. Ibid., pp. 903, 904, 901.
65. Lockhart, *Return to Malaya*, p. 223; Stark, Jelebu Memories, pp. 3, 4, 12–13.
66. J. W. S. Reid, 'H.B.'
67. Morkill, Malay Memories, pp. 27–8.
68. J. W. S. Reid, 'H.B.'
69. Heussler, *British Rule in Malaya*, p. 126.
70. Bowen, 'British Malaga as it was', p. 905.
71. Ibid., p. 903.
72. Singam, *A Hundred Years of Ceylonese*, p. 112. Singam was the son of the Ceylonese Tamil station master of Port Weld, a pioneer of the 1890s. A schoolmaster, he witnessed the rise to prosperity and later decline of the west-coast railway ports.
73. Bowen, 'British Malaya as it was', p. 905.
74. Richards and MacKenzie, *The Railway Station*, p. 77.
75. Ibid.; Wright and Cartwright, *Twentieth Century Impressions*, p. 178.
76. Cited in Andaya and Andaya, *History of Malaysia*, p. 197.
77. The purchasing power of the dollar, fixed at 2/4d (about 12p) was only equivalent to the dollar's former value of 1/7d (about 8p).

78. Blain, *Home is the Sailor*, pp. 167, 146.
79. Ferguson-Davie, 'Memories of Malaya', p. 79.
80. Blain, *Home is the Sailor*, p. 146.

3: PRIVATE LIVES, PUBLIC VALUES

1. Newton, More Exquisite When Past, ch. 1, p. 17. Lillian Newton was the great-grand-daughter of Governor Edmund Blundell of the Straits Settlements. Her father, Howard Newton, had worked in Singapore from 1877 to 1896 and, after transferring to Bombay, had died of cholera in 1897. The family had then returned to Singapore, where Mrs Newton's widowed mother, Mrs Robertson, lived. An *ayah* was a nursemaid; later, Chinese *amahs* were favoured in place of Malay or Indian *ayahs*.
2. Braddell, *The Lights of Singapore*, p. 2, though the expression was first coined by Frank Swettenham in *British Malaya*, p. 342.
3. Newton, More Exquisite When Past, ch. 2, p. 6, ch. 8, p. 1.
4. Wright and Cartwright *Twentieth Century Impressions*, pp. 232–5; E. A. Brown, *Indiscreet Memories*, pp. 43–5.
5. Binnie, 'Malaya – the Years Before'.
6. Ibid. A *Pagar* was a section of the beach enclosed for safe swimming.
7. Newton, More Exquisite When Past, ch. 2, pp. 7–8.
8. Ibid., ch. 15, pp. 1–2.
9. Ibid., ch. 5, p. 4, ch. 15, p. 4.
10. Ibid., ch. 5, p. 6.
11. Binnie, Life in Singapore before 1914.
12. Bird, *Golden Chersonese*, pp. 184–5. Parian ware was produced by the English porcelain manufacturers Copeland & Garrett, *c.* 1840, in imitation of Sèvres.
13. D. Munro, *It Passed Too Quickly*, p. 15.
14. Lockhart, *Return to Malaya*, p. 102. Caldecott's successor as District Officer, Jelebu, discovered some of his musical compositions accidentally hidden in a writing table: Stark, Jelebu Memories, p. 2.
15. Newton, More Exquisite When Past, ch. 13, pp. 10–11.
16. Ibid., ch. 1, p. 20, ch. 9, p. 1, ch. 13, pp. 8–9.
17. For a summary of the trial and its implications, see Butcher, *The British in Malaya*, Appendix 2, '"The Letter" Case', pp. 233–8; for a longer, albeit tendentious, account see Lawlor, *Murder on the Verandah*.
18. The case and trial were fully reported in the editions for 24 April, 1, 3 May, 7–10, 12–16 June 1911.
19. *The Times*, Thursday 29 June 1911, p. 5.
20. Horace Bleackley, letter to the *Daily Mail*, cited in Butcher, *The British in Malaya*, p. 238.
21. 'The Letter' (in Maugham, *Complete Short Stories*, Vol. 3) was also turned into a stage play and twice into a film, the second starring Bette Davis. For Maugham and fellow writers Bleackley and Cyril Connolly, the case provided further evidence of decadence. In Maugham's short story the central character (based on Ethel Proudlock) was found not guilty and acquitted to popular applause, but was subsequently shown to have murdered

her lover in revenge for his taking a Chinese mistress, while her lawyer connived at the destruction of crucial evidence – 'the letter'. Lawlor comes to another swingeing judgement (*Murder on the Verandah*, p. 256): 'What sealed her [i.e. Ethel's] fate was that, in addition to being a killer and an adulteress she was also almost certainly Eurasian' – and this was why the authorities brought her to trial.

22. Winstedt, *Start from Alif*, p. 18.
23. H. Clifford, 'Up Country', from *In Court and Kampong*, in *Stories*, pp. 201, 206.
24. Bowen, 'British Malaya as it was', p. 903.
25. Purcell, *Memoirs of a Malayan Official*, pp. 250–1.
26. Newton, More Exquisite When Past, ch. 9, p. 6.
27. Ibid., ch. 2, pp. 11–12, ch. 17, p. 1.
28. Heussler, *British Rule in Malaya*, p. 169; Butcher, *The British in Malaya*, p. 194. Turnbull, *History of Singapore*, p. 87, mentions the importation of Hainanese boys to supply the demand for homosexual prostitution; Purcell, *Memoirs of a Malayan Official*, p. 250, refers to a notorious incident leading to suicide in the 1930s.
29. Fauconnier, *The Soul of Malaya*, p. 45.
30. Winstedt, *Start from Alif*, p. 18.
31. Butcher, *The British in Malaya*, p. 200. He discusses the subject of relations between European men and Asian women at length on pp. 194–222.
32. Winstedt, *Start from Alif*, p. 18.
33. Bryson, Twenty-nine-and-a-half Years, para. 23.
34. Gent, The Jungle in Retreat, pp. 66–7.
35. Hutchinson, Junior Assistant, p. 44. As proof, he added, 'I can truthfully say that I knew two men who committed suicide because of their "Keeps".'
36. Lockhart, *Return to Malaya*, p. 122; see also Heussler, *British Rule in Malaya*, p. 168, n. 19; Butcher, *The British in Malaya*, pp. 193–9.
37. Hutchinson, Junior Assistant, p. 43.
38. O'Grady, If You Sling Enough Mud, p. 146.
39. According to René Onraet, who served in the police force from 1907 to 1939, 'chi-chi' owed something to the way English was taught by French missionaries, and once it was ingrained in children it was difficult to eradicate. For this reason, British Malayans were reluctant to become very friendly with Eurasians: Onraet, *Singapore – A Police Background*, p. 134.
40. Butcher, *The British in Malaya*, pp. 186–7, citing Ridley's dictum in his essay, 'The Eurasian Problem'.
41. Bird, *Golden Chersonese*, pp. 130, 132.
42. Ferguson-Davie, 'Memories of Malaya', p. 81; Newton, More Exquisite When Past, ch. 14, p. 10.
43. Ibid., ch. 2, pp. 1 and 10, ch. 14, p. 6.
44. A reference to the successful Wu-ch'ang rising under Sun Yat-sen and the formation of a republic in China, which boosted Chinese pride and self-esteem and was greeted with wild excitement by overseas Chinese, such as those in Singapore. Ibid., ch. 17, p. 2.
45. Binnie, 'Malaya – the Years Before', p. 1.
46. Newton, More Exquisite When Past, ch. 9, p. 4, ch. 15, p. 2, ch. 9, pp. 4–5, ch. 14, p. 10.

4: PYROTECHNICS IN PENANG

1. Wright and Cartwright, *Twentieth Century Impressions*, pp. 231–2; Turnbull, *History of Singapore*, p. 122.

2. Binnie, 'Malaya – the Years Before', p. 1.

3. Coe, 'Malay States Volunteer Rifles', pp. 10, 14.

4. Ibid., p. 9.

5. Harrison, 'Last of "the Creepers"', p. 349.

6. Coe, 'Malay States Volunteer Rifles', p. 10.

7. Harrison, 'Last of "the Creepers"', p. 349.

8. Kemp, Singapore Mutiny, letter, 7 March 1915, p. 1. For details of this crisis, see Chapter 5.

9. Among the liberal Chinese donors to the Aircraft Fund were Mr Tan Jiak Kim, the Hon. Mr Eu Tong Sen, the Hon. Mr Lee Choon Guan, Mr Lim Peng Siang and Dr Lim Boon Keng; the Asian communities also contributed generously to the 'Our Day' Fund for wounded soldiers and sailors.

10. For instance, the pioneer Tamil planter Mr Solomon Ramanathan of Perak gave $1,000 towards the cost of the war plane *Kuala Kangsar*.

11. Thompson, Sinking of the 'Zemchug', pp. 3–4.

12. Binnie, 'Malaya – the Years Before', pp. 1–2.

13. Christie, Malaya in 1904, p. 46.

14. E. A. Brown, *Indiscreet Memories*, p. 2.

15. Newton, More Exquisite When Past, ch. 12, p. 4.

16. This state of readiness did not apply to the whole German fleet. In 1914 Geoffrey Cator CMG, of the 1907 intake into the Malayan Civil Service, was serving in Labuan, off north Borneo, then part of the Straits Settlements. He remembered, 'we were ordered to seize the N.D.L. (*Norddeutscher* liner) SS. *Sandakan*, which was in port. This we duly did, much assisted by the fact that the German officers, being creatures of routine, did not let the outbreak of war disturb their practice of an afternoon siesta. Fortunately, Roberts, the ex-Engineer, was by profession a Marine Engineer, for nobody else had the faintest idea how to disable a ship's engine': Cator, 'A Malayan Cadet in 1907', p. 160.

17. Newton, More Exquisite When Past, ch. 13, pp. 7–8.

18. Kemp, 'Singapore Mutiny', p. 6.

19. Braddell, *The Lights of Singapore*, pp. 51–2.

20. *The Times*, 22 October 1914; van der Vat, *The Last Corsair*, pp. 96, 103.

21. Hillier, Malacca Memories, p. 137.

22. R. K. Walker, Destruction of the 'Zemshug'.

23. Hillier, Malacca Memories, p. 138.

24. Blain, *Home is the Sailor*, p. 215.

25. R. K. Walker, Destruction of the 'Zemshug'.

26. Thompson, Sinking of the 'Zemchug', pp. 3–4. Sabang was the port of Pulau or Pulo Weh, the most westerly island of the Malay archipelago.

27. Hillier, Malacca Memories, p. 140.

28. Ibid., pp. 139–40.

29. Blain, *Home is the Sailor*, p. 213.
30. Ibid., pp. 215–16.
31. van der Vat, *The Last Corsair*, p. 92, suggests that thirty-six Frenchmen were picked up. See also Hillier, Malacca Memories, p. 140.
32. R.K. Walker, Destruction of the 'Zemshug', p. 1.
33. Thompson, Sinking of the 'Zemchug', p. 3.
34. R. K. Walker, Destruction of the 'Zemshug', p. 2.


5: MUTINY!

1. Ferguson-Davie, 'Memories of Malaya', p. 80.
2. Binnie, Account of the Mutiny, p. 1. All subsequent remarks attributed to M. Binnie or Mrs Howell in the narrative of the mutiny come from this source.
3. Thompson, The Singapore Mutiny, pp. 2–3. Much of the narrative of the mutiny is taken from this source.
4. Thompson, The Malay State Guides, p. 1.
5. Thompson, The Singapore Mutiny, p. 1.
6. Binnie, Account of the Mutiny, p. 1.
7. V. Allen, '"I Remember . . .'", p. 269.
8. 'The Riot in Singapore. A Woman's Story', *The Times*, 26 March 1915, p. 9.
9. Kemp, Singapore Mutiny, letter, 7 March 1915, p. 1.
10. Thompson, The Singapore Mutiny, p. 1.
11. Shelley, With the M.S.V.R., p. 2.
12. Ibid.
13. Binnie, Account of the Mutiny, pp. 1–2.
14. 'A Lady's Experiences', p. 784.
15. V. Allen, '"I Remember . . .'", p. 269.
16. 'A Woman's Story', *The Times*, 26 March, p. 9.
17. 'A Lady's Experiences', p. 783.
18. Thompson, The Singapore Mutiny, pp. 1–2.
19. Binnie, Account of the Mutiny, p. 2.
20. Ibid., pp. 2, 4.
21. Thompson, The Singapore Mutiny, pp. 3–34.
22. Binnie, Account of the Mutiny, p. 4.
23. 'A Lady's Experiences', p. 784.
24. 'A Woman's Story', *The Times*, 26 March, p. 9.
25. V. Allen, '"I Remember . . .'", p. 270. However, the kindness of the *Ipoh*'s captain was so appreciated by the women that they presented him with a silver bowl inscribed 'From the Refugees': 'A Lady's Experiences', p. 793.
26. Binnie, Account of the Mutiny, p. 3.
27. 'A Lady's Experiences', p. 789.
28. 'A Woman's Story', *The Times*, 26 March, p. 9.
29. 'A Lady's Experiences', p. 786.
30. Binnie, Account of the Mutiny, p. 4; Shelley, With the M.S.V.R., p. 3.

31. Thompson, The Singapore Mutiny, p. 12.
32. 'A Woman's Story', *The Times*, 26 March, p. 9.
33. Thompson, The Singapore Mutiny, p. 5.
34. Shelley, With the M.S.V.R., p. 4.
35. 'A Lady's Experiences', p. 793.
36. Kemp, Singapore Mutiny, p. 3. Having been appointed officer of the guard at Government House and orderly to General Ridout, he was very involved in the pursuit of many of these alarms, day and night.
37. Ibid., p. 5.
38. Morkill, Malay Memories, p. 11.
39. Hamilton, Account of the Outbreak in Kelantan. The following summary of the To' Janggut affair is taken from this source. Another personal account is to be found in Morkill, Malay Memories, pp. 10–12.
40. Hamilton, Account of the Outbreak.
41. Pepys, 'Kelantan during World War I', p. 37.
42. Morkill, Malay Memories, pp. 11, 12.
43. Ibid., p. 11.
44. Shelley, With the M.S.V.R., p. 6.
45. 'A Lady's Experiences', p. 793.
46. Shelley, With the M.S.V.R., p. 6.
47. Dalton, *A Child in the Sun*, p. 273.
48. Binnie, Account of the Mutiny, p. 5.
49. Braddell, *The Lights of Singapore*, pp. 97–8.
50. Binnie, Account of the Mutiny, p. 3.
51. E. A. Brown, *Indiscreet Memories*, p. 7.
52. 'A Lady's Experiences', p. 794.
53. Kemp, Singapore Mutiny, p. 6.
54. Winsley, Papers.
55. V. Allen, '"I Remember . . ."', p. 270.
56. Braddell, *The Lights of Singapore*, pp. 98–9.
57. Makepeace, Brooke and Braddell, *One Hundred Years of Singapore*, Vol. 1, pp. 417–25, discusses the legislation at length.
58. Ferguson-Davie, 'Memories of Malaya', p. 81.
59. For newspaper accounts of these Amateur Dramatic Committee productions, see Newton, More Exquisite When Past.
60. Coe, 'The M.S.V.R. 1919–1927', p. 77.
61. Harrison, 'Last of "the Creepers"', pp. 349–50.
62. Harrison was twenty-eight at the time and therefore at the height of his strength.
63. Blain, *Home is the Sailor*, pp. 229–32.

6: HALCYON DAYS

1. Tomlinson, *Malay Waters*, p. 34.
2. Cunyngham-Brown, *Crowded Hour*, p. 52.

3. Peel, BECM tape 349.
4. Froggatt, Nothing Lasts for Ever, p. 6.
5. G. I. G. Munro, 'Malaya through a Woman's Eyes', p. 225.
6. Forbes, *The Heart of Malaya*, p. 117.
7. Glover, *In 70 Days*, p. 19.
8. Ibid., pp. 18–19.
9. Potter, Reminiscences of Malaya, p. 2.
10. Sim, *Malayan Landscape*, p. 13.
11. M. Price, Malayan Memories, p. 2.
12. Sim, *Malayan Landscape*, p. 50.
13. Hutchinson, Junior Assistant, p. 13.
14. Ainsworth, *Confessions of a Planter*, p. 217.
15. Hutchinson, Happy Return, p. 42.
16. Sim, *Malayan Landscape*, p. 23.
17. Ibid., pp. 49–50.
18. Pearce, 'Memories of Tin Town', p. 259.
19. Sim, *Malayan Landscape*, p. 47; British Malaya, Watkins, p. 3.
20. Pearce, 'Memories of Tin Town', p. 260.
21. Braddell, *The Lights of Singapore*, p. 3; Lockhart, *Return to Malaya*, p. 140 (the present author's italics).
22. Lockhart, *Return to Malaya*, p. 113.
23. Glover, *In 70 Days*, p. 26.
24. Froggatt, Nothing Lasts for Ever, pp. 6–7.
25. Sim, *Malayan Landscape*, pp. 56, 66–7.
26. Hutchinson, Happy Return, p. 36.
27. E. T. Campbell, 'The Magic of Malaya', p. 200.
28. Scott, *Eastern Journey*, p. 29.
29. Cameron, *Wanderings in South-Eastern Seas*, p. 31.
30. E. T. Campbell, 'The Magic of Malaya', p. 198.
31. Emerson, *Malaysia*, p. 488.
32. Bryson, Twenty-nine-and-a-half Years, para. 18.
33. Sources vary as to precise figures, so an average has been given: see Butcher, *The British in Malaya*, p. 130, cf. Soper, Experiences in Malaya, ch. 2.
34. Lockhart, *Return to Malaya*, p. 86.
35. Ibid.
36. Potter, Reminiscences of Malaya, p. 3.
37. Froggatt, Nothing Lasts for Ever, p. 8.
38. O'Grady, If You Sling Enough Mud, pp. 54–5; Hutchinson, Happy Return, p. 53.
39. Purcell, *Memoirs of a Malayan Official*, p. 252.
40. Barnes, *Mostly Memories*, p. 6.
41. Soper, Experiences in Malaya, ch. 2. Sim, *Malayan Landscape*, p. 35, describes the cinema in Parit Buntar as a 'Bug house'.
42. Hutchinson, Happy Return, p. 36.
43. Letters from Nancy Wynne to her parents in Hull, 27 April 1940 and n.d. 1940.

44. Friend, 'Acme of Advertising', p. 158; Lockhart, *Return to Malaya*, p. 143. Tiger Balm was an all-purpose ointment patented by the Aw brothers, who became millionaires as a result.

45. Sim, *Malayan Landscape*, p. 14.

46. Ibid., p. 215.

47. Froggatt, Nothing Lasts for Ever, p. 5.

48. Dixon, For Entertainment Only, pp. 1, 3, 4.

49. Ibid., p. 7.

50. Ibid., p. 5.

51. Cunyngham-Brown, *Crowded Hour*, p. 72.

52. Sewill, The Great Pahang Flood, p. 1.

53. Cameron, *Wanderings in South-Eastern Seas*, pp. 31–2; Sim, *Malayan Landscape*, p. 88.

54. Moreton, *An Irishman in Malaya*, p. 65.

55. Hutchinson, Happy Return, p. 33.

56. Soper, Experiences in Malaya, ch. 2; B. Kitching, ed., *Life and Death in Changi*, p. 196.

57. Hutchinson, Junior Assistant, p. 101. See below, p. 385, note 39.

58. Snell, Memories of British Malaya, 1998, p. 1.

59. Norman Price, interview, 6 August 1998; Hutchinson, Happy Return, p. 34.

60. Barnes, *Mostly Memories*, p. 12.

61. Lockhart, *Return to Malaya*, p. 113.

62. Snell, Memories of British Malaya, p. 1.

63. Froggatt, Nothing Lasts for Ever, p. 7.

64. Potter, Reminiscences of Malaya, pp. 2–3.

65. Hutchinson, Happy Return, p. 52.

66. Barnes, *Mostly Memories*, p. 8.

67. Morkill, Malay Memories, p. 24.

68. Bryson, Twenty-nine-and-a-half Years, paras 30, 32.

69. Hutchinson, Happy Return, pp. 20–1.

70. Lockhart, *Return to Malaya*, p. 80.

71. Cunyngham-Brown, *Crowded Hour*, p. 54.

72. Hutchinson, Happy Return, p. 14.

73. M. Price, Malayan Memories, p. 2.

74. Hutchinson, Junior Assistant, p. 74.

75. Morkill, Malay Memories, pp. 18, 32.

76. Sim, *Malayan Landscape*, pp. 34, 47, 63.

77. Purcell, *Memoirs of a Malayan Official*, p. 261.

78. Ridgway, Singapore 1926–1929, p. 17(h).

79. Captain's notebook, Miscellaneous papers on the Girl Guide movement, BAM VI/2.

80. Froggatt, Nothing Lasts for Ever, pp. 3–4.

81. Butcher, *The British in Malaya*, p. 163.

82. Mr J. B. W. Fairchild of the Public Works Department designed the golf course and played an important part in the design and construction of the Tanah Rata Hotel and the two schools in the Cameron Highlands, the Pensionnat Notre Dame and Tanglin School.

83. Letter from Nancy Wynne, 18 May 1940.

84. Sim, *Malayan Landscape*, p. 136.

85. Snell, Memories of British Malaya, p. 3.
86. Purcell, *Memoirs of a Malayan Official*, pp. 298, 303.


7: PYRAMIDS OF POWER

1. Braddell, *The Lights of Singapore*, p. 3.
2. Glover, *In 70 Days*, p. 11.
3. Oliver, BECM tape 174 (1995).
4. BECM tape 037 (1992).
5. Hutchinson, Happy Return, p. 24.
6. George V's Christmas Day Message 1934; George VI's New Year and Christmas Day Messages 1937.
7. Gray, *Looking Forward, Looking Back*, p. 47.
8. Hutchinson, Happy Return, pp. 53–4. Bruce de Burgh Thomas was the character who drank to Edward VIII. The British press led by Beaverbrook kept up a conspiracy of silence over the King's affair, but the foreign press made capital out of it.
9. Purcell, *Memoirs of a Malayan Official*, pp. 252–3.
10. Barnes, *Mostly Memories*, p. 9.
11. Lockhart, *Return to Malaya*, p. 84.
12. *The Times*, 29, 30, 31 March, 2, 24, 27 May 1922.
13. Blain, *Home is the Sailor*, p. 245. This prescient remark anticipated the later rift between the British colonials and the British at home over the importance of defending and cherishing the Empire. However, the great irony was that, unknown to all the Malayans who fêted the Prince of Wales out of respect for King and Empire, he was privately disparaging about both the British colonials and the Asians in Malaya: see Godfrey, *Letters from a Prince*.
14. Forsyth, Malayan Experience, p. 6.
15. Potter, Reminiscences of Malaya, p. 2.
16. Lockhart, *Return to Malaya*, p. 33.
17. Padfield, *Beneath the House Flag of the P. & O.*, p. 107.
18. Thatcher and Cross, *Pai Naa*, p. 6.
19. BECM tape 037 (1992).
20. Hutchinson, Junior Assistant, p. 6.
21. Shennan, *Missee*, p. 24.
22. Hutchinson, Junior Assistant, p. 7.
23. Letter from Nancy Wynne, 1 May 1940.
24. BECM tape 037 (1992).
25. Ibid.
26. Hutchinson, Junior Assistant, p. 27.
27. Bryson, Twenty-nine-and-a-half Years, para. 29.
28. Thatcher and Cross, *Pai Naa*, p. 6.
29. Bird, *Golden Chersonese*, p. 113,
30. British Malaya, Pybus, p. 1.
31. Report of Brigadier-General Sir Samuel Wilson, Permanent Under-Secretary for the

Colonies on His Visit to Malaya 1932, London, 1933, cited in Turnbull, *History of Singapore*, p. 156.

32. Bryson, Twenty-Nine-and-a-half Years, para. 46.
33. Cunyngham-Brown, *Crowded Hour*, pp. 73–4.
34. Morkill, Malay Memories, p. 4.
35. Bryson, Twenty-nine-and-a-half Years, para. 18.
36. Ibid., para. 27.
37. Hutchinson, Happy Return, p. 46. Mrs Nancy Wynne of Johore also commented, 'I believe we have to behave ourselves when His Highness is in residence', but she found his son 'charming': Letter, 12 November 1940.
38. Erina Batt, letter to the author, 7 December 1998.
39. Hutchinson, Happy Return, pp. 32, 46.
40. One such case was Captain Macdonald, killed by a Malay seaman. Tomlinson, *Malay Waters*, p. 64.
41. Bryson, Twenty-nine-and-a-half Years, para. 13.
42. Morkill, Malay Memories, p. 25.
43. Cator, 'A Malayan Cadet in 1907', p. 161.
44. Guillemard, *Trivial Fond Records*, p. 84.
45. Morkill, Malay Memories, p. 22; Bryson, Twenty-nine-and-a-half Years, para. 38.
46. The Sultan's closest friend for many years was a British planter, Colonel Teddie Bryce, and one of his wives was the daughter of a Scottish doctor in Singapore.
47. Guillemard, *Trivial Fond Records*, p. 83.
48. Morkill, Malay Memories, pp. 20–1.
49. Ibid., p. 22.
50. Thatcher and Cross, *Pai Naa*, p. 10.
51. Potter, Reminiscences of Malaya, pp. 2–3.
52. Bryson, letter to Gerald Hawkins, 6 April 1966.
53. Gent, The Jungle in Retreat, pp. 156–61; Butcher, *The British in Malaya*, p. 178.
54. W. G. Price, Notes on Sungei Nyok Dockyard, pp. 21–2.
55. Sim, *Malayan Landscape*, pp. 58–9.
56. Federal Council Proceedings, 1932, B19, cited in Heussler, *British Rule in Malaya*, p. 184.
57. Potter, Reminiscences of Malaya, p. 4.
58. Shennan, *Missee*, p. 94.
59. Roger Barrett, letter to the author, 30 August 1998.
60. Davison, Some Autobiographical Notes, p. 12.
61. Letter from Nancy Wynne, 12 November 1940.
62. Turnbull, *History of* Singapore, p. 142; Peet, *Malayan Exile*, p. 9.
63. Bryson, Twenty-nine-and-a-half Years, para. 31.
64. Ibid.
65. Ibid.
66. O'Grady, If You Sling Enough Mud, p. 262.
67. Davison, Some Autobiographical Notes, p. 11; Sim, *Malayan Landscape*, pp. 37–8, 93–4.
68. Thatcher and Cross, *Pai Naa*, p. 10.
69. Hutchinson, Happy Return, p. 46.

70. Sim, *Malayan Landscape*, p. 177.

71. Soper, Experiences in Malaya, Introduction. John Soper was the nephew of the pioneer planter, Robert 'Coconut' Munro (see Chapter 2) and also of Air Vice-Marshal Sir David Munro. He was a Cambridge graduate, and served in the Colonial Agricultural Service in East Africa before moving to Malaya.

72. Ibid. In 1969 Alan Morkill acknowledged that 'In the hindsight of later years it is obvious that we were making its [British rule's] passing inevitable by education, which included sending men to Britain to get degrees and professional qualifications; here too they learned all about democracy': Malay Memories, p. 30.

73. Cf. the daily wage rates of Chinese and Tamil shipbuilding workers in Province Wellesley from the mid-1920s to the late 1930s: carpenters and boilermakers $1.65; moulders and patternmakers $2.12; fitters, turners and machinists $1.50 to $3.00 depending on ability; coolies or labourers 65 cents: W. G. Price, Notes on Sungei Nyok Dockyard, p. 14. In the 1930s 'wages varied naturally with length of service but I recall [monthly] rates of $25–30 for cooks, $25 for boys, $18–20 for tukang ayers, $25 for amahs, and about $18 for gardeners': Bryson, Twenty-nine-and-a-half Years, para. 20.

74. Dickinson, The Political Situation in Malaya, p. 5. Guy Madoc of the FMS Police remembered some unpleasant rioting among factory workers in 1936 which was Communist-inspired, but noted that it was quite easily suppressed by the riot squad.

## 8: OFFICIALS AND UNOFFICIALS

1. Potter, Reminiscences of Malaya, p. 15.

2. Soper, Experiences in Malaya, Introduction. The 'boxwallah' never lost his inferior image: when one young English woman returned to Malaya in the post-war years, her mother's last words were, 'All I ask you, please don't marry a boxwallah, darling!'

3. Bryson, Twenty-nine-and-a-half Years, para. 38.

4. Guillemard, *Trivial Fond Records*, p. 99.

5. Turnbull, *History of Singapore*, p. 160.

6. Wilson, 'Men You Have All Met', p. 472.

7. Tregonning, *Home Port Singapore*, p. 162.

8. Savage-Bailey's service was prematurely ended when he suffered a fatal accident on Singapore dock in 1936.

9. Cunyngham-Brown, *Crowded Hour*, p. 74; see also Purcell, *Memoirs of a Malayan Official*, pp. 296–7, 299.

10. Hutchinson, Junior Assistant, p. 40.

11. Shennan, *Missee*, pp. 22–4.

12. Hutchinson, Junior Assistant, p. 4.

13. Ibid., p. 16.

14. Moore, *We Live in Singapore*, p. 283.

15. Thatcher and Cross, *Pai Naa*, pp. 8–9, 14. Sungei Lembing had suffered greatly from the effects of the Great Pahang Flood of 1926–7. In 1929 Baker had succeeded J. T. Marriner, who had supervised the mine's recovery and initiated diversification into rubber through a subsidiary company, Kuala Reman Estates.

16. *Straits Times*, 1 July 1933, cited in *Sixty Years of Tin Mining*, pp. 36–7

17. *Sixty Years of Tin Mining*, pp. 38, 42.

18. British Malaya, Edington.

19. For a good account of the tin smelting industry and the unofficials involved, see Tregonning, *Straits Tin*.

20. The other ships built between 1925 and 1941 were *Rompin, Ampang, Gemas, Tapah, Tronoh, Jarak, Klias, Rantau, Rasa, Rimau, Relau* and *Rejang*.

21. Cameron, *Wanderings in South-Eastern Seas*, p. 30.

22. Guillemard, *Trivial Fond Records*, p. 99.

23. Ibid., pp. 76, 78.

24. Bryson, Twenty-nine-and-a-half Years, para. 26.

25. Keay, *Last Post*, p. 41.

26. Glover, *In 70 Days*, p. 37.

27. Ibid., pp. 172–3.

28. Froggatt, Nothing Lasts for Ever, p. 9.

29. Purcell, *Memoirs of a Malayan Official*, p. 179. His duties included District Officer, Magistrate, Assistant District Judge, Port Officer, Port Health Officer, Postal Agent, Assistant Protector of Chinese, 'and half a dozen other things as well'.

30. Cunyngham-Brown, *Crowded Hour*, p. 67.

31. Heussler, *British Rule in Malaya*, pp. 295–6.

32. Cobden-Ramsay, Memories of Kemaman District.

33. Heussler, *British Rule in Malaya*, p. 296.

34. Sheppard, *Taman Budiman*, p. 4.

35. Bryson, Twenty-nine-and-a-half Years, para. 4.

36. Ibid., paras 6, 11.

37. Ibid., para. 22.

38. Stark, Jelebu Memories, p. 14.

39. Purcell, *Memoirs of a Malayan Official*, pp. 96, 99.

40. Cunyngham-Brown, *Crowded Hour*, p. 70.

41. Guillemard, *Trivial Fond Records*, p. 91.

42. Soper, Experiences in Malaya, ch. 2.

43. Ibid. The work of the Government Welfare Clinics was exemplified by the achievements of Elizabeth Darville in Penang and Province Wellesley from 1927 to 1935: see her Maternity and Child Welfare Work. The record of the Public Works Department, detailed by G. J. O'Grady in If You Sling Enough Mud, also seems impressive.

44. Heussler, *British Rule in Malaya*, p. 315.

45. Purcell, *Memoirs of a Malayan Official*, p. 286.

46. Wilson, 'Men You Have All Met', p. 472.

47. Hutchinson, Junior Assistant, p. 4. John Davis of the police service was equally convinced of the incorruptibility of almost all British civil servants in Malaya.

48. Bryson, Twenty-nine-and-a-half Years, para. 15A.

49. Soper, Experiences in Malaya, ch. 2.

50. Madoc, interview transcript, 1981.

51. Soper, Experiences in Malaya, ch. 2.

52. Wilson, 'Men You Have All Met', p. 472.

53. Bryson, Twenty-nine-and-a-half Years, para. 26.

54. Soper, Experiences in Malaya, ch. 2.

55. Bryson, Twenty-nine-and-a-half Years, para. 46.

56. Orwell, 'The Lion and the Unicorn' (1941), in *Collected Essays, Journalism and Letters*, Vol. 2, p. 73.

57. Bowen, 'British Malaya as it was', p. 897.

58. Soper, Experiences in Malaya, ch. 2.

59. Lockhart, *Return to Malaya*, p. 106.

60. Heussler, *British Rule in Malaya*, pp. 274, 329.

61. A cartoon in the 25 December 1922 edition of the satirical magazine *Straits Produce* portrayed Mrs A.D.O. quizzing Mrs P.W.D. on social protocol – an indication of the confusion posed by colonial language.

62. Sim, *Malayan Landscape*, p. 17.

### 9: THE RUBBER MEN

1. Lockhart, *Return to Malaya*, p. 199.

2. Hutchinson, Junior Assistant, p. 64.

3. Harrison, 'Last of "the Creepers"', p. 341.

4. Hutchinson, Junior Assistant, p. 2.

5. In 1896 the first Chinese rubber farmer, Tan Clay Yan, was persuaded by Ridley to plant rubber on a small estate at Bukit Lintang, Malacca, which thrived so well that three years later he planted another 3,000 acres with rubber.

6. Hutchinson, Junior Assistant, pp. 68–9.

7. Potter, Reminiscences of Malaya, p. 1.

8. Hutchinson, Junior Assistant, pp. 3, 5.

9. Ibid., p. 5.

10. Allgrove, Recollections of Rubber Estate Life, p. 23.

11. Hutchinson, Junior Assistant, pp. 38–9.

12. Ibid., pp. 40–2.

13. Ibid., p. 44. 'Those who were "unlucky" called at "the other club", the Government V.D. Clinic where they were well attended to, and soon cured': Ibid., p. 42.

14. Ibid., pp. 14, 26.

15. Allgrove, Recollections of Rubber Estate Life, p. 1.

16. Hutchinson, Junior Assistant, pp. 5, 25.

17. Allgrove, Recollections of Rubber Estate Life, p. 15.

18. Potter, Reminiscences of Malaya, p. 2.

19. Ainsworth, *Confessions of a Planter*, p. 156.

20. Lockhart, *Return to Malaya*, p. 198.

21. A.B.H., 'Housekeeping and Life in the Malayan Rubber', p. 607.

22. Allgrove, Recollections of Rubber Estate Life, pp. 9–10.

23. Hutchinson, Junior Assistant, p. 73.

24. Allgrove, Recollections of Rubber Estate Life, p. 22.

25. British Malaya, Tanner, p. 1; British Malaya; R. Barrett, p. 1.

26. A.B.H., 'Housekeeping and Life in the Malayan Rubber', p. 598.

27. Beauclerk, *The Mimosa and the Mango*, pp. 72–3, 74.

28. Hutchinson, Junior Assistant, p. 17.

29. A.B.H., 'Housekeeping and Life in the Malayan Rubber', p. 600; Beauclerk, *The Mimosa and the Mango*, p. 96.

30. Hutchinson, Junior Assistant, pp. 18–19.

31. Beauclerk, *The Mimosa and the Mango*, p. 90.

32. Hutchinson, Junior Assistant, pp. 27–8; Hutchinson, Happy Return, pp. 8–9.

33. His manager was A. W. Robertson, known universally as 'Lord Arthur', 'a knowledgeable planter, humorous and likeable but infuriating': Allgrove, Recollections of Rubber Estate Life, pp. 10–11.

34. Hutchinson, Junior Assistant, pp. 67, 71, 74, 64–5.

35. Ainsworth, *Confessions of a Planter*, p. 203.

36. Hutchinson, Happy Return, pp. 47–8.

37. Hutchinson, Junior Assistant, pp. 21, 24, 30.

38. Potter, Reminiscences of Malaya, pp. 3–4.

39. Hutchinson, Junior Assistant, p. 32.

40. Sim, *Malayan Landscape*, p. 111.

41. Hutchinson, Junior Assistant, pp. 21–4.

42. Allgrove, Recollections of Rubber Estate Life, pp. 7, 8–9, 13, 14, 15.

43. Hutchinson, Junior Assistant, p. 37.

44. Ibid., pp. 72, 106, 122, 125, 126, 129.

45. Ibid., pp. 134, 135, 138.

46. Cunyngham-Brown, *Crowded Hour*, p. 56.

47. *The Planter*, April 1921, p. 35. January 1921, p. 26.

48. Sir William Peel, cited in Butcher, *The British in Malaya*, p. 127.

49. For example 'Cost of Living', *The Planter*, May 1932, pp. 2289–90; 'A Planter's Lot is Not a Happy One?', *The Planter*, May 1936, p. 216; 'Rubber Planting in Malaya, An Unsound Career?', *The Planter*, January 1936, pp. 15–17. The planters' plight was also encapsulated by the press in popular verses or jingles linked to the alphabet.

50. Hutchinson, Happy Return, p. 1.

51. Ibid., pp. 1–2.

52. Ibid., p. 15.

53. 'Rubber Planting in Malaya', *The Planter*, 17, January 1936, p. 16.

54. Hutchinson, Happy Return, p. 49.

55. Maugham, *A Writer's Notebook*, p. 225. Dr Michael Pallister recalls the fury felt towards Somerset Maugham by both his father, a well-known doctor in planting circles, and his mother: conveyed in conversation, 8 May 1998. Another very hostile doctor was 'old Doc Hickey' – according to Hutchinson, 'rumour had it that his sister-in-law was one of the main characters from which Somerset Maugham drew "The Letter". I do know that one was advised not to mention that author to the Hickeys!': Happy Return, p. 44.

56. Hutchinson, Happy Return, p. 44.

57. Cunyngham-Brown, *Crowded Hour*, p. 72.

58. Hutchinson, Junior Assistant, p. 4.
59. Allgrove, Recollections of Rubber Estate Life, pp. 23–4 (written in the 1960s).
60. Hutchinson, Junior Assistant, p. 117.
61. Allgrove, Recollections of Rubber Estate Life, p. 24.
62. J. A. S. Edington, letter to the author, 22 April 1999.
63. Hutchinson, Junior Assistant, p. 4.

10: THE *MEM*, THE *MISSEE* AND THE *TUAN KECHIL*

1. Hutchinson, Junior Assistant, p. 42.
2. BECM tape 036 (1992).
3. Gent, The Jungle in Retreat, p. 54, quoting John Theophilus.
4. Hutchinson, Junior Assistant, p. 44.
5. Bruce Lockhart noticed a dramatic difference from 1907; also Morrison, *Malayan Postscript*, p. 37.
6. Hutchinson, Happy Return, p. 57; Gent, The Jungle in Retreat, p. 54.
7. The total European civilian population was almost 31,000 at that time: Maxwell, *The Civil Defence of Malaya*, p. 3.
8. Wilson, 'Some Ladies You Have All Met', p. 539.
9. Ibid.; Heussler, *British Rule in Malaya*, p. 210.
10. Yet Dr Pallister Snr saw a career in the Colonial Medical Service as financially providential, enabling him to marry in England before taking up a post as Medical Officer of Health, Seremban: conversation with Dr Michael Pallister, 8 May 1998.
11. Hutchinson, Junior Assistant, p. 102.
12. Barnes, *Mostly Memories*, p. 4.
13. Hutchinson, Happy Return, p. 56.
14. Ibid., p. 58.
15. Davison, Some Autobiographical Notes, p. 11.
16. Darville, Maternity and Child Welfare Work.
17. Gent, The Jungle in Retreat, p. 234.
18. Foss, Early Teaching Experiences in Malaya, p. 2.
19. Gent, The Jungle in Retreat, p. 238.
20. Beauclerk, *The Mimosa and the Mango*, p. 87.
21. G. I. G. Munro, 'Malaya through a Woman's Eyes', p. 227.
22. Sim, *Malayan Landscape*, pp. 65, 84, 123, 166, 177, 178, 180.
23. G. I. G. Munro, 'Malaya through a Woman's Eyes', p. 227.
24. Wilson, 'Some Ladies You Have All Met', 539–40.
25. Moore, *Far Eastern Agent*, p. 111.
26. British Malaya, Snell, p. 1.
27. Froggatt, Nothing Lasts for Ever, p. 5; Purcell, *Memoirs of a Malayan Official*, p. 249.
28. BECM tape 036 (1992).
29. Peel, BECM tape 349.
30. Sim, *Malayan Landscape*, p. 145.
31. Letter from Nancy Wynne, Segamat, Johore, 27 April 1940.

32. G. I. G. Munro, 'Malaya through a Woman's Eyes', p. 225.

33. 'Ladies' Page', *The Planter*, May 1932, p. 307; 'Household Hints', *The Planter*, February 1923, p. 473, May 1923, p. 577.

34. G. I. G. Munro, 'Malaya through a Woman's Eyes', p. 226.

35. British Malaya, N. Price, p. 2.

36. G. I. G. Munro, 'Malaya through a Woman's Eyes', p. 226.

37. Sim, *Malayan Landscape*, p. 17.

38. Holttum, A Housewife in Singapore, p. 17.

39. *Federal Council Proceedings* (1929), p. B77, cited in Butcher, *The British in Malaya*, p. 164.

40. Forsyth, Malayan Experience, p. 4.

41. *The Malayan Primer: Now We Can Read*, 3rd edn, The Malayan Publishing House, Singapore, 1936; letter from J. W. D. Kelley, 29 May 1998, Royal Commonwealth Society, Kelley Collection.

42. Beauclerk, *The Mimosa and the Mango*, p. 110.

43. 'Hill Schools: Support from the Press', *The Planter*, October 1922, pp. 317–18.

44. Oliver, BECM 174 (1995).

45. Gray, *Looking Forward, Looking Back*, pp. 31, 33.

46. Ibid., p. 35.

47. Footner, 'A Talk on the Cameron Highlands', p. 466.

48. Forsyth, Malayan Experience, p. 4.

49. British Malaya, Snell, p. 2; also conversations of the author with William Vowler, Maureen Heath, Ray Forsyth and Christopher Cannell about their experiences at Tanglin; Shennan, *Missee*, for an account of life at the school in 1940–1.

50. British Malaya, Watkins p. 2; the Edington brothers were very young when they were sent home to Edinburgh.

51. Gent, The Jungle in Retreat, p. 88: Norman Bewick's account of the exploits of Captain Lefevre.

52. British Malaya, Watkins, p. 1.

53. Christopher Cannell, conversation with the author, 9 November 1998.

54. Barnes, *Mostly Memories*, pp. 6–7.

55. British Malaya, Watkins, p. 2.

56. Hutchinson, Junior Assistant, pp. 98–9.

57. British Malaya, Watkins, p. 3; he adds, 'The pharmacy was still in the same spot in 1994 but there were fewer jars, containing less interesting exhibits.'

58. British Malaya, Pybus, p. 1.

59. J. A. S. Edington, letter to the author, 21 April 1999.

60. British Malaya, Watkins, pp. 2–3.

61. Shennan, *Missee*, p. 44.

62. British Malaya, Watkins, p. 2.

63. Barnes, *Mostly Memories*, p. 41.

64. British Malaya, Snell, p. 2.

65. Ibid., p. 1.

66. British Malaya, D. Cullen, p. 1; conversation with the author, 9 January 1999.

67. Barnes, *Mostly Memories*, p. 3.

68. Forsyth, Malayan Experience, p. 3.
69. British Malaya, Snell, p. 2.
70. Froggatt, Nothing Lasts for Ever, p. 7.
71. British Malaya, Snell, p. 2.
72. British Malaya, R. Barrett, p. 1.
73. British Malaya, N. Price, p. 1.
74. British Malaya, R. Barrett, p. 1; British Malaya, Cannell, p. 2.
75. British Malaya, Tanner, p. 2.
76. Barnes, *Mostly Memories*, p. 12.
77. British Malaya, Snell, p. 1.
78. Ibid., p. 2.
79. Barnes, *Mostly Memories*, p. 16.
80. Jette Barrett (née Rawcliffe), conversation with the author, 21 November 1998.
81. Forsyth, Malayan Experience, p. 7.
82. Susan Tanner (née Malet), conversation, 25 January 1999.
83. Barnes, *Mostly Memories*, p. 9.
84. British Malaya, Snell, p. 1.
85. British Malaya, Batt, p. 2.
86. British Malaya, R. Barrett, p. 2.
87. British Malaya, Tanner, p. 2.

### II: THE UNPREPARED SOCIETY

1. *The Times*, Saturday 1 January 1938.
2. R. Barrett, notes on Memories of British Malaya, August 1998.
3. Dickinson, The Japanese Community, in Various Papers p. 2.
4. Encountering Japanese troops for the first time, Spencer Chapman described them dismissively as 'little, evil, blustering, spectacled popinjays with huge ears, projecting front teeth, and toothbrush moustaches': *The Jungle is Neutral*, p. 14.
5. Froggatt, Nothing Lasts for Ever, pp. 8–9.
6. Glover, *In 70 Days*, p. 65.
7. Froggatt, Nothing Lasts for Ever, p. 9.
8. Vlieland, Disaster in the Far East, p. 8.
9. Kirby, *The War Against Japan*, Vol. 1, p. 27
10. Lockhart, *Return to Malaya*, p. 98.
11. Ibid., p. 96.
12. Letter from Nancy Wynne, 12 November 1940.
13. Lieutenant-Commander Kaseda, a Japanese secret service agent, was expelled from Singapore in March 1935 for attempting to smuggle out secret documents relating to the naval base; his contact, Nishismura, a prominent businessman, committed suicide in Special Branch headquarters to avoid questioning over the mission.
14. Later Tom Kitching, Chief Surveyor, Singapore, recalled, 'there is no doubt that Nakajima, the photographer, was a spy . . . And we fostered Nakajima and treated him very well for 46 years. When I arrived in Singapore in 1913, the railway coaches were plas-

tered with his pictures and very good photographs they were . . . How blind we were!':
B. Kitching *Life and Death in Changi*, p. 187.

15. Sim, *Malayan Landscape*, p. 179.
16. Froggatt, Nothing Lasts for Ever, p. 2.
17. Soper, Experiences in Malaya, ch. 3.
18. Vlieland, Disaster in the Far East, pp. 5–6.
19. Eric Robertson was a member of the unit, and I am deeply indebted to Mrs Peggie Robertson for this information and for bringing his book *The Japanese File* to my attention. See also Peter Elphick's wide-ranging *Far Eastern File*.
20. Froggatt, Nothing Lasts for Ever, p. 1.
21. Sim, *Malayan Landscape*, p. 117.
22. Ibid.
23. *Straits Times*, 4 September 1939, cited in Turnbull, *Dateline Singapore*, p. 103.
24. Soper, Experiences in Malaya, ch. 3.
25. Smyth, *Percival and the Tragedy of Singapore*, p. 41.
26. Froggatt, Nothing Lasts for Ever, p. 1.
27. Letter from Nancy Wynne, undated, *c.* June 1940.
28. Ibid., 27 April 1940.
29. Ibid., undated, *c.* June 1940, 19 August 1940.
30. Froggatt, Nothing Lasts for Ever, p. 2.
31. Sim, *Malayan Landscape*, p. 168.
32. Froggatt, Nothing Lasts for Ever, p. 2.
33. Sim, *Malayan Landscape*, p. 174.
34. M. Price, Malayan Memories, pp. 4–5; N. Price, notes on Memories of Malaya, August 1998.
35. Soper, Experiences in Malaya, ch. 3.
36. Moreton, *An Irishman in Malaya*, pp. 86, 90.
37. Letters from Nancy Wynne, 12 November 1940, 30 January 1941.
38. Letter from Alex Cullen to his wife, Dorothy, in Australia, 27 April 1941.
39. Sim, *Malayan Landscape*, p. 131.
40. Soper, Experiences in Malaya, ch. 3; income tax varied on a sliding scale from 3 per cent on incomes of $400 a month (£560 a year) up to 12 per cent on the highest (£2,500 a year and upwards).
41. Vlieland, Disaster in the Far East, p. 20.
42. Cited in ibid., p. 1.
43. Froggatt, Nothing Lasts for Ever, p. 10.
44. Letter from Alex Cullen, 30 July 1941.
45. Letter from Nancy Wynne, 3 March 1941.
46. Sim, *Malayan Landscape*, p. 205.
47. Roger Barrett, note to the author, 30 August 1998.
48. Froggatt, Nothing Lasts for Ever, p. 6.
49. Letter from Nancy Wynne, 3 March 1941.
50. Letters from Alex Cullen, 10 May, 28 May 1941.
51. Letter from Nancy Wynne, 20 June 1941.

52. Letter from Alex Cullen, 28 July 1941.

53. Ibid.

54. Letter from Nancy Wynne, 26 July 1941.

55. Soper, Experiences in Malaya, ch. 3: 'an incredible blunder was committed in the erection of a government rice mill north of Alor Star and less than 20 miles from the Thai border'.

56. Froggatt, Nothing Lasts for Ever, p. 10.

57. Soper, Experiences in Malaya, ch. 3.

58. Hutchinson, The Rhinoceros of Johore, p. 1.

59. Soper, Experiences in Malaya, ch. 3.

60. Sim, *Malayan Landscape*, p. 174.

61. Potter, Reminiscences of Malaya, p. 5.

62. Quoted in Froggatt, Nothing Lasts for Ever, p. 4.

63. Sim, *Malayan Landscape*, p. 141; Wigmore, *The Japanese Thrust*, cited in Owen, *The Fall of Singapore*, p. 34.

64. Shennan, *Missee*, p. 241.

65. Letter from Alex Cullen, 23 June 1941.

66. Froggatt, Nothing Lasts for Ever, p. 9.

67. Sim, *Malayan Landscape*, p. 216.

68. Snell, Memories of British Malaya, p. 3.

69. Owen, *The Fall of Singapore*, p. 33.

70. Froggatt, Nothing Lasts for Ever, p. 6.

71. Morrison, *Malayan Postscript*, p. 38.

72. Soper, Experiences in Malaya, ch. 3.

73. Ibid., ch. 6.

74. Ibid., ch. 3.

75. Reilly, Diary, p. 1.

76. Glover, *In 70 Days*, p. 72.

12: A CAMPAIGN OF CARDS

1. I. Innes Miller, MCS, *Changi Guardian*, No. 55, Wednesday 13 May 1942.

2. Barber, *Sinister Twilight*, p. 28.

3. Soper, Experiences in Malaya, chs 5 and 6.

4. Order of the Day issued on 8 December 1941 by R. Brooke-Popham, Air Chief Marshal, Commander-in-Chief, Far East, and G. Layton, Vice-Admiral, Commander-in-Chief, China Station.

5. The specific role in these opening days of the so-called Singapore traitor, Captain Patrick Heenan, an army-airforce liaison officer at Alor Star, has been detailed by Peter Elphick and Michael Smith in *Odd Man Out*. On the wider front Vice-Admiral Layton admitted, 'To put it bluntly, the civil population had taken the optimistic public statements before the Japanese attack at their face value; they were shattered by the gulf between them and the reality; and they were never given time to recover': cited in Wylde, Duff Cooper's Case against the Malayan Civil Service Reconsidered, p. 8.

6. The civilian population was stunned by the realization of Malaya's defencelessness; for instance, Bill Price's wife wept uncontrollably: Shennan, *Missee*, p. 241.

7. Churchill, *The Second World War*, Vol. 3, p. 551. Churchill was personally responsible for ordering the two capital ships to Singapore, even when it proved impossible for the carrier HMS *Indomitable* to accompany them and so provide air support.

8. The official history was Major-General S. Woodburn Kirby's *The War Against Japan*, and the same author's personal account is *Singapore: The Chain of Disaster*. Among the many other published accounts consulted were Barber, *Sinister Twilight*; Braddon, *The Naked Island*; Glover, *In 70 Days*; Bennett, *Why Singapore Fell*; Lee, *Sunset of the Raj*; Morrison, *Malayan Postscript*; Owen, *The Fall of Singapore*; and Tsuji, *Singapore 1941–1942*.

9. The order to hold fast and fight to the last man was repeatedly issued by General Percival, reflecting higher orders from Churchill.

10. Hay, Diary, p. 6.

11. Gent, The Jungle in Retreat, p. 116, citing Ken Hartley.

12. Soper, Experiences in Malaya, ch. 5.

13. A fortnight later at Ipoh some of the Kedah Volunteers, who were good drivers, were drafted into an armoured-car unit; the vehicles were in such a poor state of repair that when they ran into a Japanese ambush in the Parit area all the cars but one were put out of action. This incident was a talking point among the Volunteers who were personal friends of the casualties. According to John Soper, eight out of twelve men were killed, 'owing to a scandalous piece of work on the part of their C.O.', though 'two of the presumed dead subsequently turned up in Singapore via Sumatra!': Experiences in Malaya, ch. 5.

14. Hartley, BECM tape 449.

15. M. Price, Malayan Memories, p. 1.

16. Leslie Forbes, Resident Councillor of Penang, 'Personal Recollections', *Changi Guardian*, No. 61, Wednesday 20 May 1942.

17. Ibid. The official history, Maxwell, *The Civil Defence of Malaya*, gives a fuller version of the Penang episode, and (p. 20) gives higher casualty figures: 'about 3,000 seriously wounded' in addition to the 1,000 deaths.

18. M. Price, Malayan Memories, p. 1.

19. Hartley, BECM tape 449.

20. M. Price, Malayan Memories, pp. 1–2.

21. Letter from Nancy Wynne, 5 January 1941: a slip of the pen – the date should obviously read '1942'.

22. Samuel, Diary, p. 36.

23. B. Kitching, *Life and Death in Changi*, p. 17.

24. In a radio broadcast after the withdrawal from Penang, Duff Cooper, an 'aristocratic survivor of the pre-1914 *jeunesse dorée*', as Cecil Lee described him (*Sunset of the Raj*, p. 59), spoke of the successful evacuation of the majority of the whole population – meaning the European population. Shenton Thomas, the Governor, was appalled by this cavalier insensitivity to the Asian population.

25. Morrison, *Malayan Postscript*, p. 69.

26. Brundle, Escape from Singapore, pp. 5, 7.

27. Froggatt, Nothing Lasts for Ever, pp. 19–20.

28. Reilly, Diary, pp. 2–3.

29. B. Kitching, *Life and Death in Changi*, p. 18 (14 January).

30. Thatcher and Cross, *Pai Naa*, p. 23.

31. Soper, Experiences in Malaya, ch. 5.

32. B. Kitching, *Life and Death in Changi*, p. 9 (19 December 1941).

33. The Vowler family left their estate on the Malacca–Negri Sembilan border very hurriedly a few hours before Japanese troops moved in. In the interim the Asian servants had carefully buried the silver in the garden. Later the house was used as an interrogation centre for the Japanese *Kempeitai* (military secret police) and the silver was discovered. Incredibly, this substantial collection was then transferred by the Japanese to Singapore, where it was weighed, labelled and stored in the vaults of the Hongkong and Shanghai Bank. In 1946 the Vowlers were contacted by the Bank and asked to collect the silver, which was still in mint condition. This they duly did: conversation with Mr William Vowler, 11 December 1998. Also B. Kitching, *Life and Death in Changi*, p. 129 (29 July 1942).

34. Soper, Experiences in Malaya, ch. 5, p. 6.

35. Reilly, Diary, p. 7.

36. T. Kitching, The Fall of Singapore, p. 8; Soper, Experiences in Malaya, ch. 5, p. 6.

37. Kroh, at the strategic Thai border crossing, and Grik, on the main east–west route, were key points for controlling northern Malaya.

38. N. F. H. Mather, British Resident, Perak, *Changi Guardian*, No. 27, Friday 10 April 1942, pp. 1–2.

39. Soper, Experiences in Malaya, ch. 5, pp. 8, 9–10.

40. Hay, Diary, p. 4. Hay was at Tapah when he heard this.

41. B. Kitching, *Life and Death in Changi*, p. 10 (25 December 1941); John Soper also, stationed briefly south of Tanjong Malim, heard 'the news that the Japs had suffered heavily at Kampar': Experiences in Malaya, ch. 5 (new book), p. 4.

42. This was the opinion of the bank manager, who stayed until the night of 4–5 January, less than a week before the Japanese occupied it: W. D. Brown, Exit Klang, p. 1.

43. Soper, Experiences in Malaya, ch. 5 (new book), p. 4.

44. G. J. O'Grady, If You Sling Enough Mud, p. 103, mentioned a Mr Shepton, who was caught by the Japanese, tied to a tree and murdered.

45. Hay, Diary, pp. 2–3.

46. Brundle, Escape from Singapore, pp. 13–14.

47. Kennedy, *British Civilians and the Japanese War*, provides a very useful introduction to the subject, but the official history of the Malayan campaign ignores the Volunteers.

48. In addition, Colonel Dalley formed 'Dalco', a force of around 200 men, many Chinese Communist ex-prisoners who volunteered for anti-Japanese operations on the Malay mainland. The Chinese recruits for Dalforce came from the whole political spectrum, also including a body of ex-Communist ex-prisoners, released for their anti-Japanese commitment, together with Kuomintang supporters. A dynamic Hokkien businessman, Lim Bo Seng, was prominent in their recruitment. The 2,000-strong force was officered by the British, and among others who were involved were Gerald Hawkins, MCS, a veteran of the First World War, and a friend of Guy Hutchinson, Dicky Calthrope, ex-guardsman, ex-Johore Volunteers Engineer. After making a brave contribution to the defence of

Singapore, Dalforce was formally disbanded on 13 February to try to protect the Chinese rank and file from Japanese reprisals.

49. John Soper's company of the Perak Volunteers was given the choice of 'commandos, machine gunning or driving motor transport . . . The idea of commandos was to send bands of men . . . behind the Jap lines to harrass their communications': Experiences in Malaya, ch. 5, p. 5.

50. Hutchinson, The Rhinoceros of Johore, pp. 7, 14. John Soper could have joined an Indian Army, for the regiments of 11th Division had suffered very heavy casualties, particularly among its British officers. He felt 'it would have been little short of madness' to take a commission in the Indian regiment and 'to go straight into action with a body of men one did not know': Experiences in Malaya, ch. 5, pp. 8–9.

51. Guy Hutchinson, The Rhinoceros of Johore, p. 14, insisted that 'in spite of all this legitimate grouse I never saw a slacker' among the sappers of the Johore Volunteer Engineers.

52. Reilly, Diary, p. 1.

53. Hay, Diary, pp. 5–6 (2–3 January 1942). Soper was equally critical of the orders coming from senior regular officers ('too far-sighted a policy for our higher command', he noted of one suggested strategy); both he and Hay felt 'the authorities never meant to make any serious use of us': Soper, Experiences in Malaya; Hay, Diary, p. 3. (24 December 1941).

54. Soper, Experiences in Malaya, ch. 5 (new book), p. 7.

55. T. Kitching, The Fall of Singapore, p. 5 (8 January 1942).

56. Gent, The Jungle in Retreat, p. 112.

57. T. Kitching, The Fall of Singapore, p. 8 (10, 11 January 1942).

58. Morrison, the *Times* correspondent, indignantly recalled how 'a stupid British officer' described the Battle of Slim River as 'a spot of bother' when it proved to be the decisive engagement of the whole campaign: *Malayan Postscript*, p. 108.

59. Kitching, The Fall of Singapore, p. 8 (10 January 1942).

60. Ibid., pp. 14, 20–2. Ironically, at Batu Pahat the Japanese fully expected to take heavy casualties, according to Norman Bewick, who got it from a Japanese officer in Changi, Takaishika.

61. Reilly, Diary, p. 19.

62. Hay, Diary, p. 8 (27 and 28 January 1942).

63. B. Kitching, *Life and Death in Changi*, p. 24.

64. After his unit of the Perak Volunteers, which consisted of both Chinese and Europeans, had crossed the Causeway to Singapore on 13 January, to be disbanded, Soper was transferred to the Brigade Group Company of the Royal Army Service Corps 53rd Infantry Brigade, which had arrived in Singapore only on the 13th, after eleven weeks at sea. Though quite unfit and unprepared for jungle fighting, the brigade was thrust immediately into the battle for Johore, but, along with all other Allied forces, was ordered to retreat back to Singapore Island by 31 January.

65. Hutchinson, The Rhinoceros of Johore, pp. 10–11. A 'Red Cap' is a military policeman.

66. T. Kitching, The Fall of Singapore, p. 26. The naval base, over a period of twenty years, had cost some £60 million to build, but it turned out to be the most expensive white elephant in the Empire. Ironically, the base was formally opened on 15 February 1938, four years to the day before Singapore's fall. The Causeway had cost £4 million.

67. Oppenheim, Diary, p. 4.
68. Douglas Wilkie talking to Brendan Rodway, *News Weekly*, 13 February 1993, p. 19.
69. The generals knew, however, that there was no way Singapore could be held if they lost Johore. In January Percival had warned Bennett, the Australian commander, and Field Marshal Wavell had also warned Churchill.

13: AN INEXCUSABLE BETRAYAL

1. Reilly, Diary, p. 8.
2. Letter from Alex Cullen to his wife, Dorothy Cullen, 17 January 1942. Cullen was a Second Lieutenant and shortly to be promoted to Captain in the Straits Settlements Volunteers.
3. Churchill, *The Second World War*, Vol. 4, p. 43.
4. Hutchinson, The Rhinoceros of Johore, pp. 13, 15.
5. Wigmore, *The Japanese Thrust*, 1957, quoted in Owen, *The Fall of Singapore*, p. 139.
6. Reilly, Diary, p. 3.
7. T. Kitching, The Fall of Singapore, p. 24 (30 January); Caffrey, *Out in the Midday Sun*, p. 160.
8. Brundle, Escape from Singapore, p. 10.
9. According to the police chief René Onraet, who retired in 1939, there were carefully prepared schemes for evacuating women and children in the event of war, but, since dominant military opinion held that any attack on Malaya would be a seaborne attack on Singapore, the plans involved sending these *bouches inutiles* north into the Malayan hinterland; there was no thought of sending them away by ship to Ceylon or India: Onraet, *Singapore – A Police Background*, p. 21.
10. A group of British families from Malaya had settled in the wool town of Geelong, Victoria, which had a reputation for good schools. May Froggatt left on 13 December with her youngest son, Kathleen Price and her daughter a week later on the Blue Funnel liner *Ulysses*, both for Fremantle. On the last day of December, nine-year-old Brian Kitching left on a Dutch ship bound for South Africa with a complete stranger, a Mrs Bell, mother of two small sons, who took care of him for the rest of the war. Brian, who never saw his parents again, was a war orphan.
11. Maxwell, *The Civil Defence of Malaya*, p. 46.
12. M. Price, Malayan Memories, p. 3.
13. Barnes, *Mostly Memories*, p. 62.
14. Letter from Alex Cullen to his wife, 5 January 1942.
15. Holttum, Four Years in Australia, p. 14.
16. Maxwell, *Civil Defence of Malaya*, p. 42, notes that 2,300 Indians and 450 Chinese women and children took the opportunity to leave, but poverty and fear of the unknown inhibited the vast majority from leaving their husbands in Malaya.
17. The other two were the American ships, USS *Wakefield* and USS *West Point*, both of which took c. 1,500 passengers to Colombo. The *Duchess of Bedford*, zigzagged its way back via the Cape to Liverpool with 1,400 women and children. The Vowlers disembarked from the *Empress* at Durban, with the result that William Vowler, like Susan Malet and her

sisters, and Brian Kitching, was among those young Malayans brought up in South Africa thanks to the exigency of war.

18. Cunyngham-Brown, *Crowded Hour*, p. 94.

19. Soper, Experiences in Malaya, ch. 5, p. 21: 'From a personal point of view, this was a very pleasant period, except that there was rather a lot of rain,' wrote Lieutenant Soper.

20. Oppenheim, Diary, p. 5.

21. Soper, Experiences in Malaya, ch. 5, p. 26.

22. Letter from Alex Cullen to his wife, 8 February 1942.

23. B. Kitching, *Life and Death in Changi*, p. 29.

24. Oppenheim, Diary, p. 5.

25. Ibid.

26. B. Kitching, *Life and Death in Changi*, p. 29 (9 February 1942).

27. There were many eyewitness reports, e.g. Oppenheim, Diary, p. 6; T. Kitching, The Fall of Singapore, pp. 34–5, 38–9; Hutchinson, The Rhinoceros of Johore, pp. 16–17. On 9 February, Hutchinson's section was trying to hold a position south-east of Tengah aerodrome when 'a mob of A.I.F. [Australian Imperial Forces] came through, in a hurry too, most of them with no arms . . . They were just a rabble and quite out of control . . . The sods pinched 90% of our rations as they went through.' While the Johore Volunteers respected some Australian units, including the Engineers – 'They were our pals, the 2/10 R.A.E.''– Hutchinson's superior officer, Jack Crosse, 'disgusted with the A.I.F. put us temporarily under the command of Stewart of the Argylls'.

28. Hutchinson, The Rhinoceros of Johore, p. 19.

29. Hugh Fraser, 'The Last Days of Singapore', *Changi Guardian*, No. 19, Wednesday 1 April 1942. As Colonial Secretary of the Straits Settlements, Fraser was summoned that morning to an urgent meeting at Government House where it was acknowledged that 'the battle was not going according to OUR plan'!

30. Morrison, *Malayan Postscript*, p. 179.

31. Gordon Bennett's own version of events was told in his *Why Singapore Fell*; independent unpublished accounts were given by Britons who accompanied him: Oppenheim, Diary, and Hay, Diary.

32. Constance Sleep's husband, Arthur, also remained at his post in the Colonial Treasury.

33. T. Kitching, The Fall of Singapore, p. 39 (12 February 1942).

34. The Captain reported that the ship carried more than 2,000, but an RAF corporal aboard put the figure at 1,200. Most were armed-service personnel, but there were at least 160 women, including Australian nurses, and thirty-five children: Kennedy, *When Singapore Fell*, pp. 28, 47.

35. Leslie Froggatt, Superintendent Engineer, scuttled the Straits Steamship Company's coaster *Rawang*, and the little *Brunei*, which had carried passengers from Clifford Pier to waiting ships, in the inner roads.

36. Cunyngham-Brown, *Crowded Hour*, p. 98.

37. Gent, The Jungle in Retreat, p. 120, citing Ken Hartley's story. Ken's father died in Sime Road Civilian Camp.

38. Captain Sinclair DSO was mentioned in dispatches for this successful voyage from

Singapore. The story of the *Kedah*, one of the few lucky ships, was told by Muriel Reilly, Diary; also in Tregonning, *Home Port Singapore, passim*, and Tomlinson, *Malay Waters*, pp. 146–50.

39. Cunyngham-Brown tells Puckridge's story with great humour. Severely shocked, Puckridge was plucked out of the dark sea from a floating raft, but he had managed to hold on to his well-polished brown shoes. Cunyngham-Brown reckoned 'he must have merely sailed through the air from his morning's bridge session, and landed in the sea without a scratch': *Crowded Hour*, pp. 101–2. Puckridge, a Volunteer in the Selangor Battalion of the FMVR, was known by many Malayans, even outside rubber planting circles. Volunteer M. C. Hay of the Malayan Civil Service recalled a verse which was composed by Puckridge and was very popular among the Volunteers, summing up their frustrations:

> Never before have so many
> Been ——— about by so few
> And neither the few nor the many
> Have ——— all idea what to do.

Hay, Diary, p. 7 (9 January 1942).

40. Gent, The Jungle in Retreat, p. 121.
41. O. W. Gilmour, *Singapore to Freedom*, p. 49.
42. Gent, The Jungle in Retreat, p. 122.
43. B. Kitching, *Life and Death in Changi*, pp. 40–1, citing the words of Nurse Margot Turner, one of the four survivors.
44. In the confusion of those days, nothing can be absolutely certain, and it was said that Mrs Hartley died when her ship was torpedoed on its way to Japan. But Ken mentioned that the old Penang ferry arrived and took his mother off at night, and this accords with the fact that the *Tanjong Pinang* was alleged to have transferred all the remaining women. At any rate, the awful truth dawned on Ken soon after that she had died. When Ken and Gordon eventually reached the safety of Ceylon, they did not know the names and addresses of their only relatives, so they were taken to Bombay. After experiencing a succession of traumas, the boys were eventually located by their Auntie Pearl, but at the end of the war they had to come to terms with being homeless orphans: Gent, The Jungle in Retreat, p. 123.
45. For Stoker Lloyd it was a second miraculous escape, as he had been picked up from the *Prince of Wales* when she was sunk on 10 December. This time he was wounded and fell into the sea, but subsequently escaped. Sister Vivien Bullwinkle was shot through the throat and feigned death. Later she scrambled into the surrounding jungle, to be found some days later, unconscious and barely alive. Saved by the devoted care of internment camp doctors, she came through the deprivation of the next three and a half years and her heroism was duly recognized after the war: Tregonning, *Home Port Singapore*, p. 181; Tomlinson, *Malay Waters*, pp. 170–2.
46. F. M. Chamberlin, 'M.V. Rantau and M.V. Relau', p. 3, cited in Tregonning, *Home Port Singapore*, p. 183.
47. W. G. Price, Notes on Sungei Nyok Dockyard.
48. T. Kitching, The Fall of Singapore, p. 41 (14 February 1942).

49. This notorious episode would often be cited as evidence of the barbarism of the Japanese. However, the planter Norman Bewick, who was a patient in the Alexandra Road Hospital at the time, felt strongly that Punjabi troops, out of ignorance, were responsible for drawing on the advancing Japanese by firing on them from the hospital verandah. 'We were being shelled by both sides,' Bewick recalled. 'The British thought the Japs were in the hospital, and the Japs were shelling us all . . . When [General] Yamashita came into the hospital . . . he stood at the end of the ward explaining to us what had happened. He said the Japanese were trained as the Germans were; the officers stayed behind their troops, and those who made the attack were shot by their own officers outside the hospital. You couldn't blame them. They didn't know where they were! Oh, that attack was a terrible thing!': Gent, The Jungle in Retreat, p. 126.

50. Differing figures appear in various books but this is the figure given in the official history, Kirby, *The War Against Japan*, Vol. 1, p. 473.

51. T. Kitching, The Fall of Singapore, p. 46 (16 February 1942).

52. G. H. Wade, 'The Medical Auxiliary Service', *Changi Guardian*, No. 51, Friday 8 May 1942.

53. Sleep, Letter to son, p. 171.

54. T. Kitching, Fall of Singapore, p. 45 (16 February 1942).

55. Hay, Diary, p. 13 (15 February 1942).

56. Hutchinson, The Rhinoceros of Johore, p. 24.

57. Soper, Experiences in Malaya, ch. 5, p. 32.

58. B. Kitching, *Life and Death in Changi*, p. 34.

59. Letter from Alex Cullen to his wife, 8 February 1942.

60. Hay, Diary, p. 13 (15 February 1942).

61. Quoted in Caffrey, *Out in the Midday Sun*, p. 170.

62. Soper, Experiences in Malaya, Interregnum, p. 33.

63. T. Kitching, The Fall of Singapore, p. 45.

64. Wade, *Changi Guardian*, No. 51, Friday 8 May 1942.

65. Soper, Experiences in Malaya, Interregnum, p. 34.

66. Milne, 'Changi Exile', p. 1.

67. Kirby, *The War Against Japan*, Vol. 1, p. 468.

68. Soper, Experiences in Malaya: The Campaign in Retrospect; Oppenheim, Diary, p. 10, quoting various people's views and assertions on some contributory causes for the fall of Singapore.

69. Malet, Diary, p. 3.

70. Despite, for example, Cunyngham-Brown's defence of Percival's moral courage in *The Traders*, pp. 273–4, Sir John Smyth's apologia, *Percival and the Tragedy of Singapore*, and Percival's popularity with members of the Far Eastern Prisoners of War Association.

71. Soper, Experiences in Malaya, ch. 6.

72. Malet, Diary, p. 55.

73. Oppenheim, Diary, pp. 11–12, states, 'There was complete chaos on the sampan . . . The General screams like a young girl and curses Gordon Walker [his ADC] who is standing up in the nude for being so, saying it would be scandalous if the Japs saw him like that. He was like that because he had swum out to collect the sampan . . .' And, as the situa-

tion in the boat became increasingly desperate, 'everyone was in a vile temper . . . Bennett completely useless, first crying and then imploring Moses [Head of the Australian Broadcasting Company] or Walker to do something.'

74. Muriel Reilly confirmed that in the closing stages of the Malaya campaign Air Vice-Marshal Pulford was in a state of great stress. 'I was shocked at his appearance. He was obviously in a state of great nervous tension – almost mental it appeared to me – and he kept walking up and down the room, muttering to himself and thumping tables and chairs as he passed, and every now and then stopping in front of me and saying, "This is a dreadful business – this is a dreadful state of affairs – the whole show is damnable – utterly damnable. An Air Force with no planes and no aerodromes – what the Hell are we to do? What can we do!"': Reilly, Diary, p. 11.

75. Resident Minister Duff Cooper was there only from September 1941 to January 1942, General Sir Henry Pownall took over as Commander-in-Chief from Brooke-Popham on 23 December, when the Japanese had already seized northern Malaya; Wavell, Supreme Commander of the American, British, Australian and Dutch forces, first appeared in Singapore on 7 January 1942 and left finally five weeks later, four days before the capitulation.

76. Brundle, Escape from Singapore, p. 21.

77. B. Kitching, *Life and Death in Changi*, pp. 19–20.

78. Charles Hartley was not surprised that only two Malays in his company of Straits Settlements Volunteers left Penang with him to continue the fight: their decision to stay with their wives and families was understandable. John Soper noted that the desertion of Malay Volunteers became an issue when the fighting approached Kampar, but he argued that it was an outcome of the Malay psyche: 'the Malay is not a true fighter: he may be quick with his "kris" when individually aroused; the pomp of a barrack square appeals to him, and he is intensely interested in weapon training. But his idea of a good fight is an ambush with the odds heavily in his favour. A losing battle, even if it be only a football match, does not appeal to him. He has learnt from the traditional wars of his rulers that it is better to get on the winning side as soon as possible. Secondly, as volunteers they were told that Government would look after their families if they were mobilised: in fact nothing whatsoever was done . . . Thirdly, to say that they refused to fight for their country is rubbish, because they do not recognise Malaya as their country; their outlook goes not further than their state, and often not so far, and to do them justice few deserted before their own particular portion of the country had fallen to the enemy. Finally, there is also no doubt that their morale was undermined by continuous air activity on the part of the enemy, with no reply from us, and this in spite of the fact that they had been led to believe by persistent propaganda that we were strong in the air. Looked at in this light we had obviously let them down: we cannot grouse at them for letting us down': Experiences in Malaya, ch. 5, pp. 2–3.

79. Barnett, *Engage the Enemy More Closely*, p. 389.

80. P. Elphick and M. Smith, *Odd Man Out*, pp. 170–98. See above, p. 379, note 5.

81. Sleep, Letter to son, p. 171.

82. Froggatt, Nothing Lasts for Ever, p. 20.

83. Malet, Diary, p. 55.

84. Mackenzie, *Eastern Epic*, Vol. 1, p. 206.

1. Churchill, *The Second World War*, Vol. 3, p. 477: regarding the forfeits, he added, 'all this would be merely a passing phase'.

2. Kennedy, *When Singapore Fell*, p. 18.

3. There were a number of cases of soldiers who escaped by feigning death by shooting or beheading. For example, a former Volunteer, Brown North, 'had been captured by the Japs and stood up against a tree and shot. The bullet however had passed clean through without doing much damage . . . and he had recovered the following day when the execution party had of course long gone. What an experience! Another officer I heard of went through the same or worse, namely he was made to kneel down and his head hacked at with a big two handed sword. They made a mess of it, however, being in a hurry, kicked him into a ditch and covered him with brushwood, and also moved off. He too recovered sufficiently to get away and was eventually brought in as prisoner with a nasty gash in the back of the neck! A pretty ghastly experience . . .': Malet, Diary, p. 23.

4. Gent, The Jungle in Retreat, pp. 109–10.

5. Malet, Diary, p. 2.

6. Colonel James, CO of the Selangor Battalion of Volunteers, in civilian life was with Whittal & Co., Estate Agents and Company Secretaries, Kuala Lumpur, and, like many of his generation in Malaya, was a Great War veteran, having been with the first Territorial battalion to land in France in 1914.

7. Malet, Diary, pp. 2, 4–5. Changi cantonment was the area around the original village of Changi, twelve miles from Singapore town. By the 1930s it included a civilian gaol and had been developed as a key part of the island's defences. Malet noted that 'Changi' included the Birdwood and Selerang camps.

8. Ibid., pp. 6–7.

9. Cheeseman, 'An Internee Presents a Picture' p. 265.

10. T. Kitching, The Fall of Singapore, pp. 49–50.

11. B. Kitching, *Life and Death in Changi*, pp. 53–5.

12. Malet, Diary, pp. 11–12. *Bushido* was the ancient Japanese code of chivalry, which Yamashita had proclaimed would apply to both armed forces and civilian personnel – a commitment that Europeans felt was rarely honoured.

13. Cunyngham-Brown, in *The Traders*, pp. 270–2, tells how, in the aftermath of vicious fighting around Bakri, Johore, eighteen wounded young soldiers of the Madras Sappers and Miners, 11th Indian Division, were bayoneted and beheaded. Two survivors, Nadesan and Perumal, miraculously escaped and were taken by boat to Singapore to tell the tale.

14. Gent, The Jungle in Retreat, p. 139.

15. Malet, Diary, p. 18.

16. B. Kitching, *Life and Death in Changi*, p. 163. Similarly, Tom Kitching had noted, 'On August 12th [1942] a huge mass meeting of Indians in Farrer Park protested against the arrest of Gandhi. Gandhi had given a very anti-British speech. He was at college with me, damn him': Ibid., p. 134. The college was Peterhouse, where Kitching had read natural sciences in 1909–12. Malet, Diary, pp. 19–20, records that 'a punishment camp run by the 'Free Indian Army', Capt. (now Colonel) Dhillan, ex-Sikhs and Staff College, Camberley,

in Singapore is now in operation and deals with all cases of recaptured escapers, bolters from working parties etc. . . . The disciplining of these British Other Ranks consists of pillory, running the gauntlet naked through ranks of Indians armed with straps, flogging etc. Such fun for the participants!'

17. While awaiting interrogation by the *Kempeitai*, Freddy Bloom's courage was sustained by the friendship of a young Sikh prisoner, Mahinder Singh: Bloom, *Dear Philip*, pp. 123–4. Dr Ryrie was deeply touched by the loyalty of a Sikh attendant at the Sungei Buloh Leper Settlement, who spontaneously became his personal protector against Japanese guards: Kennedy, *British Civilians and the Japanese War*, pp. 141–2. Cunyngham-Brown's morale was also buoyed by a covert salute from a Sikh sentry he had known at the Havelock Road Police Court Building in Singapore: *Crowded Hour*, p. 139.

18. Like many of his fellow workers, Cherian came from Kerala in southern India and had moved to Selangor at the time of the rubber boom in 1939. During the Japanese occupation he was accosted by two armed Japanese soldiers, who hit him with rifle butts and took him prisoner. Hearing stories of the Japanese practice of abusing and killing young Tamils, he was determined to avoid such a fate. While being transported away, he picked his moment to escape when the lorry slowed down, and, despite being shot at repeatedly by guards, made the cover of the jungle. After hiding in a monsoon drain underneath a bridge for a week, he caught malaria but was found by Malay fishermen, who looked after him for the duration of the war. On hearing about the Japanese surrender, he walked all the way to Singapore, joining a cousin there. Always pro-British, his ambition to serve the Crown led him to join the RAF, in which he worked as a civilian storekeeper: information conveyed by his daughter, Elizabeth Cherian, 8 December 1998.

19. Captain Raja Aman Shah, Tunku Abdul Rahman's brother-in-law and a cousin of the Sultan of Perak, was among the officers shot on 28 February 1942, though the truth did not emerge until after the war.

20. Two distinguished officers were Hussein, who joined on 8 February 1935 in Malacca and made a career in the Army, and Tunku Haji Mohamed Mohaidin, a son of the last Rajah of Patani, who fought down the peninsula and took part in the last-ditch stand on Kent Ridge, Singapore, before escaping.

21. Brundle, Escape from Singapore, pp. 23–4, where a different spelling of the Tunku's name is used.

22. Gent, The Jungle in Retreat, p. 136.

23. B. Kitching, *Life and Death in Changi*, pp. 214–15; other accounts in ibid., p. 161, and Malet, Diary, p. 57.

24. Gent, The Jungle in Retreat, p. 135.

25. B. Kitching, *Life and Death in Changi*, p. 135.

26. Ibid., pp. 135, 217.

27. Malet, Diary, p. 16.

28. Gent, The Jungle in Retreat, pp. 137–8.

29. Nona Baker and her brother Vincent, who escaped from Sungei Lembing and hid from the Japanese in the high jungle of Pahang, were entirely dependent on local Chinese men for supplying them with food, shelter and news, as told in Thatcher and Cross, *Pai Naa*.

30. Chew and Lee, *History of Singapore*, p. 102.

31. In the opinion of Christopher Blake, who ran the office dealing with the honours system as Secretary to the Governor, Sir Franklin Gimson, Elizabeth Choy was given the OBE but deserved the George Cross. Among the Eurasians who showed supreme courage were a pro-British family from Ipoh, Dr and Mrs Sybil Kathysagu, who held out repeatedly against torture for treating wounded Chinese guerrillas.

32. Captain Malet, Diary, p. 15, described the initial distribution of the prisoners of war: the AIF occupied the old Selarang Barracks, the British 18th Division Artillery, Herts. and Beds., Cambridgeshires, Norfolks etc., and Malet himself in the Southern Area which included Changi village, the Point, Government House, the Yacht Club, 'very pretty and surrounded by sea on the North and East. Here are Gunners, Sappers, 2 Malayan Infantry Brigades, the Loyals, Gordons, Manchesters, Straits Settlements, Federated Malay States and Unfederated States Volunteer units. The Robert Barracks was all hospital and soon very full with dysentery, malaria and wounded – 3,000 cases, and no electric lighting or running water, and little equipment.'

33. Gent, The Jungle in Retreat; p. 129. Bewick is quoted giving other examples of the selfish and irrational behaviour of senior officers on pp. 130–1.

34. Soper, Letters, p. 4 (15 May), pp. 12, 15 (17 May), p. 35 (26 July).

35. Ibid., p. 48 (29 November).

36. Foss, Letters, 24 August 1945.

37. Froggatt, Nothing Lasts for Ever, p. 22. Padre Duckworth was greatly praised for his humanity and inspiration; the Assistant Chaplain General, 'a professional radio broadcaster', was said to be 'quite alone in the preaching field'; others mentioned were the Catholic priest Fr Bourke, 'a pretty hard-hitting Irishman, a fine preacher', and the Presbyterian Padre Webb: Malet, Diary, p. 23. A number of chaplains died in prison camps in Thailand, such as Padre Parr at Upper Kanyu Camp in June 1943. More widespread praise went to the leadership and humanity of the medical profession; for example, in the Thai railway camps Major Kevin Fagan was remembered for his extraordinary courage, gentleness and endurance, and Captain Hugh Edward 'Ginger' de Wardener for his devotion to cholera patients.

38. Bishop Wilson had enjoyed thirteen months of freedom before internment, largely thanks to the good offices of a Japanese Christian, Lieutenant Ogawa. The Bishop was to be one of the first prisoners to be released, in mid-August 1945, which was resented in some quarters. He arrived in Changi with a load of supplies, wearing – to some disapproval – a top hat. He was able to cash cheques through intermediaries, using the money to buy food from the black market; he also borrowed money for himself and other internees using the name of the Anglican Church. His refusal to hand over the tinned food he brought with him to the camp quartermaster created considerable controversy and added to an initial reputation in Changi for arrogance and hypocrisy. He was resented by British internees for apparently putting the interests of Asian Christians above theirs. McKay, *John Leonard Wilson*, pp. 28, 40–2. His reputation for strength and courage was, however, redeemed when he endured eight months of torture by the *Kempeitai* and emerged to continue his ministry and his spiritual leadership, first in Changi and later back in Britain.

39. Froggatt, Nothing Lasts for Ever, pp. 22–3. They had been taken prisoner as representatives of the AIF. One of them, George McNeilly, was very popular and much respected for his musical talent.

40. Ibid., p. 21; Malet, Diary, pp. 13, 24.

41. Malet, Diary, p. 10.

42. Froggatt, Nothing Lasts for Ever, p. 21. This became a universal catch phrase of the prisoners.

43. B. Kitching, *Life and Death in Changi*, pp. 75, 84, 250.

44. A former British internee who was a pupil in a similar school in the Kuching Civilian Internment Camp said schooling was set up to provide necessary discipline for traumatized children who would otherwise have run wild: conversation with Mrs Anne Graham (née Atkinson), 9 September 1999.

45. Tom Kitching notes 226 seamen, 876 government officers, 331 planters, 302 merchants, 188 miners and mining engineers, 153 engineers, 144 medical and associated professions (102 government), 103 municipal officers, 85 accountants, 59 bankers, 35 brokers, 37 lawyers, 50 clergymen and other religious workers, 6 farmers, 12 entertainment and catering staff, 16 managers of hotels, boarding houses and clubs, 8 musicians, 32 retailers and 11 horse-trainers and jockeys. Of 402 women, 70 were nurses, 258 housewives, 6 doctors, 13 teachers and 11 typists.

46. Braddon, *The Naked Island*, p. 165.

47. Malet, Diary, pp. 29–30.

48. Soper, Letters, p. 56 (14 March 1943), p. 55 (14 February 1943).

49. Potter, Reminiscences of Malaya, p. 7. Another prisoner, Nigel Conder Halsey of the FMS Police, recorded some humorous anecdotes in letters – for example, 'A P.O.W. got a letter from a friend who wrote to the following effect. "Very sorry to hear you are a P.O.W. I hope those Japanese bastards are treating you reasonably well." The Japanese censor only altered one word, and then passed the letter into the camp. He had cut out the word "Japanese" and substituted the word "Niponese" [*sic*]!'

50. B. Kitching, *Life and Death in Changi*, pp. 61, 102.

51. Soper, Letters, p. 51. The prisoner, a middle-ranking military officer, died on Boxing Day 1942.

52. Ibid., pp. 17, 54, 55.

53. Ibid., pp. 2–3.

54. Letter from Alex Cullen to his wife, 31 January 1942.

55. Warin, Changi Diary, pp. 13, 27, 32.

56. B. Kitching, *Life and Death in Changi*, pp. 143, 161, 197, 205, 227. Nora Kitching, a passenger on the *Kuala*, had died aboard the *Tanjong Pinang* in mid-February 1942; gradually Tom Kitching came to the bitter realization that she had probably died at sea.

57. Soper, Letters, p. 32 (12 July 1942 – the eve of his wife's birthday) and p. 51 (Christmas Day 1942).

58. Letter from Fr Gerard Bourke to Mrs Dorothy Cullen, 7 January 1946. Mrs Cullen's father was Revd Stephen Band, minister in charge of the Presbyterian Church in Singapore (1929–41) and effective leader of the Church in Malaya: Cheeseman, An Appreciation.

59. Malet, Diary, p. 31 (5 July 1942). His wife's family were Catholics; Malet also attended Anglican services. Mrs Malet and her children were then in South Africa.

60. Ibid., p. 20.

61. Soper, Letters, pp. 36, 56, 58.

62. Warin, Changi Diary, p. 13.

63. Letter from Dorothy Cullen to Alex Cullen, 16 February 1942.

64. Ibid., 5 November 1944.

65. See, for example, Holttum, Four Years in Australia, pp. 3–4; Reilly, Diary, pp. 3, 18–19.

66. M. Price, Malayan Memories, p. 3.

67. Ibid., pp. 3–4.

68. Holttum, Four Years in Australia, pp. 3, 13.

69. M. Price, Malayan Memories, p. 3.

70. Geelong, in 1942 a small port on Corio Bay, was known affectionately as 'Sleepy Hollow', but it boasted some fine church schools: Geelong Grammar, Geelong College, Morongo Presbyterian Girls' College and the Hermitage. At the same time in Perth, Western Australia, Norman Price of Penang, who experienced many changes of schooling, had 'probably my best education' at Nedlands State School and Scotch College: response to author's questions, August 1998, p. 2. The Barnes brothers transferred to the Hale School, Perth. They were among a group of ex-Malayans who attended schools in the 'big five' institutions, which included Hale, Scotch and Wesley Colleges.

71. Snell, Memories of British Malaya, p. 3.

72. Allton, Guildford Grammar School Recollections, p. 1.

73. However, two further incidents sent shock waves through the Australian public and some of the British wives: the sinking off Queensland of the hospital ship *Centaur* (a British ship which in peacetime was on Blue Funnel's Western Australian run) in May 1943 and the penetration of Sydney harbour by Japanese midget submarines.

74. This was the message of John Soper's first card home.

75. Warin, Changi Diary, p. 89 (Easter Sunday 1944). Warin came out to Malaya in 1920 as a rubber planter with Boustead & Co. At the outbreak of war he was manager of Cheras Estate, near Kajang. At Christmas 1941 he gave up a flight booking to join his wife and two children who had moved for safety to Victoria, Australia, and instead stayed to defend his estate until forced to leave. He then served as an auxiliary fire officer in Singapore from 15 January 1942. After the fall of Singapore he remained with the Auxiliary Fire Service until interned in Changi Gaol on Easter Monday, 6 April 1942: note from his son, Jack Warin, accompanying Changi Diary.

76. Soper, Letters, p. 15.

77. Ibid., p. 19.

78. B. Kitching, *Life and Death in Changi*, p, 187.

79. Cheeseman, An Internee Presents a Picture, p. 266.

80. One of the women was crippled and was struck while trying to rise from her chair; another was ill and asleep when struck.

81. Soper, Letters, pp. 40–1.

82. The fate of all the Double Tenth victims is listed in Kennedy, *British Civilians and the Japanese War*, pp. 157–8.

83. B. Kitching, *Life and Death in Changi*, p. 273 (1 April 1944).

84. Froggatt, Nothing Lasts for Ever, pp. 18–19. His party who returned to Singapore included Bill Price, Deputy Manager of Sungei Nyok Dockyard, and his assistant, G.R. Jones,

Thornton Draggett and Bobby Moffatt, Assistant Superintendent Engineers, Jurgen Thomson and Freddie Harper. The only survivor of Mansfield's Sumatra group was Cecil Starkey. 'Joe' Penrice, Dennis Peterkin, Freddie Adams, George Andrews and 'Tamby' Messenger all died as prisoners.

85. Mr Asahi, the Japanese Custodian of Enemy Civilians in Malaya and Sumatra, assured the internees in Changi on 18 December 1942 that conditions there were better than in the other twenty internment camps he had visited.
86. Samuel, Diary p. 64.
87. Froggatt, Nothings Lasts for Ever, pp. 18–19.
88. Malet, Diary, pp. 28, 41, 53, 59.
89. Soper, Siam Diary, 28 October 1943.
90. Ibid., 26 October 1943. His last camp in Thailand was Tameron Pah, above Takanun and some fifty miles from the Burmese border.
91. Coast, *Railroad of Death*, p. 247; Soper, Siam Diary, 26 October 1943; Sheppard, *Tunku*, p. 49, gives the 1945 estimate of at least 100,000 Malayan men, including Malays.
92. Peacock, *Prisoner on the Kwai*, p. 282.
93. Letters from Robin Band to Dorothy Cullen, Nakon Nyok Camp, 25 August 1945, and Bombay, 10 September 1945, and from Fr Gerard Bourke to Mrs Cullen, Singapore, 7 January 1946. Amoebic dysentery was fatal in most cases, because the camp doctors had no emetine. David Waters died at Chungkai, having been evacuated with a party of sick men.
94. Soper, Siam Diary, 23 December 1943.
95. Warin, Changi Diary, pp. 90–2.
96. Band, The Heights and the Depths, p. 107. For their remarkable courage and technical skill Max Webber was awarded the MBE.
97. For example Dr and Mrs Chong Tak Nam of Ipoh, who belonged to the pre-war educated elite, took immense risks to help the anti-Japanese cause.
98. Lee, *Sunset of the Raj*, p. xv.
99. Gent, The Jungle in Retreat, p. 130.
100. Soper, Diary, 16 March 1945.
101. Ibid., 28 March 1945.
102. Ibid., 11, 20 May, 5 June, 1, 3, 4 July 1945.
103. Coast, *Railroad of Death*, p. 247. Documents were later made available to the military tribunals in Tokyo and elsewhere, set up to prosecute war crimes, confirming plans for the 'final disposition' of all prisoner of war, e.g. by mass bombing, poisonous smoke, drowning, decapitation, the aim being 'to annihilate them all and not to leave any traces': Doc. 2701, p. 1, from the Journal of the Taiwan POW Camp, 1 August 1944, submitted to the International Prosecution Section 2015, British Division.
104. Cunyngham-Brown, *Crowded Hour*, p. 146.
105. Winton, *The Forgotten Fleet*, p. 339.
106. MacDonald's grave had been twice dug in Thailand. Then the ship taking prisoners from Thailand to Japan was sunk by a US submarine and he spent two or three days in the water before being picked up by the Japanese: Letter from J. A. S. Edington, Assistant to Mr MacDonald on Kulai Young Estate, Johore, to the author, 21 June 1999.

107. Letter from Dorothy Cullen to Alex Cullen, 15 August 1945; she was still unaware of her husband's death in 1943.
108. Duncan-Wallace, Diary, p. 2.
109. Soper, Diary, 19 August 1945.
110. Hardie, *The Burma–Siam Railway*, p. 176.
111. Soper, Diary, 20 August 1945.
112. Warin, Changi Diary, pp. 105–6.
113. Moreton, *An Irishman in Malaya*, p. 123.
114. Potter, Reminscences of Malaya, p. 9. Suzanne Fesq believed her planter-father found happiness and a certain revelation in the austerity of Changi life.
115. Warin, Changi Diary, pp. 105–6.

### 15: FALSE DAWN

1. Moreton, *An Irishman in Malaya*, pp. 134–6, but Purcell, *Memoirs of a Malayan Official*, p. 346, states that these were erected in honour not of the British but of their allies, the Chinese-dominated Malayan People's Anti-Japanese Army.
2. Life in Malaya and Singapore after 1945, Browne; Life in Malaya and Singapore after 1945, Kerr. Mrs Brown's husband, Ted, went out to Malaya in 1946 and they were married in 1952 when he was Assistant Manager of the Rubber Research Institute's Experimental Station at Sungei Buloh, Selangor. From 1958 to 1962 he was attached to Kepong Estate, Kepong, and from 1962 to 1972 they lived in Kuala Lumpur. After three years at Sungei Way, Mr Kerr was Manager at Klang from 1951 to 1958 and at Sungei Siput in Perak from 1959 to 1967.
3. Life in Malay and Singapore after 1945, Menneer. Mr Meneer was a shipping assistant with Harrison & Crosfield from 1955 to 1962 and worked in commodity marketing from 1963 to 1984.
4. Life in Malaya and Singapore after 1945, Read. Mr Read was sent out by J. & P. Coats of Glasgow to establish a marketing and sales operation throughout Malaya, taking over from agents Boustead & Co. Ltd in Kuala Lumpur and Harper Gilfillan Co. Ltd in Singapore. His was among the first British companies to take over business formerly handled by local agents.
5. Life in Malaya and Singapore after 1945, Anderson. Mr Anderson spent thirty-five years in Malaya in the plantation industry, during which he worked in Selangor, Kedah, Negri Sembilan and Johore.
6. Bloom, *Dear Philip*, p. 157.
7. Potter, Reminiscences of Malaya, p. 10.
8. Close confinement with the Communists had given Miss Baker insight into their mentality, and, though like Bob Chrystal and John Creer she deplored their ruthless anti-traitor tactics, she attended a farewell feast in her honour at the camp of the 7th Regiment before leaving for Kuantan under escort. After three and a half years in the jungle, the sight of the Union Jack flying over Chapman's headquarters was overwhelming. So, too, was the kindness of the Sultan of Pahang in the warmth of his hospitality.
9. Gullick, *Malaya*, p. 85.

10. Conversations with James Robertson, 17, 29 June 1999. As a pre-war planter, Mr Robertson was fortunately familiar with Malay. The citation for this MBE (Military) records his 'Firmness, coolness and tact and his knowledge of the language'.

11. Author's conversation with John Davis, 23 August 1999.

12. Captain Rawcliffe was later presented with the Japanese commanding officer's samurai sword, which decorated the Rawcliffe family home.

13. For a full account of naval and military events in the Pacific in 1945, see Winton, *The Forgotten Fleet*.

14. Gent, The Jungle in Retreat, p. 143.

15. Chris Noble, an Australian of the Malayan Survey Department in Kuala Lumpur, had left Singapore with seventy-one crates of materials, including all the first-quality maps needed for future military operations to reconquer Malaya. The second-grade maps were sent to India. Although Noble reached Australia safely, he was unable to gain release from the RAAF until October 1944, when he went to England to assist with Operation Zipper. His arrival was too late, however, to alter the plans which had been based on the Indian maps: Lee, *Sunset of the Raj*, p. 38.

16. Pawle, BECM tape 319 (1996).

17. Brundle, Escape from Singapore, p. 33.

18. Soper, Diary, 1 September 1945.

19. Warin, Changi Diary, pp. 108–10.

20. Langlands, BECM tape 420 (1997).

21. M. Price, Malayan Memories, p. 5.

22. Bloom, *Dear Philip*, p. 155.

23. Warin, Changi Diary, p. 49.

24. Gent, The Jungle in Retreat, p. 143.

25. Ibid., p. 131.

26. Cunyngham-Brown, *Crowded Hour*, p. 149.

27. Gent, The Jungle in Retreat, p. 133.

28. Ibid., pp. 142–3.

29. Potter, Reminiscences of Malaya, pp. 9–10. His points were borne out by Post-War Malaya and Malaysia, J. Barrett; conversation with Norman Price, August 1998; conversation with Alastair Reid, grandson of E. R. Reid, editor of the *Straits Times*, 27 June 1999.

30. Holttum, A Housewife in Singapore, p. 11 (9 May 1948).

31. Letters to Dorothy Cullen from Chinese in Singapore.

32. Holttum, A Housewife in Singapore, p. 11 (9, 23 May 1948).

33. Gent, The Jungle in Retreat, p. 187.

34. Ibid., p. 224. Datuk Puan Halimahton became a tireless champion of the Malays and a campaigner for women's rights in an independent state.

35. The government of the Federation, conducted by the High Commissioner in the name of the Malay rulers and the British Crown, had strong financial powers and a Federal Legislative Council of official and nominated unofficial members, with authority over the whole peninsula, together with Penang, while each state had a Malay chief executive (Mentri Besar) and deputy and a British Adviser.

36. Life in Malaya and Singapore after 1945, Stewart.

37. Soper, Malayan Correspondence, Marjorie Soper to Ray Soper, 7 February 1948.

38. In an eloquent testimony to Guthrie's losses, Cunyngham-Brown counted the human toll, 'the grim cavalcade of fine men' who passed down to immortality in Singapore, Sumatra, and on the Burma–Thailand railway: Barnes, Baxter, Baxter-Phillips, Bennett, Burns, Burnside, Cranna, Crawford, Craig, Deighton, Gibb, Giles, Godfree, Godward, Gray, Gulland, Harvey, Hogan, Hutchison, Mountain (old 'Sam'), Richardson, Stark, Sly, Wooding and Wright: *The Traders*, pp. 280–1.

39. Tregonning, *Straits Tin*, pp. 59–60. Tregonning, reports that, although they were instructed to leave Singapore at the end, only Sir John Bagnall, the Managing Director, and B. J. Cramer, General Works Manager, eventually reached the safety of South Africa. H. B. and W. A. Hall and R. J. Trotter were killed on the docks, D. Heddle, W. A. Corkill, S. W. Gooding, J. Newman, P. J. O'Dwyer, F. G. Stiff, P. B. Taylor and head-office men Messrs, Armstrong, Cornelius, Monteiro and Aeria all died as prisoners or internees in Malaya, Borneo or Thailand.

40. Those who died included Brian Tyson, the underground mine manager, who had volunteered to operate a secret radio transmitter on a 'stay-behind' mission and died of malaria in January 1943; Dr Reid, the resident medical officer, Harry Knight, an electrical engineer and captain in the Federated Malay States Volunteer Force, who died in Changi, W. R. Davis, an engineer, and Mr C. Wicksteed, assistant accountant, who died in Borneo, and Mr McEachern, a mechanical engineer and his wife who were lost at sea trying to escape. The seventeen remaining European staff survived as internees in Changi.

41. W. G. Price, Notes on Sungei Nyok Dockyard, p. 23.

42. For example the Barretts' home at Kuala Muda Estate, Kedah, had been destroyed, and Valerie Henebrey (née Walker) recalls her father had to rebuild their estate house near Telok Anson before his family could return, as it had been used as a 'dying house' during the occupation: Life in Malaya and Singapore after 1945, June 1999; Hutchinson, Junior Assistant, p. 71.

43. J. A. S. Edington, letter to the author, 9 June 1999. Mr Edington had a distinguished career in Malaya from 1948 to 1971 and subsequently in West Africa from 1971 to 1986.

44. The reports by Creer and Chrystal were ignored by the BMA, and Chrystal reported how he had been patronizingly told, 'You've been too long in the jungle. What you need, old boy, is a good long rest': Holman, *The Green Torture*, p. 185.

45. Bryson, Twenty-nine-and-a-half Years, para. 43.

46. Gent, The Jungle in Retreat, p. 181. Malcolm MacDonald was then Governor-General of Malaya and Singapore.

47. Bryson, Twenty-nine-and-a-half Years, paras 43, 44.

48. J. A. S. Edington, notes to the author: The Emergency, 21 June 1999.

49. Gent, The Jungle in Retreat, p. 182.

50. Dr Tweedie, who was considered a remarkable doctor, was repeatedly called to casualties in the Emergency but insisted on treating Europeans and Communists with complete impartiality: Gent, The Jungle in Retreat, pp. 182–3.

51. Soper, Malayan Correspondence, John Soper to Ray Soper, 27 June 1948.

52. The Palestine Police had been disbanded after the end of the British Mandate on 15 May 1948. Hugh Bryson was one senior civil servant who criticized their imposition on

the Federal Police Force, feeling it was bad for morale. Gray was also believed to under-value the importance of intelligence work in fighting the terrorists, and to be responsible for forcing the retirement of Colonel Dalley. However, he adapted to his very difficult brief.

53. J. A. S. Edington, notes to the author: The Training of Special Constables, 21 June 1999. John Edington had been a lieutenant in the Royal Scots Fusiliers, in which he had recently been involved in training new National Service recruits. Some months after these events, Sergeant Graver and Corporal Osman of the Midland Estate Special Constabulary were ambushed by Communist terrorists while travelling in their jeep. Both jumped off the vehicle, chasing after and killing four of their attackers, for which they were later awarded the George Medal.

54. Gent, The Jungle in Retreat, pp. 193–4.
55. J. A. S. Edington, notes to the author, 21 June 1999.
56. Gent, The Jungle in Retreat, pp. 187–8.
57. D. A. Macpherson, letter to the author, 26 May 1999.
58. Gent, The Jungle in Retreat, p. 188.
59. Life in Malaya and Singapore after 1945, Macpherson.
60. Life in Malaya and Singapore after 1945, Kerr.
61. Life in Malaya and Singapore after 1945, Anderson.
62. Post-War Malaya and Malaysia, Winchester.
63. J. A. S. Edington, notes to the author: The Incorporated Society of Planters, 21 June 1999.
64. J. Loch, BECM tape 366 (1996).
65. Ibid.
66. Norman Price, a resident of Penang, remembered the murder there of Jerry Fitzgerald by 'bandits' during a police operation in about 1951: 'British Malaya', August 1998. As a fit young man Price 'did his bit' by joining the Malayan Auxiliary Police in the early 1950s and carried out pay drops (supplying money by air) to tin mines and rubber plantations.
67. J. Loch, BECM tape 366 (1996).
68. E. J. Winchester, letter to the author, 16 June 1999.
69. Gent, The Jungle in Retreat, p. 190.


16: THE BATTLE FOR HEARTS AND MINDS

1. J. Loch, BECM tape 366 (1996).
2. J. A. S. Edington, paper on The Communist Insurrection in Malaya, lent to the author.
3. G. T. M. de M. Morgan, note to author on Sir Donald MacGillivray, 27 September 1999. Tom Morgan worked with him as the senior civilian member of the Director of Operations' personal team in Malaya.
4. J. Loch, BECM tape 366 (1996).
5. Brian Stewart, letter to the author, 14 August 1999.
6. Life in Singapore and Malaya after 1945, Anderson, p. 4.
7. Potter, Reminiscences of Malaya, pp. 12–13.
8. J. Loch, BECM tape 366 (1996).
9. For anecdotes of his exchanges with the European membership of the Rotary Club and the Lake Club in Kuala Lumpu, see Cloake, *Templer, Tiger of Malaya*, pp. 223, 263–5.

10. Quoted in Cloake, *Templer, Tiger of Malaya*, p. 213.

11. Ibid.

12. Madoc, interview transcript, 1981; Cloake, *Templer, Tiger of Malaya*, p. 325.

13. See Cloake, *Templer, Tiger of Malaya*, pp. 307–9, 327–9.

14. Morgan note on Sir David MacGillivray; Humphrey, BECM tape 442 (1997).

15. Cloake, *Templer, Tiger of Malaya*, p. 206.

16. Humphrey, BECM tape 442 (1997).

17. Gent, The Jungle in Retreat, pp. 69–70.

18. Hislop's colourful career – as Guthrie's planter, commando, soldier-hero, naturalist, conservationist (as Game Warden of Pahang and Perak, Protector of Aborigines in Perak and finally Chief Game Warden of the Federation of Malaya until 1960), linguist, piper, sharebroker, factor and woodturner – makes him one of Malaya's most remarkable Europeans, and an outstanding member of the Scottish expatriate community.

19. Humphrey, BECM tape 442 (1997).

20. Potter, Reminiscences of Malaya, pp. 13–14, 18–19.

21. Madoc, interview transcript, 1981.

22. Ibid.

23. Potter, Reminiscences of Malaya, p. 15.

24. Brian Stewart, letter to the author, 14 August 1999.

25. Bryson, Twenty-nine-and-a-half Years, para. 41. Although Howe was awarded an MBE, Bryson felt that neither he nor Negri Sembilan got the credit they deserved for this important social-engineering initiative, which was taken up by Gurney and by Briggs in his Plan, and exploited further by Templer.

26. Brian Stewart, letter to the author, 14 August 1999.

27. Gent, The Jungle in Retreat, pp. 189–90.

28. Ibid.

29. Ibid., p. 191.

30. Brian Stewart, letter to the author, 14 August 1999.

31. Ibid.

32. Gent, The Jungle in Retreat, p. 192.

33. Ibid., p. 191.

34. J. Loch, BECM tape 366 (1996).

35. Margaret Barton, interview, 10 August 1999.

36. Ibid.

37. At a dinner party given by the Sultan of Selangor in 1947, John Soper noted that the Sultan's consort was 'very keen on Malay embroidery work and has several women regularly engaged on it; it is mostly with gold and silver thread on thick material like velvet': Malayan Correspondence, letter to Ray Soper 4 May 1947.

38. Margaret Barton, interview, 10 August 1999.

39. Ibid.

40. D. Loch, BECM tape 366 (1996).

41. Margaret Barton, interview, 10 August 1999.

42. Darren Jeffery, interview with Mrs Margaret Mackenzie, *Courier* (East Lothian), 24 April 1998. Mrs Mackenzie became the Chief Commissioner for Guiding, Malaya, in 1951.

43. Margaret Barton, interview, 10 August 1999.

44. BECM tape 097.

45. Mrs Deirdre Edington, interview, 21 August 1999. For her work in welfare and charities, she was invested by Sultan Sir Ismail with the Pingat Ibrahim Sultan – the Sultan Ibrahim Medal. Dr Comber was, as Han Suyin, the author of the best-selling book *A Many-Splendoured Thing* (origin of the film *Love is a Many-Splendoured Thing*), based on her relationship with the journalist Ian Morrison. He died during the Korean War, and the Eurasian doctor married Leonard Comber of the Malayan police service. While working in Johore, she wrote another successful novel based on the Communist Emergency: *And the Rain My Drink*.

46. Kerr-Peterson, BECM tape 156.

47. Gent, Jungle in Retreat, pp. 198–9.

48. Ibid., pp. 199–200.

49. Ibid., p. 200.

50. Royle, *The Best Years of Their Lives*, p. 101.

51. British Malaya, N. Price; Price was only twenty when he left Malaya in 1953 with experience of flying and police work.

52. E. J. Winchester, letter to the author, 16 June 1999.

53. Life in Malaya and Singapore after 1945, Duffton. Mr Duffton was Assistant and then Plantation Manager, serving in Johore, Kedah and Malacca (1954–68).

54. BECM tape 047 (1992).

55. Barton, interview, 10 August 1999.

56. BECM tape 097 (1993?).

57. BECM tape 047 (1992).

58. British Malaya, N. Price.

59. Post-War Malaya and Malaysia, R. Barrett.

60. J. Loch, BECM tape 366 (1997).

61. Darby, BECM tape 050 (1993).

62. Coates, BECM tape 225 (1999).

63. E. J. Winchester, letter to author, 16 June 1999.

64. D. Loch, BECM tape 366 (1997).

65. Potter, Reminiscences of Malaya, p. 19.

66. Royle, *The Best Years of Their Lives*, p. 161.

67. Ibid.

68. Life in Malaya and Singapore after 1945, Menneer.

69. Kaye, BECM tape 084 (1993).

70. E. J. Winchester, letter to author, 16 June 1999.

71. Post-War Malaya and Malaysia, R. Barrett.

72. Margot Massie recalls that when her husband, 'Lt Col. L. A. Massie landed in Singapore the War had been over for two days . . . Leslie, who was already a qualified lawyer was sent up to deal with all legal matters in Kedah.' Many malicious letters came in criticizing Tunku Abdul Rahman. Colonel Massie discounted these, invited the Tunku into his Chambers, and asked, "Can you dine with us in the Mess tomorrow evening?" The Tunku never forgot that and always referred to Leslie as "Tuan Mas" (Mas is the Malay

for gold), and we were his guests in the Lodge up Fraser's Hill': letter to the author, 10 August 1999.

73. Life in Malaya and Singapore after 1945, Stewart.
74. J. Loch, BECM tape 366 (1996).
75. Brian Stewart, letter to the author, 14 August 1999.
76. BECM tape 097.
77. Potter, Reminiscences of Malaya, p. 13.
78. Dermot Barton, interview, 10 August 1999.
79. The 'Member' system for shadowing ministerial departments had been started under Gurney: ibid.
80. This arose when the Singapore government decided that Maria Hertogh, a Dutch Eurasian girl, separated from her parents and brought up by a Muslim Malay family during the war, and who had since married a Muslim, should be returned to her Christian Dutch parents in Holland. The decision aroused fierce opposition from the Malay Nationalist Party and Malay, Indian and Indonesian Muslims.
81. John Davis's war-time experience with the MPAJA taught him that Chin Peng was very different from any other Communist he met. He was always direct, and gave straight answers to straight questions. He had a captivating personality, was immensely likeable, and above all was a great survivor.
82. A summary of the new constitution, together with an account of the political developments in Malaya before and after independence, can be found in Gullick, *Malaya*, pp. 120–1 and chs 11 and 13.
83. BECM tape 056 (1993). Lee Kuan Yew came from a prestigious group in the Chinese community, the 'Babas' or 'The King's Chinese'. According to Helen Tan, who came from the same protected background, they believed passionately in the education of society. Lee was educated in the Raffles Institution, Singapore, and at Cambridge, where he achieved a double first in law; there he was socially snubbed by the English, which perhaps influenced his political agenda. A man of formidable intellect, when he was elected in 1959 he only spoke English and bazaar Malay. He began to speak Chinese in 1960, and by 1962 he spoke fluent Mandarin. During the negotiations for the merger with the Malay Federation he learnt fluent Malay, and finally he took up Tamil: Gent, The Jungle in Retreat, p. 170.
84. Darby, BECM tape 050.
85. BECM tape 056 (1993).
86. Life in Malaya and Singapore after 1945, Stewart.
87. Madoc, interview transcript, 1981.
88. Life in Malaya and Singapore after 1945, Stewart.
89. Life in Malaya and Singapore after 1945, Gold.
90. Darby, BECM tape 050.
91. Life in Malaya, Anderson.
92. Ibid.
93. Ibid. This author's italics.
94. Life in Malaya, Browne. Mrs Browne's brother, who was visiting, judged the competition. He discovered an old Scotsman who was a patient there for many a years – an old pupil

of the Royal High School in Edinburgh – and who, although cured of the disease, did not want to leave the Valley of Hope.

95. Darby, BECM tape 050; he was pleased to be invited by the Malay government to attend the official *merdeka* celebrations in Penang the following day.

96. Post-War Malaya and Malaysia, Winchester.

POSTSCRIPT

1. Potter, Reminiscences of Malaya, p. 18.
2. Madoc, interview transcript, 1981.
3. Post-War Malaya and Malaysia, Winchester. The same point was made by a planter on Carey Island: Life in Malaya after 1945, Gilbert.
4. Life in Malaya after 1945, Macpherson; Life in Malaya after 1945, Menneer.
5. For example J. Gilbert in a thirty-five-year career moved from being Assistant Manager to Director Plantations, Visiting Agent and subsequently Director in 1980: Life in Malaya after 1945, Gilbert. John Anderson, Manager of a 4,000-acre estate in north Johore in 1957, became successively Planting Adviser to a group of estates, Regional Director and finally Chief Executive of a state plantation enterprise in Sabah, east Malaysia, until 1986: Life in Malaya after 1945, Anderson.
6. Life in Malaya after 1945, Read.
7. Having started as an officer in the British Military Administration in 1945, he ended his career in Malaysia as Director of the Rubber Growers' Association from 1979 to 1982: Life in Malaya after 1945, Stewart.
8. The new directors were Mr Tan Chin Tuan CBE, a prominent businessman, Dato Loke Wan Tho and a distinguished Malay, Dato Nik Ahmed Kamil bin Haji Mahmood.
9. John Anderson to the author on Life in Malaya after 1945, 9 June 1999.
10. Life in Malaya after 1945, Edington; Life in Malaya after 1945, Henebrey.
11. Life in Malaya after 1945, Armstrong.
12. Life in Malaya after 1945, Edington.
13. Ibid.
14. Ibid.
15. For example planter Donald Macpherson worked for two years, from 1982 to 1984, in Sabah; John Anderson also ended his career there. In May 1971 John Edington left Malaysia and continued his career in Nigeria. E. M. Dickson, of the Singapore Harbour Board, resigned in 1957 and became Assistant Port Manager in Sierra Leone in 1958.
16. Life in Malaya after 1945, Anderson.
17. Life in Malaya after 1945, Menneer.
18. Signs of racial intolerance were touched on in, for example, Life in Malaya after 1945, Menneer, especially after 1975; Life in Malaya after 1945, Browne; Life in Malaya after 1945, Gold; Life in Malaya after 1945, Kerr; Life in Malaya and Singapore after 1945, Read.
19. For example M. J. Henebrey, T. Kerr, I. Harness, J. Anderson, E. J. Winchester and R. Armstrong, in their various reflections on Life in Malaya and Singapore after 1945.
20. Kerr-Paterson, BECM tape 156.
21. Lee, *Sunset of the Raj*, p. xvii.

22. Davison, Some Autobiographical Notes, p. 13.
23. Shennan, *Missee*, p. 187.
24. McKay, *John Leonard Wilson*, p. 113.
25. Margot Massie, interview, 30 June 1999.
26. Sim, *Malayan Landscape*, p. 17.
27. Gent, The Jungle in Retreat, p. 246.
28. Life in Malaya after 1945, Harness.
29. Onraet, *Singapore – A Police Background*, p. 25.
30. Holt was a member of the famous shipping family, but, rather than return to post-war England, he preferred to live a simple life in a remote Malay bungalow, looked after by an old Chinese retainer (to whom he left his bungalow).
31. Moreton, *An Irishman in Malaya*, pp. 151, 170.
32. Life in Malaya after 1945, Gold.
33. Hugh Bryson, Twenty-nine-and-a-half Years, para. 51.
34. Life in Malaya after 1945, Browne.
35. I am grateful to Professor Peter Rowe, Professor of Law at Lancaster University, for pointing this out to me.
36. Potter, Reminiscences of Malaya, pp. 17–18.
37. Sheppard, *Tunku*, p. 197.

# Bibliography

ABBREVIATIONS

BAM     British Association of Malaya Papers, Royal Commonwealth Society Records, Cambridge University Library
PP      Private papers
RHL     Rhodes House Library, Oxford


UNPUBLISHED SOURCES

Allgrove, J., Some Recollections of Rubber Estate Life in Malaya from 1920 to 1953, BAM III/16

Allton, D. R., Guildford Grammar School Recollections 1940–49, PP

Anderson, J., Letters elaborating Notes on Life in Malaya after 1945, PP

Band, R. W. I., The Heights and the Depths, Imperial War Museum Archives 74/112/1

Binnie, Marjorie, Account of the Mutiny of the 5th Light Infantry in Singapore, BAM XI/2

——, Life in Singapore before 1914, memoirs of Mrs Binnie, BAM III/7

Blackwell, K. R., Malay Curry, 1945, RHL MSS. Ind. Ocn s. 90

British Malaya: responses to questionnaires and letters to the author from D. R. Allton, Roger Barrett, Jette Barrett, Erina Batt, Christopher Cannell, Derick Cullen, John Edington, Valerie Henebrey, P. V. Morris, Norman Price, Anthony Pybus, Sheila Rawcliffe, Gordon Snell, Susan Tanner, William Vowler, Christopher Watkins, E. J. Winchester

Brown, W. D., Exit Klang: Extract from the Madras A.R.P. Journal, May 1943, BAM XII/2

Brundle, K. A., Escape from Singapore 1942: An Architect's Memories of Malaya and Singapore 1941–1942, BAM Addenda

Bryson, H. P., Correspondence on aspects of the Malayan Civil Service, BAM I/17

——, Twenty-nine-and-a-half Years in the Malayan Civil Service, BAM III/8

Cantrell, G., Notes and Recollections about Rubber Planting, c. 1909–11, BAM IV/15

Changi Guardian, extracts April–May 1942, anon., Leslie Forbes, Hugh Fraser, N. F. H. Mather, I. Innes Miller, N. Rees, G. H. Wade, BAM XII/29

Cheeseman, H. R., An Appreciation of Rev. Stephen Band and His Wife, Mrs Helen Band (Cullen Collection, PP)

# Bibliography

Christie, Ella, Diary and letters concerning Malaya in 1904, BAM III/3

Cobden-Ramsay, A. B., Memories of Kemaman District, Trengganu, 1934–6, BAM IV/28

Collinge, C. E., et al., Preliminary Report on the Internment of Civilians in Singapore by the Nipponese Authorities, February 1942 to August 1945, BAM XI/11

Cullen, Alexander, Notebook of Journey to Singapore 1928, PP

Cullen family of Singapore, Private correspondence, 1941–45, PP

Darville, Elizabeth, Maternity and Child Welfare Work in Penang, 1927–1935, RHL MSS. Ind. Ocn s. 134

Davison, Mrs Agnes, Davison papers, inc. Some Autobiographical Notes and General Reminiscences, RHL MSS. Ind. Ocn s. 112

Dickinson, A. H., Fifth Column and Political Security, various papers relating to World War II, BAM XII/25

——, The Political Situation in Malaya Immediately Preceding the Outbreak of the Malayan War, BAM I/25/3

Dixon, Alec, For Entertainment Only, BAM IV/18

Duncan-Wallace, A. M., Diary of a Civilian Internee in Singapore, 1942–1945, BAM XII/17

Edington, J. A. S., Letters and miscellaneous papers, PP

Forsyth, Ray (née Soper), Malayan Experience, PP

Foss, Josephine, MBE, Early Teaching Experiences in Malaya, BAM VI/1

——, Letters, RHL MSS. Ind. Ocn s. 83

Froggatt, Leslie, Nothing Lasts for Ever: Singapore Swan Song – and After, memoir, Melbourne, 1945, PP

Gent, Marian, The Jungle in Retreat, MSS. (250 pp.), 1975, PP

Gilman, E. W. F., Personal Recollections, RHL MSS. Ind. Ocn s. 127

Graham, A. McD., Formation of the Volunteer Movement in the F.M.S., Malaya, BAM X/1

Hall, J. D., Diary: Early Jap Attack on North Kedah, BAM XII/4/8

Hamilton, Haji, Account by Haji Hamilton of the Outbreak in Kelantan, April 1915, BAM XI/3

——, Letter to A. H. Dickinson, 9 June 1960, BAM XI/3

Hay, M. C., Diary of Escape, F.M.S.V.F., BAM XII/4

Hillier, Maurice, Malacca Memories, BAM III/5

Holttum, Mrs Ursula, Four Years in Australia, May 1941 to September 1945, BAM III/13

——, A Housewife in Singapore, April 1948 to September 1949, BAM III/6

Hutchinson, Guy, The European Volunteers of the State of Johore: The Rhinoceros of Johore, BAM XII/20

——, A Happy Return, 1934–38, BAM III/15/2*

——, A Junior Assistant on a Rubber Estate, Malaya, 1928–1932, BAM III/15/1*

Kemp, W. Lowther, Singapore Mutiny, 15th February 1915, BAM XI/4

Kitching, Thomas, Diary, January 1942–February 1942, The Fall of Singapore, BAM XII/1

Life in Malaya and Singapore after 1945: responses to questionnaires from John Anderson, R. Armstrong, G. D. Brown, Christina Browne, Robert W. Duffton, John Edington, Mary Elder, J. Gilbert, D. M. Gold, I. Harness, M. J. Henebrey, Valerie Henebrey, T. Kerr, D. A.

---

* In the BAM catalogue these are attributed to 'Guy Hutchings', but contemporaries confirm that they are in fact by Guy Hutchinson.

Macpherson, John Menneer, H. Naysmith, J. R. Pippet, E. R. Read, Brian Stewart, E. J. Winchester

Madoc, Guy, transcript of interview, 1981, 'End of Empire' series, RHL MSS. Brit. Emp. S 527–9(2)

Mahmud bin Mat, Dato' Sir, Some Features of Malay Life in East Pahang at the Close of the 19th and the Beginning of the 20th Centuries, BAM IV/24

Malet, Captain Henry, Diary of P.O.W. Camp, 1942, PP

Miscellaneous papers on the Girl Guide Movement in Malaya, BAM VI/2

Milne, J. C., Changi Exile, BAM XII/9

Morkill, A. G., Malay Memories, 1969, BAM Addenda

Newton, Lillian, More Exquisite When Past, Royal Commonwealth Society Records, Cambridge University Library, Y030311/1

Nias, S. J., A Selangor Volunteer's Escape, BAM XII/5

O'Grady, G. J., If You Sling Enough Mud, 1945, RHL MSS. Ind. Ocn r. 6

Oppenheim, H. R., Diary of an Escape from Singapore, BAM XII/3

Peach, Rev. Preston L., Recollections of 35 Years as a Missionary Teacher in Malaya, BAM IV/26

Post-War Malaya and Malaysia: responses to questionnaires and letters to the author from Mrs Jette Barrett (10 April 1999), Roger Barrett (10 April 1999), E. J. Winchester (12 May 1999), PP

Potter, J. S., Some Reminiscences of Malaya, 1934–1957, BAM III/1

Price, Mrs Mabel, Malayan Memories, 1988, PP

Price, Norman, Miscellaneous papers, August 1998, PP

Price, W. G., Notes on Sungei Nyok Dockyard, n.d., PP

Reid, J. W. S., 'H. B.': Memories of Hubert Berkeley, 1959, RHL MSDS. Ind. Ocn s. 82(2)

Reilly, Mrs Muriel C., Diary of her Experiences in Singapore and of her Escape to Australia, dated March 1942, BAM XII/24

Ridgway, Major Leonard, RASC, Singapore 1926–1929, A Reminiscence, BAM Addenda

Samuel, C. R., Diary 1941–42, RHL MSS. Ind. Ocn r. 7

Sewill, J W., The Great Pahang Flood of 1926, BAM III/2

Shelley, M. B., With the M. S. V. R. in the Singapore Mutiny, 1927, BAM XI/5

Sleep, Constance, Letter to son from Changi Internment Camp, RHL MSS. Ind. Ocn s. 130

Snell, Gordon, Memories of British Malaya, 1998, PP

Soper, J. R. P., Diary, 13 February 1944 to September 1945, PP

——, Experiences in Malaya, MSS., 1942, PP

——, Letters to Marjorie Soper, May 1942 to May 1943, PP

——, Malayan correspondence 1947–48, PP

——, Siam Diary, PP

Stark, W. J. K., District Officer's Day: Klang 1927, BAM IV/31

——, Jelebu Memories, 1913–14, BAM IV/31

Stewart, Brian, Recollections of Life in Malaya after 1945, 1999, PP

Thompson, Arthur M., The Malay States Guides, BAM XI/6/2

——, The Singapore Mutiny of the 5th Indian Light Infantry 1915, BAM XI/6/1

——, Sinking of the Russian Cruiser 'Zemchug' (handwritten notes), BAM XI/6

# Bibliography

Vlieland, C. A., Disaster in the Far East 1941–42: Memoir of the Secretary for Defence, Malaya, 1938–41, Liddell Hart Centre for Military Archives, Kings College, London

Walker, R. K., Eye Witness Account of the Destruction of the Russian Cruiser 'Zemshug' by the German Cruiser 'Emden', October 1914 in the Penang Harbour, written 21 September 1961, BAM XI/1

Warin, T. P., Changi Diary – World War II, PP

Williams, Captain G. A. Garnon, RN, Collected papers and reports, Imperial War Museum Archives

Winchester, E. J., Letter to the author, 16 June 1999, elaborating notes on British Malaya and Post-War Malaya, PP

Winsley, Captain T. M., Papers relating to the history of the Singapore Volunteer Corps, BAM X/5

——, Service of Malayan Volunteers in the Imperial Forces 1914–18, BAM X/5

Wylde, A. J. B., MA Dissertation, Royal Holloway College, London University, September 1994: Duff Cooper's Case against the Malayan Civil Service Reconsidered, BAM Addenda

Wynne, Mrs Nancy (Mrs Bateson), Letters from Malaya to her family in Hull, 1940–41, Mrs N. Bateson Donation, Centre for South-East Asian Studies, University of Hull


ORAL SOURCES

Author's interviews with Dermot and Margaret Barton (August 1999), Ray Forsyth (July 1998), Margot Massie (June 1999), Norman Price (August 1998), Peggie Robertson (April 1998), Professor Peter Rowe (September 1999). Author's conversations with Ken Barnes, the late Col. Christopher Barrett, Roger and Jette Barrett, Dr Erina Batt, Christopher Cannell, Elizabeth Cherian, Derick Cullen, Fenella Davis, John Davis, Anne Douglas, John and Deirdre Edington, Mary Elder, Dulcie Gray, Anne Graham, Maureen Heath, Edward Morris, Dr Michael Pallister, Anthony Pybus, Alastair Reid, James Robertson, Gordon Snell, Susan Tanner, William Vowler

British Empire and Commonwealth Museum, Bristol, recorded interviews with the following (all numbers refer to tapes in the Oral History archive): Christopher Blake (tape 192), J. Coates (tape 225), Jeremy Darby (tape 050), M. E. Dickson (tape 095), C. W. S. Hartley (tape 449), Kenneth Hellrich (tape 263), Hugh Humphrey (tape 442), Geraldine Kaye (tape 084), Mrs Kerr-Peterson (tape 156), Mrs Anne Langlands (tape 420), John Loch and Mrs Daphne Loch (tape 366), Major M. Lockhead (tape 033), Robert Oliver (tape 174), Lieutenant-Colonel G. Pawle (tape 319), Sir John Peel (tape 349), Mrs M. Wheatley (tape 460); also tapes 036/7, 047, 056 and 097


PRINTED SOURCES

(The place of publication of books is London unless otherwise stated.)

A.B.H. [Alice Berry Hart], 'Housekeeping and Life in the Malayan Rubber', *Blackwood's Magazine*, Vol. 221, May 1927

Ainsworth, Leopold, *The Confessions of a Planter in Malaya*, H. F. & G. Witherby, 1933

Allen, Charles, *Tales from the South China Seas*, Deutsch, 1983, repr. Abacus, 1996

# Bibliography

Allen, Victoria, '"I Remember . . ." February 15th 1915 – The Singapore Mutiny, February 15th 1942 – the Fall of Singapore', *British Malaya*, February 1946

Andaya, Barbara Watson and Leonard Y., *A History of Malaysia*, Macmillan Education, Basingstoke, 1982

Barber, Noel, *Sinister Twilight*, Collins, 1968

——, *The War of the Running Dogs. How Malaya Defeated the Communist Guerrillas, 1948–60*, Collins, 1971

Barnes, Geoffrey, *Mostly Memories: Packing and Farewells*, Mulu Press, Royston, Herts, 1996

Barnett, Corelli, *Engage the Enemy More Closely*, Hodder & Stoughton, 1991

Barr, P., *Taming the Jungle: The Men who Made British Malaya*, Secker & Warburg, 1977

Bartlett, Vernon, *Go East, Old Man*, Latimer House Ltd, 1948

Beauclerk, S. M. A., Duchess of St Albans, *The Mimosa and the Mango*, W. H. Allen, 1974

Bell, Leslie, *Destined Meeting*, Odhams, 1959

Bence-Jones, Mark, *The Catholic Families*, Constable, 1992

Bennett, H. Gordon, *Why Singapore Fell*, Angus & Robertson, 1944

Binnie, Marjorie, 'Malaya – the Years Before', *Singapore Free Press*, 15 March 1932, BAM IV/12

Bird, Isabella, *The Golden Chersonese and the Way Thither*, John Murray, 1883, new edn, OUP, Kuala Lumpur, 1967

Blain, William, *Home is the Sailor. William Brown, Master Mariner and Penang Pilot*, Hurst & Blackett, 1940, repr. Cedric Chivers, Portway, 1969

Bloom, Freddy, *Dear Philip: A Diary of Captivity, Changi 1942–45*, Bodley Head, 1980

Bowen, C. D., 'British Malaya as it was', *Asiatic Review*, Vol. 46, 1950

Braddell, Roland, *The Lights of Singapore*, Methuen, 1934

Braddon, Russell, *The Naked Island*, Werner Laurie, 1951

Brown, Edwin A., *Indiscreet Memories*, Kelly & Walsh, 1936

Brownfoot, Janice, 'Memsahibs in Colonial Malaya: A Study of European Wives in a British Colony and Protectorate, 1900–1940', in Hilary Callan and Shirley Ardener, eds, *The Incorporated Wife*, Croom Helm, 1984

Bryan, Rev. J. N. Lewis, *The Churches of Captivity in Malaya*, SPCK, 1946

Buckley, C. B., *An Anecdotal History of Old Times in Singapore 1819–1867*, 2 vols, Fraser and Neave, 1867, repr. University of Malaya Press, Kuala Lumpur, 1965

Buckoke, Lilian, 'Tin Mining Operations in Malaya', *Crown Colonist*, December 1948

Burton, Reginald, *The Road to Three Pagodas*, Macdonald, 1963

Butcher, John G., *The British in Malaya 1880–1941: The Social History of a European Community in Colonial South East Asia*, OUP, Kuala Lumpur, 1979

Caffrey, Kate, *Out in the Midday Sun: Singapore 1941–45*, Deutsch, 1974

Cameron, Charlotte, *Wanderings in South-Eastern Seas*, T. Fisher Unwin, 1924

Campbell, Arthur, *Jungle Green*, Allen & Unwin, 1953

Campbell, E. T., 'The Magic of Malaya', *Empire Review*, LIII, 1931

Cator, G. E., '"I Remember . . ." A Malayan Cadet in 1907', *British Malaya*, February 1941

Chapman, F, Spencer, *The Jungle is Neutral*, Chatto & Windus, abr. edn 1964

Cheeseman, H. R., 'An Internee Presents a Picture of Internment in Singapore', *British Malaya*, February 1946

Chew, Ernest C. T., and Lee, Edwin, eds, *A History of Singapore*, OUP, Kuala Lumpur, 1991

Churchill, Winston S., *The Second World War*, 6 vols, Cassell, 1948–54

Clifford, Sir Hugh, *Stories by Sir Hugh Clifford*, selected and introduced by William R. Roff, OUP, Kuala Lumpur, 1966

Cloake, John, *Templer, Tiger of Malaya: The Life of Field Marshal Sir Gerald Templer*, Harrap, 1985

Clutterbuck, Richard, *The Long Long War: The Emergency in Malaya 1948–1960*, Cassell, 1966

Coast, John, *Railroad of Death*, Commodore Press, 1946

Coe, T. P., 'The Malay States Volunteer Rifles 1911–15: Some Personal Reminiscences', *The Volunteer*, 1937, BAM X/2

——, 'The M.S.V.R. 1919–1927: More Personal Reminiscences', *The Volunteer*, 1937, BAM X/2

Crawford, Oliver, *The Door Marked Malaya*, Rupert Hart-Davis, 1958

Cross, John, *Red Jungle*, Robert Hale, 2nd edn 1975

Crozier, L. A., 'The Raub Gold Mines and the Emergency', *Malaya*, Vol. 2, 1953

Cunyngham-Brown, Sjovald, *Crowded Hour*, John Murray, 1975

——, *The Traders: A Story of Britain's South East Asian Commercial Adventure*, Newman Neame, 1971

*Daily Telegraph*, 26 February 1999, Obituary of Lieutenant-Colonel James Hislop

Dalton, Clive, *A Child in the Sun*, Eldon Press, 1936

*The Directory and Chronicle of China, Japan, Corea, Indo-China, Straits Settlements, Malay States . . . for the Year 1930*, Hong Kong Daily Press 1930

D. K., 'A Woman's Life in an Up-Country Bungalow', *British Malaya*, July 1926

Duval, Arthur, 'Life on a Malay Plantation', *The Westminster*, Vol. 28, 1916

Elphick, Peter, *Singapore: The Pregnable Fortress: A Study in Deception, Discord and Desertion*, Hodder & Stoughton, 1995

——, *Far Eastern File: The Intelligence War in the Far East, 1930–1945*, Coronet Books, Hodder & Stoughton, 1997

Elphick, Peter and Smith, Michael, *Odd Man Out: The Story of the Singapore Traitor*, Hodder & Stoughton, 1993

Emerson, R., *Malaysia: A Study of Direct and Indirect Rule*, Macmillan, New York, 1937, repr. University of Malaya Press, Kuala Lumpur, 1964

Fauconnier, Henri, *The Soul of Malaya*, trans. Eric Sutton, OUP, Kuala Lumpur, 1965

Ferguson-Davie, Bishop, '"I Remember . . ." Memories of Malaya', *British Malaya*, November 1944

Footner, C. C., 'A Talk on the Cameron Highlands', *The Planter*, October 1935

Forbes, Duncan, *The Heart of Malaya*, Robert Hale, 1966

Friend, Julius F., 'The Acme of Advertising: The Hand-Painted Hoardings of Singapore', *British Malaya*, February 1941

Gilmour, O. W., *Singapore to Freedom*, E. J. Burrow, 1943

Glover, E. M., *In 70 Days: The Story of the Japanese Campaign in British Malaya*, Frederick Muller, 2nd edn 1949

Godfrey, Rupert, ed., *Letters from a Prince: The Letters of Edward Prince of Wales to Mrs Frieda Dudley Ward*, Little, Brown, New York, 1998

# Bibliography

*The Golden Jubilee Celebration (1935–1985)*, magazine of the SRK Convent, Cameron Highlands, Pahang

Gray, Dulcie, *An Autobiography: Looking Forward, Looking Back*, Hodder & Stoughton, 1991

Guillemard, Sir Laurence, *Trivial Fond Records*, Methuen, 1937

Gullick, J. M., *Malaya*, 2nd edn Ernest Benn, 1964

——, and Hawkins, G., *Malayan Pioneers*, Singapore Eastern University Press, Singapore, 1958

Gwinnell, J. K., 'Christmas in Captivity', *Malaya*, January 1958

Hake, Egmont, *The New Malaya and You*, Lindsay-Drummond, 1945

Han, Suyin, *A Many-Splendoured Thing*, Jonathan Cape, 1952

——, *And the Rain My Drink*, Jonathan Cape, 1956

Hardie, Dr Robert, *The Burma–Siam Railway: The Secret Diary of Dr Robert Hardie, 1942–45*, Imperial War Museum, 1983

Harper, R. W. E., and Miller, Harry, *Singapore Mutiny*, OUP, Singapore, 1984

Harrison, C. R., 'Ramblings of the Last of "the Creepers" – I', *The Planter*, 37, 1961

Heussler, Robert, *British Rule in Malaya: The Malayan Civil Service and Its Predecessors 1867–1942*, Clio Press, Oxford, 1981

——, *Completing a Stewardship: The Malayan Civil Service, 1942–1957*, Greenwood Press, Westport, Conn., 1983

Hodgson, G. A., 'The Incorporated Society of Planters, 1919–1969', *The Planter*, December 1969

Holman, Dennis, *The Green Torture*, Robert Hale, 1962

Howarth, David and Stephen, *The Story of P. & O.: The Peninsular and Oriental Steam Navigation Company*, Weidenfeld & Nicolson, 1986

Innes, Emily, *The Chersonese with the Gilding Off*, 2 vols, Richard Bentley, 1885, repr. OUP, Kuala Lumpur, 1974

Innes, J. R., 'Old Malayan Memories', *British Malaya*, July 1926

Jackson, Robert, *The Malayan Emergency: The Commonwealth's Wars 1948–1966*, Routledge, 1991

Keay, John, *Last Post: The End of Empire in the Far East*, John Murray, 1997

Kendall, Franklin, *'Dearest Mother': The Letters of F. R. Kendall*, ed. Brian McDonald, Lloyd's of London Press, The Peninsular and Oriental Steam Navigation Company, 1988

Kennedy, Joseph, *British Civilians and the Japanese War in Malaya and Singapore, 1941–45*, Macmillan, Basingstoke, 1987

——, *When Singapore Fell: Evacuations and Escapes, 1941–42*, Macmillan, Basingstoke, 1989

Kirby, Major-General S. Woodburn, *Singapore: The Chain of Disaster*, Cassell, 1971

——, *The War Against Japan*, 5 vols, HMSO, 1957–69

Kitching, Brian, ed., *Life and Death in Changi: The Diary of Tom Kitching Who Died in Japanese Hands in Singapore in 1944*, Brian Kitching, 20 Beechgrove Drive, Perth PH1 1JA, 1998

'A Lady's Experiences in the Singapore Mutiny', *Blackwood's Magazine*, Vol. 198, December 1915

Lawlor, Eric, *Murder on the Verandah: Love and Betrayal in British Malaya*, HarperCollins, 1999

Lee, Cecil, *Sunset of the Raj – the Fall of Singapore 1942*, Pentland Press, Edinburgh, Cambridge, Durham, 1994

Leggatt, W., 'A Visit to Cameron Highlands', *The Planter*, October 1935

Lockhart, Sir Robert Hamilton Bruce, *Return to Malaya*, Putnam, 1936

# Bibliography

Ludbrook, Juliet, *Schoolship Kids of the Blue Funnel Line Western Australia Service*, Black Swan Press, Perth, WA, 1998

McFadyen, Sir Eric, 'Twenty-one Years of Rubber', *British Malaya*, July 1931

McKay, Roy, *John Leonard Wilson, Confessor for the Faith*, Hodder & Stoughton, 1973

Mackenzie, Compton, *Eastern Epic: Vol. 1, Defence*, Chatto & Windus, 1951

MacKenzie, John M., *Propaganda and Empire: The Manipulation of British Public Opinion, 1880–1960*, Manchester UP, Manchester, 1964

Makepeace, Walter, Brooke, Gilbert E., and Braddell, Roland St J., *One Hundred Years of Singapore*, 2 vols, John Murray, 1921

Maugham, W. Somerset, *Complete Short Stories of Somerset Maugham*, Vol. 3, Heinemann, 1951

——, *A Writer's Notebook*, Heinemann, 1949

Maxwell, Sir George, ed., *The Civil Defence of Malaya: A Narrative of the Part Taken in it by the Civilian Population of the Country in the Japanese Invasion*, Hutchinson for Association of British Malaya, n. d.

Miller, Harry, *Menace in Malaya*, Harrap, 1954

Moore, Donald, *Far Eastern Agent or the Diary of a Nobody*, Hodder & Stoughton, 1953

——, *We Live in Singapore*, Hodder & Stoughton, 1955

Moreton, D. E., *An Irishman in Malaya: John Lowe Woods*, Volturna Press, Peterhead and Hythe, 1977

Morrison, Ian, *Malayan Postscript*, Faber, 1942

Mugliston, G. R. K., '"I Remember . . ." Penang 1904–1908', *British Malaya*, January 1942

——, '"I Remember . . ." Singapore 1908–1927', Part 2, *British Malaya*, May 1942

Munro, Air Vice-Marshal Sir David, *It Passed Too Quickly*, Routledge, 1941

Munro, G. I. Gun, 'Malaya through a Woman's Eye', *Crown Colonist*, April 1932

Nash, Ogden, *Collected Verse from 1929 on*, Dent, 1959

*News Weekly*, 13 February 1993

O'Ballance, Edgar, *Malaya: The Communist Insurgent War, 1948–60*, Faber, 1966

Onraet, René, *Singapore – a Police Background*, Dorothy Crisp, 1947

Orwell, George, *The Collected Essays, Journalism and Letters*, 4 vols, Secker & Warburg, 1968

Owen, Frank, *The Fall of Singapore*, Michael Joseph, 1960

Padfield, Peter, *Beneath the House Flag of the P. & O.*, Hutchinson, 1981

Parkinson, C. N., 'The British in Malaya', *History Today*, VI, 1956

Peacock, Basil, *Prisoner on the Kwai*, Blackwood, 1966

Pearce, J., Cyprian, 'Memories of Tin Town', *British Malaya*, January 1931

Peet, G. L., *Malayan Exile*, Singapore, 1934

Pepys, W. E., 'Kelantan during World War I', *Malaysia in History*, Vol. 6, July 1960

*The Planter*, January, April 1921; October, December 1922; February, March, May 1923; May 1932; January, May 1936

Postgate, Malcolm R., *Operation Firedog: Air Support in the Malayan Emergency, 1948–1960*, HMSO, 1992

Purcell, Victor, *The Chinese in Malaya*, OUP, 1948

——, *The Memoirs of a Malayan Official*, Cassell, 1965

Reid, T. H., 'The Miracle of Malaya. A British Triumph in the Handling of Native Races', *The Empire Magazine*, Vol. 9, No. 1, 1914

# Bibliography

Rennie, J. S. M., 'The Old Singapore Club', *British Malaya*, January 1930

Richards, Jeffrey, and MacKenzie, John M., *The Railway Station: A Social History*, OUP, Oxford, 1986

Robertson, Eric, *The Japanese File*, Heinemann, Singapore, 1979

Roff, William R., *The Origins of Malay Nationalism*, Yale UP, New Haven, 1967

Royle, Trevor, *The Best Years of Their Lives: The National Service Experience 1945–63*, Michael Joseph, 1986

Sandhu, Kernial Singh, *Indians in Malaya: Some Aspects of Their Immigration and Settlement (1786–1957)*, CUP, 1969

Scott, J. MacCullum, *Eastern Journey*, J. Gifford, 1939

Scrivenor, J. B., 'Recollections of Cameron Highlands and Fraser's Hill', *Journal of the Malayan Branch of the Royal Asiatic Society*, Vol. IX, Pt 1, 1931

Shennan, Margaret, *Missee*, Kensal Press, Bourne End, Bucks., 1986

Sheppard, Tan Sri Dato Mubin, *Taman Budiman: Memoirs of an Unorthodox Civil Servant*, Heinemann, Kuala Lumpur, 1979

——, *Tunku: His Life and Times*, Pelanduk Publications, Petaling Jaya, 1995

Short, Anthony, *The Communist Insurrection in Malaya, 1948–1960*, Frederick Muller, 1975

Sim, Katharine, *Malayan Landscape*, Michael Joseph, 1946

Singam, S. Durai Raja, *A Hundred Years of Ceylonese in Malaysia and Singapore (1867–1967)*, privately published, Kuala Lumpur, 1968

*The Singapore and Malayan Directory for 1935, 1937*, Printers, 10 Collyer Quay, Singapore, 1935, 1937

*Sixty Years of Tin Mining. A History of the Pahang Consolidated Company 1906–1966*, Pahang Consolidated Co. Ltd, 1966

Smyth, Sir John, VC, *Percival and the Tragedy of Singapore*, Macdonald, 1971

Song Ong Siang, *One Hundred Years' History of the Chinese in Singapore*, John Murray, 1923

Swettenham, Sir Frank, *British Malaya*, Allen & Unwin, 2nd edn 1948

——, *Stories and Sketches by Sir Frank Swettenham*, selected and introduced by William R. Roff, OUP, Kuala Lumpur, 1967

——, *Watercolours and Sketches of Malaya 1880–1894*, The Malaysian–British Society, Kuala Lumpur, 1988

Thambipillay, R., ed., *'God's Little Acre' 1948–1998: A Commemorative Book on the 50th Anniversary of the Malayan Emergency (1948–1960)*, Perak Planters Association, Ipoh, 1998

Thatcher, Dorothy, and Cross, Robert, *Pai Naa [Nona Baker]: The Story of an Englishwoman's Survival in the Malayan Jungle*, 2nd edn White Lion Publishers, 1974

Thomson, J. T., *Glimpses into Malayan Lands*, OUP, Singapore, 1984

*The Times*, 29 June 1911; 11, 12 November 1914; 26 March 1915; 28, 30, 31 March, 2, 24, 27 May 1922; 1 January 1938; 17 November, 20 December 1941; 17 June 1942; 29 January 1999

Tomlinson, H. M., *Malay Waters: The Story of the Little Ships Coasting out of Singapore and Penang in Peace and War*, Hodder & Stoughton, 1950

Tregonning, K. G., *Home Port Singapore: A History of the Straits Steamship Company 1890–1965*, OUP, Singapore, 1967

——, *Straits Tin: A Brief Account of the First Seventy-five Years of the Straits Trading Company Limited*, The Straits Times Press, Singapore, n. d. (1962?)

# Bibliography

Tsuji, Masonobu, *Singapore 1941–1942: The Japanese Version of the Malayan Campaigns of World War II.*, trans. Margaret E. Lake, 2nd edn OUP, Singapore, 1988

Turnbull, C. M., *Dateline Singapore: 150 Years of the Straits Times*, Singapore Press Holdings, Singapore, 1995

——, *A History of Singapore 1819–1985*, 2nd edn OUP, Singapore, 1989

van der Vat, Dan, *The Last Corsair: The Story of the Emden*, Hodder & Stoughton, 1983

Vlieland, C. A., 'Singapore: The Legend and the Facts', *Daily Telegraph*, 13 February 1967

*Voices and Echoes: A Catalogue of the Oral History Holdings of the British Empire and Commonwealth Museum*, BECM, Bristol, 1998

Walker, E. A., *Sophia Cooke, or Forty-two Years' Work in Singapore*, Elliot Stock, 1899

Wigmore, Lionel, *The Japanese Thrust*, Australian War Memorial, Canberra, 1957

Wilson, W. Arthur, 'Malayan Types. Men You Have All Met', *The Planter*, February 1923

——, 'Malayan Types. Some Ladies You Have All Met', *The Planter*, April 1923

Winstedt, Sir Richard, *Start from Alif: Count from One*, OUP, Kuala Lumpur, 1969

Winton, John, *The Forgotten Fleet*, Michael Joseph, 1969

Wright, Arnold, and Cartwright, H. A., eds, *Twentieth Century Impressions of British Malaya*, Graham Brash, Singapore, 1908, 2nd edn (abrd) 1989

# Index

# Index

# Index